On the Law of Nature, Reason, and Common Law

On the Law of Nature, Reason, and Common Law

Selected Jurisprudential Writings

Matthew Hale

EDITED BY

Gerald J. Postema

OXFORD
UNIVERSITY PRESS

OXFORD
UNIVERSITY PRESS

Great Clarendon Street, Oxford, OX2 6DP,
United Kingdom

Oxford University Press is a department of the University of Oxford. It furthers the University's objective of excellence in research, scholarship, and education by publishing worldwide. Oxford is a registered trade mark of Oxford University Press in the UK and in certain other countries

First Edition published in 2017

Published in the United States of America by Oxford University Press
198 Madison Avenue, New York, NY 10016, United States of America

British Library Cataloguing in Publication Data
Data available

Library of Congress Control Number: 2017947439

ISBN 978–0–19–923492–9

Contents

Preface ix
Acknowledgements xi
Abbreviations xiii
Editor's Introduction xv
Matthew Hale: Life, Career, Works xv
Jurisprudence in Seventeenth-Century England xix
Hale's Common-Law Jurisprudence xxxi
Major Events in Hale's Life and English History lix
A General Note on the Texts lxi

Part I. Treatise of the Nature of Laws in General and Touching the Law of Nature

1. Touching the Nature of Law in General 3
2. Touching the Effect of Laws in General 16
3. Touching the Several Kinds of Laws 20
4. Touching the Description of the Law of Nature in Man, and Whence It Is to be Gathered 22
5. Concerning the Several Heads of that *Lex Naturalis* whereof before 31
6. That these Natural Laws Have in their Matter an Intrinsic Moral Goodness and Congruity to Right Reason, and Conveniency to the Condition of Mankind Antecedent to and Abstractive from any Law Enjoining them 60
7. Touching the Formal Reason of the Law of Nature and its Obligation 62
8. Concerning the Publication of this Law of Nature under the Manner of the Communication thereof to Mankind 67
9. Concerning the Second Kind of Publication of the Moral or Natural Law by the Institution or Engraving of it by the Finger of God in the Crasis of the Human Soul 81
10. Touching the Third and Fourth Methods of the Natural Publication of the Natural Law; Namely of the Intellective Faculty and the Natural Conscience and the Actings thereof in the Reasonable Nature 93

11. Concerning those Other External or Adventitious Publications of the Law of Nature 99
12. Concerning Human Laws and their Use in Relation to the Law of Nature 107
13. Concerning the End of the Laws of Nature 112

Appendix: Law in the Natural Order 122

Part II. The History of the Common Law of England

1. Concerning the Distribution of the Law of England into Common Law and Statute Law. And First, Concerning the Statute Law, or Acts of Parliament 129
2. Concerning the *Lex non Scripta*, i.e., the Common or Municipal Laws of this Kingdom 133
3. Concerning the Common Law of England, its Use and Excellence, and the Reason of its Denomination 139
4. Touching the Original of the Common Law of England 141
5. How the Common Law of England Stood at and for Some Time after the Coming in of King William I 148

Part III. Hale's Preface to Rolle's Abridgement of the Cases and Resolutions of the Common Law

Preface 159

Part IV. Considerations Touching the Amendment or Alteration of Laws

1. Concerning the Several Extremes Relating to the Amendment and Alteration of Laws; and therein Touching the Extreme in the Excess of Overhastiness and Forwardness to Alterations in Laws 167
2. Touching the Reasons and Grounds that Ordinarily Move Men to this Excess, and Itching after Changes in Laws 171
3. Touching the Other Extreme, the Over-Tenacious Holding of Laws, Notwithstanding Apparent Necessity for and Safety in the Change; the Danger and Occasions thereof 178

Part V. Reflections on Mr Hobbs his Dialogue of the Law

1. Of Laws in General and the Law of Reason 187
2. Of Sovereign Power 195

Part VI. Prerogatives of the King

1. Of Government in General; the Original, Alterations, and Trials thereof 207
2. The Application of the Former Generals to the Government of the Kingdom of England 215
4. Concerning Allegiance; What It Is; What It Binds to; and the Kinds of It 223
14. The Great Council and Court of Parliament 226
16. The King's Temporal Power in General and of the Power of Making Laws, Proclamations, and Dispensations with Laws 227
17. Concerning the King's Power of Jurisdiction in Distributing Justice according to Law *in Foro Contentioso* 231

Part VII. Jurisdiction of the Lords House or Parliament

Chapter 1 237
Chapter 2 238
Chapter 15 239
Chapter 17 240
Chapter 27 241
Chapter 32 242
Chapter 34 243

Select Bibliography 247
Name Index 249
Subject Index 251

Preface

Lawyer, judge, public figure and Member of Parliament, legal historian, theologian, and amateur natural philosopher, Sir Matthew Hale worked and wrote in the middle decades of the seventeenth century, that most turbulent period of English political history. A deeply reflective practitioner, he observed, analysed, and gave theoretical expression to the common law from many different vantage points. His reflections on reason, law, and the foundations and limits of political authority, set out in a number of works, most unpublished in his lifetime, are of continuing theoretical and historical interest.

This collection sets two of Hale's pivotal but nearly inaccessible jurisprudential works—his *Treatise on the Nature of Laws in General and Touching the Law of Nature* and his "Reflections on Mr Hobbs his Dialogue of the Laws"—in context of other key works of legal history and legal and constitutional theory. *Treatise*, when read together with other more familiar writings, reveals a complex general understanding of law and moral and legal reasoning. "Reflections" brings these very general considerations to bear on English common law, through a critical response to Hobbes's all-out attack on common-law jurisprudence. While fragmentary, "Reflections" suggests a conception of judicial reasoning and an understanding of political authority that deepen the view articulated in Hale's longer and more systematic work. In each work, key themes are sounded and, in some cases, elaborated. But these themes are best understood, and the range and the depth of Hale's jurisprudence are best appreciated, when these two works are read in conjunction with other works, some more systematic, some less so, in which these and cognate themes are discussed and argued. Hale's views on practical reasoning, discussed in *Treatise*, are elaborated and related explicitly to the necessary discipline of law in his "Preface to Rolle's Abridgement," in parts of his *History of the Common Law*, and, crucially, in "Reflections." The view, suggested in *Treatise*, that "human law" is necessarily instituted in the "constitutions" (practices, customs, and ways) of specific communities—manifesting therein their "consent"—is enriched and deepened in *History* and "Considerations Touching the Amendment or Alteration of Laws." His views about the foundations of political authority, sounded in *Treatise*, are argued at length in *Prerogatives of the King* and, to a lesser extent, in "Reflections." Key views about the necessary legal limits of ruling power, mentioned in "Reflections," are set in a systematic discussion of the nature and limits of political authority in *Prerogatives*.

This collection does not present, either in any part or in the whole, a systematic jurisprudential theory of authority, law, and reason. The closest Hale came to a systematic theory was his *Treatise*, but he intentionally limited it to articulating an account of the natural-law foundations of common law, not a fully developed theory of the latter. Nevertheless, there emerges from these writings a rich, subtle, sophisticated articulation of a classical common-law understanding.

Durham, North Carolina

Acknowledgements

This book was many years in the making and over those years I have been expertly assisted by many people. Several research assistants have aided me along the way, including Erin Ashworth-King, Kiran Bhardwaj, Ian Cruise, Katie Dickson, Theodore Graham, Elyse Hamilton, Caleb Harrison, R. L. Hunter, John Lawless, Sydnor Roy, and Joseph Sampson. I am very grateful for their excellent work. For guidance and advice I am indebted to colleagues and fellow scholars Reid Barbour, John Bell, Alan Cromartie, John Orth, C. D. C. Reeve, Philip Schofield, Victor Tunkel (for the Selden Society), D. E. C. Yale, and an extremely helpful anonymous reader. I could not have produced this book without the help of Dave Hansen and his staff at the library of University of North Carolina School of Law, and the library officials at the British Library, the library at Lambeth Palace, the National Humanities Centre, and the Beineke Library/Yale University. I owe a special debt of gratitude to Michael Lobban for his generous assistance and good counsel at many points in the evolution of this text, and for invaluable assistance regarding historical annotations of it. He helped me track down legal references, clarified many matters of English legal history for me, and saved me from mistakes too many to count. I fear even his heroic efforts did not prevent all of them and for those that remain I accept full responsibility.

Abbreviations

BL	BL Add MSS 18,235 (copy of *Treatise*)
BL Add MSS	British Library Additional Manuscripts
Draught	"Reflections on Mr Hobbs his Dialogue of the Law—Draught"
Ed	Introduces an editor's gloss on unfamiliar words or phrases
H	British Library MS, Hargrave 485 (copy of *Treatise*)
Harley	Harley 7159 [copy of *Treatise* in British Library]
Lambeth	MH's MSS in Lambeth Palace Library, London
MH	Sir Matthew Hale
OED	*Oxford English Dictionary* (2000)
Rights of the Crown	*Preparatory Notes Touching the Rights of the Crown* (Lincoln's Inn Library, Hargrave MS 9)—an early draft of *Prerogatives of the King*
RP	*Rotuli Parliamentarium*, 6 vols (London, 1767–77). English edition: *Parliamentary Rolls of Medieval England 1275–1504*, ed. Chris Given-Wilson (Leicester, 2005) available online at Scholarly Digital Editions, <http://www.sd-editions.com/PROME/home.html>
St. Realm	*Statutes of the Realm*, ed. A. Luders et al., 11 vols (London Eyre and Strahan, 1810–28); available at HeinOnline
YB	Yearbook, cited by term, regnal year, folio, and *placitum*

Editor's Introduction

Sir Matthew Hale (1609–76) was an advocate, parliamentarian, judge, and writer on legal, moral, scientific, philosophical, and theological topics. Deeply engaged in legal practice, he wrote about the common law with penetration and insight. He worked and wrote in the middle decades of seventeenth-century England, a tumultuous period of constitutional struggle, civil war, regicide, parliamentary and dictatorial rule, and eventual restoration of the monarchy. Although his Royalist sympathies were known, Hale sought to "steer himself between the rocks of contesting factions without shipwreck."[1] He was, however, a resolute partisan of the law and defender of its claim to govern the exercise of power whatever its stripe. He articulated his understanding of reason, law, and political authority in a large number of works composed over the course of his career. The writings collected here, composed in the last fifteen years of his life, represent his most mature thoughts on these topics.

Matthew Hale: Life, Career, Works

Hale was born 1 November 1609 in Alderley, Gloucestershire, six years after James I became king of England.[2] His father, a moderately successful barrister, died before Matthew reached the age of five. Young Matthew was educated by Antony Kingscot, a man of strong Puritan convictions. In 1626, Hale went up to Magdalen College, Oxford, where he was tutored by Obadiah Sedgewick, noted scholar and Presbyterian preacher. Hale began his study of law at Lincoln's Inn in 1629 and was called to the bar in 1636. In his student years, Hale was a hard-working student and a voracious reader. Throughout his life he read widely in Roman and English law, Greek and Latin classics, history, theology, and philosophy. Although he was reared on Calvinist theology, he was inclined towards theological rationalism. This led him to study classical, medieval, and contemporary philosophy and theology, including writings of Plato, Aristotle, and the Neo-Platonists and Neo-Stoics; Duns Scotus, Aquinas, and Suarez; Maimonides, Avicenna, Averroes, and Roger Bacon; and Descartes, Gassendi,

[1] Matthew Hale, "Observations" on "The Life and Death of Pomponius Atticus Written by his Contemporary and Acquaintance Cornelius Nepos" (probably written in the late 1670s) in *The Works, Moral and Religious, of Matthew Hale*, ed. T. Thirwall (London, 1805), vol. I, 467. In Hale's view, Pomponius conducted himself with utmost integrity and grace during a period of political upheaval in Rome. He regarded Pomponius as his model.

[2] Alan Cromartie offers the most comprehensive and balanced assessment of MH's life and body of writing in his book, *Sir Matthew Hale: 1609–1676* (Cambridge: Cambridge University Press, 1995). For a very helpful study of Hale's jurisprudence, see Michael Lobban, *A History of the Philosophy of Law in the Common Law World, 1600–1900* (Dordrecht: Springer, 2007), ch. 3.

Hobbes, and Selden.[3] In the late 1630s, he met intellectual giant, John Selden, who became his mentor, intellectual model, and friend. "That treasury of all kind of learning," he called him.[4] The impact of Selden's scholarship can be seen in much of Hale's work, notably his *Treatise of the Nature of Law* and *History of the Common Law of England.* Yet Hale was no mere disciple of Selden. From his own reading of classical and contemporary sources Hale developed nuanced views of law, reason, judgment, authority, obligation, and the relevance of history for law and politics.

Hale began his legal career as England's political conflicts escalated into civil war. In the 1640s and early 1650s, he defended political figures on both sides of the conflict, all the while avoiding entanglement in deadly partisan disputes. He gained a reputation for integrity, political moderation, and deep understanding of the law. In 1652, the Rump Parliament, keen on pushing forward a program of law reform, appointed Hale to a commission charged with examining the legal system as a whole. He presided over the commission initially and influenced discussions early on, but seemed to lose interest later. He argued vigorously against certain sweeping reforms of the court system and land law. This conservatism did not follow from fundamental opposition to correction or "amendment" of the law (see Part IV); rather, he resisted making substantial changes in the law in politically unstable times. He favoured a measured approach, guided by judges who, he thought, were best informed about law's quotidian operations.

In 1654, Hale represented Gloucestershire in the Protectorate's first parliament and sat for Oxford in Richard Cromwell's parliament in 1658, where he moved for restoration of the monarchy. He played an active role in negotiating the restoration in the Convention Parliament of 1660, urging that the king be returned, subject to limits on the royal prerogative. "We are like foolish passengers in a storm, that when the boat reels too much on one side, run all to the other; which doth not cure, but increase the danger," he mused. Before the regicide, "our king and his council would govern without a parliament: our cure was—the parliament to govern without a king." Now, he feared, "the detestation of the latter extreme under which we last smarted . . . will carry us over to the former extreme."[5]

Hale's reputation for integrity, learning, and command of the common law inclined Cromwell to offer him a position on the Court of Common Pleas in 1654. Hale explained to Cromwell that his reluctance to accept the commission stemmed from his view that the legal grounds of the Protector's authority were shaky. Cromwell

[3] Richard Baxter observed that MH studied Roman and canon law and during his years at Oxford read Aquinas, Scotus, Suarez, and other scholastics. R. Baxter, "Preface" to Matthew Hale, *Discourse of the Knowledge of God and of our Selves* (London, 1688), a2–a3. This observation is borne out by a catalogue of MH's books at Acton (dated 20 January 1668 in MH's hand), which includes works by authors mentioned above. (I am grateful to David Yale for allowing me to see a copy of this catalogue.)

[4] "Preface to Rolle's Abridgement," 159.

[5] Hale, "Considerations concerning the Present and Late Occurrences, for my own use and observation," (13 May 1660), quoted in J. B. Williams, *Memoirs of the Life, Character and Writings of Sir Matthew Hale* (London: Jackson and Walford, 1835), 63.

replied that he got possession of the government and was determined to keep it, but that he wished to rule according to the law and thus looked to men of law to administer justice. He add ominously that if he was not permitted "to govern by red gowns, he was resolved to govern by red coats."[6] Hale accepted the commission, serving on the court until Cromwell died. One might read Hale's decision and subsequent service on the court as opportunistic collaboration with an illegitimate government, but it is likely that they issued from his deep loyalty to the common law and his conviction that ruling power, however constituted, must be held accountable to that law. His refusal to try a case in which Cromwell packed the jury lends credence to this interpretation.[7]

In 1658, Hale resigned from the court, refusing the commission offered by Richard Cromwell, who, in Hale's view, lacked legitimacy. Despite his service under the Protectorate, Hale attracted the attention of Charles II. Upon his restoration in 1660, the king quickly appointed Hale to the Court of the Exchequer as Chief Baron. He served on that court until 1671, when the king made him Chief Justice of King's Bench. The Chief Justice was reputed to be impartial, independent, and a scrupulous adherent to the law, even in politically sensitive cases. Unlike Mansfield of a later generation, Hale was no great legal innovator, and his judicial opinions were not collected in written form, although at the time they were reputed to be authoritative and "incontestable."[8] In serious ill health, he resigned from the bench in February 1676.[9] On Christmas Day 1676, Hale died of congestive heart failure.

In his judicial career, he sought to follow the biblical injunction never to "respect the person of the poor nor honour the person of the mighty" (Lev. 19:15); however, he was known to be solicitous of the poor and inclined to favour "that side that most seemed to be oppressed."[10] After an especially gruelling few days on circuit in Bury St Edmonds, in which he presided at the trials of people charged with theft, arson, and murder, Hale wrote in his diary,

> I had rather through ignorance of the truth of the fact or the unevidence of it acquit ten guilty persons than condemn one innocent.... It is the grace and goodness of God that I myself have not fallen into as great enormities as those upon which I give judgment. I have the same passions and lusts and corruptions that even those malefactors themselves have.... But even while the duty of my place requires justice and possibly severity in punishing the offense, yet

[6] Sollom Emlyn reports the substance of Cromwell's reply in his preface to Matthew Hale, *History of the Pleas of the Crown* (London, 1736), vi.

[7] Edmund Heward, *Matthew Hale* (London: Robert Hale, 1972), 49.

[8] Heward, 110, quoting Roger North, *The Lives of Francis North, Dudley North, and John North* (London: George Bell, 1890), vol. I, 121.

[9] In his letter of May 1676 to MH, Richard Baxter writes with MH's imminent death clearly in mind: "An Unpublished Letter of the Reverend Richard Baxter to the Chief Justice Sir Matthew Hale," *Bulletin of the John Rylands Library*, 24 (Manchester: Manchester University Press, 1940), 173–5.

[10] Roger North, *Examen, or an Inquiry into the Credit and Veracity of a Pretended Complete History* (1740), 530, quoted in John Hostettler, *The Red Gown: The Life and Works of Sir Matthew Hale* (Chichester: Barry Rose, 2002), 139.

the sense of common humanity and human frailty should at the same time engage me to great compassion to the offender.[11]

This admirable compassion for the vulnerable, however, was notably lacking six years earlier in a case he also tried in Bury. In that case, two women were charged with bewitching several girls in the village. During the trial, one of the accusing girls was subjected to a test which raised serious doubts about the allegations. But, in his charge to the jury, Hale failed to review the evidence or call attention to the test; he merely directed the jury to strictly observe the evidence. In addition, he affirmed his belief that witchcraft was condemned by scripture, and the laws of all nations, and instructed the jury that it was criminal in the eyes of the laws of England. The women were convicted. Hale sentenced them to death, without consideration of mercy. Belief in witchcraft was common at the time, of course, even among the educated, but from the eighteenth century onward Hale's complicity in the death of these women has been judged a serious moral failing.[12] Apparently, the same devout religious convictions which moved him to compassion even for those who have committed serious crimes blinded his judgment and compassion in this case. However, there is some evidence that Hale may have had second thoughts later about his handling of this case.[13]

Hale's career also raises another question. Hale's biographer says "Hale was a fluent writer who liked to do his thinking pen in hand."[14] His prolific writings range from detailed studies of the law of customs on imported goods, to systematic analyses of English criminal law and royal prerogatives, to long theological treatises and occasional devotional essays. He even wrote scientific studies of magnetism. But only his "Preface to Rolle's Abridgement" (Part III) and a few writings on scientific

[11] Selections from MH's diary of autumn 1668 are reproduced in Maija Jansson, "Matthew Hale on Judges and Judging," *Journal of Legal History*, 9 (1988), 204–13. The above passage comes from pages 208, 209, 210.

[12] More recently, critics have cited another example of what they take to be MH's misogyny and antagonism against the interests of women. (See D. Lanham, "Hale, Misogyny and Rape," *Criminal Law Journal*, 7 (1983), 148–66 and Gilbert Geis, "Rape-in-Marriage: Law and Law Reform in England, the United States and Sweden," *Adelaide Law Review*, 6 (1977), 85–6; challenged by Wilfrid Prest in "Hale as Husband," *Legal History*, 14 (1993), 142–4.) They trace the common-law rule (not challenged until the 1970s), according to which a husband cannot be guilty of rape of his lawful wife, to a passage in MH's *History of the Pleas of the Crown*, vol. I, 629 (published posthumously in 1736). The judgment of these critics is unwarranted. Although MH clearly states the rule in this work, we cannot draw any conclusion about MH's attitude toward women from that fact. MH was no legal innovator, and he cannot reasonably be taken as the originator or even defender of this rule. *History of the Pleas of the Crown* was not a piece of legislation or even an authoritative judicial opinion, but rather a treatise outlining the criminal law at the time, based on MH's extensive knowledge of King's Bench records. Moreover, the work was not prepared for or destined for publication, so it could not have been intended to influence the development of the law. While it may reveal much about the attitude toward women in the common law at the time, it indicates little about MH's own attitude.

[13] See Cromartie, *Hale*, 239.

[14] Alan Cromartie, "Hale, Sir Matthew," *Oxford Dictionary of National Biography* [online version] (Oxford: Oxford University Press, 2004–14).

topics were published in his lifetime.[15] His vast production of work on law remained unpublished until well after his death. Some works were published in the late seventeenth century; Francis Hargrave edited and published several others in the eighteenth century; others remained unpublished until late in the twentieth century. (His *Treatise of the Nature of Law in General* is published in this collection for the first time.) Why were these works not published, we must ask?

We may never know the answer to this question. Hale wrote on some topics that were very controversial at the time, but it is unlikely that he kept the work from the public out of fear for himself or out of fear of waking the dogs of contention that had warred disastrously in the years before the Restoration. This explanation is implausible because among his unpublished writings are many that did not address hotly contested topics. A more likely explanation is that Hale wrote almost exclusively for purposes of self-education and self-articulation.[16] Hale was driven by curiosity and he explored without restraint the natural and intellectual world around him. Also, being a man of action, he sought through his writing to clarify, understand, and gain perspective on matters he dealt with in his work and life. We might add a further, more speculative, explanation. In addition to being professionally reflective, remarkable in a lawyer of his time, Hale was also unusually self-aware. He sought to integrate the legal, juridical, and political activities, and the understandings on which they rested, with his deeper moral and religious convictions. Self-education and self-articulation might have been part of a larger project of self-accounting and, ultimately, accounting before his God.

Jurisprudence in Seventeenth-Century England

In seventeenth-century England, the deepest and most deadly conflicts—conflicts over the nature, grounds, and limits of ruling power—were carried on in legal terms. The language of political contestation was drawn largely from the language of law. The dominant dialect was the language of indigenous common-law jurisprudence. This frame of thought, generated and sustained by common-law judges and lawyers, shaped the political thinking of England's populace.[17] But a second jurisprudential dialect, emerging from the continental natural-law tradition, could also be heard. Common law was Hale's native tongue, but he also spoke natural law fluently. He used both to articulate his contribution to jurisprudential thought. We can best begin

[15] Hale's collection of devotional writings, *Contemplations Moral and Divine* (London, 1676), was published shortly before he died, but it may have been published against his will.

[16] See Charles Gray, introduction to Hale, *History of the Common Law of England* (Chicago: University of Chicago Press, 1971), xvii–xix; D. E. C. Yale, "Hale as Legal Historian" (London: Selden Society Lecture, 1976), 9, 13–14.

[17] "To seventeenth century Englishmen, politics was a branch of the law." Alan Cromartie, "The Rule of Law," in John Morrill (ed.), *Revolution and Restoration: England in the 1650s* (London: Collins & Brown, 1992), 55; see also Johann P. Sommerville, *Royalists and Patriots*, 2nd edition (London: Longman, 1999), 82.

our exploration of the basic themes in Hale's jurisprudence with a sketch of these two traditions and their role in the political debates to which he addressed his thought.

The Natural-Law Tradition. Stemming from work of Aristotle and Cicero, natural-law jurisprudence was influentially articulated by Aquinas in the late thirteenth century and developed further by canon-law jurists and scholastic theologians thereafter. Although it was a product of ancient and medieval thought, its presence and importance were undiminished in the seventeenth century. Around the time Hale was writing his *Treatise*, Samuel Pufendorf published *Elements of a Universal Jurisprudence* (1660) and *The Law of Nature and Nations* (1672) and John Locke wrote *Essays on the Law of Nature* (1660–1). At the beginning of the century, two monumental contributions to the tradition were made by Francisco Suarez (*On Laws and God as Law-Giver*, 1612) and Hugo Grotius (*On the Laws of War and Peace*, 1625). In England, Thomas Hobbes published *De Cive* (1642) and *Leviathan* (1652), and the Cambridge Platonist, Nathanial Culverwell, wrote *Discourse of the Light of Nature* (1646/52). Some of these works, especially those of Suarez and Culverwell, maintained a strong connection to the tradition's scholastic roots, while other works, notably those of Hobbes, took the tradition in a new direction.[18] The older tradition, culminating in the work of Suarez, was still vital in the seventeenth century. Hale was much drawn to this tradition, although the influence of the work of his mentor, John Selden, is also much in evidence.[19]

Natural-law jurisprudence typically seeks to deepen our understanding of the law in and of political communities (secular or human law) by locating it in a larger theoretical—philosophical and theological—context. It offers an account of the generic concept of law and then explains various kinds of law, including human law, in its terms. Conventionally, the history of this tradition is told in terms of the dialectic between two camps that take opposed positions on the generic nature of law. Rationalists, according to this story, identify law with a rational ordering or a system of practically rational principles accessible to human reason. Voluntarists, in contrast, see law as the set of directives made and made known by someone in a position of authority. Both are inclined to speak of law as a kind of dictate, but the source of the dictate in one case is impersonal reason and in the other the very personal will of someone in power.

The rationalist account faces an immediate problem as the starting point of an explanation of human positive law, for, it is often pointed out, law does not merely *indicate* to an agent that something is right or good to do, it *demands* that the agent perform the action; it *obligates* the agent. What makes something good or right to do

[18] Some scholars have traced modern natural law to the work of Grotius, but, like other writers in this period, he mixed an emerging new understanding with substantial elements of the older tradition.

[19] MH's theory of law is often treated as heavily dependent on Selden's work. See Richard Tuck, *Natural Rights Theories* (Cambridge: Cambridge University Press, 1979), 132–3; Cromartie, *Hale*, 30; Lobban, *History*, ch. 3, esp. p. 63. However, I believe that this emphasis has obscured the evident and important influence of Suarez and the older scholastic tradition in MH's thought.

are the reasons in favour of the action, but what makes it legally binding, it is argued, involves something more. That something more, the voluntarist argues, is a person in a position of authority who imposes a demand on the law-subject, who makes the action obligatory. The voluntarist, however, also faces an obvious problem, for on that account law seems to be reduced to the arbitrary exercise of power, Moreover, if law is nothing more than the product of a ruler's lawmaking, law cannot govern the ruler; unavoidably, the ruler is above the law. The problems facing these two positions were familiar to medieval natural-law theorists and they sought to solve them in different ways. In legal theoretical writing from the thirteenth century on, rather than finding rationalists opposed to voluntarists, we find a series of attempts to combine rationalist and voluntarist elements in different ways, in different proportions, often mixed with other elements.

Aquinas's (1225–74) view is instructive in this respect. While he defined *ius* (right) as a kind of rational ordering,[20] he defined *lex* (law proper) as an "ordinance of reason," a "rule or measure" that *directs* actions of free, rational agents; law, he argued, is a directive of a someone in a position of superiority addressed to another, commanding some (rationally grounded) action.[21] *Lex* must have this directive force because it does not merely recommend actions, it makes them *obligatory*. Moreover, it is essential to law so understood that the ordinance of reason is made known ("promulgated") by a party in a position of authority, who is entrusted with "the care of the community."[22] Although Aquinas is conventionally put in the rationalist camp, he subtly combined rationalist and voluntarist elements.

Similarly, William of Ockham (1287–1347), conventionally assigned to the radical voluntarist camp, argued that an action is truly virtuous only if it is dictated by right reason and freely willed for the sake of the intrinsic value of the action and ultimately because right reason requires it.[23] Right reason identifies the natural goodness of actions and thus gives reasons to the agent to will, but it does not guarantee that the agent wills the action, nor does it constitute a binding moral precept. Precepts come from law, but law presupposes deliverances from right reason. *Ius fori* (positive law) must be established by human ordinance or pact, while *ius poli* (law of the heavens, i.e., natural law) is non-positive, a matter of harmony of action with right reason.[24]

[20] Aquinas, *Summa Theologiae*, IIaIIae, 57, a. 1, a. 2, in *Aquinas: Political Writings*, ed. R. W. Dyson (Cambridge: Cambridge University Press, 2002), 158–63.

[21] Aquinas, *Summa Theologiae*, IaIIae, 90, a. 1 and a. 4; 91, a. 1; 93, a. 5; 97, a. 3; in Dyson, 76–8, 82–5, 102, 153–5.

[22] Aquinas, *Summa Theologiae*, IaIIae, 90, a. 3, in Dyson, 80–2.

[23] William of Ockham, *Opera Theologica*, 9 vols (St. Bonaventure, NY: Franciscan Institute Press, 1967–86), vol. 8, 335. Marilyn McCord Adams, "The Structure of Ockham's Moral Theory," *Franciscan Studies*, 46 (1986), 1–35; Adams, "Ockham on Will, Nature, and Morality," in Paul Vincent Spade (ed.), *The Cambridge Companion to Ockham* (New York: Cambridge University Press, 1999), 245–72.

[24] Ockham, *The Work of Ninety Days*, chapter 65 in Ockham, *A Letter to the Friars Minor and Other Writings*, ed. Arthur Stephen McGrade and John Kilcullen and tr. John Kilcullen (Cambridge: Cambridge University Press, 1995), 49–51. Ockham makes room in his moral theory for both "positive moral science"—"the science that contains human and divine laws that obligate one to pursue or to avoid that which it neither good nor evil except because it is commanded or prohibited by a superior"—and

Natural law on his view is accessible to the ordinary exercise of human reason, and even the divine lawgiver directs human action only to the good and the right which exist apart from the exercise of his will.

In the early seventeenth century, the late-scholastic philosopher and theologian Francisco Suarez (1548–1617) articulated a nuanced hybrid of rationalist and voluntarist elements. Suarez started from the common premise that law has two essential features: it is a rational order and it obligates.[25] Debates among the late scholastics turned on what can account for the obligating force of law.[26] Domingo De Soto (1495–1560) argued that bare will can never obligate: a mere expression of will is just a wish and a wish does not obligate. Command is more than a mere wish; and the more, he argued, is supplied by reason. Suarez countered that reason is connected not to will but to intellect and judgment, and a mere act of judgment is not sufficient to obligate. Human reason or intellect can point out a (moral) necessity, but law *confers* necessity, brings it home to the agent, as it were. Law can do this only through an act of will, the will of a superior. The object of the superior's will, however, is not the subject's action; for the superior's willing gives rise to a "moral necessity" rather than a physical one. The superior wills to bind the subject—that is, the superior wills that the subject be under obligation.[27] Will alone, of course, is not sufficient either; will reinforces that which is already morally necessary by making it obligatory.[28] Both reason and will are necessary if we are to explain the special kind of normativity possessed by law, Suarez argued. Law and its distinctive binding force are rooted in the will of the lawgiver. Thus, law needs a lawmaker, but the lawmaker's will is not sufficient for the making of law. Lawmaking is governed by standards independent of the lawmaker's will.

Suarez's natural-law theory was influential in seventeenth century. Hale was surely familiar with it. He owned fifteen volumes of the Spanish philosopher's work and had studied them carefully already early in his life. He may also have been familiar with the theory Culverwell (1620–51) offered in lectures delivered in Cambridge in mid-century.[29] God's creation is rationally ordered, Culverwell maintained, and human good, which is rooted in created human nature, is a part of this ordered universe. The content of the law naturally governing human action is determined by rational

"non-positive moral science," which "directs human acts apart from any precept of a superior." Ockham, *Quodlibital Questions* (Second Quodlibit, q. 14), tr. Alfred Freddoso and Francis Kelly (New Haven: Yale University Press, 1991), 149.

[25] Francisco Suarez, *Treatise on Laws and God the Lawgiver*, in *Selection from Three Works*, ed. Thomas Pink and tr. Gwladys L. Williams, Ammi Brown, John Waldron, and Henry Davis (Indianapolis: Liberty Fund, 2015), Bk I, 1–6.

[26] Annabel Brett, "Later Scholastic Philosophy of Law," in Fred D. Miller and Carrie-Ann Biondi (eds), *A History of the Philosophy of Law from the Ancient Greeks to the Scholastics*, 2nd edition (Dordrecht: Springer, 2015), 335–75.

[27] Suarez, *On Laws*, Bk I, 4.7–9.

[28] Suarez, *On Laws*, Bk I, 1.1, 12.3.

[29] Nathaniel Culverwell, *An Elegant and Learned Discourse of the Light of Nature* (1652), ed. Robert A. Greene and Hugh MacCallum (Indianapolis: Liberty Fund, 2001).

principles of this ordered universe, but its formal character as law is not. The "sinew, life and soul" of a law is obligation, he maintained, and obligation presupposes a relationship to another. To be under obligation is to be accountable for one's actions to another.[30] Law makes certain actions obligatory and the obligation is owed to another party who is in a position to hold one accountable for one's actions. At the heart of law's formal obliging nature is not a fact of power, the imposition of one party's will on another, but a certain kind of normative relationship, that of one party's having standing to hold another to account and the other being liable to being held to account.

Thus, natural-law theory provided an account of the fundamental precepts of morality, in which both the divine lawgiver and natural human reason play a role. God's directive will makes binding precepts that direct action to that which is independently and intrinsically good and away from that which is intrinsically evil; yet the precepts themselves are accessible to human reason. Human or secular law must fit this pattern, too, according to the natural-law tradition. Human law is formally instituted: it is either explicitly made or it emerges as custom from the interactions of many people over time. Like natural law, secular law presupposes an authority that makes or at least adopts and endorses its norms and holds subjects accountable to them. It also presupposes natural law as its measure.

By what warrant can one make and enforce this positive law and what role does the established natural law play in the daily life of this law? Answers to these questions emerge from attempts to answer the prior question: what need is there for secular law if natural law is already in force and functioning? The typical answer, inaugurated by Aquinas and developed in various ways in later scholastic theories, offers three related reasons. First, positive law is needed to make up for weaknesses of human reason and motivation. It may be difficult for ordinary individuals to work out what natural law requires of them, especially in contexts of complex social interaction, and even where practical reason gives clear direction, motivation to act accordingly is often lacking. Second, natural law does not provide a detailed code of behaviour for all contexts and circumstances. Its principles are general and to a degree silent with regard to specifics. Secular law is needed to specify the sometimes indeterminate principles of natural law. Natural law guides without determining the content of secular law, by providing a framework of general principles which can be worked out in potentially many different ways. Third, natural-law theories typically recognized that determinations of the natural law must be made for and addressed to people with limited rational capacities, who must interact in complex social contexts in which what seems best for them to do individually often depends on what they expect others to do. Thus, although natural law ultimately grounds both secular law and the

[30] Culverwell, *Discourse*, 57.

authority of those empowered to make and enforce it, its role in the daily life of this law might be indirect.

English Common-Law Jurisprudence. Natural-law concepts and modes of thought were not absent from English jurisprudence before the seventeenth century, but English jurists found them uncomfortable and tended to push them to the margins of their thought. For example, Fortescue (1395–1479) conceded that common law was ultimately grounded in natural law, but he thought the more immediate and important ground of common law was the fact that it existed unchanged as the law of the English people from time immemorial.[31] St German (1460–1540), writing in the early sixteenth century, drew on Aquinas and later Thomist jurists.[32] His *Dialogue* argued that the validity of human law depends on conformity to first principles of natural law, but that natural law of itself cannot obligate. A wise man may discover a precept of natural law, but his judgment does not bind unless it has authority, he argued.[33] For obligation, the authority of custom or statute is necessary. He argued that the common law is fundamentally founded on custom, "the law of secondary reason,"[34] and on "maxims" that give rational structure to the common law and guide judicial deliberations. The strength and warrant of maxims, however, lay not in independent principles of natural law, but rather in their coherence with and integration into the body of the common law.[35] St German thought that "conscience" or "equity" played an important role in judicial reasoning, but this natural power of the soul,[36] oriented to the good and the just, must be structured and made orderly by existing law, only rarely modifying or reforming it.

Like Fortescue, St German rooted English law in common customs of the people, although he insisted that it was for the courts to determine the existence and shape of those customs. The authority of the deep principles ("maxims") of English law lay in their approval by the king and people, evidenced in their continued use over long periods of time. Likewise, Richard Hooker (1554–1600), writing on the eve of the seventeenth century, argued that while human law must accord with natural and divine law, its force lies in the consent of the people and the king, evidenced in their continued use.[37] Hooker also echoed a theme that had been central to common-law jurisprudence since the thirteenth century. The work known as *Bracton* asserted that the king is subject to no man but only to God and the law.[38] Likewise, Hooker argued that the monarch, although supreme in the realm, is nevertheless subject to

[31] See Lobban, *History*, 7–14. [32] See Lobban, *History*, 14–25.

[33] Christopher St German, *Dialogue betwixt a Doctor of Divinity and a Student of the Common Laws of England* (1523, 1530), ed. T. F. T. Plucknett and J. L. Barton (London: Selden Society, 1974), 27.

[34] St German, *Dialogue*, 33. [35] St German, *Dialogue*, 57–9. [36] St German, *Dialogue*, 81.

[37] Richard Hooker, *Of the Laws of Ecclesiastical Polity: Preface, Books I and VIII*, ed. Arthur Stephen McGrade (Cambridge: Cambridge University Press, 1989), 92–3.

[38] *Bracton on the Laws and Customs of England*, ed. Samuel E. Thorne and George E. Woodbine (Cambridge, MA: Harvard University Press, 1968–77), vol. 2, 339.

the law—not merely the natural or divine law, but the common law of England. "What power the King hath," he wrote, "he hath by law"; the law gives dominion to the king and the king "must hold it of and under the law."[39]

Thus, common-law jurisprudence in Hale's time inherited and to a degree absorbed from the natural-law tradition a language for thinking about law and authority, but this language was differently inflected and in some ways substantially altered by the local circumstances in which it was used.[40] Rooted in and shaped by the practice of judges and lawyers, common-law jurisprudence was less systematic and more pragmatic. Its core concepts formed a web rather than a hierarchy, each modified by and modifying the others. Common-law understanding of English law was formed by the interaction of four central notions: custom, reason, time (the past), and consent. It is a measure of the interdependence of these concepts that one prominent common-law jurist could write "Common law is nothing else but common custom," while another could write, "Common law is nothing else but common reason," without seeming to contradict the first.[41]

Common law was said to be, or to be rooted in, "reasonable usage." This was not meant to imply that its rules or doctrines had their origin in custom to the exclusion of explicitly enacted statutes or royal charters. Nor did it imply that unwritten rules were originally matters of popular custom or usage. But essential to the claim was the thought that the legislative power of the king (or King-in-Parliament) was grounded in something with deep roots in the political community—that at a fundamental level law made the king, not king the law. It also implied that, regardless of the source of a given rule or doctrine, the law was not to be understood as something laid down by the exercise of ruling power, but rather something taken up, having their content and force in the regular use of the doctrines in the practical reasoning, first of all, of the courts, and by extension, of the people generally. The doctrines used in the courts had ultimately to be approved by the crown and the people in their daily activities.

Time was thought to play an important role in the ordinary functioning of this law and its proximate force and appeal. Common-law reasoning sought to anchor present and precedent-setting decisions in actions, decisions, and practices that could be seen to be continuous over time. The rules that shaped ordinary life in the political community, as well as the rules defining the powers and prerogatives of royal government—defining the rights and liberties of subjects and rulers alike—were seen as an inheritance, a birthright. Their normative claim on the deliberations and actions of those subject to them was usually not thought to rest in their ancient

[39] Hooker, *Laws of Ecclesiastical Polity*, 140, 146, 217.

[40] Generally, see Gerald J. Postema, "Classical Common Law Jurisprudence," *Oxford University Journal of Commonwealth Law*, 2 (2002), 155–80 and 3 (2003), 1–28.

[41] John Davies, "Irish Reports," in *The Works in Verse and Prose... of Sir John Davies*, ed. Alexander B. Grosart (Blackburn, 1869–76), II, 251–2; Henry Finch, *Law, or a Discourse Thereof* (1627) (New York: Kelly, 1969), 75. See Postema, "Classical Common Law Jurisprudence, Part I," *Oxford University Journal of Commonwealth Law*, 2 (2002), 168–80.

wisdom so much as in the fact of their having shaped the common life of people in the kingdom, continuously and adroitly adapting to the changing circumstances of that life. Time was not enough; rather, over time the rules and doctrines, whatever their origin, took root in and were integrated into the body of the law and the practices of the people. The common law was thought to be the constitution, not of government only, but of the political community as a whole, not only of the king but also of the kingdom. Such integration was thought to manifest, perhaps to constitute, a kind of common consent. This "ancient constitution," refined and adjusted over time, was thought to define and protect the liberties and rights of the English people.

Yet common law was, on this view, not only community-constituting usage, but also "common reason." This reason of the law, however, was not immediately accessible to any person of ordinary capacities of human reason, nor could it be measured by an independent and transcendent standard (of, for example, natural or divine law); rather, law's reason was thought to be internal to the law. When actions or rules were said to be "against reason," this meant that they were inconsistent with the law as a whole. Law was *summa ratio*, highest reason, because it was thought that those who wished to understand its doctrines must approach them on the working assumption that they fit together as a coherent, pragmatically workable whole. Their claim to reasonableness lay in the fact that they were the products of a distinctive mode of *reasoning*. Thus, the rules and doctrines of the common law were said to have their standing and force not because they are rational or right, but because they are *reasoned*, having emerge from and survived a formal and public process of discursive reasoning. The reason of common law, argued Sir Edward Coke, is not untutored natural reason, but rather the "artificial reason" practised paradigmatically in the courts.[42] Law's reason is a disciplined practice of reasoning mastered through long study and experience in the company of other students and practitioners of law. It was "artificial" not in the sense of being arbitrary, but rather in the sense of being the reason of the pragmatic craftsman (*artifex*)[43] of practical reasoning within the law, a craft practised in open courts, subject to challenge and rebuttal.

Thus, the characterizations of law as common custom and as common reason, existing from "time immemorial" and the product of "artificial reason," travelled together in classical common-law jurisprudence. On this view, rules and doctrines could find their way into the common law by various routes—royal charter, acts of parliament, judicial articulation, or general custom identified and elaborated by the

[42] "The common law itself is nothing but reason," Sir Edward Coke wrote in 1628, but he hastened to add that this is not "every man's natural reason," but rather "an artificial perfection of reason gotten by long study, observation, and experience"; for "*nemo nascitur artifex*" [no one is born a craftsman]. *First Part of the Institutes of the Laws of England*, 97b, in *The Selected Writings of Sir Edward Coke*, ed. Steve Sheppard (Indianapolis: Liberty Fund, 2003), 701. For a general discussion of the common-law idea of "artificial reason," see Gerald J. Postema, "Classical Common Law Jurisprudence: Part II," *Oxford University Commonwealth Law Journal*, 3 (2003), 1–11.

[43] Coke linked law's reason to Aristotle's notion of craft (*techne*) in his report of "Calvin's Case," in *Seventh Report*, 19a, Sheppard, *Coke: Selected Writings*, I, 210.

courts—but their place in the body of the law was determined by their role in the reasoning of the courts, reasoning disciplined by a common, public practice. Common-law writers often claimed, further, that this law rests on "consent," a kind of constructive consent manifested in the ordinary operation of the law.[44]

Debates over England's Political Constitution. In the first half of the seventeenth century, perennial questions of political theory took on special urgency as common lawyers, parliamentary partisans, and radical republican forces challenged the increasingly authoritarian rule of the Stuart monarchs. By the 1660s, when Hale was writing the works included in this collection, the civil war had ended and monarchy was restored; yet, the issues that divided the country remained salient. Two issues were of special interest to royalists and their opponents:[45] (1) the scope of the king's legislative power, and (2) the ground and limits of royal prerogative powers (powers uniquely assigned to the crown to act on its initiative and discretion alone without advance guidance of the law or accountability after the fact). Debates about these issues soon drove participants to opposing positions on fundamental questions regarding the source and limits of ruling authority and the role of law in governing and guiding the exercise of that authority. Both natural-law and common-law traditions provided resources for these debates.

Perhaps the dominant common-law position (albeit not the position of all common-law judges) took its point of departure from Bracton's dictum (echoed by Hooker) mentioned earlier: although the king is supreme in the land, he is subject to the law and all rightful royal power is power ordained by the ordinary law of the land. On this view, ruling power is subject to reason, and law is the means by which reason orders and ordains ruling power. Thus, law not only constrains ruling power, but it alone constitutes and grounds it. The common law, rooted in time immemorial, was regarded as the "ancient constitution," defining and limiting the powers of the prince and determining and protecting the rights and liberties of the people.

This common-law perspective did not yield a univocal answer to the questions of the scope of the king's legislative or prerogative powers. Rather, it focused the high-stakes political debate on the content, and hence the history, of the common-law constitution.[46] One central issue in this debate concerned the nature of William I's accession to the throne in 1066. Some argued that in battle he defeated Harold, a rival to the throne, but took the crown by rightful title. While he made major changes in

[44] Before MH, John Selden sought to bring together the natural-law and common-law modes of thought. His influence is seen at various points in MH's thought.

[45] Lobban, *History*, 41–51.

[46] On the role of the idea of the "ancient constitution" in seventeenth-century English politics, see Sommerville, *Royalists and Patriots*; Alan Cromartie, *The Constitutionalist Revolution* (Cambridge: Cambridge University Press, 2006); Glenn Burgess, *The Politics of the Ancient Constitution* (University Park, PA: Pennsylvania State University Press, 1992); Janelle Greenberg, *The Radical Face of the Ancient Constitution* (Cambridge: Cambridge University Press, 2001), chs 4–6.

English law, initiating the system of feudal tenures throughout the land, nevertheless he did so within the four corners of the ancient constitution. Others insisted that William acquired the crown through right of conquest alone, imposing Norman institutions and law on a conquered nation. On the latter view, the Norman Conquest marked a major constitutional discontinuity in the history of the English and their law. Some argued from this premise that limits on ruling power recognized in contemporary law were merely the gracious self-limiting concessions of an all-powerful sovereign. Others, drawing a revolutionary conclusion, argued that the ancient constitution, distorted by the "Norman Yoke," must be recovered, and the institutions introduced after the Conquest eliminated. Political debate focused on the law and the debate about the constitutional principles of law focused on its history. The history of the common law was a major battleground of politics in seventeenth-century England.

Some common-law writers argued that the monarch, while in certain respects limited by the law, nevertheless retained some powers that transcended the law, the exercise of which were never accountable to common-law courts.[47] However, defenders of a more robust and expansive understanding of the sovereignty of the monarch tended to draw on natural-law sources, although that support was also equivocal. Natural-law writers from the late medieval period onward tended to agree broadly on the need for political authority. They argued that human individuals are by nature radically dependent on others for survival, but also have diverse and potentially complementary capabilities, such that working cooperatively together they can live better than living apart. Moreover, human beings tend naturally toward social union and thrive only when united in communities. Yet, they argued, their diversity and their narrow, self-oriented perspectives make it difficult for spontaneous associations and cooperative arrangements to arise and survive. Ruling authority is both necessary and useful. And for these reasons, God ordained all political power, and all political authorities are subject to God and the natural law. Governments are bound by a special overarching duty to serve the *salus populi*, the safety and well-being of the community and its members.

God ordained all political power, on this view, but natural-law theories divided over the way in which the forms and modes of the institution of government were determined. Some, like divine-right theories, insisted that God is directly involved in instituting government, having granted all dominion to Adam and to his proper descendants. The Stuart monarchs in England embraced this view. It had the welcome implication that sovereign authority rested on God and not on human law, and hence the sovereign was above that law, although not above divine law.

[47] Chief Baron Fleming, "Bates's Case," in T. B. Howell, *A Complete Collection of State Trials* (London, 1816–26), II, 389; Sir John Davies, *The Question Concerning Impositions, Tonnage, Poundage* (London, 1656), 30–2. See Francis Oakley, "Jacobean Political Theology: The Absolute and Ordinary Powers of the King," *Journal of the History of Ideas*, 29 (1968), 323–46.

Another extra-legal mode of institution was conquest, which was, again on these views, a means of direct divine institution—for the outcome of battle was thought to manifest the judgment of heaven. Like divine-right theories, conquest theories tended to reject legal-constitutional constraints on sovereign power.

Other theories accorded God only an indirect role in the institution of government. These theories typically saw some mode of popular consent as the proximate source of political authority. But this idea, too, developed in different ways. On one such theory, popular consent was seen as the device by which divine authority was transmitted, delegated to particular human individuals or groups. The people select their rulers, but selection was seen as a mode of designating the God-ordained ruler, rather than a mode of transfer of a power originally located in the people. On other understandings, political power originally held by the people (collectively, according to late medieval theories) was transferred to the rulers thus selected. Designation theories could be used to support absolutist constitutional arguments, but so too could transfer theories; for what enables and empowers constitutional constraints on the exercise of ruling power—legal limits on sovereign power—are institutional means by which those exercising power are held accountable to the ordinary law. On some transfer theories, sovereignty was transferred to the governing power voluntarily, but unconditionally and irrevocably. On this view, sovereign power was portrayed as unconditioned by any human force and beyond all human judgment (although subject, of course, to God and the natural law).

However, consent theories also offered resources for building a foundation for constitutional limitations on sovereign power. On the transfer model, if the transfer was conditioned on respecting certain constitutionally defined limits, or if certain rights or powers were not transferable (i.e., if they were inalienable), secular law might enshrine these limits and the sovereign might then be held accountable to them. Again, the nature and potential conditions of the transfer, and hence the principles of the existing political constitution, were thought to rest on events or processes rooted in the history of law.

Hobbes. The most sophisticated philosopher of politics and law of mid-seventeenth-century England was Thomas Hobbes. He staked out a distinctive and now familiar position in this hotly contested domain. In Hale's *Treatise*, Hobbes is a frequent, but unidentified, interlocutor and opponent. He appears as the sole antagonist in Hale's *Reflections*.

Hobbes argued from a distinctive, "modern" natural-law framework for a (near) absolutist account of law and political authority. The central aim of his most mature work, *Leviathan*,[48] was to demonstrate the rational necessity of a sovereign, the ultimate maker and interpreter of the law, who is not subject to its governance or

[48] Thomas Hobbes, *Leviathan* (1651), ed. Richard Tuck (Cambridge: Cambridge University Press, 1991).

limits. Only political authority of this kind, he argued, can solve permanently the problems of social conflict that human beings, who are prone to narrowness of interest and judgment, face when forced to live together. In the absence of a common power (in the "state of nature"), human beings judge what is just and right by their own lights;[49] and, given their radical uncertainty about how others will behave, in particular uncertainty about whether others will respect their rights, they find pre-emptive violence in protection of their rights rationally unavoidable. The state of nature inevitably erupts in a war of all against all.[50]

However, Hobbes maintained, natural-law precepts—directing each individual to the best means to their survival—require that rational human beings seek peace on the condition that others do as well, and so require them to consent to any political arrangement that guarantees escape from this state of nature and prevents risk of return to it. These natural-law precepts are, in Hobbes's view, dictates of practical rationality, true and accessible to individual human reason in the same way as principles of mathematics are; they are laws, properly speaking, just insofar as they can be seen as commands of God.[51] For, he insisted, laws are commands, acts of authority not wisdom, and they bind just insofar as there is someone in a position to enforce them. Secular law is nothing more than the commands of the secular sovereign, who holds his position of authority by virtue of his subjects' voluntary transfer of (nearly) all of their rights of judgment. Although law is command and "not philosophy or other disputable arts," law is *summa ratio*;[52] indeed, in civil society, "law is all the right reason we have."[53] But Hobbes understood this typical natural-law and common-law slogan in a non-typical way. Law is reason, first, in that it is the product of the exercise of the (essentially private) judgment and will of the sovereign, whose will is *deemed* by all to be public reason *for them*, the authorized surrogate for the private reason and judgment of each. Second, law is reason in the sense that it is rational (as dictated by the precepts of security-promoting natural law) for each subject to obey without question one who articulates and enforces common public standards, and thereby guarantees personal security.

For Hobbes, the sovereign is above the law. He makes, applies, and enforces it, or revocably delegates such power to others. He is bound by the natural law to seek the *salus populi* and must govern by means of law. However, no human entity—person, people, or institution—has standing to judge him or hold him accountable to civil or natural law. The sovereign must rule by law, because the fundamental problems of the state of nature are problems of the privacy of judgment due to the absence of common standards of judgment and behaviour. This duty, like the general duty to

[49] Hobbes, *Leviathan*, 91. [50] Hobbes, *Leviathan*, chapter 13. [51] Hobbes, *Leviathan*, 111.

[52] Thomas Hobbes, *Dialogue between a Philosopher and a Student of the Common Laws of England*, in Thomas Hobbes, *Writings on Common Law and Hereditary Right*, ed. Alan Cromartie and Quinten Skinner (Oxford: Clarendon Press, 2005), 19.

[53] Thomas Hobbes, *English Works*, ed. Sir William Molesworth (London: 1839–45), vol. V, 194.

seek the *salus populi*, imposes constraints on the behaviour of the sovereign. But, again, no one, save God, has standing to judge whether the sovereign has complied with these natural-law imposed duties.

Hale's Common-Law Jurisprudence

Taken together, the works collected in this volume offer a general account of the nature and foundations of English law and of law in general. They highlight Hale's views on three issues fundamental to classical common-law jurisprudence: the nature and binding force of law, the nature of practical reasoning within the law, and the nature, grounds, and limits of political authority. Hale's *Treatise* (Part I) addresses all of these issues from a general point of view. In the remaining selections, he discusses them with English common law in view. The selection from Hale's *History of the Common Laws of England* (Part II) addresses all three. "Reflections on Mr Hobbs his Dialogue" (Part V) offers an account of practical reasoning within common law; other elements of common-law reasoning are presented in his "Preface to Rolle's Abridgement" (Part III) and "Considerations Touching the Amendment or Alteration of Laws" (Part IV). Hale directly addresses the question of the grounds and limits of political authority in the selection from *Prerogatives of the King* (Part VI) and offers further insights on it in "Reflections" and again in "Jurisdiction of the Lords House" (Part VII). We begin with Hale's discussion of the nature of law in his *Treatise*.

Law

In a manner reminiscent of scholastic treatises on law, Hale opens his *Treatise* with a characterization of law in general, which informs his account of divine law, natural law, and instituted law, in particular English common law. Law, he writes, is a rule of moral (i.e., voluntary) actions given to beings capable of understanding and will by one with the authority to give law and exact obedience (*Treatise*, 3). This might seem an unpromising beginning for an account of English common law, at least, for a jurist who gives a large role to unwritten law (*lex non scripta*) in common law. So we must look carefully at Hale's elaboration and defence of the various components of this sketch of his conception.

In Hale's view, two features of law drive this characterization of law. First, a law is a rule addressed to "intellectual creatures" regarding their voluntary actions, directing them to some independently existing good or against some independently existing evil (or, if the actions are in themselves morally indifferent, then to some good that is to be achieved by compliance with the rules). Law guides behaviour by engaging the understanding and the will of agents. It "discovers" or indicates the good or evil in the actions to which it calls attention (the "*vis indicativa*" of law) and directs actions accordingly (*Treatise*, 63). But directives grounded in the intrinsic moral quality of actions are not *laws*, by that feature alone, for laws are fundamentally obligatory (*Treatise*, 4–5). Thus, secondly, laws necessarily have a *vis preceptiva* or *vis imperativa*—prescriptive or imperative force (*Treatise*, 63). Obligation, in Hale's view, is a relational notion: obligations place an agent in a special kind of (normative) relationship with another agent (*Treatise*, 9, 64–5). Obligatory actions are not merely reason-supported or morally required; they are owed to someone, someone who can hold the obligated agent accountable for acting in accord with directives. Since one cannot hold oneself accountable,[54] there must be another party, someone in authority, to hold one accountable.[55]

This relationship of authority involves "the just right" or standing of one party to obligate another (*Treatise*, 13). The party in authority has standing to put another party under obligation through the exercise of will or command. It should be noted that Hale does not define obligation in terms of liability to suffer punishment (or even less, the probability of doing so),[56] but rather in terms of answerability to another. For Hale, the capacity to exact obedience is auxiliary to the primary task of holding a party accountable (*Treatise*, 4–5, 14, 64). Moreover, according to Hale, the characteristic attitude of those who recognize they are under obligation is not fear of punishment, but recognition of being bound by and to the will of another. It follows from this view of the two fundamental features of law that the "intellectual creatures," who are bound by obligations, must be capable of (1) understanding and freely following directives, (2) grasping the good to which their behaviour is directed, and (3) appreciating and participating in a certain kind of normative relationship.

The product of combining these two core features of law is what we might, with Hale's encouragement, call his "thetic" conception of law: laws are directives for voluntary actions of rational agents given by a *nomothetes* (lawgiver) who has authority to give (make or endorse) those directives and exact obedience to them. This conception is meant to capture the distinctive normative features of law. Hale makes clear that law requires a *nomothetes*, but the *nomothetes* need not be the *author* of the law, as long as its endorsement *authorizes* it. Divine "natural" law is implicitly "thetic"; similarly, customary law, he maintains, has fully "the force of law"

[54] Like many other philosophers, MH holds that to be accountable to oneself is to be accountable to no one. See *Treatise*, 5, 63. The argument MH makes in this passage is common in the early modern period. See Jean Bodin, *On Sovereignty: Four Chapters from "The Six Books of the Commonwealth,"* ed. and tr. Julian H. Franklin (Cambridge: Cambridge University Press, 1992), 10–13; Hugo Grotius, *The Rights of War and Peace*, Bk II, ch. 2, paragraph 12, ed. Richard Tuck (Indianapolis: Liberty Classics, 2005); Hobbes, *Leviathan*, 184.

[55] In an early essay, "Of doing as we would be done unto," MH seems to embrace the possibility that one might be accountable to oneself. The golden rule, he writes "sets up a tribunal within every man's breast, which will infallibly and impartially direct him; and his own will, and the determination thereof, is become his law and his judge" (*Works*, I, 400–1). However, in *Treatise*, 97, MH makes clear that conscience is witness not to the rightness/wrongness of certain actions, but to the obligatory nature of the actions, that is, to their binding *as law*, and so to the relationship that exists between moral agents and God who holds them accountable.

[56] Here MH departs from Selden who held that being under obligation logically entailed being liable to punishment. The idea of obligation without punishment is no more conceivable than the idea of paternity without a child. Selden, *De jure naturali et gentium juxta disciplinam Ebraeorum* (London, 1640), I.4, p. 47.

even if it lacks the explicit, formal character of enacted law (*Treatise*, 14). As we proceed, we will see how Hale attempts to reconcile this thetic conception with both natural law and common law.

Natural law. Hale distinguishes two broad classes of law: divine law and human law. Human law is exclusively *instituted* (*ex instituto*), but divine law can be either "natural" or "positive." The latter is explicitly made, announced, and addressed by God to specific communities (for example, the Mosaic Law, addressed to the Israelite people) or to people generally (for example, the seven "Noachide" laws of the Talmudic tradition, which were addressed to Noah and his offspring, and all human beings living thereafter). The Mosaic Law concerned both matters of "natural right" and matters that were morally indifferent, for example, ways in which people ought to worship God. However, in neither case was the divine positive law merely arbitrary, in Hale's view, for laws regarding matters of worship defined ways appropriately to express the awe, love, and gratitude naturally due to God, and the remainder of the decalogue explicitly articulated and endorsed matters that were independently required by natural law, adding penalties for disobedience. Natural law, in contrast, is not explicitly or expressly commanded, Hale maintained; nevertheless, its ground and status as law lies in the will of God communicated to intellectual creatures.

Natural law, in Hale's view, is a hybrid of two essential features: (1) directives regarding matters of intrinsic moral goodness or evil that are logically prior to God's judgment and will and (2) the communicated will of God (*Treatise*, 63, 95–6). Without God's willing his creatures to be under obligation, there would be no law, but only morally good or evil actions; equally, no directives willed by God could be law without "discovering" to God's intellectual creatures actions that are intrinsically good or evil. Hale's conception of natural law, like Suarez's, is *thetic* but not *voluntarist*.[57] God's prescribing an action is not sufficient to make it good (except for morally indifferent actions);[58] yet nothing that is morally good is obligatory by virtue of that fact alone, because, as we have seen, obligation is rooted in a kind of relationship, not

[57] MH expresses a standard voluntarist view in "Of doing as we would be done unto." He writes, "The moral goodness of every act or action of mankind, whether internal or external, relating to God or man, consists in the conformity thereof to the will and command of God, which is the primitive rule of all moral goodness: and the moral evil of any act or action is the deformity, deviation, or contrariety thereof to the will or law of God" (Hale, *Works*, I, 388–9). But this view is not echoed anywhere in the *Treatise* or other jurisprudential writings. Moreover, later in the same essay he writes that, although God commands that I not do that which I would not have another do to me, yet "if there were no such express commands . . . the very precept itself includes a most evident conviction of an eternal and indispensable justice in it; for if I judge this action should not be done to me, and that it were unjust and unreasonable if it were so done, why should I go about to do that to him that I would condemn as unjust if done to me?" (*Works*, I, 413–14).

[58] "That which is morally good is eternally and intrinsically so, and that which is morally evil is eternally and intrinsically evil, and therefore the matter of this natural law is in that which is eternally or intrinsically good or evil, though there were no law superadded commanding or prohibiting it" (*Treatise*, 95).

just the moral quality of the obligatory act. Thus, Hale's account of the relationship between God and human creatures lies at the centre of his account of natural law.[59]

Hale divides the subject matter of natural law into three broad groups: matters relating to God, matters regarding the self, and matters relating to others. He spends a good deal of time listing duties falling into each of these groups (*Treatise*, Chapter 5). For jurisprudential purposes, the third group is the most important, but before we consider it, two themes that emerge from his discussion of duties regarding the self deserve attention. First, like many philosophers of the time, Hale argues that it is right for one to defend one's life and to secure what is necessary to support life, although he quickly insists that this justification is limited (*Treatise*, 42–3, 49). It is weaker than the right of self-defence defended by Grotius and much weaker than Hobbes's right of nature. Moreover, it plays no significant role in his account of the natural duties we have towards others. The foremost principle of natural law that generates duties to others, according to Hale, is the principle of faith-keeping or fidelity: *fides est servanda* (*Treatise*, 48). Second, his account of natural duties owed to others rests on an assumption of the fundamental moral equality among all human beings. Natural and social differences exist among human beings, but they have no intrinsic moral significance, according to Hale, and advantages attached to such differences are not deserved. Quoting Paul's epistle to the Corinthians, he pointedly asks, "What hast thou which thou hast not received?" (*Treatise*, 47; see also 42). This moral equality implies natural political equality, Hale maintains: no person has a natural right of governance over another (*Prerogatives*, 208).[60]

In Chapter 5 of his *Treatise*, Hale argues that fundamental principles of moral right that prescribe just, decent, and honourable behaviour of one person to another exist and are binding prior to established civil society and its law (*Treatise*, 48). He explicitly rejects the Hobbesian thesis that in the state of nature each person has a right to act on his judgment of what best serves his own security.[61] One has a limited right of self-defence, Hale concedes, and outside civil society there may be no impartial judge to determine when that right has been properly exercised. Nevertheless, one chooses to act in self-defence at one's peril, for God judges whether one has judged aright.[62] Also, Hale argues that in the pre-social condition, the resources of the material world were given to all in common for their survival and mutual enjoyment, so no one has a right to exclude another from access to those resources.[63]

59 See the discussion of MH's view of divine authority in the section "Political Authority and Obligation."

60 However, MH does accept that a right to parental rule is "settled in the father by the law of nature" (*Treatise*, 54). But like Locke, MH regards the parental right as limited and sharply distinguished from a political right to rule.

61 Hobbes, *Leviathan*, 91; Hobbes, *On the Citizen*, ed. Richard Tuck, tr. Michael Silverthorne (Cambridge: Cambridge University Press, 1998), 1.7–10 (pp. 27–8).

62 *Treatise*, 49, 52. MH takes a similar view of the limits of political obligation. Although refusal to obey a legitimate, albeit unjust, ruler may be justified in some circumstances, one acts against the law at one's peril. He recognizes no right to act on one's conscientious judgment (*Treatise*, 59).

63 *Treatise*, 50. MH follows medieval natural-law and canon-law doctrine.

Hale concludes that, in view of this fact, and the fundamental moral equality of all human beings, exclusive property rights to portions of the material world can justifiably exist only in a society established on the basis of consent.[64]

Hale distinguished two broad levels of natural-law truths (*Treatise*, 35–7). At the primary level are self-evident principles, known directly and universally without discursive reasoning, and their immediate logical implications. Among these are very abstract principles like, "do that which is right," or only slightly less abstract like the golden rule and "do not harm the innocent." Immediate implications from self-evident truths include: "God is to be worshipped and obeyed," which follows directly from a grasp of the kind of being God is, and "*fides est servanda*," which follows from an elementary understanding of the fact that society would not be possible if the principle were not observed. The class of secondary moral truths includes all further implications and applications of these fundamental truths to the vast variety of particular circumstances of daily moral life. These moral truths are accessible to human beings through exercise of their faculties of discursive reasoning. Hale does not doubt that moral truths, from the most abstract to the most concrete, exist and are accessible to rational creatures, at least in principle. But he concedes that the further a morally serious and intellectually competent person moves from abstract and self-evident first principles, the greater are the demands on the intellect to appreciate the moral complexities of daily life and judge aright with respect to them. Moral truths that fall into the first group are truly common to (and commonly acknowledged by) all human beings. But those that fall into the latter are not common in the sense of being immediately accessible to all. Instituted law is needed to supplement natural law, where natural law is difficult to determine or is indeterminate. This is the domain of natural law's *lex permissiva*.[65]

Hale recognizes three kinds of natural-law indeterminacy. First, some matters of daily life are simply morally indifferent (*Treatise*, 14, 108). Different options may present themselves to a given agent, or several ways of organizing social life may be available, none of which is mandated by the natural law. No moral good or evil is directly implicated in the choice among the options. In these cases we might say that natural law permits any choice. Hale thinks that such situations exist, but are rare. More likely, natural law will exclude some options and may at least prefer, if not mandate, others.

[64] The notion of individual natural rights makes only one explicit appearance in the texts selected here (see *Treatise*, 49–50), although MH often talks of the ancient rights and liberties of individual subjects defined in and protected by the (instituted) common law. Protection of natural rights does not play a prominent role in his theory of the grounds of political authority.

[65] *Treatise*, 14, 108–10. Here MH probably follows Selden. In *De synedriis*, Selden writes, "the divine law is and always was twofold, either preceptive (as in commands and interdicts) or permissive, as concerning things and actions left to human decision" (Selden, *Opera Omnia*, ed. David Wilkins (London, 1726), vol. 1, 794). See also Selden, *Of the Dominion of the Sea* (1631), tr. Marchamont Nedham (London, 1652), 12–13, 42–4. However, the notion of *lex permissiva* was common among medieval natural-law theorists, although it was understood in a variety of different ways. See Brian Tierney, "Permissive Natural Law and Property: Gratian to Kant," *Journal of the History of Ideas*, 62 (2001), 381–99.

Second, some matters are guided by principles of natural law, but at certain points the general principles must be made concrete in order to guide actions in particular circumstances. Natural law leaves further specification of its demands to rational, informed, and responsible human judgment (*Treatise*, 109–10). Such cases call for what scholastic legal theorists, following Aquinas, called *determination*.[66] Hale recognizes two subclasses of cases calling for determination. In one class, the kind of behaviour prescribed is relatively determinate, but matters of time, place, or manner may be left indeterminate (*Treatise*, 108). In the other class, what the more general principles require in particular circumstances can vary, so their application must be settled, made determinate, by human judgment. Such determination is not a matter of arbitrary choice, but rather involves careful, wise, and responsible judgment, judgment trained by long experience in mediating general principles and particular circumstances. This class comprises cases that are indeterminate by nature, as it were—matters left indeterminate at some level by natural law itself.

Third, however, some matters are indeterminate by virtue of limitations of our reason (*Treatise*, 37). In this class, while there may be (relatively) determinate requirements of natural law, nevertheless its principles apply to circumstances in ways that ordinary human beings find difficult to grasp. As a result, wise and responsible agents may come to quite different conclusions about what natural law requires or permits. In such cases, especially when it is important for there to be common, public rules of behaviour, or where fairness or impartiality calls for consistency of treatment across a number of cases, natural law may support explicit, public specification of its principles even when the public rules do not exactly accord with determinate natural-law requirements. Such determinate arrangements are consistent with permissive natural law because it recognizes the value of the publicity of social norms and consistency of treatment under them. "We may reasonably think," writes Hale, that "those remoter consequences and conclusions were not intended as the common rule of all mankind, but at most for such that having their faculties exercised were able to follow the clue of reason to such degree" (*Treatise*, 24).

Note that, with respect to each kind of indeterminacy, even though natural law is in one sense "permissive," determination of the natural-law principles is not arbitrary, in Hale's view. Practical reasoning, not mere choice, is essential to the process of determining natural-law principles. Hale argues that common law plays an important role in training that faculty of practical reason.

Instituted law. So understood, *lex permissiva* links natural law and secular or civil law. Civil law is instituted law; it necessarily involves human intervention and invention. As law, it is rooted in the choices and actions of some person, council,

[66] Aquinas, *Summa Theologiae*, IaIIae, 93, a. 3; 95, a. 3, in Dyson, 105–6, 129–31. Selden seems to run together permission and determination; see Selden, *De jure naturali & gentium juxta disciplinam Ebraeorum* (London, 1640), Bk I, ch. 8, p. 108.

or community that is in a position of authority with respect to those subject to the law. Humanly established law may be the product of explicit law*making* (modelled on the command of one in authority), but it also may be instituted by the custom or usage of a community, or by the acts of individuals establishing a covenant or pact (*Treatise*, 11). The latter Hale calls *intervenient law* (*lex interveniens*):[67] it is *law*, by virtue of its being endorsed by a civil authority independent of the parties involved in the rule-making (for example, individuals making a pact or whole communities instituting customary practices); it is *intervenient* in the sense that the institutive actions of the agents or communities and the consent manifested in those actions mediate the general principles of natural law, on the one hand, and human agents subject to the rules, on the other.

Instituted human law is distinct from natural law and ultimately grounded in it. Instituted law has its standing as law by virtue of either explicit authoring or implicit authorization by civil authority. No valid inference can be made from determinate judgments of moral right or wrong as recognized by natural law to their place in a given community's civil law; likewise, one cannot infer from the fact that a rule is established in civil law that it is endorsed by natural law. Nevertheless, instituted law is grounded ultimately in natural law in two ways. First, all legal norms are grounded ultimately in the fundamental natural-law principle of fidelity (*fides est servanda*) either directly, because they are the immediate product of agreement, or indirectly, because they are enacted or endorsed by civil authority, which rests on community-wide mutual consent. Second, instituted law finds its place within the *lex permissiva* of natural law. Civil law determines that which was left indeterminate by natural law. This fact about civil law is rooted in the nature and purpose of such law. Instituted law is needed precisely because natural law is indeterminate, either by nature or by virtue of the limitations of our reason, and it recognizes the fundamental need of (at least relatively) determinate common, public rules for orderly, decent, and just social life. In addition to this primary task, instituted law also serves as an auxiliary to natural law (*Treatise*, 109–12), publicly articulating its norms. These public norms compensate for the temporal astigmatism of those who are otherwise well-motivated[68] and add sanctions to deter those who are insufficiently motivated by natural law.

Thus, on Hale's understanding, civil law is positive, rooted in the creative, institutive actions of human individuals, groups, and agencies. But his account is not positivist in the modern sense of that term: it is not motivated by any form of moral scepticism, by a theoretical aim to reduce normative matters to empirical facts, or by a methodological desire to separate the study of civil law from morality or from larger theoretical questions about the fundamental nature and purpose of law. On the

[67] MH may have borrowed the term *lex interveniens* from Selden (*Of the Dominion of the Sea*, 15), but the idea is common in medieval natural-law theory.

[68] Hale thinks that human beings typically find it difficult to appreciate long-term consequences of their behaviour.

contrary, in his view, we can only understand instituted law and account for its binding force when we set it in its larger natural-law context. Instituted law is a product of will and rests ultimately on consent in some sense, but it is not simply a product of will, and practical reason is actively involved in its production even if its precepts cannot be deduced directly from principles of natural law.

Common law. Hale's account of English common law fits into the general framework just described. English law is "common," Hale observes, in the sense that (1) it is common to the whole kingdom, and (2) it fits the specific complexion or constitution of the English people (*History*, 139–41). This latter respect is of fundamental importance for instituted law, because in order for law to function well it must take root in the community, according to Hale. Only in this way can it be stable. (This is a dominant theme running through "Amendment.") Although, in Hale's time it was a familiar theme in common-law jurisprudence that English law was, or was rooted in, popular custom, Hale was keenly aware that the custom of the common law was primarily seen to be the custom of common-law courts and the legal profession. His view was that common law consisted primarily in "general customs," but that judicial decisions, and more broadly, the custom and practice of the courts, were the best evidence of this custom.[69] Moreover, he insisted, law can function well only when it is congruent with popular practice. Law must be of the community it serves and integrated into the practical vernacular of the people it seeks to guide. Thus, the law of one political community might be quite different from the law of another without being any less wise or appropriate. Determination of natural law must take into account the distinctive characteristics and practices of each community. "That law is best that is best for the people whose law it is," Hale argues, as the oyster's shell is better for an oyster than the shell of a scallop ("Amendment," note 2).

Formal law must be congruent to a significant degree with a community's customs and practices, but the process of fitting law to its community works in both directions: the law is refined and shaped to fit the community and the community's practices are shaped by the law. This process takes much time and never reaches anything like perfection, because our grasp of the vastly varying circumstances and complexity of human interests is always limited and because those circumstances and interests are always changing. At any point in time, one can take an abstract perspective on the law of a community and evaluate it in comparison to the law of other communities and to principles of natural law. However, only when it is seen operating in the context of the actual activities and practices of the community it addresses can its merits be assessed and its general norms wisely interpreted and applied.

[69] Alan Cromartie, "The Idea of Common Law as Custom," in Amanda Perreau-Saussine and James Bernard Murphy (eds), *The Nature of Customary Law* (Cambridge: Cambridge University Press, 2007), 221–2.

Hale tells us in *History*, Chapter 1, that English common law is a composite of *lex scripta* and *lex non scripta*. These terms, in Hale's usage, refer to laws distinguished neither by their form (written vs unwritten) nor by their origin (explicit lawmaking vs emerging from usage of the community or the courts). Rather, they refer to the current legal status or "force as law" of legal norms—that is, the mode of their standing as law and the proximate root of their binding force. *Lex scripta* comprises laws that have their current legal standing as *enacted* by a recognized lawmaking body (King-in-Parliament, or some subordinate body on which lawmaking power has been devolved), which are committed to writing prior to enactment. The entitlement to make law, the formal constituents of lawmaking authority, lay not in ancient pedigree or abstract reason, but simply in the continuous reception—ultimately, in the kingdom in general and proximately in the courts—which is rooted in mutual fidelity. *Lex non scripta*, in contrast, comprises laws (including both enacted laws and those that emerge *ex instituto*) that have standing by virtue of their being continually taken up and practised. "The formal and obliging force and power" of the common law "grows by long custom and use" (*History*, 134). Such practice is not simply a matter of compliance, but rather a matter of their incorporation into the systematic body of law, that is, a matter of their being based on some norms of that system and grounding others, supporting some resolutions and regarded as consequences of others.

Lex non scripta, in Hale's understanding, is the "great substratum" of English law (*History*, 148) and the foundation or constitution of civil government. All governing power—legislative as well as adjudicative, royal as well as parliamentary—is ordained, constituted, structured, and limited by this law. Thus, *lex non scripta* underwrites *lex scripta*; the terms and "formal constituents" of lawmaking power are determined by and are an integral part of this unwritten common law (*History*, 146). *Lex non scripta* also supplies the matrix within which individual enactments of parliament are to be understood and interpreted.

Judicial opinions, on Hale's view, do not themselves count as laws (as, for example, enacted statutes do), but they count as persuasive evidence of the law, persuasive because judges are greatly learned in the law, are committed to judge according to law, and are bound to decide matters in tribunals only after hearing extended argument in a public forum (*History*, 147). Hale identifies three appropriate sources or grounds of judicial decisions within common law (*History*, 147–8). Judges will, first, be guided directly by enacted or practised rules of common law. Secondly, where necessary, they will base their decisions on rules or principles derived by analogy from these explicit rules. Third, where these are not sufficient to determine a matter before the court, judges will appeal to "the common reason of the thing" (*History*, 148). But, in Hale's view, this appeal to the common reason of the thing does not license judges to appeal directly to natural law or encourage them to rely on the common faculty of practical reason shared with lay people. "The common reason of the thing" is most reliably identified and appreciated by persons skilled in what Sir Edward Coke called the "artificial reason" of the common law.[70] To fully appreciate this element of Hale's view we must first explore his understanding of practical reason in general and the special discipline of practical reasoning characteristic of common law.

Practical Reasoning

Hale's view of practical reason is as nuanced as his view of law. He opens "Reflections" with the observation that, when we speak of "reason," we have one of three things in mind. First, we may speak of the reason *in things*, apart from our grasp or appreciation of them, the objective ordering of things according to rational principles. Second, we may speak of reason *in us*, the faculty of reason—that by which we come to know about what is or what ought to be done, and that by which we deliberatively determine to do something. This is a discursive and deliberative faculty, but also a discerning and apprehending one. It is common to all human beings, although it may be refined and strengthened in some and distorted by temperament or passions in others. Third, we may have in view disciplined or habituated reason—the faculty of reason in us that is directed or specially attuned to some range of rationally ordered objects through training in a particular practice. So we speak of the reason of a mathematician, doctor, statesman, watchmaker, or lawyer. In such disciplines, Hale maintains, "the understanding is governed by the special reason of the thing into which it is thus determined" ("Reflections," note 14). The special reason of the lawyer is the common faculty of reason directed to and disciplined in certain practical matters—matters of moral good and evil *as instituted* in law. Before exploring the special discipline of common-law reasoning, consider first Hale's account of natural practical reasoning.

Natural reasoning. Hale believes that there is a rational natural and moral order. He believes there are truths about laws obligating behaviour of human agents, as well as truths about moral good and evil and what, morally speaking, ought or ought not to be done by them. Since these laws are meant to guide and direct voluntary human actions, they must address human agents and human agents must have access to them. Thus, he found it necessary to explore how human beings come to know the natural law. His discussion of the "publication" or "promulgation" of natural law offers accounts of (1) the human rational or cognitive faculty, (2) the matter or "objects" to be cognized, and (3) the medium of access, or process of communication, of these objects.

Hale distinguishes two "methods" by which natural law is made known to, and impressed upon, human agents. Divine positive law—the decalogue and the seven Noachide laws—makes known the natural law by an artificial method; it supplements the more "primitive" or "natural" method (*Treatise*, ch. 11). Consider the latter first.

[70] See note 42.

Hale distinguishes three different tasks for this "internal" method of "publication" of the natural law. (1) It must give human agents access to the requirements of natural law; it must make its "content" or "matter" available to them. (2) It must make clear to human agents that they are obligated to comply with them. And, (3) it must incline those agents to comply with the law's demands. The centrepiece of Hale's discussion focuses on the first question, and we will return to it presently, but the importance for him of the other questions shows that he regards the problem of "publication" of the natural law as not merely an epistemic one, a problem of determining *what* to do, but also a problem of communicating to human agents that these are demands *of law* that are *addressed to* them.

Hale argues in *Treatise*, Chapter 10, that conscience is the part of the human reasoning faculty that detects the status—the "formal nature"—of the requirements directing us to good and away from evil as requirements of *law*. By it, we sense that some action is not only good or even right to do, but also that we are under obligation to do. We sense that our doing so is owed to someone as the proper or necessary response to that party's rightful expectation or demand. Awareness of obligation, for Hale, involves not fear of punishment but an appreciation of the appropriateness of the demand for one's compliance and of the rightfulness of sanctions for one's failure to comply, and hence of a secondary duty to submit to that penalty.

Distinct from this recognition, Hale argues, are inclinations or "propensions" to comply with the natural law that God implants in us (*Treatise*, 82). These "rational instincts," analogous to instincts implanted in other species of animals, direct human beings to seek moral goodness and their moral well-being.[71] They are intimately linked to the understanding. The will is the last act of the practical understanding (*Treatise*, 8). Elsewhere he writes, "The will is a rational power in man ... the complement of the rational procedure in the soul, and that which doth, or should, immediately follow the last act of the understanding."[72] The distinction between intellect and will is merely notional, in Hale's view. Indeed, he confesses, "it is a hard matter to conceive how the understanding can deliberately and plenarily conclude an object to be particularly good or evil unless the will go along with it, for such a conclusion is in effect the conjunction of the act of understanding to the will."[73] Will

[71] In his *On the Primitive Origination of Mankind* (London, 1677), MH writes, "there are lodged in the very *crasis* [constitution] and construction of the soul certain rational instincts whereby it is pre-disposed, inclined and byassed to the good and convenience proportionable to a rational and intellectual life" (61). Hale supposes that these instincts operate like internal natural appetitive principles, but he also associates them with "common notions of moral good and evil, of *decorum* and *turpe*" (ibid.) to which the intellective faculty has cognitive access. God's implanting of these instincts underwrites divine "promulgation" of them to the intellect. See generally, *Primitive Origination*, 60–1, 353, 365.

[72] Hale, "Of Doing as we would be done unto," in *Works*, I, 385. In this respect, MH's view accords more closely to that of Aquinas, *Summa Theologiae*, IaIIae, 17, a. 1, a. 5, than to that of Suarez, *On Laws*, Bk I, chs 4–5. His view differs sharply from that of Hobbes, who held that the will is just the last *appetite* or *aversion* before action. Hobbes, *Leviathan*, 45.

[73] Hale, Lambeth 3505, 211 (quoted in Cromartie, *Hale*, 171).

is the rational faculty which "moves indeterminately to all good,"[74] which movement is guided and made determinate by human understanding. The key faculty of reason is the intellect, to which we now turn.

Human cognition: the active intellect. Hale devotes a long chapter of his *Treatise* (Chapter 8) to a discussion of the "publication" of the matter or content of natural law. The main outlines of his view are reasonably clear, although the details become obscure rather quickly. This is due in part to the eclectic and somewhat undisciplined character of the discussion, but in larger part to the technical language he employs and the philosophical tradition on which he draws, both of which are unfamiliar to twentieth-first-century readers. Some stage setting will be useful.

Hale sets his account of the promulgation of natural law at the convergence of three ancient philosophical traditions. From the Stoic tradition he draws two elements of his theory: (1) the view that all human beings are endowed with certain fundamental first principles—"common notions" or "preconceptions"—which are self-evident, immediately recognized by every human being without exercise of their reasoning powers;[75] (2) the view that these common notions are so abstract and indeterminate that they provide limited guidance in themselves.[76] Human beings must exercise their deliberative reasoning capacities to work out how they are to act in particular cases, and, given the difficulty of applying the common notions to complex circumstances (and inevitable distortions of judgment by bias and interest), human beings are often likely to arrive at different conclusions about what natural law requires of them. This Stoic doctrine, while useful for his purposes, did not help him explain how the rational faculties worked or how the requirements for actions that are discovered could be regarded as laws, that is, as directives from an authorized lawgiver.

Hale sought an account of the nature of intellective activity in individual thinkers that also explained the possibility and conditions of the convergence of individual thinkers on common, true judgments. Although he was primarily concerned with practical or moral judgments, he drew on traditions that sought to explain the possibility and nature of knowing in general. For this purpose he turned to the developments of Augustinian and Aristotelian philosophies of mind or intellect in the twelfth and thirteenth centuries, traditions which still exerted influence on philosophical thought in the mid-seventeenth century.[77]

[74] Hale, *Discourse of the Knowledge of God and of our Selves* (London, 1688), 56–7.

[75] *Treatise*, 23–4, 35 (note 85), 68, 76, 85. On the Stoic (and earlier Epicurean) roots of the idea of "preconceptions" (*prolepseis*), see Leen Spruit, *"Species Intelligibilis": From Perception to Knowledge* (Leiden: Brill, 1994), vol. 1, 50–65.

[76] MH is fond of quoting a passage from Epictetus's *Dialogues* (I.22) that makes this point; see, e.g., *Treatise*, note 85.

[77] See Richard C. Dales, *The Problem of the Rational Soul in the Thirteenth Century* (Leiden: Brill, 1995).

The basic Augustinian (Hale often refers to it as "Platonist") tradition, represented by William of Auvergne, Bonaventure, Roger Bacon, and others,[78] held that cognition was an activity of each individual human soul, which takes deliverances from the five senses and converts them into thoughts suitable for the intellective faculty. According to this tradition, this cognitive activity is made possible by divine illumination. God sheds "uncreated light" as a "regulative and motive principle," certifying the deliverances of the mind's abstraction of ideas from sense experience.[79] Some in this tradition held in addition that God aided thought by implanting in the human soul fundamental first principles akin to the Stoic common notions.

The third tradition stemmed from an obscure passage in Aristotle's *De Anima* (3.4–5, 429a–b) that drew extended comment and elaboration by later Greek philosophers in the third and fourth centuries CE and by Arab philosophers in the tenth and eleventh centuries CE.[80] These commentaries and treatises were read, debated, developed, challenged, revised, and refined in the Latin West (especially Paris and Oxford) in the twelfth and thirteenth centuries.[81] According to this tradition, human cognition necessarily involves two key elements: (1) "sensibles"—images or representations of concrete objects in the world—delivered to the intellect by the human senses—and (2) "intelligibles"—thinkable objects or concepts—with which intellect reasons. For Aristotelians, intelligibles are "forms" and they thought that to think is to be "in-formed,"[82] that is, the thinker in some sense becomes the form. Commentators on Aristotle's *De anima* found a distinction between two faculties of the intellective soul: the *potential* or *possible* (later: *material*) intellect, which "becomes all things," and the *active* or *agent* intellect, which "brings forth all things." That is, the agent intellect (Greek: *nous poetikos*, Latin: *intellectus agens*) makes the potential intellect *actual* by "in-forming" it. It does this by operating on "sensibles" presented to the potential intellect by the senses. Aristotle's Greek commentators maintained further that if human communication and common knowledge are possible, there must be a common source of concepts or intelligibles.

This basic view was developed in a variety of different ways, especially by Arab commentators. Their different accounts shared the following framework of ideas. First, the human soul was thought to share imagination (*phantasia*) with other animals. Imagination was seen as a capacity to receive, sort, and store images, and to think in a

[78] See Dales, *Rational Soul*, 31–6, 75–8, 99–107; Z. Kuksewicz, "The Potential and the Agent Intellect," in Norman Kretzmann, Anthony Kenny, and Jan Pinborg (eds), *The Cambridge History of Later Medieval Philosophy* (Cambridge: Cambridge University Press, 1982), 595–601.

[79] Dales, *Rational Soul*, 105–6.

[80] See Herbert A. Davidson, *Alfarabi, Avicenna, and Averroes on Intellect* (New York: Oxford University Press, 1992); Deborah L. Black, "Psychology: Soul and Intellect," in Peter Adamson and Richard C. Taylor (eds), *The Cambridge Companion to Arabic Philosophy* (Cambridge: Cambridge University Press, 2005), 308–26.

[81] See Dales, *Rational Soul*.

[82] Marilyn McCord Adams, "Whose Thought Is It? The Soul and the Subject of Action in Some Thirteenth and Fourteenth Century Aristotelians," *Philosophy and Phenomenological Research*, 85 (2012), 626.

rudimentary way. Human beings were thought to be capable of something more, namely, intellective or rational thinking, which involves grasping and reasoning with ideas or concepts. But, these philosophers argued, concepts or intelligibles are immaterial and universal, and the human intellect needs help moving from logically particular sensibles to universal intelligibles. The potential or material intellect receives the images, which are at that point only potential thoughts; active intellect transforms them into intelligibles. Aristotle and his commentators thought the active intellect is to the human intellective soul as the sun is to sight.[83]

This analogy was not greatly illuminating; it begged for further elaboration. Three different explanations of the activity of the *intellectus agens* emerged and were often combined or conflated. According to the first view, the active intellect casts light on images present to the material intellect, enabling it to discern that which is intelligible in them. It does so by abstracting (or enabling the abstraction) of the universal from the concrete sensibles, removing or "purifying" them of their "matter" or particularity. In this way, sensible images are made graspable by the intellect, and once grasped they can be deployed in ordinary reasoning. By this process of extraction the material intellect is populated with thinkables "from below." On a variation of this and of the analogy to the activity of the sun, Averroes held that the active intellect does not so much do the abstraction or extraction, but it prepares the medium in which the abstract or universal propositions (or concepts) are communicated to the receiving intellect.[84]

On the second view, the active intellect was thought to serve also as a "cosmic transmitter,"[85] communicating concepts and propositions to the material intellect, "from the top down," as it were. These are communicated by the active intellect to the material intellect immediately without active ratiocination by the receiving intellect. Most philosophers working in this tradition restricted this activity to the communication of first principles or axioms of thought or action, the most abstract practical notions (like the "common notions" of the Stoic tradition). However, Avicenna maintained that all truths received by the material intellect have their source, not in abstraction from deliverances of the senses, but in emanation from the active intellect.[86]

Third, prompted by the Aristotelian thought that the active intellect actualizes the potential intellect, some in this tradition held that, like the sun, the active intellect activates the capacities of the potential intellect. It enables or empowers discernment of what is intelligible in the sensible (through abstraction) and waking up and fuelling the reasoning process.[87]

Debates raged within this tradition, and between its partisans and Augustinians, over the details of this account of human cognition. Some argued that the material

[83] Davidson, *Alfarabi, Avicenna, and Averroes*, 14, 19–29, 50–1, 92–3, 316–20.
[84] Davidson, *Alfarabi, Avicenna, and Averroes*, 318–19.
[85] Davidson, *Alfarabi, Avicenna, and Averroes*, 20.
[86] Black, "Soul and Intellect," 319–20; Davidson, *Alfarabi, Avicenna, and Averroes*, 93.
[87] Davidson, *Alfarabi, Avicenna, and Averroes*, 26, 29 (discussing Themistius).

and active intellects were two distinct substances; others argued that they are just two powers or operations of a single unified intellect. Some argued that because the intellects (actually or potentially) deal with immaterial objects—concepts, universals, and the like—they cannot themselves be material or located in embodied human individuals. Averroes argued that the active and potential intellects are ultimately unified, but they exist entirely apart from individual human thinkers; they are "one for all," but not identified with any one human being, and so not individuated.

Critics, like Aquinas, thought that although Averroes may have made a strong case for a common source of knowledge, he failed to explain how ordinary human individuals have access to it. Against Averroes, others, especially those trying to achieve a synthesis of the Augustinian and Aristotelian traditions, argued that the active and the potential intellects are complementary powers operating within individual human beings, aided by a second, external active intellect. The latter was sometimes identified with God or some created intelligence acting on God's behalf.

For an understanding of Hale's view, three features of this debate are key. First, contributors to the debate sought to explain how it is that human beings come to grasp and judge truly of their world, through an analysis of the capacities of the human mind and the structure of the knowable world. Their aim was not to answer scepticism. It was widely agreed, of course, that the unaided human mind can never rise above the level of brute thinking, but no one doubted that human beings could and did acquire knowledge. They sought an account of how knowledge is acquired. Intervention of a (quasi-)divine intellect was not regarded as a *deus ex machina* deployed to rescue human thinkers from epistemic darkness, but rather as a component intrinsic to the realization of the human rational soul. Second, this intervention was thought to be necessary for shared knowledge, and thus for an understanding of, and an ability to navigate together, a common, public world. Third, the debate concerned human cognition generally, including both theoretical and practical matters. There was no special concern to address scepticism about moral judgments that the appeal to divine intervention was meant to answer. However, this general approach faced the mirror image of the challenge of scepticism: in view of the knowability of the world and the divinely aided capacities of human thinkers to grasp it, it was necessary to explain how the failure to know and judge is evidently so prevalent.

Human cognition: Hale's account. With materials drawn from this debate, Hale constructed in *Treatise* and other works his own account of human cognition, and, on that basis, his account of the nature of divine publication of the moral law. Cognition, on Hale's account, is intrinsic to each human being, an essential part of the rational soul which consists of the understanding (the intellective faculty) and the will (the executive faculty).[88] The will, although spontaneous, is nevertheless naturally directed to the good as discovered and determined by the intellect. Will is capable

[88] Hale, *Primitive Origination*, 28–9, 54–60.

of purpose or resolution, choice, and command of subordinate natural faculties.[89] The understanding engages in two kinds of activity: (a) immediate recognition or intuitive grasp of intelligible objects or truths and (b) active discursive and deliberative reasoning. This intellective faculty is suitably accommodated or specially attuned to its intelligible objects just as sight is accommodated to visible objects.[90] Two kinds of objects are accessible immediately: (a) abstract first principles ("common notions or anticipations") regarding both empirical and speculative matters and practical, especially moral, matters; and (b) intelligible concrete objects or states of affairs including truths regarding the moral qualities of particular actions. Implications and applications of more general truths are accessible through the activities of discursive reasoning, including distinction, definition, determination, deliberation, and argumentation.

Human beings share with non-human animals certain primitive capacities. Through "imagination" or "phantasy" they have access to particular objects in the world of which they form sensible images. They are also capable of primitive forms of thinking (*ratio* or *discursus imaginativus*), in which they put together simple propositions and form something like conclusions about what to do.[91] But this faculty is not capable of grasping or using universals (concepts), the stuff of rational thought. Grasping universals is only available to the intellective faculty, which, guided by axioms of thought, acquires more specific concepts, the basic materials of discursive reasoning, through abstraction from particular representations presented to the intellect by the imagination.[92] In addition, the intellective faculty corrects deliverances of our senses, grasps and reasons with concepts of number, time, causation, and God, and traces logical and practical consequences from established propositions.[93] Intellective perceptions or judgments at the concrete level arise through attending to and generalizing (or abstracting) from the specific features of particular cases, an activity structured and guided by the general resources of the intellect—in particular, the directly received first principles and implications derived from them by discursive reasoning.

However, intellective activity in all its aspects proceeds only with the aid of divine illumination. In Hale's account, echoing the medieval Aristotelian account, divine illumination operates on the human intellect in three ways (*Treatise*, 68, 73–4). First, through a kind of "irradiation," it makes accessible the abstract common notions necessary for thought and the common stock of moral notions needed for direction of action. Second, it activates the intellective faculty in its perceptive, abstractive, and discursive activities. Third, it unites the intelligible empirical and moral world with the intellective faculty. The intellective faculty is attuned to objects

[89] Hale, *Primitive Origination*, 28, 58–9. [90] Hale, *Primitive Origination*, 2, 365.
[91] Lambeth 3504, 113, quoted in Cromartie, *Hale*, 230–1.
[92] Lambeth 3504, 102, quoted in Cromartie, *Hale*, 231; Hale, *Primitive Origination*, 2–3.
[93] Hale, *Primitive Origination*, 2, 22, 55, 364.

in those worlds. Divine illumination provides a medium in which the objects of judgment can be grasped.

Moreover, this illumination is communicated to all rational creatures (*Treatise*, 68), so they can agree on first principles and fundamental moral notions and can communicate with each other regarding their common world. The intellective faculty, Hale maintains, is equally aware of itself (capable of "turning... the intellectual eye inward upon its own actions")[94] and of other minds. Not only are human cognition and human capacities common to us all, but also this commonality is evident to us through conversation. Speaking with each other, we find that we have similar intellective faculties, that we "divide, define, abstract, purpose, determine [and] will" using the same "operations of mind." And we find that even when we come to different conclusions, we recognize that we "maintain [our] conclusion[s] by the like method of reason and discursive ratiocination."[95]

Thus, regarding practical reasoning in particular, Hale concludes that, just as the sun sheds light on the object, wakens the eye, and brings eye and object together in the medium of light, not for this or that viewer only but for all viewers properly disposed, so divine illumination enables and empowers the human intellect, properly disposed and uncorrupted, to grasp that which is naturally good or evil as something to be sought or avoided, energizes the conscience to grasp it as a matter of obligation owed to one in whom the law is grounded, and provides all human beings with the natural instinct and compliant will to act as directed. In this way, Hale argues, natural law can be seen properly as law, not only indicating and manifesting that which is good or evil to do, but also prescribing and publishing obligations addressed to those subject to that law.[96]

Common-law reasoning. Despite the manifold ways in which the intellect is equipped and enabled to discern, derive, and deliberate about moral good and evil and the natural law bearing on it, Hale insists in his jurisprudential writings that natural reason is insufficient for public purposes. Natural reason alone cannot equip people to navigate the complexities of civic life and the positive law instituted to order that life. Although it is universal among human beings, natural reason is nevertheless a faculty of individual thinkers and deliberating agents. They may arrive at common conclusions or judgments, but this convergence is not guaranteed. Natural reason is vulnerable to misdirection by passion, interest, and the influence of corrupted education, culture, and custom. It also typically suffers from a kind of

[94] Hale, *Primitive Origination*, 22–4. [95] Hale, *Primitive Origination*, 24.

[96] In "Of doing as we would be done unto," MH adds that the golden rule provides a powerful heuristic by which the human intellect can discover "the whole duty of man in relation to others," "accommodated to every action of a man's life" (*Works*, I, 379). On this model, the "visive" capacity of the intellect is not limited to grasping abstract common notions of moral good and evil, but is also involved in discerning what is morally to be done or avoided—what is intrinsically just, honourable, and right—in all particular circumstances. However, MH gives voice to a more robust sense of the limitations of the intellective faculty in "Reflections" and "Abridgement."

myopia, finding it difficult to focus clearly on practical matters that are temporally or socially distant (*Treatise*, 111–12). It can be improved through exercise, but also it can be more developed in some people and less in others ("Reflections," 189). Hence, Hale argues, natural reason must be supplemented with instituted law and a special discipline of practical reasoning tailored to it, which seventeenth-century common-law writers (notably Sir Edward Coke) referred to as the "artificial reason" of the law.

In his *Dialogue between a philosopher and a student of the common laws of England*, Thomas Hobbes accepted the common-law claim that "reason is the soul of law," but he ridiculed the idea of the "artificial reason" of the law.[97] He insisted that the reason of the law was nothing other than the natural reason of the sovereign. In the first chapter of "Reflections," Hale answers Hobbes's challenge. "Reason" either is *in things*—the rational ordering of things, empirical, social, or moral—or is *in us*—the natural intellective faculty involving an immediate intuitive capacity and a discursive capacity. His aim in "Reflections" is to distinguish this natural reason, analysed in the *Treatise* and other systematic works, from reason trained and disciplined in a specific way and "governed by the special reason of the thing unto which it is thus determined" ("Reflections," note 14). The human intellective faculty is often fitted or attuned to some particular rationally ordered subject matter and habituated to this use by extended exercise in this domain, guided by methods distinctive to it, and by other practitioners skilled in those methods. It is a practised, common skill or art, a discipline of reasoning shared among those engaged in its practice but not (or not to the same extent) by others. In this way, the reason of the mathematician differs from that of the philosopher, the reason of the doctor from that of the engineer or watchmaker or smith. Reason in and of the common law is just such a disciplined practice, Hale argues.

Distinctive features of natural law make the need for such a discipline acute. First, the moral domain is exceptionally complex. Judgments of the rightness or wrongness of actions depend greatly on widely varying and constantly changing circumstances ("Reflections," 192; "Preface," 163; "Amendment," *passim*). Abstract notions of justice and fitness are common to all and are universally appreciated, but they must be articulated and applied to these circumstances by individuals. For this, more than general skills of discursive reasoning are needed. Moral philosophers and men of great learning are inadequate to the task because they are "transported from ordinary measures of right and wrong... above the common staple of human conversations" ("Reflections," 190). Especially needed for this exercise of reason are wide practical experience and engagement in "human affairs and conversation between man and man," and the refined skill of combining a grasp of general principles with a full appreciation of the practical significance of particular circumstances. Second, as we have seen, natural law is indeterminate, needing specification appropriate to the

[97] Hobbes, *Dialogue*, 9–10. The "student" largely echoes the views of Coke.

concrete conditions of social life in particular communities. Because determination must be reasoned, not arbitrary, it calls for a special kind of creative but especially skilled practical reason. Third, reasoning within the law always concerns matters for the public and for a length of time, so it cannot be satisfied with the exercise of essentially private natural reason, no matter how conscientious or even correct for the particular circumstances. Natural reason, even of the greatest minds, Hale argues, is unlikely to converge on judgments that can serve for the long term the public purposes of law.

The special discipline of common-law reasoning, however, fulfils this need. This special discipline is shaped by the need to bring to bear a secure grasp of broad principles with a refined understanding and appreciation of the details of human affairs and conversation to forge practical judgments regarding the regular interactions of daily civic life. Moreover, in their daily activities over many years, "these great traders in learning" bring their several acquisitions "into a common stock by mutual communication," and thereby each becomes the participant in and common possessor of each other's learning and knowledge ("Preface," 159–60). This discipline is a shared practice, a common activity, continually contributing to and drawing from a common stock of examples and principles, developing measures and methods that shape the discursive and deliberative skills distinctive of this discipline. An intensely practical deployment of reason, common-law discipline is focused on practical, moral matters in all their complexity, but it is guided and constrained by broad, general principles and by concrete, "instituted" determinations of them, drawn partly from formally enacted provisions and partly from the common stock of decisions to which practitioners constantly contribute. The special discipline of legal reasoning is always *ex instituto*. It is bound not only by its fixed and already determinate rules, but also by the systematic connections that join them together into a coherent whole, each piece mortised together with others, like the frame of a house ("Amendment," 176–7). It is also bound to fit the current decision or rule into the trajectory of a body of law that extends and is meant to guide over a significant stretch of time. Thus, the discipline of common-law reasoning is never free to consider matters wholly afresh, from a moral perspective entirely above or apart from what has already been established. Common-law reasoning is reasoning *in media res*, tethered simultaneously to broad principles of justice, the common stock of experience and decision and the enacted rules which determine them, and systematic connections within the body of law. In addition, because law can function well only if it takes root in the community, it must be always mindful and seek integration of its determinations and of the law in general into the political community's constitution.

Political Authority and Obligation

The second part of Hale's "Reflections" sketches a critique of the views of Hobbes on sovereignty and political obligation. His argument draws on the analysis of these central jurisprudential notions developed in his *Treatise* and *Prerogatives of the King*.

He grounds civic obligation and political sovereignty ultimately in natural law and God's "natural authority," so we begin our discussion with that root notion.

Natural authority. The proximate ground of legal obligations, Hale argues, lies in the relationship of authority between lawgiver and law-subject. Authority is an asymmetrical relationship between two distinct parties; the idea of a person's being her own authority, he thinks, is nonsense. Authority is a normative relationship, defined not by the capacity of one party to make another act as he wills, but by one party's "just right to obligate" another and the subject's reciprocal duty of obedience owed to the party in authority. In Hale's view, this reciprocal right and duty are rooted in a prior relationship of allegiance.

Obligation—one side of the relationship of allegiance—is an important moral fact about persons that is affirmed by the obligated person's internal sense of being bound. In Chapter 2 of his *Treatise*, Hale offers an account of the "formal reason" of obligation and a complementary account of the root of this internal sense. He offers two arguments for divine authority based on (or perhaps two ways of viewing) the fundamental fact that human beings are utterly dependent on God for their being and well-being. This fact is ontological rather than practical; it is the fact of God's power to create and sustain, rather than to threaten and punish. Viewing our ontological dependence on God in one way, we are utterly powerless in God's infinitely powerful hands. In the prophet Jeremiah's image, God is the *potter*, we are the clay.[98] God can shape or reshape, sustain or annihilate us as God pleases. As *maker*, God has the absolute right of dominion so to act.[99] Yet, this same Maker of infinite power and absolute dominion is infinitely good and just; and these are not two independent properties of God competing for pre-eminence, but just two ways that limited human beings think of God.[100] Viewed in this way, to be utterly dependent on God's power is just to be protected and preserved by an infinitely just being.

This thought leads Hale to describe the allegiance-grounding facts in a rather different way: not as non-relational facts about God, on the one hand, and about human beings, on the other, but rather as facts about a certain kind of relationship between God and human beings. He represents God not as potter but as *pater*, as giver and sustainer of life, whose infinite goodness is expressed initially in our creation and continually in our preservation. Life and well-being are experienced by us creatures, Hale argues, not merely as good and welcome things, but as gifts expressive of a fundamental commitment of the giver, who has undertaken to link his good with ours.[101] This divine commitment calls forth love and gratitude on the part

[98] Jeremiah 18:1–8; Hale, *Primitive Origination*, 354–5 (see *Treatise*, note 42); Lambeth 3488, 151v, quoted in Cromartie, *Hale*, 234.

[99] *Treatise*, 39; Hale, *Primitive Origination*, 354–5 (*Treatise*, note 42).

[100] MH embraces the doctrine of divine simplicity in *Discourse*, 12–13.

[101] "The wise God hath as it were twisted his own honour and glory with man's felicity and happiness," Hale writes (*Primitive Origination*, 379).

of creatures, not as required by a yet more fundamental moral principle (e.g., a duty of gratitude), but as the natural, fitting, and willing response constitutive of recognition and appreciation of this relationship (*Treatise*, 39).

These two arguments sit side-by-side in Hale's discussion of natural divine authority. Always mindful of God's infinite power, Hale nevertheless seems to accord priority to the second, relational view of the root fact of dependence. He regards motivation from love and gratitude as "nobler" than fear. Fear binds only to compliance rather than obedience; love and gratitude are more appropriate to "intellectual" beings capable of acting freely and capable of appreciating and participating in significant relationships (*Treatise*, 18). "The love of God," he writes, "is the only true principle of all obedience."[102]

Civil authority. In contrast to his account of natural authority, Hale's account of civil authority starts from the assumption of fundamental political equality among human beings (*Prerogatives*, 208). Outside the domestic context, no human being has an original natural right to govern another person, unless the latter has submitted to that rule. Thus, civil authority is not natural but rather instituted, the product of human actions and invention (albeit not always the product of explicit human design) that in some way involve the voluntary submission of each subject. In this respect, Hale's view is similar to Hobbes's, but, *pace* Hobbes, Hale insists that in the "state of nature" the universal demands of justice, honesty, and decency are in full force (*Treatise*, 48).

Civil authority, in Hale's view, rests on two complementary grounds: necessity (or utility) and civil compact.[103] The necessity of government is the product of three factors. (1) Human beings are naturally inclined toward social relations and to accept government, which (2) they recognize is necessary for human life and well-being, providing security against injuries from others and opportunities for mutual benefit from combining complementary abilities and resources (*Treatise*, 55–6). (3) Although social relations are ordered and governed by natural law, determinate, consistent, and fully public laws must be established to guide members of society, fix penalties for wrongdoing, and prevent arbitrary exercise of power. Recognizing these facts about his human creatures, God ordains authority (*Prerogatives*, 208).

Political authority is necessary, but it exists in determinate form only if it is instituted through compact, according to Hale. The "mutual interposition of faith" among the governed and between the governed and those who govern unites ("twists") them into one body, creating a *fides publica*, a civic association based on mutual commitment, in which each subject has an interest in the good faith

[102] Hale, *Discourse*, 259.
[103] MH here follows a long tradition of medieval political thought, including Islamic, Jewish, and Christian writers.

allegiance of the others (*Prerogatives*, 209).[104] Hale speaks of this mutual commitment or compact as either expressed or implied. But we should note two things about what Hale has in mind. First, he does not take the "implied" or "virtual" form of this relationship of allegiance as merely a shadowy version of the more concrete "expressed" version. On the contrary, he treats "expressed" consent, for example in the form of oaths or public promises, as merely a way of "attesting and witnessing" the more fundamental ("intrinsic" and "primitive") moral phenomenon.[105] Second, although he takes the historical (as opposed to "hypothetical" or merely notional) character of this compact seriously, he does not think of it as a discrete event. Hale often uses "consent" in a broad sense to refer not to present, mindful undertaking of an obligation, but rather community-wide agreement or concurrence in some practical opinion or some ongoing practice.[106]

The compact underlying civil authority is consensual in this sense, but it is also reciprocal, a "mutual interposition of faith." There may have been a discrete compact-forming event, but even that event would not explain fully either the content or the moral character and force of the compact. What is critical to its content and moral significance is the continuous pattern of interaction and the mutual commitments evident in it. Moreover, it is a pattern acknowledged and articulated in the practical reasoning of judges, who are trained to appreciate the practical complexity of social life and the historical continuity of the community's commitment enacted in the daily practice of its members. It is mutual reliance on that commitment that is the lifeblood of the compact.

This civic association, characterized by fidelity and allegiance, is underwritten by the fundamental principle of natural law—and first principle of all civic relationships—*fides est servanda*: honour your agreements. While the reasons for the commitments grounding the civic association lie in the necessity and utility of ordered social life and the role of government in it, the root obligation, the core of allegiance, lies in this principle of fidelity.

The structure of government and hence the definition, allocation, and limits of governing powers are determined, according to Hale, by the founding compact and subsequent modifications of it. Governments can arise in a number of different ways. The two most common are compact and conquest. Both modes ultimately rest on consent, Hale argues, although they come about in different ways. Overwhelming force never by itself gives rise to authority or the relationship of allegiance, but it can

[104] Similarly, Coke speaks of the reciprocal bond between sovereign and subject: "As the ligatures or strings do knit together the joints of all the parts of the body, so doth ligeance joyn together the Sovereign and all his Subjects ... for as the subject oweth to the King his true and faithful ligeance and obedience, so the Sovereign is to govern and protect his Subjects ... so as between the Sovereign and subject there is *duplex et reciprocum ligament* [dual and reciprocal tie]." Edward Coke, "Calvin's Case," *Seventh Report*, 4b–5a, in Sheppard, *Coke: Selected Writings*, 175–6.

[105] Hale, *History of the Pleas of the Crown*, I, 61–2, quoted in *Prerogatives*, note 55.

[106] *Treatise*, 26–7, 29, 76; Hale, *Primitive Origination*, 240–1.

bring parties together who then, through mutual stipulation and submission, establish the terms and limits of the governing power and the conditions of obligation to its rule.

Hale discusses with great care different kinds of conquest (*victoria in regem* vs *victoria in populum*), and the resulting just claims that might arise from them,[107] but he seems relatively unconcerned about the apparent threat to the moral validity and bindingness of consent posed by the conditions of duress under which the conqueror extracts the initial submission. When he considers the thesis that it is possible to acquire a right to rule by conquest (as he does in *History*, Chapter 5), he does so either from the point of view of the law of nations (considering whether nations have good reason to recognize such a right) or the pragmatic point of view of the ruler (who may be moved to offer concessions by the need to stabilize his hold on power), ignoring the issue of moral principle that is obvious to us.

Hale's relative lack of interest in this question stems, perhaps, from his view of the moral significance of such "origins" stories. The actual origin of a polity and its government, whether in conquest or more or less explicit compact, is of far less normative or moral importance, in Hale's view, than the community's current constitutional practice.[108] However they may have begun, political communities and their governments are subject to constant change over time, the people extracting concessions from those who rule, and rulers sometimes acquiring new or additional powers recognized by the people.[109] Some such arrangements result from explicit negotiations at critical junctures, moments of explicit constitutional adjustment; other may arise gradually by custom or usage. And custom and usage, embodied and elaborated in the common law of a political community, he maintains, is not merely evidence of some more ancient pact or agreement. It has "a kind of introductive or institutive power" (*Prerogatives*, 215), initiating on its own fundamental changes in the constitution of the political community or its government. Hale regards this process and mode of interaction as a kind of compact, the most important and enduring kind in his view, because in most political communities it replaces explicit compacts or conquests, stabilizing, enhancing, and transforming them. Hale regards it as a kind of compact because it represents an ongoing process of mutual

[107] "Reflections," 196 and *Prerogatives*, 211, 216–17. MH does so because he found it important to maintain the continuity of the common-law constitution in the face of William I's invasion of England in 1066 and installation of Norman institutions of government.

[108] Even the usurper, without valid legal title, acquires a right to rule based on community consent. Hale writes: "although the rightful heir, or inheritor of the crown, hath an unresumable right, yet the usurper hath no other right but immediately from the people; that so long as, de facto, he continues king, he hath the right of a king, as against this or that particular man or society, but not against the whole people: that so long as he continues in possession, though by power, so long, by judgement of law, he continues king; because in judgement of law, he hath so long an influence from the major, at least most powerful, part of the people" (Lincoln's Inn, Hargrave MS 9, 86; quoted in Cromartie, *Hale*, 77).

[109] MH is very fond of the image of the ship of Theseus (or as he refers to it, the ship of the Argonauts), the basic materials of which over a span of many years had all been replaced, while the ship retained its identity (*History*, 142; "Amendment," 173).

adjustment of terms of association understood against the background of mutual commitments ultimately underwritten by the principle *fides est servanda*. Of course, adjustments rarely are made in the absence of duress, because they are adjustments of arrangements of political power made in the presence and through the exercise of that power.

The authority of and allegiance to civil government, then, rest in the founding compact and ultimately in the natural-law principle of fidelity, *fides est servanda*.[110] But he argues in *Treatise*, Chapter 5, that natural law also demands that governments comply with principles of justice, honesty, and decency, and, although natural law gives wide leeway to positive law to determine its requirements, it is not completely silent. Positive law and governmental power may violate this more fundamental law, and in cases of conflict, the primary allegiance of citizens is to God and to God's law (i.e., natural law). Citizens can never be bound by civil law to offend God, Hale argues, but this does not free them from their obligations to honour the civil law in all such cases. Rather, first, individual citizens who violate instituted law on conscientious grounds are justified only when the judgments are correct. "The decision of such a contradiction requires great judgment and integrity in the subject; for if he err in his judgment, his disobedience is at his peril." *Treatise*, 18; see also 59). When it comes to civil obligation, Hale recognizes no right of conscientious action. Second, even when citizens are released from their obligation to obey actively, they remain "under the obligation of non-resistance and passive subjection" (*Treatise*, 59). Otherwise, Hale argues, "every man would thereby be put into a condition, not only to dispute the lawfulness of everything commanded, but also the power and authority of laws in inflicting punishment in whatsoever they should judge not lawful, wherein every man would be a judge of the lawfulness of inflicting the penalty and consequently of the lawfulness of resistance when and how he please" (*Treatise*, 59).

Limits of Sovereignty. Civil order, according to Hale, is *instituted* order, established by and rooted in a continuous but ever-changing compact. This compact determines the nature and form of the civil order and government of a political community. It defines the powers of sovereignty (the *jura summi imperii*) for that community, distributes them to various organs of government, and delimits their exercise ("Reflections," 198; *Prerogatives*, 207–8). As we have seen, this compact is not merely evidenced or recorded in the community's evolving law; it is embodied in it and evolves with it. Thus, on Hale's view, all ruling power is ordained by law. Sovereignty is not a natural or original property of a ruler, but entirely the product of the compact embodied in the political community's law. Law does not merely limit

[110] In *Treatise*, 54, Hale clearly distinguishes the duty of allegiance generated by this mutual commitment from another, lesser duty of gratitude for received benefits.

sovereign power, law constitutes it.[111] There is no residual sovereign power beyond the legally ordained powers, including royal prerogatives, accorded to it.[112] Hale does not trumpet this feature of his theory of sovereignty, but it is fundamental to his understanding of sovereign power.

Echoing Bodin,[113] Hale maintains that the constituted powers of sovereignty comprise (1) powers of empire—including the power to make war and peace, to establish the currency (and more generally to regulate commerce and the economy), and the right of pardon—and (2) powers of jurisdiction—including powers to make law (and therewith to abrogate and dispense with them) and to give judgment in execution of them ("Reflections," 198; *Prerogatives*, 228)—and (3) certain prerogative powers. The sovereign's prerogative, taken broadly, includes all the powers allocated to the sovereign ruler, but more specifically refers to those assigned powers the exercise of which is left largely to the sovereign's discretion. Within the relaxed boundaries of *lex permissiva*, instituted government can take many different forms, according to Hale, and can range from a wholly unqualified ("absolute") form to a highly qualified one (*Prerogatives*, 220).

Writing after the Restoration, Hale maintains that, in England, royal power is basically monarchical, but qualified. Having no equal in the kingdom, the king is subject to no other power on earth; in particular the king is not subject to the people considered distributively or collectively (*Prerogatives*, 218–19). Nevertheless, royal power is qualified by law in several respects, among the most important of which are the following. First, the king can make law and impose taxes only with the advice and assent of parliament, and has very limited powers of dispensation. It is parliament (that is, Lords and Commons acting only with the assent of the king) that has "sovereign and sacred authority in making, confirming, repealing and expounding laws."[114] Second, although all adjudicative power was originally lodged in the king, it has over time irrevocably devolved onto his courts which now operate independently of his oversight or intervention (*History*, 138; *Prerogatives*, 231–4). Third, the king—and all departments of government—are bound by the laws duly instituted. In a brief but intriguing discussion in *Prerogatives* (echoed in "Reflections") Hale elaborates this thesis.

He begins by distinguishing three "powers" or "effects" of law (with which he associates different kinds of "obligation"): (1) *potestas directiva*, (2) *potestas coercens*,

[111] MH here follows familiar, if not uncontested, common-law doctrine. For example, Sir Edward Coke wrote, "the King hath no Prerogative, but that which the Law of the Land allows him" (*Twelfth Report*, 76; Sheppard, *Coke: Selected Writings*, 489). See Hooker at note 39.

[112] Yet, according to MH, in the English constitution these rights are bestowed "absolutely, perpetually and hereditarily and [the king] cannot be deprived of them either in whole, or in part, without his consent" (BL Add MS 14291, 222v; quoted in Michael Lobban, *History*, 70).

[113] Bodin, *On Sovereignty*, Bk I, ch. 10, esp. 58–88.

[114] Hale, *The Original Institution, Power and Jurisdiction of Parliaments* (London, 1707), 49 (see *Prerogatives*, note 73).

and *potestas irritans*. In his *Treatise*, Hale further analyses directive power into (a) law's *vis indicativa* and (b) law's *vis preceptiva* or *imperativa* (*Treatise*, 63–4). That is, law presents to the understanding that which is to be done or not done (and in the case of natural law, that which is morally good or evil) and it *prescribes it*, making it obligatory. He distinguishes the latter into two distinct but complementary "obligations": *obligatio ad officium*, obligation proper, and *obligatio ad poenam*, the duty to submit to punishment in the case of violation of the first obligation. The primary obligation rests mainly in conscience and is owed to the authority that prescribes the law. In *Prerogatives* and "Reflections" these two obligations are allocated to distinct powers of law—its directive power and its coercive power. The third power—law's invalidating power—is the most intriguing. Hale's idea is that the law has the power to nullify or deny legal standing to acts contrary to existing law.[115] It is central to Hale's understanding of the sovereign's subjection to the law.

Against those who argued that the sovereign is and must be above the civil law,[116] Hale, following a long medieval tradition,[117] argued that while the sovereign is not subject to the civil law's coercive power, the sovereign is subject to law's directive power. The directive power binds in conscience, we have seen, and in Hale's view that makes the sovereign accountable to God, in virtue of the *fides est servanda* principle in which sovereign authority is grounded. But Hale goes beyond this familiar medieval doctrine. Implicit in the directive power of law is the invalidating power of law, the power of "putting an inefficacy or civil nullity upon those acts that are within the institution or restraint of the law" ("Reflections," note 44). In some cases, law can nullify acts done contrary to the law. In these cases, he argues, although the king himself cannot legally be punished directly, his "instruments and ministers that are the immediate actors of such unlawful things are subject to the coercive power of the law" (*Prerogatives*, 221). Acting contrary to the law, even when acting pursuant to the king's policies or on the king's explicit orders, officials are denied the protection of the law: "The king's act in such case being void doth not justify or defend the instruments" (*Prerogatives*, 221). Thus, "the king is obliged by his own laws, for these acts that are done by his command against the laws are void and the instruments therein are not indemnified by such command" ("Reflections," 197, note 41).

[115] This idea is familiar in canon law and prominent in Suarez's theory of law. See Thaikoottathil James, *Leges Irritantes et Inhabilitantes* (Rome: Pontificia Universitas Urbaniana, Facultas Juris Canonics, 2003); Edward Roelker, "The Concept of Invalidating Laws," *The Jurist*, 3 (1943), 32–63 and "The Interpretation of Invalidating Laws," *The Jurist*, 3 (1943), 364–403, 550–66; Suarez, *On Laws*, Bk II, ch. 33.1, 12–14; Bk III, ch. 35.24–5. Suarez devotes a large part of *De legibus ac deo legislatore* (Bk V, chs 19–34) to a discussion of law's invalidating power, but this text has not been translated into English.

[116] See, e.g., Hobbes, *Leviathan*. "Absolutists" never claimed that the sovereign is above natural or divine law, of course, but rather that the sovereign is not subject to human or civil law and hence subject to no earthly judge.

[117] See, e.g., Aquinas, *Summa Theologiae*, IIaIIae, 96 a. 5, ad 3.

The potential scope of this doctrine is masked by Hale's modest statement of it; for, although the king in his person and property is immune from prosecution for violation of the law, the king's government is subject to the full force of the law. And the king cannot indemnify the actions of government officials that are found to be contrary to standing common law (unless the law specifically authorizes them to do so). Combined with Hale's earlier thesis that all sovereign power is the product of law, this yields a potentially powerful endorsement of the rule of law. The monarch's officials, and thereby the policies and practices of the king's government, are subject to the judgment of the regular common-law courts.

However, Hale locates ultimate sovereignty not in some supreme judicial body that sits in judgment on the king's government and parliament, but rather in the composite body of King-in-Parliament, which alone determines with finality the content of the laws made ("Jurisdiction," 243–5). Not only does parliament have "transcendent and absolute" power of making laws, he insists, but also "being the highest and greatest court," its decisions are final and beyond any further appeal, conceding that "if by any means a misgovernment should any ways fall upon it, the subjects of this kingdom are left without all manner of remedy."[118]

In light of above complex view of sovereignty, Hale's critique of Hobbes's doctrine of sovereignty takes on special importance. Against the common-law doctrine, which Hale largely defends, Hobbes had argued that there cannot be any limits on ruling power. The sovereign has the power to make, alter, and repeal laws, to tax, and even to act contrary to the rights and property of citizens at the sovereign's pleasure. Of course, the sovereign is wise to govern with law and publicly to follow it, except in times of public danger. But in that case, Hobbes had argued, the sovereign is always the judge of public danger. In "Reflections," Hale argues that Hobbes is wrong about English constitutional law ("Reflections," 199–201). But even more he is also wrong as a matter of political principle: Hobbes's absolutist constitution is pernicious to the government and to the governed ("Reflections," 202–3). It betrays sovereign power with a kiss, Hale argues, for government rests morally and practically on mutual confidence between the governed and governors. But if the sovereign claims a right to rule by arbitrary will, popular trust will be undermined and with it the sovereign's capacity to rule. Likewise, the sovereign's claim to rule absolutely harms the governed, because, when property rights are insecure and citizens cannot count on stable laws, their willingness to labour, invest, and trade withers and the community becomes impoverished. Finally, it is especially dangerous to put such arbitrary powers in the hands of the sovereign, when they may be needed only in rare circumstances. It is better to be governed by certain laws and duly constrained sovereign powers, even if they prove inadequate for certain circumstances, than always to be subject to the arbitrary whim of government. Even in times of crisis,

[118] Hale, *Original Institution*, 49 (see "Jurisdiction of the Lords House," note 2).

constrained power, forced to act deliberately and with parliamentary consultation, is not only possible, but is the wiser course.

Conclusion

The views and arguments we find in the selections contained in this volume are more suggestive than determinative, offering basic materials for a common-law jurisprudence rather than a systematic theory of it. Yet, Cromartie correctly observes that "no one gives more insight into the intellectual implications of the constitutional role of common law" than Sir Matthew Hale.[119] In our hyper-specialized era, Hale's irrepressible intellectual curiosity may strike us as undisciplined and promiscuous; yet it enabled him to cross the boundaries of the province of jurisprudence effortlessly; he moved without change of gauge from discussion of feudal tenures to constitutional law to political theory to epistemology to theology and back again. Questions about the constituents of the human soul were as important to him as the limits of royal prerogatives.

119 Cromartie, *Hale*, 6.

Major Events in Hale's Life and English History

55–54 BCE	Romans invade Britain
Mid-5th century CE	Last Romans driven from Britain
450–600 CE	England settled by Angles, Saxons, and Jutes
787	Danes attack Anglo-Saxon England and settle in the North, Centre, and East
924	Saxons regain control of former Danish central England
1042–1066	Edward the Confessor, the last Anglo-Saxon king, reigns
1066	William I defeats Harold at Battle of Hastings, begins Norman rule in England
1215	King John and Barons agree to terms of the Magna Carta; soon after it is annulled by Pope Innocent III
1225	Henry III reaffirms Magna Carta, establishes canonical version
1272–1307	Edward I, the "English Justinian," reigns, consolidates existing law; Yearbooks begin to record and report decisions of courts
1530s	Henry VIII separates the English Church from Rome and spurs the Henrician reformation
1603–1625	Reign of James I, first Stuart monarch in England
1609	Matthew Hale is born
1625	Charles I succeeds James I; parliament passes Petition of Right
1629–1640	Period of personal rule by Charles I
1636	Hale is called to the bar
1642–1649	English Civil War
1649	Charles I executed; Interregnum begins
1652	Hale participates in law reform commission established by Rump Parliament
1653–1658	Oliver Cromwell rules as Lord Protector
1654	Hale represents Gloucestershire in Protectorate's first parliament; Cromwell appoints Hale to the Court of Common Pleas
1658	Hale resigns from the Court of Common Pleas

1659	Richard Cromwell succeeds Oliver Cromwell
1660	Convention Parliament restores Charles II to the throne; Hale participates in negotiating the restoration; Charles II appoints Hale Chief Baron of Exchequer
1671	Charles II appoints Hale Chief Justice of King's Bench
1676	In February, Hale resigns from King's Bench. Hale dies on Christmas Day

A General Note on the Texts

So far as we can tell, all of the texts included in this collection were written in the last fifteen years of Matthew Hale's life, when he was at the height of his judicial career. Only his "Preface to Rolle's Abridgement" was published in his lifetime. All have since been published in either eighteenth-century or twentieth-century editions. Manuscript sources for all the works exist, some in Hale's own hand, some only in a copyist's hand. Wherever possible I have followed manuscript sources, aided by consulting the published sources. In preparing *Treatise* and "Reflections," I followed manuscript sources directly. Because spelling, punctuation, and capitalization varies widely across manuscript, autograph, and published sources, I have edited the selections to conform to modern standards in order to achieve a uniform text accessible to twenty-first-century readers.

Francis Hargrave (1740/1–1821) edited a number of the texts used in this collection. Hargrave was a chancery lawyer and government advisor. In 1772, he successfully argued the habeas corpus application of escaped slave James Somerset and persuaded Lord Mansfield that slavery was contrary to English common law (*Somerset v Stewart*, 98 ER 499 (1772)). He collected and edited many important legal manuscripts in the late eighteenth century. Prominent among the 500 Hargrave manuscripts in the British Museum and Lincoln's Inn are a large number of Hale's unpublished works. Hargrave may have undertaken to edit all of Hale's works. He did not complete the project, but he did edit and publish several of them; others he prepared for but did not see through to publication, among them the text of Hale's *Treatise*.

PART I

Treatise of the Nature of Laws in General and Touching the Law of Nature

Introductory Note

Hale wrote his *Treatise* sometime after 1668, probably in the mid-1670s. A diary entry for autumn of 1668 contains what appears to be a sketch of chapter 1.[1] The autograph manuscript appears to be lost, but the British Library holds three fair copies: BL Add MSS 18,235 (fos 42–147), Harley 7159, and Hargrave 485 (fos 1–93). There is no reason to doubt the authenticity of the text. In addition to the above-mentioned diary entry, the title page of the BL 18,235 copy reads "Some chapters touching the Law of Nature. By the late Lord Cheif [sic] Justice Hale and copied from his own writing. Sent to Sr Robt Southwell by his grandson Matthew Hale of Lincoln's Inn Esqr 1693" (fo. 41). Also, the work ("Of the Law of Nature") appears in the catalogue of Hale's works appended to Burnet's "Life and Death of Sir Matthew Hale."[2] The Harley MS was made in 1696 and perhaps a century or more later, Francis Hargrave prepared the text for publication; however, the task was never completed.

The three copies are very close, but some discrepancies between them exist. I have largely followed the Hargrave copy, but in instances where there was good reason to prefer the BL or the Harley reading (or both) to Hargrave's I have indicated this as follows: *XX* = text inserted from BL MSS; †XX† = text inserted from Harley MSS; ^XX^ = text inserted from BL and Harley. The current editor's emendations or corrections are indicated by enclosing text in square brackets. Numbers in square brackets indicate Hargrave MS folios (recto and verso). I have silently altered spelling, punctuation, and capitalization to conform to modern conventions. The Appendix

[1] "Circuitus Autumnalis 1668," Osborn Manuscript, Beinecke Library, Yale University, 6450, fos 15–16.
[2] Hale, *The Works, Moral and Religious, of Matthew Hale*, ed. T. Thirwall (London, 1805), vol. I, 77.

adds a selection from Hale's *Primitive Origination of Mankind* (London, 1677) in which he discusses laws of the natural order. It is not part of Hale's *Treatise* text.

In this *Treatise*, Hale sets out and defends his general conception of law and gives a detailed account of morality, which, following a very long tradition, he calls "natural law," and of forms and structures of practical reasoning associated with it. He also explains in general the nature of instituted or positive law (both divine and human) and its relationship to natural law. Finally, the *Treatise* addresses questions of the nature and ultimate grounds of sovereign authority (again, divine and human) and the obligations entailed by it. For an extended discussion of the main themes and arguments of this *Treatise*, see the Editor's Introduction.

[3r, 1]

1

Touching the Nature of Law in General

Being now about to write somewhat concerning the law of nature, it may be convenient to premise somewhat concerning law in general.[3] Wherein, as also in the subsequent discourses, I shall neither bind myself to the sentiments of other men that have written touching this subject, nor to those forms of expression that others have used, nor to their method or order of writing; but shall follow my own thoughts and conceptions, and render them under such terms and expressions as I shall think sufficient to give an account of my thoughts and to render them legible and intelligible, though perchance not in the phrases or the appropriate words of the philosophers, schoolmen, divines, or philologers.[4] And since words and phrases are but a sort of institution chosen or agreed upon to signify things or notions, I shall take the liberty to be master of my words, and use such as I think fit and sufficient to be the image of my thoughts, without being solicitous of using those modes, or obliging myself to the strict rules or artificial terms, now or formerly in fashion among many learned men.

A law, therefore, I take to be a rule of moral actions, given to a being endued with understanding and will, by him that hath power or authority to give the same and exact obedience thereunto *per modum imperii* [in the manner of ruling], commanding or forbidding such actions under some penalty expressed or implicitly contained in such law.

I have chosen this long description of a law; because it takes in most of the several ingredients [3v, 2] necessary to be considered in the notion of a law.

I. I call it a *rule*.

This is the general term, under which I describe a law. But yet singly in itself it is too large and comprehensive, and extends to such rules as are not properly laws; and

[3] On the title page, the MS reads: "Of the Nature of Laws in General"; in the table of contents for Chapter 1 and in the text for Chapter 1, it reads: "touching the nature of law in general." This discrepancy may have been the work of copyists rather than MH himself, so readers should not attach much significance to it.

[4] OED: literary scholar.

therefore I have subjoined those restrictive differences that confine the generality of it to the formal or proper notion of law.

Almost in all kind[s] of natural and artificial actions, there are certain prescript rules, which are but directions to attain certain ends proposed to those actions, which yet are not properly and strictly laws. The grammarian hath his rules of words and their composition into sentences; the rhetorician hath his rule of expression, persuasion, and gesture; the logician hath his rules for argumentation; the physician hath his rules for administering physic[5] and prescribing diet, and the patient in order to the attaining of his health is under the direction of those rules. Nay, every mechanical art or operation hath its rules, whereby the artifice is to be effected; and without the due observance of those rules none of these can well attain their ends. But yet these come not under the strict denomination of laws, though in respect of their analogy thereunto they are often so called. The physician prescribes a rule of diet to his sick patient and tells him that if he observe it not, his sickness will increase and probably become mortal: and the patient obediently observes his direction; and the opinion he hath of the skill and fidelity of his physician, the love and desire of health, the incommodity and painfulness of sickness, and the fear of death are strong and forcible and powerful motives of his observance. But all this while the prescription of the physicians is not his law; for it is a rule indeed, but not *juncta cum imperio* [joined with command]. He will die perchance, if he observes it not; but the physician hath no authority to exact his observance under any penalty to be inflicted by him or by [4r, 3] his authority, but only to withdraw himself and leave his unruly patient to taste and undergo the fruit and inconvenience of his own wilfulness.

And upon this account, if atheistical persons could, as they would, exterminate the great God of heaven from having to do in this world, that which they call reason and the law of reason would be indeed a rule, but not truly and formally a law.[6] For let us suppose any one man to be of the most exquisite reason that human nature is capable of; and that he hath that reason chalked out to him, the just end and exquisite measure and order of all his moral actions in order thereunto. Yet this rule of reason would not be a law to him, unless there were some superior that gave this rule to him

[5] Ed: medicine.

[6] Thomas Hobbes says this explicitly in *Leviathan* (1651), ed. Richard Tuck (Cambridge: Cambridge University Press, 1991), 111, 183. See also Francisco Suarez, *A Treatise on Laws and God the Lawgiver*, in *Selection from Three Works*, ed. Thomas Pink, tr. Gwladys L. Williams, Ammi Brown, John Waldron, and Henry Davis (Indianapolis: Liberty Fund, 2015), Bk II, ch 6.14, 17 and II, ch. 9.4. It is often thought that Hugo Grotius denied this in a much discussed passage from his "Prolegomena" to *De jure belli ac pacis libri tres* (vol. II: translation), ed. Francis W. Kelsey (Oxford: Clarendon Press, 1925), para. 11, where he writes, "What we have been saying would have some validity even if we should concede [*etiamsi daremus*] that which cannot be conceded without utmost wickedness, that there is no God." However, it is clear Grotius is not claiming that without God as lawgiver, there still would be natural *law* and *obligation*, but rather that the rational grounds of such law and obligation, rational requirements on human behaviour, would still be valid. In this respect, MH follows Suarez, Grotius, and Hobbes.

per modum imperii et sub ratione legis [in the manner of ruling and on the basis of law]; for he could be under no obligation to observe this rule of reason but only to himself, and therefore may absolve himself by the liberty of his will from observing of that rule and from all obligation to it.[7] As he is lord of himself, so he would be lord of that rule which they call the law of reason, and keep it or break it at his pleasure, without giving account thereof to any but himself; for though he remain a reasonable creature, and is well acquainted with the rule of his reason, yet he remains still a free and voluntary agent, and as to the exercise of his actions is lord still of himself and them.

And what is said of the rule of reason of a single man, the same will be [said], if that rule of reason were as to the perfect exercise thereof universally and equally and uniformly communicated to all mankind. If once we preclude the supreme legislator out of the world with Epicurists and atheists,[8] this rule of reason will not, cannot, be a law. What is said of one man will be said of any, of every man. He will not be under the law of reason as truly a law; because he may absolve himself from any obligation to anything whereof he is lord. And though perchance fear of other superinducted[9] laws, and government, mutual pactions, and such like, give an external and adventitious coercion to him to observe [4v, 4] those common rules of reason, by which such laws are superinducted, and in conformity whereunto they are made; yet still the rule of reason simply considered, excluding the authority of the supreme legislator, would still be without the true formal nature of a law; because, though it were an excellent rule, yet it would induce no obligation upon him that hath it, but he might use or not use it at his pleasure, if he can but deliver himself from the difficulties of other external subservient *government*, laws, or penalties either by secrecy or power.

So that every rule, nay, the best of human rules, the rule of reason itself, considered abstractedly from any superior authority, is not a law or a rule *juncta cum imperio*, but of this more hereafter.

II. It is a rule of *actions moral*.

[1] Some actions, especially of the human nature,[10] are *simply natural* that have no influx of the will, nor any spontaneity in them, but are performed without the immediate concurrence of either. Thus the heart beats, the blood circulates, the meat when once received in the stomach is digested and distributed. These and

[7] MH may have in mind the view expressed by Hobbes in *Leviathan*, 184, 224.

[8] The Epicurean tradition (third to first centuries BCE; Epicurus lived 341–271 BCE) denied the divine origins of justice and law and held that they are products of mutual, consensual arrangement. Because of their materialist metaphysics, Epicureans were often regarded, especially in the seventeenth century, as atheist. Pierre Gassendi (1592–1655) was the most influential Continental Epicurean, but he did not embrace atheism. In the mid-seventeenth century, British critics frequently attacked Hobbes as neo-Epicurean and atheist. See Jon Parkin, *Taming the Leviathan* (Cambridge: Cambridge University Press, 2007), 133–5, 152–3, and *passim*.

[9] OED: instituted or appointed in the place of.

[10] Ed: especially issuing from the nature of human beings.

the like actions are not properly the subject of this law whereof we speak. Indeed there is something analogical to a law, by which these actions that are simply natural are governed; namely, the wise disposition and order that the great God of heaven and earth hath substituted in things, and which appears in things inanimate as well as animate.[11] Thus the elementary bodies act according to the prevalence of active qualities; heavy things descend; vegetables are nourished, grow, and increase, according to that pre-instituted order that the divine wisdom hath settled, which we ordinarily call the law of nature. To this law, indeed, the vital and natural actions in man are subject. But this, as it is not properly a law, so it is not that law whereof we are speaking. But of this more hereafter.

Again [2] there be some actions that are *mixt*, partly [5r, 5] natural, and partly voluntary, or at least spontaneous;[12] and such are most of the spontaneous actions that are subservient to and flow from the animal life in man *quâ talis* [as such], which are in a great measure common to the human and animal nature. The condition of our animal nature makes it natural for us to eat and drink and sleep, and the like; because otherwise our individual nature could not be supported. The desires of sexes are natural, because otherwise our species could not be preserved. It is natural for us to preserve ourselves from the injuries of the weather, and to defend ourselves from other injuries. But the timing of those actions, the measure, the manner, the order, [and] the degree of those actions are subject to our choice and election. I can eat now or forbear for a while. I can eat thus much, or of this kind, and forbear the rest; and so in other things. Now, although these spontaneous actions belonging to the animal life are in a great measure common to the human and brutal[13] nature; yet there is this difference universally between them: though those are in a great measure even spontaneous in the brutes and other animals, yet they are under the regiment[14] only of their phantasy[15] and natural appetite. But in men they are in a great measure under the regiment of a superior faculty, namely, the understanding and will; and therefore they are not only natural and spontaneous, as in brutes, and directed to a natural end and use, but they are also voluntary and under the regiment of that governing faculty in man, namely his will; and that will, though not commanded by his reason, yet is enlightened and directed by it. And by this power or faculty those spontaneous actions of the animal life, which in brutes become almost necessary, yet in man are in a great measure arbitrary or voluntary, [5v, 6] at least as to the times, seasons, degrees, measure, order, and other circumstances accompanying their exertions. In this respect these *mixt* actions, though they come not under a law properly so called in brutes, yet in men they are the proper subject of a true and

[11] In the Appendix to Part I, MH applies this concept of law to laws of the natural order.

[12] Ed: free from external stimulus.

[13] Ed: animal.

[14] OED: rule or governance. Hargrave corrects this to "regimen" several times on this page, but in the remainder of the text he allows "regiment." I follow the latter practice.

[15] Ed: from the Greek, *phantasia* = imagination; a primitive faculty (shared with human beings) of forming sensible images but not capable of grasping universals. See Editor's Introduction, pp. xliii–xliv, xlvi.

formal law: sobriety, chastity, temperance, moderation of passions, and many more moral virtues, being to be exercised about these animal actions of the human nature; because, though the actions themselves are such as belong to the province of the animal life in him, yet the circumstances and modifications thereof are under the regiment of the superior faculties of the rational nature, namely, the understanding and will, and consequently the subject of a law properly so called; for though the actions themselves are in their kind natural, yet the modifications and circumstances thereof render them moral, and capable to be under the sanction of a law in man.

Again, [3] there be some actions that are purely and *simply moral*, and such as can only concern the reasonable or intellectual nature, and are immediately and simply directed to the concerns of a rational life. Such are those that either are relative to Almighty God, as the love, fear, *and* obedience of his commands, sincerity, integrity, and worship of him; or such as concern directly human society, as justice and equity, charity, friendship, beneficence, longanimity,[16] veracity, and the various offices[17] of human society. And these and the like are called actions moral, and come under the *commanding*, and the contrary under the *prohibiting* sanction of a law properly so called.

III. This law is to be *given*, by which I intend these two things:

1. The institution or application of the law to the persons or things for which it is intended.

2. The promulgation of that law to the persons whom it is intended to oblige: This promulgation of a law is not of one kind only, but different in its manner. Thus in some laws the promulgation thereof is by printing, or public inscription thereof in tables or upon pillars, in some by proclamation, as it was in others by constant and known usage. And we shall [6r, 7] find that among the laws of Almighty God himself there are various kinds of promulgations of his laws. Some were delivered by an audible voice from Sinai with thunder. Some were immediately received by Moses, and by him declared to the people; and, as we shall have occasion hereafter to instance, the natural law, whereof we treat, was secretly insinuated and engraven in the mind and conscience, yet so that this still voice, this silent promulgation, is as real and true a promulgation, as if it had been given by the trumpet of Sinai and the voice of thunder.

IV. The *persons*, for whom it is instituted, are *natures endued with understanding and will*. And these natures are, for aught we know, only the angelical and human nature.

The understanding faculty is requisite, because without it the law cannot be known as a law. And the will, and consequently the intrinsic liberty thereof, is required;

[16] OED: long-suffering, forbearance, patience.

[17] OED: positions to which certain duties are attached.

because otherwise it cannot be obeyed as a law, neither can the obedience or disobedience thereof reasonably be attended with their reward or punishment properly so called. For if we shall suppose the subject, to whom such law is given, to be already *necessarily* determined, I say *necessarily* to observe the tenor of what is commanded as a law, the law is needless; and if he be necessarily determined to the contrary, the law would be unreasonable, because impossible to be observed, and it were unreasonable to exact a punishment by the sanction of a law from one that were under an invincible intrinsic necessity to disobey it or not to obey it. It is requisite therefore that the *subjectum cui* [subject to whom], the person or being to whom a law properly and formally so called is given, should have a liberty **ad oppositum**[18] at least intrinsic and connatural to him, which is that we call *will*.

[6v, 8] It is true that the true stating of the liberty of the will, what it is, wherein it consists, whether it be determined intrinsically by the judgment or decision of the understanding, what kind of liberty of will the glorious angels or glorified souls have or shall have who are yet capable of a law, are enquiries that at this time are not pertinent to my purpose. That which I design is the disquisition touching laws as they relate to those natures with which we are acquainted.

And although possibly it may be true that in the true method and actings of the reasonable soul, and in its proper and orderly motion, the will, being a reasonable faculty, should follow the decision of the understanding, and possibly the understanding and will are not so much two distinct faculties, but rather the will is the last act of the soul in things practical, and so it were the consummation of the act of the practical understanding;[19] yet it is certain, we find in ourselves a power to suspend the decision of the understanding, and sometimes we act contrary to it. *Video meliora, deteriora sequor.*[20] So that there is some kind of regent power in the human nature that is free *ad opposita* which we call the will; and the liberty and dominion thereof which the soul exerciseth, whereby a man hath within himself a dominion over what he doth though it be *regnum sub graviore regno* [a dominion subject to a greater power], namely, the determining and commanding power of God.

And upon this account it is that the brutal or bare animal nature is not a proper subject of a law properly so called; for though the animal nature hath in its constitution a kind of inferior shadow or analogy to the rational nature, this phantasy carrying

[18] Ed: freedom to perform an act or its opposite; freedom to do otherwise.

[19] This may remind readers of Hobbes's definition of will as "the last appetite or aversion adhearing immediately to the action" (*Leviathan*, 44). However, like Aquinas (*Summa Theologiae*, IaIIae, qu. 17, a. 1) and other scholastic philosophers, MH sees a close link between reason (rather than "appetite") and will. "For it is a hard matter to conceive how the understanding can deliberately and plenarily conclude an object to be particularly good or evil unless the will go along with it for such a conclusion is in effect the conjunction of the act of understanding to the will ..." (Lambeth 3505, 211, quoted in Alan Cromartie, *Sir Matthew Hale: 1609–1676* (Cambridge: Cambridge University Press, 1995), 171). See also Hale, *Discourse of the Knowledge of God and of our Selves* (London, 1688), 56–7.

[20] "I see the better and approve it, but I follow the worse." Ovid, *Metamorphoses*, VII, 25, tr. Frank Justus Miller, vol. I (Cambridge, MA: Harvard University Press, 1966). See also St Paul in Romans 7:19.

something analogical to intellect, and his appetite something analogical to will, and his spontaneity something analogical to liberty; yet certain it is that he hath not the very faculties or prerogative of intellection, will, or liberty, but is more rigorously determined in and to the actions of an animal life, which seems to have some [7r, 9] spontaneity, than the human nature is, even in relation to actions of the same kind.

V. I mention the *author of a law*; and under this part of the description above given of a law there are these things implied or expressed:

1. That for the constitution of a law truly and properly so called there must be an author thereof as a legislator.
2. That the person, that is the lawgiver or *nomothetes*,[21] must be distinct from the person to whom it is given or that is to be obligated by it.

And the reason is plain: because there doth, and must necessarily, by every law truly and properly so called, arise an obligation, from the party to whom the law is given, unto the party by whom it is given, to observe and perform it. Otherwise it is but a nominal law, and not a real or true law. And in all obligation, because it is a term of relation, there must be *correlata*. No man can oblige himself simply to himself, *for he cannot from himself exact an obedience to himself,* but is absolved at his own pleasure.

It is true, in the case of human laws and constitutions, [that] a legislator may be constituted by the persons who are to be afterwards obliged by that authority that he himself, either wholly or at least as one of the community, transfers to that person or these persons to whom this nomothetical power is thus entrusted. And therefore if we should suppose the new erection either of kingly or aristocratical or democratical government by the paction or stipulation[22] of any society or community of men, [then] by this paction, if I am one of that community, I do together with the next [person] transfer to this government a power to oblige me by the laws which such governors shall make. And *per circuitum* [by circumlocution], it may be said I oblige myself by my own laws, that is, by such laws, which my governor hath made by a power derived from myself, at least as one of the community.

But there are in this two things to be observed, which solve the difficulty. For [i] though the legislator may in some [7v, 10] cases have an authority in their first constitution partly derived from me, yet here [there is a] distinction of persons. The legislator is one [person], and I that am obliged am another person, and between us there may arise an obligation. But this is not all. He that rests here rests before he comes at his journey's end. [ii] By the pact and stipulation that is made whereby the government is transferred to another person or company of men, I have given my

[21] Ed: from the Greek, *nomos* (law) + *tithemi* (to set, put, lay down, make). Compare the Latin *lex* (or *ius*) + *ponere*, from which medieval theorists derived *lex* (or *ius*) *positiva* and in modern English, positive law.

[22] OED: agreement or contract.

faith to that person or society that I will obey them and their laws. And this faith I am bound to keep, not only by an obligation between me and the party to whom it is given, for then if I could avoid his coercion I may loosen myself again; but I am obliged hereunto by a more sovereign and uncontrollable law, the law of Almighty God, who hath given this law to me and to all mankind, [namely,] that *fides est servanda* [faith (i.e., promises or agreements) must be kept], and till God himself shall cancel that obligation, which I owe thereby to Almighty God, I cannot deliver myself from the obligation that I have given by my faith to my governors. And this is the great foundation of the obligation of all civil contracts made between man and man, and the root of all civil government: *fides est servanda*, which is the uncontrollable law of the sovereign Lord of heaven *and earth*.

And this consideration solves that common mistake that some casuists have taken up, even upon this very consideration, who, because [they have held that] a man cannot oblige himself to himself, have thought that no legislator is bound by his own laws. And this is true in two cases. [i] When the laws in themselves and in their matter concern not the legislator, but the community or some of them. [ii] When the absolute power of making laws is solely and simply in that legislator; for then he may retract his law, when and how he please, and so may set himself loose even from those laws that otherwise might for the matter have concerned himself.[23]

[8r, 11] But in other cases of human laws and human legislators, according to the various *constitutions* of government and the various pacts and contracts that either at first or in process of time intervened between the governors and governed, it may fall out that the governors, not only civilly, but by the law of God himself, may be bound by [their][24] own laws; because the governors in such cases are bound under that sovereign law of *fides* [*est*] *servanda*, as well as the governed. If such pactions can sufficiently appear, either by the pacts themselves, or by long usage interpretatively evidencing them, they [i.e., the governors] are under the directive obligation of their own laws, and sometimes under the protectors and rulers thereof, though according to the constitution of such government they may not be under any external coercion to enforce their observance of them.[25] But this is not the present business.

And now if any shall object that in commonwealths purely popular,[26] and where the nomothetical power is lodged in the whole community, there the same persons oblige themselves by their own laws, I say:

1. That the community considered as a community, is a distinct thing from the particular persons that are the integrals of that community; and so the lawgiver is not

[23] See Jean Bodin, *On Sovereignty* (*Four Chapters from "The Six Books of the Commonwealth"*), ed. and tr. Julian H. Franklin (Cambridge: Cambridge University Press, 1992), 10–13; Hobbes, *Leviathan*, 184. See p. 63.

[24] All MSS: his.

[25] See MH's discussion of this theme in "Reflections," 197 and *Prerogatives*, 221–2, 230.

[26] OED: deriving from, or consisting of, the people as a whole.

the same with the persons obliged to the law, but there may be a separate obligation from every particular person of that community to the aggregate body of the community; as any, yea every, freeman of London personally and individually considered may be bound in a bond to the mayor and commonalty or bound by the laws of the mayor and commonalty.

2. Still there is further to be remembered that every particular person of the commonalty, having bound themselves by the faith or paction to obey the laws of that commonalty, there lies a higher and another obligation upon the particular persons to observe their faith, namely the sovereign law [8v, 12] of God that saith *fides est servanda*, so long as the commonalty continues and the matter of that stipulation is not altered. And thus, as there is a difference of persons civilly considered between the commonalty and every particular *person* thereof naturally considered, which may sustain the relation of an obligation; so there is a third person (with humility be it spoken), the glorious God of heaven, whose law requires the observance of the faith as well of the community as of every particular person.

And as this is so in matters relating to laws and government; so there is the very same obligation of contracts between man and man. Titius promiseth Gaius a sum of money for his goods. If Titius were bound to himself only by his promise, he were loose if he please. If he were only bound to Gaius, if Gaius have no power to exact the performance of his obligations, it were fruitless and nothing. But here lies the strength of the obligation by the divine law of Almighty God that saith *fides est servanda*. Titius is bound to the sovereign power of Almighty God. And although a kind of intervenient right[27] of propriety happens between Titius and Gaius by this promise, and therefore Gaius may change the matter of it by releasing that obligation; yet so long as that obligation continues not so released, the contract stands under the signature and law of Almighty God, who in the voice of nature hath proclaimed this law to be observed by all men, *fides est servanda*. And under the obligation of that law Titius remains so long as the matter of his promise stands unaltered by the consent of Gaius.

3. The third thing observable in this particular of the author is the necessary qualification of the author of law, namely authority to give, and power to exact obedience to, such law.

[A] For the former of these, namely nomothetical [9r, 13] authority, it is of two kinds: *natural* or *civil*.

[27] Following Selden, MH treats property rights as a matter of *lex interveniens* (law that comes between or after, or that happens to emerge, i.e., is merely contingent). Intervenient law or rights have their roots not directly in natural law nor in explicitly posited law of an authorized lawmaker, but in the "intervenient" consensual acts of individuals or people either through explicit agreements or compacts or through custom or prescription. They are indirectly binding under the natural-law principle, *fides est servanda*. See John Selden, *Of the Dominion or Ownership of the Sea* (London, 1652), 12–16, 170. The notion is used extensively in Selden's *De jure naturali & gentium juxta disciplinam Ebraeorum* (London, 1640), for example at Bk I, ch. 6; Bk II, chs 2, 8.

[i] The natural authority nomothetical is again of two kinds: either absolute or limited.

[a] That nomothetical authority, that is absolute, ariseth from the absolute dependence of one thing upon another both as to being and to preservation or support. In such a case, that being, upon which anything hath such absolute dependence, must needs have naturally a plenitude and absoluteness of power of imposing a law upon such dependent being; because he is absolute lord thereof. And upon this account the great God of heaven and earth, and only he, hath naturally the sovereign and absolute authority of giving a law to any created being, for all things have their original being and their preservation from him and their dependence upon him; and therefore he is most absolute lord, governor, and proprietor of all things, and consequently hath most naturally a just authority, independent upon any one creature, to give that [creature] a law, which [God] not only gave but continues in being.

If it were possible to conceive that anything had a being from Almighty God, but having once obtained it could preserve itself in that being by its own power, it might abate somewhat of the plenitude of the natural nomothetical authority of Almighty God. But all things are essentially depending upon him both for their origination and preservation. And he is therefore the most absolute lord and proprietor and governor of all things in heaven and earth, angels and men, and not only their lord and creator, but also their bountiful benefactor, and filleth everything according to their several capacities with goodness, so that upon all accounts, by the greatest justice and reason imaginable, and by the very nature of things, he hath the most absolute nomothetical authority to give law to his creatures of all kinds, and they do most naturally owe an universal obedience to him.

And as his authority to give laws to his creatures is most just and natural and universal, so his power to exact obedience to those laws is plenary and sufficient, it being [9v, 14] infinite and boundless.

[b] That other natural authority, which I call limited, is the parental power, which certainly, till the necessity of civil authority was superinduced upon it, was very large; yet [it was] limited, not only by civil constitution and government superinduced, but even in its own nature.

This parental nomothetical authority is therefore natural, 1. because the child[,] subordinately unto the divine causality and influence[,] had his being from his parents, especially the father, or at least the chief active instrument under God of his generation; [and] 2. because during minority the child hath a great dependence upon the care and provision of the parent.

But yet it is a limited authority by nature, 1. because the child owes more of his being and preservation to Almighty God then he can possibly owe to his parents, and therefore the parental nomothetical authority is naturally subordinate to the nomothetical authority of Almighty God and controllable by it; [and] 2. because after a competent age the child hath less dependence upon his parent than in his infancy for support, and so gradually the parental authority nomothetical doth decline and by emancipation after a complete age seems to decay.

Again [3] it is limited civilly by superinduced civil government, which in all ages and places hath much abridged that parental authority, which naturally [the parent] had before instituted civil government. And according to degrees of parental nomothetical authority, such are the degrees of the parental executive power limited and restrained upon the same account that the nomothetical parental power is limited or abridged.

And thus far concerning the natural authority nomothetical and the executive power in order thereunto.

[ii] As touching the *civil* authority nomothetical and the executive power in order thereunto, I need not say much.[28] It is the subject of infinite political discourses. [10r, 15] Only thus much: the means of acquisition of the legislative authority are various. Sometimes it is acquired by descent, sometimes by investiture or ordination from another that hath it; sometimes by victory or conquest; sometimes by pact and convention between the governor and governed, and that either in the first institution of that government, or by succeeding conventions or concessions or capitulations between the governors and governed.

It is hard to find any conquest so absolute but as to the modification of the legislative authority there is something of convention or agreement, which directs or qualifies that authority, either by pactions intervening between the conquered and conquerors, or upon dedition[29] or subsequent capitulations, or even among the victors themselves, where the very army or officers model or moderate or order their future governments by pactions among themselves.

And upon this account it comes to pass that the nomothetical authority is variously modified in several states and kingdoms, and in the same states and kingdoms variously in several seasons. In some kingdoms, it seems to be more absolutely settled in the prince alone. In some it is placed in the prince with the assent of the nobility or optimates. In some there is also necessary assent of the people or their delegates. In some, the legislative authority is lodged in one society, as in Rome in the senate, and the executive power in others, as in the consuls. In some, both the legislative authority and the executive power are lodged in the same person.

And thus among men the legislative authority is variously modelled according to various customs, pactions, concessions, and capitulations.

And thus far touching that which I call authority nomothetical, which is nothing else but a just right of [10v, 16] making laws to oblige others, whether that right

[28] In the *Treatise*, Hale is primarily concerned with natural law, rather than civil law; MH's views of the latter are set out in "Reflections," Ch. 2 and *Prerogatives*, Ch. 1.

[29] OED: surrender.

be acquired *jure naturae* or *jure civili* or *jure belli* [by laws of nature or by civil laws or by laws of war]; which is partly a civil right introduced upon necessity to avoid worse inconveniences. This is that which the Greeks call ἐξουσία [*exousia*] or authority, *jus ferendi leges* [the right of making laws], which is essentially necessary to the due constitution of the law.

Customary laws introduced by long usage do obtain the force of laws, though their original or first perfection from the legislative authority be not extant, upon two accounts, both consonant to what is delivered. 1. Because by long usage they carry a presumption of their origination and †perfection†[30] at first from the just legislative authority of him or them that at first had it. 2. Because the long usage carries with it, not only the consent of the community that is bound by it, but also of the legislative authority that tacitly consents to it; and so though it hath not the formality of other instituted laws, yet it hath the substance and equivalence of an institution by the legislative authority; I mean in relation to civil laws.

[B] But besides the ἐξουσία or *authoritas nomothetica*, which is essential to the due constitution of a law, so to the due execution of a law there is required power that which the Greeks call δύναμις [*dynamis*].

This alone is not sufficient without the former for the constitution of a law; for there may be a power over a man enforcing him to do a thing, which nevertheless doth not truly obtain the right of a law; as when a man falls into the hands of a company of robbers or riotous persons that are too strong for him. Neither doth the absence of this power or force always invalidate the efficacy of a law; for a prince or state, having a lawful authority, may make a law that is obliging to his subjects, when yet by reason of some emergency, as of a sudden commotion or rebellion or tumult, the executive [11r, 17] power of that prince or state is suspended.

But this δύναμις, power to execute the laws when made, is necessary to be somewhere to the end and efficacy of the law, which without it will be dead and ineffectual to the end of its institution.

And thus far concerning the qualification of the lawgiver.

VI. I have in the description of a law said that it is not simply a rule, but *regula juncta cum imperio* [a rule joined with command], whereby it is distinguished from a bare rule of direction and from a bare counsel or advice. But of this enough before. And this empire of a law[31] consists commonly in these two branches of commands and prohibitions according to the various objects of either; for as to that of permission, or *lex permissiva* [permissive law],[32] it is nothing else but an omission of anything out of a law, at least as to some circumstances of person, time, or place, which leaves the thing indifferent or free to be done or omitted till that indifferency be determined by some human law.

30 H: promanation.
31 Ed: the domain of its *imperium*, i.e., of its governance.
32 See Chapter 12.

VII. We have in this description the sanction or *sepimentum legis*;[33] namely, the penalty or pain of the violation of it: which is punishment either expressed or determined, as in some laws; or left undetermined to the *arbitrium judicis* [decision of the judge] to inflict prudentially under various degrees proportionable to the circumstances of the offence or contempt, as in other laws.

Punishments or penalties either expressly or implicitly annexed to laws have three special ends or uses. First, to be a satisfaction or compensation of that debt, which is contracted by the violation of the law. For as we have before shown, and shall more fully show in the next chapter, there is an obligation in case of every law truly so caused[34] to the obedience of it, and by the act of disobedience there grows a kind of forfeiture to the governor from the governed, which, because what is done by such violation [11v, 18] cannot be *infectum* [undone], thence *there* ariseth a just exaction of a penalty or mulct upon the offender as the compensation or retribution thereof in point of justice. But this I take to be the less principal reason or end of the penalty of a broken law.

Secondly, the principal end of the sanction annexed to a law is not so much that the penalty may be inflicted, as that the law may be observed and the penalty avoided. The exacting of the penalty is the thing least intended by every good and wise legislature. But the principal end is thereby to secure the law from violation by the fear of the penalty annexed to it. So that the penalty annexed to the law is, as I before said, the security and *sepimentum legis*, the means to keep the subjects in obedience to it; and not so much, or at least not primarily intended to be, the satisfaction for the disobedience of it.

Thirdly, and as thus the sanction of the law is principally intended to contain subjects in their duty, so the punishment, when inflicted, is neither purely nor principally for the retribution or satisfaction of the offence by the party offending, but to be exemplary and medicinal to others. And therefore the wise lawgiver in his injunction of penalties doth so frequently repeat this clause that all Israel may hear and fear and do no more so wickedly.[35]

It is true that these two[36] ends of punishment do not answer altogether the institution of everlasting punishment by the great God of heaven upon the contemptuous violators of *his* law, as shall in their due time be shewn.

But this everlasting punishment is inflicted upon other accounts. 1. As to a just retribution of the contempt of the divine justice and goodness, in respect whereof Almighty God is a just judge and *per modum vindicate* [by way of punishment] inflicts that everlasting *poena sensus* [pain or punishment of sense][37] as an *instituted*

[33] Literally, "the fence of law," that is, that which keeps agents within the bounds of law. Elsewhere, MH writes that ecclesiastical government is "a great help to the preservation of [religion] in its purity and unity, and may well be called *Sepimentum Religionis Christianae*, as the *Jews* call their oral traditions *Sepimentum Legis*, 'the fence of the law.'" Hale, "A Discourse of Religion," in *Works, Moral and Religious*, I, 297.

[34] So read all MSS; should it be "truly so called"?

[35] MH probably has in mind Deuteronomy 13:11—"And all Israel shall hear, and fear, and shall do no more any such wickedness as this is, among you." (See also Deuteronomy 17:13 and 19:20.)

[36] Ed: presumably, the latter two.

[37] Ed: in Christian theology, the torment of fire.

punishment of their contempt and wilful rebellion. 2. As a kind of necessary consequence [12r, 19] or natural effect of that *ataxy*[38] and disorder occasioned by the parting from the station, which God Almighty hath ordained for the human nature, whereby it comes to pass that by a kind of natural consequence they may suffer the *poena damni* [pain of loss][39] and at least some measure of the *poena sensus* that the damned must suffer as sickness or fever or palsy to an intemperate man is not only the just punishment but the natural consequence of that intemperance; the poverty of a slothful, negligent, or profuse man is as well the effect as the punishment of his fault; and death the natural consequence, as well as the punishment of him that destroys himself or rejects the necessary means of preserving life. But of this hereafter.

As touching the other incentive of obedience, namely rewards of obedience, though the bounty and goodness of God hath for the most part annexed to his laws as well rewards of obedience as punishments of disobedience, as appears both in the Mosaical and evangelical laws:[40] yet it is not always necessary that express rewards be annexed to laws; partly because obedience is the duty of every subject to a just law, and therefore not necessary to be purchased by the annexation of rewards; and partly, because every just and wise law carries with itself and in itself a benefit to those that obey it, or at least to the community whereof they are members.

And thus much touching the formal nature of the laws and the necessary incidents[41] to their constitution. I shall subjoin a few words touching the effects of laws which shall be the subject of the next chapter.

[12v, 20]

2

Touching the Effect of Laws in General

The effect of laws is considerable under the two terms of the relation of laws, namely, on the part of the governors and on the part of the governed or subjects.

[38] OED: lack of order or discipline, irregularity, confusion.
[39] Ed: in Christian theology, pain of radical separation from God.
[40] Ed: laws of Moses (i.e., Torah) and of the Gospel (i.e., New Testament).
[41] Ed: matters necessarily connected with.

First, on the part of the governors the effect of the laws is that the governors do govern their subjects according to such just laws, as are duly made, so long as they stand in their due force. And yet this doth not exclude the governor from a prudent relaxation of penalties by pardoning offenders or mitigating penalties, where the conveniences of government may require or permit it, especially in case of the submission and reformation of the offender.

Secondly, on the part of the subject the effect of law is that which we call obligation; and this is of two kinds. 1. An *antecedent* obligation, whereby the subject is bound to obey such laws as are justly made. 2. An obligation *secondary* or *subsequent*, whereby the subject in case of disobedience is obliged to the penalty or sanction of the law.

As to the former of these, the antecedent obligation is that whereby the subject is intrinsically bound actively to obey what the law requires him to do and to forbear to do what the law forbids.

Now in relation to the laws of Almighty God we are to consider two things. 1. The formal reason of that obligation. 2. The reference of this obligation in the rational creature.

First, the sense of that obligation is the reason of the former of these: namely, the intrinsic or formal reason of this obligation of obedience to the laws of Almighty God consists in that natural and original subjection of the creature to the will of God, and that [13r, 21] essential dependence of the creature upon him both for his being and for his preservation, whereby he is sovereign and absolute lord of his creature by all the right and justice imaginable.[42]

[42] In *On the Primitive Origination of Mankind* (London, 1677), MH argues that "the root of all Obligation in Mankind... is the law and command of him that hath sovereign authority to command, and infinite power to exact obedience, and punish the want of it" (355). "[T]he true foundation, root, and extent of that subjection that the created nature owes to almighty God, namely, on the part of man there is dependence upon God, as the root and support of his existence, there is the obligation of love, gratitude, and duty, as to his greatest and most sovereign benefactor. But this is not all the foundation of subjection on the part of man, and authority on the part of God, but there are certain radical foundations of the divine authority and sovereignty over man; namely, 1. A right of propriety, nothing can be more a man's own than that which he gives a being to. But the propriety that any man can have in what he makes, is still limited and qualified, first, because he is not himself his own, he owes his being to God, and therefore without the help of divine indulgence his acquests are like the acquests of a servant, *acquirit domino* [the lord's acquisition]. And besides, the matter is not his own, whatsoever he makes, he makes out of that matter that was not his own. But the propriety that almighty God acquires in his creatures is absolute, because he himself is a supreme and sovereign efficient [cause], none is above him, and because the matter out of which he effected man and all corporeal existences was perfectly his own; it was matter of his own making. 2. A right of absolute dominion and sovereignty over his creatures; where the property is circumscribed, limited, or qualified, the dominion is so too; but an absolute sovereign property carries with it an absolute sovereign dominion in the proprietor. 3. An infinite irresistible power to exert the right of his dominion according to his will: The two former considerations give him a sovereign authority over his creature, a right, *jus disponendi* [right to dispose at will]; but authority or right being divided from power to execute the authority and exact obedience to it is lame, but the glorious God hath not only an absolute right of propriety and dominion over his creature, but an infinite irresistible power to rule, order, and dispose it according to his will.... And yet this infinite power of God is under the management of a most wise, and holy, and pure, and gracious will; and therefore though his propriety be absolute, his dominion boundless,

Secondly, the nature or reason of the impression of the sense of this obligation upon the creature, which seems to be of this kind: 1. A connatural inbred impression upon the human nature of that dependence it hath upon Almighty God, antecedently to any distinct ratiocination or experimental observation,[43] not altogether unlike that instinct in the young birds or other animals, which, together with their own very being, receive an impression of their dependence upon the old ones before they have any experimental observation of the usefulness of such dependence. 2. An acquired sense of that dependence, either by ratiocination or by experience, whereby the soul is more distinctly informed of its own dependence upon God, of his power, goodness, and beneficence. And hereupon all the passions of the mind come in and elevate and improve the sense of its obligation to the will of God. Fear comes in and gives a sense of its obligation in relation to the divine justice and power. Hope and love and gratitude come in and give a farther and nobler sense of its obligation to obey Almighty God as the greatest benefactor of mankind.

And all or some of these make up that which we call obligation in conscience, as that internal primitive sense of that obligation, which the creature owes to the law of her maker.

But in [the] case of human laws this obligation of an active obedience in the subject to the laws of his sovereign is under this limitation: so far as the same is not repugnant to the law of God. For it is an eternal truth [that] in the contradiction of human laws to the law of God, it is better to obey [13v, 22] God than man, though the decision of such a contradiction requires great judgment and integrity in the subject; for if he err in his judgment, his disobedience is at his peril.

And upon the same reason it is that even in human laws made by a subordinate legislator, whose laws are subject to control or invalidation by a contrary law of a supreme one, the active obedience to such subordinate law is as subordinate as the law itself. And therefore in the contradiction of the particular laws of a city to the laws of that kingdom whereof it is a city, the active obedience of the laws of the city is suspended or discharged by the contradictory law of the kingdom; because, as before is said, where the law is subordinate, the active obedience is and must be with the same subordination.

his power infinite, yet the exercise of his dominion and power is full of goodness, suitable to the most perfect nature of God" (354–5).

[43] I.e., observation from experience. In *Primitive Origination*, 8, MH writes: "When we consider how many things in nature escape our senses, and the discoveries thereof; and yet how much we stand in need of the discoveries of sense, and sensible and experimental observation, to bottom any sound conjecture concerning the nature, causes, and effects of the things in nature, and how uncertain, fanciful, and imaginary our suppositions are without it, whereby it comes to pass, that we many times frame suppositions and conclusions concerning things supposed to be in nature, before we have any certain evidence, whether in truth the very things about which we frame our suppositions or conclusions have at all any real existence, or if they have, yet for want of a clear, and sensible, and experimented observation of them, our positions and conclusions touching their causes, effects, order and methods of their procedure are but fictions and imaginations."

But where the human law is duly made and not contrary or contradictory to a more sovereign law, the obligation of obedience by the subject thereunto is necessary; because the subject either expressly or tacitly hath given his faith so to do, to the observance whereof the divine law obligeth. The consequence whereof is that, although the immediate obligation ariseth by the express or tacit paction or stipulation of the subject; yet, that being once supposed, the supreme lawgiver of heaven and earth hath set his fiat to it by that law of his, *fides est servanda*.

And therefore as the ancients have said that the supreme or uppermost link of the chain of natural causes is fastened to the chair of God;[44] so in the last contracts between the governors and governed and between man and man, though the terms of the stipulation be between such as by nature are equal, yet the uppermost link of that stipulation is fastened to the throne of the glorious God; and therefore the violation of that contract is not only a violation of the law of man, but of the law of God himself, who hath set his signature to it and requires performance of it.

[14r, 23] And hence it is that as a man is bound in conscience to the law of God in his promises and contracts between man and man, so he is bound in conscience to the same law of God to observe the laws of his governor that are possible and not contradictory or contrary to the law of God. And this is the true foundation and establishment of all justice, commutative and distributive, of all government, [and] of ^all^ laws. And they that go about to remove God or his providence or his sovereign law, even that of nature, out of the world, do in a moment dissolve the foundations of all human government and human societies and all justice between man and man, all which stand bottomed only upon the sovereign authority and law of Almighty God; and without this great *substratum*, men of power or boldness or subtlety would with as much facility break the bonds of government, as Samson broke the *withes* or the new cords with which he was bound.[45]

2. The *subsequent* obligation is that which is after an offence committed or supposed against a law duly made; which is an obligation to punishment, or a passive subjection to the sanction of the law that is oftentimes called guilt, *reatus*, or obligation to punishment.

And this guilt or obligation to punishment with respect to the violation of God's law is called guilt of conscience; because the divine law is that, which only either mediately or immediately lays hold upon the conscience, as I shall have occasion at large to declare, when I come to the particular discussion of the part of the divine law which is called the law of nature.

[44] MH may have in mind the Stoic doctrine of the chain of causes. See Susan Sauvé Meyer, "Chain of Causes," in Ricardo Salles (ed.), *God and Cosmos in Stoicism* (Oxford: Oxford University Press, 2009), 71–91.

[45] See Judges 15:9–17.

3

Touching the Several Kinds of Laws

Laws are distributed, in relation to the immediate author of them, into divine laws or the laws of Almighty God, [14v, 24] and human laws or laws of men. Touching the latter it is not my purpose to discourse at this time.

Touching the laws of God or divine laws, either they are positive laws given by the express command of Almighty God to intellectual creatures whether angels or men, or [they are] natural laws.

The positive laws of God are distinguishable in relation to the matter or subject of them.

They are such as either command or prohibit some things that antecedently to such law had no intrinsic good or evil in them, but stood indifferent to be done or not; and this is properly the subject of a divine positive law. For God Almighty, being the supreme lawgiver and governor of all things, may by a positive law determine the indifferency of things in their nature indifferent,[46] and by virtue of such command or prohibition they cease to be indifferent as they were before, and the reasonable nature is most justly obliged to obey such positive institution. And of this kind seems to be the command or law given to the first man touching the not eating of the tree of knowledge of good and evil, as also many of the Levitical and ritual and judicial laws given to the Jews in the Mosaical dispensation, and perchance the sacramental institutions of baptism and the Eucharist under the gospel, which, though they were designed to a great moral good, yet simply considered in themselves their institution seems to be positive.

Again sometimes the positive law of God hath for its object or matter some things that are either commanded or prohibited by an antecedent natural right by the intrinsic good or evil of such things. Thus Almighty God did as it were re-enact by a positive law the natural law contained in the Decalogue. And this positive law of God hath in respect of the natural law thus given these effects. First it is a more explicit publication of that natural law, which obliged before. Secondly it superadds a further obligation to those to whom such law is so given, and consequently enhanceth the crime and guilt of their disobedience; [15r, 25] because in such case disobedience is as it were *crimen duplicatum* [a double crime], being committed

[46] Ed: make determinate matters that are indeterminate and are not either intrinsically good or evil.

against a double obligation, namely that of the divine law of nature and that of positive law of God superadded thereunto. And this was the case of the Jews, to whom the natural law contained in the two tables was, as it were, positively re-enacted by that new promulgation thereof upon Mount Sinai.

But the consideration of the positive law of God is not my business at this time, and therefore I shall say no more concerning it.

The divine natural law or the law, commonly called the law of nature, hath a double acceptation.

First, more large and comprehensive, as it imports that order of the universe or of the several parts thereof instituted by Almighty God and his most wise, powerful, and sovereign will, whereby the works of nature are directed, ordered, and governed to their several ends regularly and with great constancy and uniformity suitable to their kinds and natures. And thus the orderly motion of the celestial bodies, their influences and *causalities*, the mutual contemporation[47] and actions of the elementary bodies, and their qualities, the method of natural generations in things animate and inanimate, the qualities and instincts and operations of vegetables and animals; and the whole order, chain, and consecution[48] of natural causes and effects: all these come under that rule and law, which is comprehensively called the law of nature, and is nothing else but that most admirable order and method, which the divine will hath with admirable wisdom instituted and with admirable power preserved and maintained in the universe and the several parts thereof, as I have elsewhere at large declared.

But *secondly*, the more limited and proper law of nature is that, which Almighty God hath given unto, settled, and [15v, 26] fixed in the natures of intellectual creatures whether angels or men. And it is called the law of nature, not as if nature were the author of it; for nature properly considered is not any real efficient [cause], but is the effect, law, or order that the supreme intellectual being hath instituted or ordered in things. But it is therefore called the law of nature or a natural law, because, as in animals, plants, and other things their instincts, order, and rule are connatural to them by the wise institution of Almighty God, so this law that I now speak of is connatural to the intellectual nature, implanted and characterized in it by the wise lord of heaven and earth in such manner as shall be hereafter declared.

Touching the law of nature connatural to the angelical nature we cannot determine anything; we are not acquainted with their natures or the frame thereof. And therefore I apply myself to that law of nature, which we suppose to belong to the human nature. And herein I shall endeavour, in what follows to give a description of that law, to show what is its author, its object, [and] the manner of its communication to the human nature. I shall also show that it is properly a law, what its force is, what the kinds, and at least some of the principal *capita legis naturae*;[49] and shall show that

[47] OED: synchronism. [48] OED: succession or sequence.

[49] Ed: tenets or principles of the law of nature [lit. "heads" and by extension "chapters" and "clauses" of legislation].

really and truly it is such a law common to the human nature; and shall herein follow that method that seems to me most natural and proper for the explication and declaration of this argument.

4

Touching the Description of the Law of Nature in Man, and Whence It Is to be Gathered

He that goes about to evince[50] anything or supposition [16r, 27] to be, must of necessity in the first place set down what that thing or supposition is, which he intends to prove that it may be understood what it is he contends for. It would therefore be a vain endeavour to prove there is such a thing as the law of nature in the human nature or given to it, unless we first give some intelligible explication what the law of nature is.

And therefore to bring this question to its proper state, we are to consider that the human nature hath something in it that is common to other things as well as itself and something that is proper, specifical, and appropriate to it as constituted in *specie humanâ* [the human species].

As to the former, man consists partly of a bodily substance as well as things inanimate, and therefore is subject to those laws of nature that bodies of that kind are subject to. He cannot be in several places at once; he moves downwards as other heavy bodies do. Again he is *corpus vivens* or *animatum* [a living or animate body], and therein participates with the laws that are common to the vegetable nature. He concocts[51] [and] grows. Again he is *corpus animatum sensibile* [a living, sensing body]. And therefore if there be due application of the object to the organ, he sees, hears, feels, tastes, as other animals do; and is subject to those laws of sensation that animals are subject to. If the distance be too great or the organ hurt, sensation is impeded. These laws, therefore, though natural to man, yet are not the subject of this enquiry; for they concern him, not under the specific nature of man, and the will hath

[50] OED: to prove by argument or evidence.

[51] OED: ripens, matures.

not to do in them taken simply and precisely in themselves. But those laws of nature that we enquire after in the human nature are such as concern him in the complement[52] and specific constitution of the human nature, as he is a reasonable creature and endued with understanding and will.

It is therefore that law that we enquire of that relates to those actions, that come under the dominion of his will; and those we call moral actions.

And it will not be material, whether those actions may be possibly terminated in that which concerns the animal [16v, 28] or vegetable life or no; for, as hath been observed before, those very actions may be, and for the most part are, under the dominion of the will, and a considerable part of the moral actions of the human nature are such as terminate in the action belonging to the vegetable or sensitive nature. If I eat, my meat is digested and distributed without the concurrence of the empire of my will: but my act of eating is spontaneous,[53] and under the regiment of my will. If I open my eye lid, my eye does see by the laws of sensation without the concurrences of my will: but the opening of my eye lids is spontaneous, and under the regiment and empire of my will.

These natural laws, therefore, that we enquire after in the human nature, are such laws that concern a man in the complement of his specific nature, that concern him as an intellectual and voluntary agent, and that concern those actions of the human nature which are under the dominion and regiment of the will, and those are called truly and properly moral actions.

This natural law, therefore, may be thus described: It is the law of Almighty God, given by him to man with his nature, discovering the moral good and moral evil of moral actions, commanding the former and forbidding the latter by the secret voice or dictate of his implanted nature, his reason and his conscience.

And now to pursue the method propounded, I shall endeavour to show,[54] (1) what those laws are that are thus given, (2) that those laws are given to mankind by Almighty God, and that not only as rules of direction but as obliging laws. (3) The manner how they are given. (4) The end for which they are given. (5) I shall consider the objections against it.

Touching the first of these, namely what the laws of nature are.

That there are laws of moral righteousness planted in the human nature is a truth confessed by most men. [17r, 29] If we look into the sacred scripture, we shall find the same soundly evinced by the Apostle (Rom. chap. 1 and 2, and *per totum* [throughout]). If we are minded to hear the learned among the heathen, Plato, Aristotle, Seneca, Tully,[55] and others, do assert and prove it; and generally the Stoics, whose

[52] OED: completeness.
[53] Ed: entirely voluntary, without stimulus from external (or internal) causes.
[54] MH here outlines the main topics of the remaining chapters.
[55] Ed: Marcus Tullius Cicero (106–43 BCE).

communes notitiae and *anticipationes*[56] are no other than several expressions of this natural law of God given to man and inserted in his heart.

But, although those learned, observing philosophers here and there mention some few of these common notions; yet none have proceeded so far as to give us a perfect catalogue thereof. And those modern writers that have attempted it have rested in[57] very few, and those very general; and those that have attempted to give them more particularly and explicitly have but made up certain conclusions finely spun by speculation, which either the generality of mankind can never expect to undergo, nor ever did they come into their minds; and with the same labour and subtlety that they have spun out these, they might deduce a thousand more equally evident or inevident with those they have enumerated. And therefore, though it may be true that the consequences and deductions that may be made by reason may be ramifications of the law of nature; yet possibly it may be hard to conclude that all those deductions and inferences are that law of nature, which was intended for the common rule or law of mankind; because, though they may be truths, yet every man is not capable of that perspicacity to follow consequences so far. But although it be difficult to set the uttermost bounds of the common law of nature, as it was intended to be common to mankind; yet we may reasonably think that those remoter consequences and conclusions were not intended as the common rule for all mankind, but at [17v, 30] most for such that having their faculties exercised were able to follow the clue of reason to such degree.

Others again have shrunk up the laws of nature into a very narrow compass, and have made in effect self-preservation the only cardinal law of human nature; and all these rules or consequences that they have observed to be conducible to that cardinal law or deducible from it, they conclude to be so many ramifications of that grand natural law.[58] Wherein their mistake hath happened by this means: that, whereas the natural laws of mankind are of that excellent frame that consequentially they produce the good of every individual, though besides that [they conduce] to many other excellent ends, they have improvidently singled out this one as the only governing law of nature, which is no other but one of these excellent effects that this excellent law produceth; and therefore they are too parsimonious, as if a man should conclude that, because architecture is a notable effect or product of geometry, therefore the building of houses should take up the whole compass, design, end, and use of that art.

The difficulty therefore of giving a catalogue of the laws of nature depends upon this difficulty—what media are proper to be used for the settling of this enquiry; and

56 Ed: common notions and precognitions or preconceptions. See note 85.

57 All MSS: have either rested in ["Have rested in" here means "have been content with offering."]

58 This was a common mid-seventeenth-century criticism of Hobbes. See Robert Sharrock, *Hypothesis ethike, De officiis secundum naturae jus* (Oxford, 1660), preface, 46. Critics are likely to have had in mind, *inter alia*, *Leviathan*, ch. 13 or *On the Citizen*, ed. Richard Tuck, tr. Michael Silverthorne (Cambridge: Cambridge University Press, 1998), chs 1–3.

the great variety and discrepancy that possibly may happen in and among the particulars that shall occur in those *media*.

And touching this enquiry these things ought to be remembered.

1. That there is a great difference to be observed in the enquiry [a] touching the matter, kind, and number of these things, which we call the law[s] of nature, and the discovery of them what they are, and that enquiry [b] that is touching the reason and ground and principle of their obligation as laws. As to the former of these, [18r, 31] we shall and must make use of the experience and observation of the usages of several nations in several ages and under several governments, especially of those that are civilized and the *moratiores* [more civilized] of nations, the sentiments of the more wise considerate men in all times, the institution of laws of wise lawgivers, the suffrage[59] of reason and the conclusions thereof, the voice of the natural conscience in men; and out of those particulars, and by an induction thereupon, collect those common sentiments, which we have reason to believe are the matter of those natural laws. But any of those or all those put together do not give us the true ground or formal reason of that obligation, whereby they become properly laws of nature; for this is to be referred to a higher original, as hath been observed and will be further manifested; namely, the sovereign authority of Almighty God, enacting those as laws to the children of men, and by that effectual promulgation and inscription thereof in the minds of men in such way, as shall be further illustrated in the ensuing discourse.

2. That to give some tolerable *elenchus capitum legis naturalis* [examination or drawing out of the tenets of the law of nature] one single *medium* is hardly sufficient: but it must be evidenced by a consonancy and concurrence of several instances concentering in the same common sentiments or notions.

And though it be true that divine revelation might be sufficient of itself for this discovery; yet there are some considerations to show that, in the state of divine revelation as it stands exhibited to mankind, it seems not of itself to answer fully this enquiry. 1. Because divine revelation, as such and manifestly appearing to be such, hath not been communicated in that amplitude answerable to the extent of mankind in all ages and places. For although I do not doubt [18v, 32] but that the spirit of God that did strive with the men of the old world (Gen. c. 6, v. 3), that exhibits itself as a light to every man that comes in the world (John c. [1, v.] 9) [and] that even in the gentile world hath in all ages produced eminent men for the reducing[60] of men to natural religion and morality, doth still by secret ways unknown to us secretly move mankind to ways of piety and morality; yet that standing revelation of the holy scriptures hath not been freely communicated to the gentile world till these but sixteen hundred years. 2. Because though there are certain indications of the natural law and discriminations of it from positive laws in the holy scriptures, which a

[59] Ed: voice, or perhaps assistance.

[60] OED: return, calling back.

considerate and attentive reader may observe by comparing of the several places of scripture; yet the holy scripture doth in no place expressly distinguish them, by saying, this is a law of nature, this is a positive law. Neither was it needful it should; because, whether the laws were positive or natural in respect of their matter, yet being given by the sovereign lawgiver they were to be obeyed by those to whom they were given and for the time they were continued; for the sovereign command of God is sufficient obligation to all creatures to obedience, without distinction of natural or positive. 3. The laws of nature, with all the helps we have for their discovery, cannot be certainly and definitively enumerated in their uttermost extent; partly by reason of mixture of the laws that are natural with the laws that are positive whether of God or man. This is partly by reason of the prevalence of corrupt education and customs among men; partly by reason of the great variety of circumstances which accompany moral actions, which strangely[61] diversify the application of the general laws, which we may suppose natural, whereby those that perchance subscribe to the same universal laws of nature, yet are contradictory in their conclusions touching particular moral actions; partly [19r, 33] because of the multitude of those particular illations[62] or conclusions, which men according to the fertility of their wits deduce from the more general laws of nature: whereby, as from the great vein in the body called *vena cava* there are derived some less and from them others less than these, till at last the ramifications of this single vein ends in innumerable company of small capillary veins, which yet are as properly veins as the greater though not equally evident; so the ramifications of the laws of nature, by deductions and ^inferences^ and conclusions inferred upon them, are carried on by trains of consequences to a great number of other particular laws, which though they are reasonable and consequential, yet they are not to be all reckoned among those laws of nature which are intended the common rule for all mankind.

Now touching the *media*, whereby the discovery of these natural laws is made, they are many; and though perchance any of them singly and apart may not be effectual enough to draw out the conclusion intended, yet the concurrence of many of them may make up a sufficient induction to frame a conclusion touching them: and they are principally these that follow.

(1) The common consent of nations in all ages and places, or at least such of them as have been civilized and reduced into culture.

It must be agreed that many people and nations have been overgrown with evil customs and barbarism; that they have imbased[63] their very human nature to a degree not much superior to beasts, as appears at this day in many of the countries of the West Indies, and appeared anciently in some remote Northern countries: and although by a strong application of those remedies of civiller laws, customs, and

[61] OED: greatly, extremely. [62] OED: inferences.
[63] OED: degraded, made base.

education, they may be reducible into a menage[64] more congruous to the true state and standard of human nature, yet it is not without great difficulty.

But even among the rudest of these nations (the Brazilians only excepted) we may find scattered under that [19v, 34] rubbish of evil customs certain common sentiments of truth and morality: as the acknowledgment and veneration of something as a deity, though they mistake in the application of that notion to such as are not truly God; somewhat of government, of keeping faith, of compassion to men in misery, and such like.

But as a man, in the inquisition[65] whether there be one common principle in human nature which essentially runs through the whole kind, will not take his measures from what he observes in small children, in idiots or madmen, in those that either by intemperance, extreme passion, or brutish customs have degraded themselves of the actual dignity of human nature;[66] but from those that are *moratiores* [more civilized], and that by their own industry or the care of others, by education, laws, and other helps, have brought or kept themselves nearer to the true standard of humanity: so in this disquisition touching the natural laws, we are to inspect the usages and common notions of these *gentes moratiores* [more civilized nations]; because in these we may reasonably suppose that the true exercise of reason, and the conformity to the true standard thereof and of the human nature, to be more vigorous and regular.

Therefore when I shall see several nations, under distinct and several ages, places, and governments, agree in certain sentiments of morality; or if perchance some one people in some one or more of these sentiments may be anomalous, yet the greater number agree in them (I speak still of those general sentiments, not in the particular modification or application of them); I have reason to believe that some one common regnant principle, which I call the law of nature, is that which inclines and disposes and carries them into this common sentiment.

Now we shall observe the several notions in several ages of the cultivated world, as Egyptians, Syrians, Greeks, Romans, Phoenicians, and others that have their peculiar positive institutions, customs, and laws *proper* to themselves, have [20r, 35] yet agreed in those general and common sentiments of morality hereafter mentioned or the greatest part of them.

And if it be said that this consent[67] in these sentiments had its rise from some imitation of one another or some common tradition that they received from the ancestors that were perchance common to all or the most of them, I answer: this doth not appear to be so; because then there might be as much reason to expect the like in other things that are of positive constitution; as the form of their government, their municipal laws, the variety of the methods of acquest and translation[68] of property.

64 OED: a social group living together.

65 Ed: considering the question.

66 BL and Harley; H: reason.

67 Ed: agreement or concurrence.

68 Ed: acquisition and transfer.

Besides, there hath not been that universality of mutual converse between many distant nations, which yet have accorded in the same common sentiments of morality. And though this concurrence may have been, either by the help of mutual intercourse and commerce, by imitation, or by some common tradition that hath pervaded all these nations, yet when I see that this tradition [and] communication, which have not altered or modified the positive or municipal laws and customs of one people to another,[69] have so generally and commonly obtained in the common rudiments of morality, I have reason to think there is some admirable consonancy thereof to the human nature itself and that which we call reason in it, and that these rudiments have a kind of secret interest and party in the human nature that sides and closeth with them by a kind of connaturality; for otherwise they could not be so readily entertained and constantly preserved among the generality of men, whose governments, interests, and laws are in other respects different and severally appropriate.

(2) But suppose we should not find this consonancy in the notion of the world in these sentiments of morality that might be of itself effectual to make up an induction sufficient to prove our conclusion. Let us look among these men that have been as it were the elixir of mankind, that have made it their business to search into the nature of things and men, as the learned philosophers and moralists, and those that have made it their care and employment to cultivate mankind and [20v, 36] improve it to the best and noblest advantage, as excellent governors and lawgivers. These of all other men are the likeliest, by their placits[70] and edicts and instructions, to give us the best account of things congruous to human nature and reason, and to propose a right standard of humanity, as far as the light of nature could lead them. And all these, scarce one excepted, no not Epicurus himself (if we may believe his apologists and advocates), have agreed in the common sentiments of morality. There may be possibly a Diagoras or a Lucian[71] that may at least despise much of the gentile religion. But where shall we find any of any note or esteem that ever held or taught that all things were equally just or honest; that there is no difference between *decorum et turpe* [decency and shame] antecedent to human laws commanding or forbidding; that ever condemned or prohibited justice, beneficence, keeping faith, modesty, sobriety, temperance, [or] reverence and worship of God; or that commended or by a law enacted impiety, injustice, injury, perfidiousness, impudence, intemperance, [or] ingratitude? Nay, further, they were not only for the most part uniform and consonant to themselves, and one to another, in their arms[72] and laws

[69] BL and Harley insert: "but still they retain their discrepancy from one another,".

[70] Ed: decrees.

[71] Diagoras of Melos, fifth-century Greek poet and sophist, was widely believed to be an atheist. Lucian, a second-century CE Greek satirist, mocked the Homeric notion of the gods in *Dialogues of the Gods.* See Loeb Classical Library edition, *Lucian VII*, tr. M. D. MacLeod (Cambridge, MA: Harvard University Press, 1961).

[72] All three MSS: "arms." FH queries this in the margin but does not suggest an emendation. OED offers "arguments for and against" as a possible synonym for "arms."

touching morals. But the most learned of them professed that these were laws of nature. (Aristotle, *Rhetoric*, L.1. cap. 15: *Est enim aliquid, quod opinantur universi, natura, commune jus, et injuria, tam etsi nullam habeant invicem ipsi communionem, nullave pactio intercedat.*)[73]

I shall not now instance in Epictetus, Tully, Seneca, and others, who all speak to the same purpose. They are collected to my hand by the industry of others; and I shall have further occasion to instance [them].

Now what can we reasonably think could make men of this sublimated[74] reason, great industry, and curious inspection thus to agree in the common rudiments of morality, but that congruity that those sentiments had to that common reason that actuated them all as men? The same thread of natural light and law [21r, 37] did run through them all and conformed them to the same common sentiments. And as when Titius and Gaius and Sempronius look upon the same visible object, and upon that perception the report is made to their several phantasies that it is red or square or thus distant, and the same report Titius and Gaius and Sempronius gave one to another, *and therefore* we may reasonably suppose the object that each of them beheld is the same, the medium through which they beheld the same and the faculty by which they saw it superficially the same, because each of them report the same thing; so we have reason to think that common consent of these learned, excellent men in these common sentiments is out of the consonancy that they bore to that common nature and reason of mankind.[75]

(3) But because we have not that opportunity to be acquainted with the sentiments of others, as we have to be acquainted with our own, I shall in the next place appeal to the particular judgment and conscience of every man that is not miserably captivated under the power of his sensual lusts, passions, or evil customs. Let any man impartially examine himself, whether he hath not a secret approbation of moral goodness, honesty, veracity, clemency, benignity, sobriety, modesty, and whether he honours and values it in others and is best pleased with himself when he contains himself within the bounds of it: and whether he hath not a secret detestation of dishonesty, perfidiousness, cruelty, intemperance, and the like, in others, and doth not blame it in himself and is not troubled and disordered and discomposed into a serious reflection upon his failings herein. And though perchance the hypocrisy of some, and superciliousness, censoriousness, and sourness of others professing religion, bring some disreputation upon others professing the same religion, because these deportments excite men's passions and animosities against them; yet where is

[73] Aristotle's text reads: "for there is, as is universally known, a common natural justice and injustice which bind even those who have no association or agreement between them." (MH's reference should be *Rhetoric* I.13, 1373b.)

[74] OED: elevated to a high degree of perfection or excellence; noble; exalted.

[75] MH supports this thesis further in Ch. 8, relying on the notion of *intellectus agens*.

that man that doth not really approve religion even whilst his passions and lusts transport him [21v, 38] to an unsuitableness of conversation to it, that bears not a secret and real veneration to that man who without ostentation or vanity practiseth it and walks according to the rules of it? The most unjust subject in a kingdom desires that his controversies may be determined by a just and a wise and an honest man. How many persons in the world that through ill customs or by the determination of his lusts and passions have been very much addicted to lying, intemperance, and immodesty, yet have reproved their children, whom they love best next [to] themselves, when they have found them in the same faults; and therefore have been unwilling that their children should be tainted with their own example, but rather choose to have them otherwise educated? What other reason can be assigned, why, when so many are transported by their own lusts and follies, by their own avarice or injustice in their particular dealings, yet oftentimes a few wise, just, [and] honest men are even by them chosen or at least desired as their leaders, governors, and judges; that the greater part of the unruly world is managed, ordered, [and] governed by the far less number of sober, wise, just, [and] impassionate men, and to these they willingly submit, and these they reverence and value? No other, or at least no better cause can be assigned than this: That though men by their lusts and passions are transported to evil courses, yet their judgments give a suffrage to goodness and virtue and honesty and those other laws of human nature whereof we speak; and there is scarce any man so perfectly divested of his natural conscience, or can so far unman himself, but that still moral goodness will keep a party in him, and hold so much interest in him as to gain and keep his judgment in a great measure, though by reason of other contingencies it obtain not the entire regiment of his life.

(4) There is no one moral precept, but carries in [itself] its own reasonableness and usefulness, and a special objective congruity [22r, 39] to that great and appropriate faculty in man called understanding, and that great engine or instrument of that faculty which we call reason. And these precepts of morality, whereof we shall more fully speak in the next chapter, carry in them such objective excellence, ^usefulness^, and congruity to the human nature and all circumstances thereof that antecedently to any †positive law that† cannot but be subscribed unto as suitable rule for a reasonable nature. But because the examination of this reason requires farther †particular†[76] instances and a further illustration and enforcement in what follows, I shall at present abstain from the farther pressing of this *medium* for the discovery of the *capita legis naturalis*.

And this is all I shall at present say touching the *media elicientia cognitionem legis naturalis* [means of eliciting knowledge of natural law]. And herein I do purposely omit that excellent instance of the 7 *precepta Noachidarum*:[77] 1. Because they have

[76] H and BL: peculiar.

[77] MH discusses these seven laws given to "the sons of Noah" in Ch. 11, where he discusses God's "positive" publication of the natural law added to their "natural" publication discussed in Chapters 8–10. For the seven laws, see *Treatise*, 101–2 and note 285.

been incomparably urged by the excellent author of the book *De jure naturale apud Hebraeos.*[78] 2. Because it may be objected upon the common tradition of the Jews that they were given *per modum legis positivae* [in the manner of positive law] to the generality of mankind, as the Decalogue was given to the Jews: and though in the one as well as the other divers of the most important laws of nature are included, yet their obligation might be *virtute precepti divini* [by virtue of the divine precept] obliging the generality of the sons of Noah. 3. Because although those express precepts did contain most of those great and important laws of nature, and possibly by deduction from them most others might be inferred and evidenced; yet there seem some natural laws *primo intuitu* [by immediate intuition] evident to mankind besides those that are expressly and *in terminis* [in express terms] delivered in those *precepta Noachidarum* though by following of consequences easily deducible from them and implicitly contained in them.

[22v, 40]

5

Concerning the Several Heads of that *Lex Naturalis* whereof before

In the former chapter we have been searching into those *media*, from whence by induction we may gather what those common propensions or notions are in the human nature, which are the matter of the law we call moral or natural. For as I have before observed, [these][79] media go no further than the discovery of the matter of the laws of nature, but do not either contain or give the formal reason of their obligation as laws; for this depends upon a higher principle.

And I now come to give some account of the particulars of these natural laws, or at least of some of them; for it is besides my purpose, and possibly beyond the capacity of any one man, to give an exact and adequate account of all the particulars of natural law in all its ramifications, and under all the variety of circumstances that make a

[78] That is, John Selden, *De jure naturali et gentium, juxta disciplinam Ebraeorum.* This work is an extended commentary on (and elaboration of) each of the seven Noachide laws. MH leans heavily on this work.

[79] All MSS: these nor any of these.

difference in the particular application of it, for what the prophet saith of the law of God in general is verified in a special manner of this Psalm 119:96, "I have seen an end of all perfection but thy commandment is exceeding broad."

Both the amplitude and perfection of the natural or moral law appears by these considerations.

1. It was instituted and given to man, by the great and wise rector of the world in the first institution of the human nature, to be the great rule and direction of all the most important moral actions of human life, and to conduct and guide and manage him in the temporary concerns of his temporal life, and also to bring him to his chief end, his felicity and happiness, and therefore [23r, 41] a law, proceeding from such an author, directed to such an end, must needs be a most excellent law, and in its full amplitude and extent very great and extensive.

2. After the great concussion that this law had in the nature of man by his fall,[80] all those various economies of the divine special providence relating to man have been principally directed to restore man into that primitive law, and to reduce, contain, and preserve mankind unto and in the conformity unto it and obedience of it. This is the reason of those *adminicula divinae gratiae* [aids of divine grace] that secret striving of the spirit of God with the old world and in all succeeding ages of the world secretly ^contending^ against the corruptions of nature which arose by evil customs and the unruliness of the sensual appetite; the reason of raising up men in all ages, even in the gentile world, wise philosophers and lawgivers and other wise men, to reduce men to the obedience of this law and containing them in it; the reason of those extraordinary and speaking[81] providences, manifesting to the children of men the regiment of Almighty God and his indignation against the violation of this law. [It is also] the reason of his giving out the compendium of the chief moral or natural laws to Noah and his sons, namely the *septem precepta Noachidarum*; the reason of the reinforcing of this natural law by the precepts of the Decalogue given from Sinai in thunder and fire; [and] the reason of raising up prophets in all ages of the church of the Jews, enforcing this law and giving a testimony of the truth of their mission by miracles and predictions. And although these two latter were immediately given to one particular nation, the Jewish church, yet [God][82] made that nation signal and eminent and conspicuous to all the [23v, 42] world by signs, wonders, and observable providence, that they might be like a beacon upon a hill, like a mighty and stately pillar set up in the middle of the world to hang up upon it those tables of natural righteousness, which might be conspicuous and legible to the greatest part even of the gentile world for many ages. And lastly this was one of the great reasons of the mission of the Messiah, his admirable doctrine, miracles, death, [and] resurrection, to republish this natural law given to mankind unto all the world; to reinforce it with

[80] Ed: the violent disturbance or distortion of the law in human nature after the fall.
[81] OED: expressive or eloquent. [82] All MSS: he.

such new and further manifestations of divine truths, with such admirable and effectual motives, that never before were so fully declared, bringing life and immortality to light by the gospel, showing explicitly and evidently the rewards of a due conformity to this law of nature and the punishment of the disobedience thereof. So that, excepting some positive institutions, which nevertheless do reasonably and clearly tend to the same great end, the whole doctrine of the gospel of Christ drives at nothing more, than the discovery of the true law of nature and the conformity of the human nature thereunto, in order to a perfect state of living here and the perfect enjoying of an intimate communion with God in this life, and the consummate and everlasting enjoying of him hereafter. And therefore let any man run over all the doctrine of the gospel delivered by Christ and his apostles, he shall find nothing in it derogatory to that law of nature, whereof we speak; but a full system of all the excellent and moral precepts of the natural law, commanding all things that are good and virtuous, and becoming the dignity of the human nature, and prohibiting the contrary. So that, whereas by the bare help of nature we may be under some difficulties of sifting out that pure gold, namely the natural law, from the corrupt usages and customs under which it many times is [24r, 43] covered; and whereas by the help barely of the natural conscience and the conduct of reason, a man without a great exercise of his understanding and self-denial, cannot follow the train of consequences to the discovery of all the laws of nature; and whereas most men, either by reason of the incompetence of their parts[83] or the want of exercise of them, or by reason of the prejudice or unhappiness of their education, or by reason of self-love or self-interest, are under great deficiencies in discovery of the full extent of natural laws: the gospel of Christ gives to all men, *quasi per saltum* [as if all at once] and without the great exercise of ratiocination, a plain, easy, [and] obvious catalogue of all these natural laws, and only superadds this, namely a command of faith to believe it, and a sufficient evidence to oblige men to that faith.

And that the great scope[84] of the gospel of Christ is to reimprint and reinforce this natural law upon the human nature, appears by the whole tenor of the gospel. Take some instances among many. When the lawyer asked Christ, what was the great commandment of the law, he sends him to those two great natural laws the love of God and the love of his neighbour (Matt. 22:36[–40]). When he gives an account of these things that defile and imbase the human nature, the catalogue he gives is of moral iniquities (Matt. 15:19). When he gives an account of the various rewards of the good and evil, his instances are in particulars of the observance of and violation of the natural law of charity (Matt. 25:31[–40]). When he gives an abstract of the law and the prophets, he gives this short excellent precept of nature all justice: "whatsoever ye would that men should do to you, that do ye to them" (Matt. [7:12]). When he gives the necessary preliminary to the kingdom of heaven, it is such righteousness, as

83 OED: personal qualities or attributes, especially of an intellectual kind.
84 OED: mark for aiming at; aim.

exceeds the righteousness of the scribes and Pharisees the strictest set of Jews (Matt. 5:20) and teacheth the perpetuity of the moral law (Matt. 5:17, 18). The whole tenor both of his [24v, 44] doctrine and life was humility, sincerity, purity, patience, justice, peace, beneficence, submission, and obedience to the divine will, adoration and invocation of him, and the whole train of those virtues which we call the natural law.

If we come to the doctrine delivered by his apostles, we shall find in every place this natural law commended, and the contraries forbidden. Take but a few instances for many: "The kingdom of God is righteousness, peace, and joy in the Holy Ghost" (Rom. 14:17). "For we are his workmanship created in Christ Jesus unto good works, which God hath before ordained that we should walk in them" (Eph. 2:10). "Put ye on the new man, which after God is created in righteousness and true holiness" (Eph. 4:24). "This is the will of God, even your sanctification, that ye should abstain from fornication, that everyone should know how to possess his vessel in sanctification and honour" (1 Thess. 4:3); and "Now the end of the commandment is charity out of pure heart, and good conscience and faith unfeigned" (1 Tim. 1:5). "For the grace of God bringing salvation hath appeared unto all men, teaching us that denying ungodliness and worldly lusts we should live soberly, righteously, and godly in this present world, looking for the blessed hope and glorious appearance of the great God and our saviour Jesus Christ, who gave himself for us that he might redeem us from all iniquity, and purify unto himself a peculiar people zealous of good works" (Tit. 2:11).

By these and the like instances that might be given out of the New Testament, and by what is said in this digression, I would have these things observed. 1. That the great end of the gospel is the conforming of men to the true standard of the natural law, consisting in godliness, sobriety, and righteousness. 2. That, consequently by this, natural law is a most excellent law, the institution of God touching man, and the image of God in man. 3. That this natural [25r, 45] law is most excellently and incomparably set forth, evidenced, and delivered in the gospel, more explicitly and fuller than even it was done since the creation of man, and evidenced to be such, not only by the divine person that published it by the supernatural miracle that attested it, but by the exact consonancy of it to the true and solid suffrage even of reason and the natural conscience.

And therefore my business of recollecting the laws of nature may seem impertinent, since the evangelical doctrine contains a perfect system of it. But because the Christian doctrine was not known to the heathen world, and yet the law of nature even then obliged them upon the light and evidence of nature and reason; and because among those that dare do no otherwise than profess they believe the gospel, yet really and truly do no further believe it than they find reason asserting it; and because it is consonant to the design of these papers to give out some *specimina legis naturalis* [examples of laws of nature], I shall make a short collection of some of them under several ranks.

And yet before I come to particulars, I shall give a general account touching the general state of natural laws.

The laws of nature seem therefore to be of four kinds.

(1) Those that are most universal, and most remote from any particular determination to this or that particular action, as that the *legis naturae primo primae, honestum est amplectendum inhonestum est fugiendum* [absolutely fundamental laws of nature are: embrace that which is honourable or right [and] flee from that which is dishonourable or wrong]. This is true in the human law of the human nature, but by reason of its generality and indeterminateness it becomes equally applicable to contradictory conclusions according to the various opinions of men touching the thing to be done. Hence in ^Arrianus^ in Epictetus (L. 1. c.22) in the controversy between Agamemnon and Achilles touching the [25v, 46] returning of Chriseis to her father both assumed the same antecedent viz. *honestum est faciendum* [what is honourable or right must be done]; yet from those general premises they framed contradictory conclusions, one for and the other against her return.[85]

(2) Certain principles of morality, which, though they are not wholly restrained to particularity, yet are of a much more restrictive nature than the former, and therefore of greater use and more directive in moral actions. *Leges naturales secundo primo* [secondary yet fundamental laws of nature]; as that it is not just to do that to another which we would not that another should do to us in the same circumstance; that I am not to do hurt to him that is innocent; that I am to be thankful for benefits received; and many more both in the preceptive and prohibitory instances of moral or natural laws.

And though all these be clearly deducible by discursive ratiocination to be highly reasonable and becoming the human nature; yet they have that congruity to the rational nature and that self-evidence in them that the understanding needs not the help of the gradual discovery or ratiocination to gain an assent to them, but takes them in *per saltum* [immediately] by a kind of intuition altogether, as the eye perceives light or colour without argumentation. And they seem, as it were, engraved in the human nature, characterized in it, growing up with it, connatural to it: and therefore they are taken up and assented unto, not as conclusion[s], but as principles[86] of natural righteousness; just as that common principle in physics or mathematics *totum est majus suâ parte* [the whole is greater than its parts], though it be demonstrable to be true by rational process, yet the evidence of the truth of it is so sensible that the intellect assents to it without any rational process or induction to make it out.

[85] Epictetus's *Discourses* (first collected by Arrian) I.22: "Preconceptions are common to all men. And preconception does not conflict with preconception. For who among us does not assume that the good is beneficial and choiceworthy, and in all cases to be strived after and pursued? Who of us does not assume that justice is fair and appropriate? Where then does the conflict arise? In applying preconceptions to particular cases.... This is the conflict you will find between Agamemnon and Achilles." Epictetus, *Discourses Book I*, tr. Robert F. Dobbin (Oxford: Clarendon Press, 1998), 42–3.

[86] All MSS: as a principle.

(3) Certain conclusions immediately and necessarily arising from some common principles admitted. For since the conclusions of every proposition are in truth virtually in the premises, though they are not yet formed [26r, 47] into the shape of a distinct conclusion, so there are some conclusions that have that evidence of inexistence in the premises, that vicinity to and necessary conjunction with them, that they are as soon known and subscribed to as the premises themselves, without the formality or *mora* [undue delay] of a discursive process, the transition from the supposition of the premises unto the conclusion being so natural, so easy, swift, and speedy, that the ^assent^ to the conclusion seems to run hand in hand with the assent to the premises. Whereby, though in nature they are not principles, but conclusions, yet they are in time congenite[87] with them, and have the same manner of entertainment as if they were the very original principles themselves, and, as before I said are assented to by a kind of intuition without the help of discursive ratiocination. Thus at the very same instant that a man entertains the notion of deity (which is as shall be shown not only a conclusion of reason but a principle connatural to man) he presently concludes without the help of a syllogism that he is to be worshipped, invoked, honoured, and obeyed. So that a man cannot tell which is first in time in the soul, the notion of a deity or the conception of that †natural† obligation of natural law to honour and obey him. Yea, many times, where the notion of a deity is confused and indistinct, yet a kind of distinct adoration is performed to him: so that after an offence committed against God, it is most rational to esteem repentance, and sorrow for what is past, and resolution to do better for the time to come, the most rational way to propitiate an offended God; because, though that which is done cannot be undone, yet the nearest method *to undoing* of it is by sorrow for it and amendment of it.

Yet even as naturally repentance is taken up upon [26v, 48] any offence committed by those that scarce even know the natural connection and consequence between repentance and pardon: so in that most necessary precept of the law of nature *fides est servanda*, any man that can give himself the leisure and can connect consequences to another, will easily show many reasons that may discursively evince this by way of conclusion: as first, that it is derogatory to the dignity and honour of the human nature to be false to this word; that it is a means to provoke others to do the like by him; that without it there can be no security to human society; and many more. Yet without all this process, and even in men that know not how to make it, every man in the world that is not lapsed into brutishness takes it for granted that a man must be as good as his word. And these two last mentioned instances in this and the former section seem to make up for the ordinary bulk of the common rudiments of the law of nature, because easily and quickly perceived and digested by most men.

[87] OED: born or made with.

(4) There may be many natural or moral laws (for I use the words promiscuously, 'moral' because concerning the morals[88] of men, and 'natural' because implanted in nature) that are really and truly natural laws, but yet are conclusions more remote from the first rudiments of natural law, and therefore not easily elicited or deducted[89] without a rational process or discourse, and according to their distance from first principles or conclusions before mentioned, sometimes by a chain of two, three, or more consequences. And this happens in relation to such moral acts or actions, as are either 1. more remote or distant from the self-evident principles or conclusions; or 2. such as are mingled with involved or difficult circumstances of particular acts or actions; or 3. such as have a mixture or complication with other laws of nature that either cross or allay[90] or are interwoven with the moral actions to be done.

[27r, 49] And, according to these various states and textures[91] of actions to be done or omitted, the decisions are more difficult and inevident, and the variety of men's judgments give different theories and make different conclusions touching them. And therefore to settle and determine them, there is required much exercise of the reasoning faculty, much judgment and advertence which doth not so commonly fall under ordinary capacities. This we may easily perceive in the curious and subtle works of many writers of moral philosophy, and in schoolmen and casuists of this and former ages. Whereas though they many times differ, yet certainly there is truth of moral or natural laws even in relation to these complicated and perplexed moral actions, if it can be attained: as in anatomy there is a real existence and use of the minutest ramifications of the veins, arteries, and nerves in the body, though the discovery thereof be not so easily attainable, and one age discovers those vessels and motions that a former age never thought of.

Yet the divine goodness is admirable in this that there is scarce any man that hath the use of reason, and will attentively exercise it in the consideration of the moral actions of his life, and that will keep a strict hand over his lusts and passions, and will curiously observe the secret inclination and voice of his conscience, but shall be directed to do that which is morally good and avoid that which is morally evil in the most intricate and complexed moral actions of his life, though he be unacquainted with the curious distinctions and definitions contained in the writings of casuists and moral philosophers: especially if he do humbly and sincerely implore the direction of Almighty God, whose secret, wise, and gracious advice will never be wanting to them that humbly and sincerely desire it and listen unto it.

[88] Harley: manners. [89] OED: derived by reasoning. [90] OED: qualify or diminish.

[91] Ed: OED traces the usage of this word in the seventeenth to nineteenth century to weaving: "the product of the weaver's art" and by extension, "any natural structure having an appearance or consistence as if woven . . . especially applied to the body"; then further extended: "the constitution, structure or substance of anything with regard to its constituents or formative elements." MH explicitly acknowledges the root of the metaphor in the weaver's art at p. 89. For other examples of MH's use of this metaphor, see *Treatise* 54, 92, and especially "Reflections," 191.

[27v, 50] I shall not go about to set down the particulars of these secondary or deducible laws of nature that may be ranged under this fourth distribution of natural laws; for it were too voluminous, and beside my purpose. But I shall proceed to the enumeration of those laws of nature that are contained under the second and third head; namely such principles or conclusions, as seem to be *primo intuitu* evident in the natural conscience or to it, or as many as I can remember or as occur to me. For I take those under that foregoing second and third heads to be the common laws of nature, being equally obvious almost to every capacity. But as to those under the fourth head, though they are or may be consonant to natural law, yet in respect of their difficulty, multiplicity, and remoteness from those first principles or near conclusions, I shall not range them under this law of nature, which is the common rule of a law for all men.

And I shall distribute them under these three relations, habitudes,[92] or ranks: I. Such as relate to Almighty God. II. Such as relate to a man's self. III. Such as relate to others either in or out of the bonds of civil societies.

I

Touching the first of these, the notion of existence of a God or supreme governor of the world is not only evident by undeniable reason and natural evidence; but it seems to be engraven in the very crasis[93] of the human nature, and congenite with it and connatural to it. And it is not only so; but there are also evident by the light of reason so very many of his attributes, and especially that great trinity of perfect and infinite power, wisdom, and goodness, as also his purity, holiness, justice, omniscience, placability, beneficence, and truth, which are but so many branches of his wisdom and goodness. And besides there is a secret consciousness in every man that all the things [28r, 51] in every man and that all the things in nature had their being from his power, their preservation from his providence, their benefit and good from his beneficence. These notions are evident to be in the nature of man, and by the experience of all nations, by the testimony of the apostle. "The invisible things of him from the creation of the world are thereby seen, being understood by the things that are made, even his eternal power and Godhead. So that they are without excuse" (Rom. 1:20).

And indeed this great principle is the foundation, not only of all natural religion, but of the obligation of all laws; and hither they are to be reduced.

And although in the particular determination of their *deities*, particular nations differed, one affirming one thing to be God, another another; yet they all in general agree in this common notion that there is such a being as God, and that he is of

[92] OED: manners of being in relation to something else.
[93] OED: composition, constitution, temperament.

immense power, wisdom, and goodness; which seems to be a clear indication that the notion of an existence of a God is connatural to the common nature of mankind.

And from this principle thus stated in nature there do naturally and without any perplexed or difficult deduction flow all those ensuing natural consequences or conclusions, which are so many laws of nature.

[A] The affirmative or preceptive laws of nature necessarily and immediately resulting from hence, as these that follow.

1. That there is to be a great reverence of mind towards this great and glorious God. This is the immediate conclusion that ariseth in relation to a being of infinite power, wisdom, and goodness, and consequently of infinite majesty, glory, and dignity. And this internal temper of the mind necessarily produceth the signs thereof in the external deportment in all those external applications and addresses to him.

2. That he ought to be feared; because of infinite power [28v, 52] and wisdom [he is] able to discern and recompense any neglect of him or disobedience to him; and because he is the rector [and] governor of the world, and he upon whose pleasure all our good or evil depends.

3. That he is to be loved with a most intense love, both because he is the most intense and sovereign good essentially in himself and full of beneficence to all his creatures, especially to the human nature; he is not only our sovereign rector, but also our greatest benefactor.

4. And upon the same account the highest gratitude of soul is due to him; which is the natural consequence in a reasonable nature towards its benefactor.

5. That he is to be trusted and rested and depended upon; because he is all-sufficient and full of beneficence, and all things in the world have an essential dependence upon him as their creator and preserver.

6. That he is to be adored, honoured, and worshipped; the principal parts of which worship consist in invocation of him; because our essential dependence is upon him. This all-sufficiency, wisdom, and goodness [deserve][94] praise and thanksgiving, because he is our most bountiful benefactor. That he ought with all humility and patience to be submitted unto without any kind of murmuring or impatience; for he is not only the rector and lord of all things and all men, but a most wise and gracious lord, and knows what is fittest for *us* as well as to suffer as to do.

7. That he is to be obeyed; because he is the sovereign rector of all things, and consequently not only endued with infinite power to exact obedience to his commands, but of most rightful and just authority to command. And that authority is grounded upon the most natural reason that can be imagined; because he is a sovereign lord and proprietor of all things, and all things have their existence and preservation from the emanation of his own most [29r, 53] free and sovereign will.

[94] All MSS: and.

And this obedience is therefore not only due to his natural law, but also to his positive laws and institutions when manifested to us; because they are the commands of him that hath the absolute dominion and just sovereignty over us; and because we may assure ourselves that the most just lawgiver in the world will impose no unreasonable or unjust laws upon us; but contrariwise all his commands are like himself, full of wisdom and justice in themselves, and full of convenience and beneficence to his creatures.

8. That consequently †all† mankind ought to give all due diligence to know what his will is, whether in such laws as are natural or in such as are positive, that thereby each may answer the will of his maker with a suitable and acceptable obedience.

9. That, in case of any deficiency on the part of man in his duty, he endeavour by all those ways that can be reasonable, to propitiate his maker, to obtain his pardon to reconcile himself to him; which is no fruitless endeavour, because his placability is an essential branch of his goodness.

10. And because after an offence committed it is impossible to make that to be ^*infectum quod semel factum est*^ [undone which once was done]; and repentance, which consists in sorrow for sin committed and a firm purpose not to do the like, is as much as can be possibly done as it were to render that *infectum quod semel factum*; for it is a returning into the way of duty and obedience: therefore repentance after an offence committed is a natural duty or due by the law of nature.

11. And because the mind is the man, and the will [29v, 54] in man is that which gives the true value and just denomination of all moral actions; and because Almighty God is of infinite wisdom and therefore knows the thoughts and purposes of the heart; hence it follows that the obligation of natural laws lays hold, not only upon the outward actions, but upon the very thoughts and purposes of the heart and soul, and requires those *sancti recessus mentis* [out of pure conscience] as well as the outward conformity of the outward man.

12. And upon the very same reason, in all that worship, service, and obedience which is performed by the law of nature, sincerity and integrity is required. The laws of man cannot reach to those *interiores animi affectus* [inner desires of the soul]; because it cannot discern them, nor have cognizance of them. But Almighty God is of infinite wisdom, searcheth the heart; and his laws extend to the deliberations, resolutions, and purposes of the mind, because he discerns them, and gives his laws principally and primarily to them, as being the roots of outward actions and that gives the true denomination and modification[95] of them.

And these are some of those preceptive natural laws which relate to Almighty God, as being immediate and necessary conclusions without any long process of ratiocination, resulting from the notion of God. More might be added and many more

[95] OED: form of existence.

secondary conclusions deducible from them, but these may give a specimen of them, and the evident reasonableness or natural consequence of them.

[B] Now as to the prohibitory laws of nature, they [30r, 55] will appear by the preceptive [law]: *Rectum est index sui et obliqui.* [the right is the guide to itself and to wrong.] The opposite of these preceptive laws are such as fall under the prohibitory ^law of nature, and the unnaturalness and unreasonableness of these, and the reasonableness of their prohibition will appear by the reasonableness and naturalness of those that I have mentioned as preceptive laws of nature. I shall but name them.^

1. Such thoughts or practices, as do tend to the abating of that natural reverence due to God, or do imbase the notion of it in the minds of men, or as are unbecoming the dignity of God. Such are the common irreverent use of the name of God, the imbasing of the notion of the deity by images, creature deities, and the like. Though the corrupt customs of the gentile world made this common, yet certainly it was against the due reverence to Almighty God, and derogatory to his dignity. Therefore excellently the Apostle says (Rom. 1:21, 22, 23) "because when they know God, they glorified not as God, neither were thankful, but became vain in their imaginations and their foolish heart was darkened and changed the glory of the incorruptible God into an image made like a corruptible man and to birds and four-footed beasts and creeping things." And upon the same account the multiplication of deities, especially those that they supposed supreme, their *Dÿ*[96] were not only things false in themselves, but derogatory to the true notion of God, who, being *ens summe perfectum* [the most perfect being] loseth both his perfection and dignity by such partition of the divine nature and power into many distinct gods.

2. Upon the same reason *maledictus manus* [accursed hand] his own perjury is prohibited by the law of nature.

3. Upon the same reason, hatred of God, bold defiance [30v, 56] of his power, denying of the regiment of his providence in this inferior world, presumptuous independence upon him or despair of assistance from him, denying all worship to him or performing it coldly, carelessly, or hypocritically, resolved and presumptuous disobedience against his known laws, impenitence after sins committed, a loose and ungoverned habit of thoughts, and secret deliberate motions of the will as being under no law—these and such of these are contrary to that natural law given to man that respects the glorious God. I have not named atheism (for, as I doubt whether there be any in the world that are perfectly dogmatical atheists, so if there are, the error is not so much in their will as it is in their understanding and judgment). But he, that either believes or but suspects there is a God, and wisheth there were none, that he might not be within the reach of his power, but might offend with impunity, is a hater of God.

[96] Ed: gods (*Diis*).

II

I come now to consider these natural laws that relate to a man's self.

And as before I observed that the true notion of God is the natural root of all those laws of nature that in special manner relate to God: so the true notion of the human nature and the constitution and value [of man] is the true fountain of those natural laws that relate to a man's self, wherein there are these *postulata*, which almost all mankind agree in, that are necessary to be premised to this purpose.

[a] That man, though he hath many of the faculties, affections, and lusts that are common to him and the animal nature, hath a specifical dignity belonging to his nature far more excellent than [31r, 57] the common animal nature, namely, his reasonable soul.

[b] That that reasonable soul of his is immortal and dies not with the body.

[c] That that reasonable soul ought to have the regiment and regency over the animal lusts and affections; otherwise in his life he should have no prelation[97] over the brutal or animal nature.

[d] That although there may be accidental or adventitious preferences that may give one man preference and prelation above another—as sharpness of wit, excellence of memory, learning, strength or health or beauty of body, power, domination, wealth, or the like—yet essentially, naturally, and in [their] specifical constitution, all men are equal.

Now these natural laws that relate to a man's self, or are immediately deducible from the due consideration of his constitution and frame, are generally the observation of those things that are convenient and suitable to his nature, and the avoiding of these that are contrary. I shall mention some of the particular instances thereof.

1. That he use all due and just means for his own preservation. This it is true is common almost to all natural beings, and appears signally even in the vegetable and animal nature. Everything desires and endeavours its own preservation both in its species and in its individual; and therefore it is no appropriate law of the human nature, because common almost to every natural being. And yet because in man it is an act or disposition of a reasonable nature and of a voluntary agent, it comes under the law of nature and morality.

And this law of nature brancheth itself into many particulars. As for instance, it is agreeable to the law of [31v, 58] nature to preserve itself with due moderation from injuries, which is a *debitum moderamen inculpatae tutelae* [due moderation of blameless defence].[98] It is consonant to the law of nature to provide for the

[97] OED: pre-eminence, superiority.

[98] MH quotes a Roman law maxim (*Codex* 8.4.1), which was the foundation of the doctrine of self-defence in civilian jurisprudence since the twelfth century. See Kenneth Pennington, "*Moderamen*

convenient supports of life in the moderate provisions of meat, drink, clothing, [and] habitation. It is likewise consonant to this law of nature to enter into societies and capitulations[99] of peace, because this is a convenient means of self-preservation.

And on the contrary, these that follow are against this law of nature: Self-destruction, exposing a man's self to needless dangers, denying a man's self the convenient supplies and supports of his natural life, idleness and neglect of due industry for the provision of the necessaries of life, aversation[100] from peace and those necessary conducibles thereunto, and divers others.

2. There is a law of self-preservation that seems more appropriate to the human nature, as being most reasonable and suitable to the structure of his nature: viz. that the greatest care and endeavour ought to be to preserve that part of man which is of greatest value, and to avoid that which may be most noxious to it, namely, his soul. Consequently by how much the soul is more noble than the body, by so much the more care is to be used in preserving it from that which must annoy and hurt it, namely, sin and iniquity; and consequently in equal dangers, †to the destruction of the body,† when both cannot be avoided, the latter must be rather tolerated than the former. We see obvious instances of the like disposition, when a danger is eminent to the head,[101] the seat of life and sense: the hand that is not of that moment or value is lifted up to receive the stroke to defend the head. It was a truth that the father of lies uttered [in] Job 2:4, "skin for skin, and all that a man hath will he give for his life." And by how much the more the soul is more valuable than [32r, 59] the body, by so much the more the life of the soul is more preferable than the life of the body: For what equal exchange can a man give for his soul? And therefore a man is to choose to undergo the death of the body from the hands of a tyrant, rather than knowingly and deliberately to commit a mortal sin against God.

3. From the consideration of the dignity of the human nature, it is a natural law for a man to avoid all such things as do degrade or imbase it. And therefore drunkenness, immoderate eating, intemperate luxury, are contrary to the law of nature, not only because they are contrary to the law of self-preservation, being the mothers of diseases and death, and contrary to the good and convenience of human societies to the ends of which they disable a man, but [also] because they are contrary to the dignity and honour of the human nature.

4. From the same consideration, those things, which carry in themselves an indecorum and undecency or turpitude, are contrary to this natural law. Such are immodesty, impudence, obscenity of language, uncleanness, *vagus et illicitus*

inculpatae tutelae: The Justification of a Justifiable Defense," *Rivista Internationale de Diritto Comune*, 13 (2013), 27–55.

99 OED: agreement on specific terms, covenant, treaty.

100 OED: turning away, aversion.

101 H has "heart" which may fit this clause; BL and Harley have "head" which fits the image in the following clause.

concubitus, obsceni ponderis propalam et publice depositu pudendorum develatio [promiscuous and illicit copulation, grossly obscene public exposure of the genitals], lying, [and] ridiculous and discomposed gestures. These seem to be *contra decorum et dignitatem humanae naturae* [contrary to the decency and dignity of human nature]. For though those or some of those do in some sort relate to the third rank of natural laws, namely such as concern others; and though it may be true that in matters of decorum and seemliness various customs and usages do much prevail in their specification and determination, so that that may be hereby a decorum in one country, which by different usages and customs may be indecorum in another or under varied [32v, 60] circumstances: yet certainly there is a certain intrinsic reverence that a man owes to the dignity of his nature, which must be observed, though no eye behold him, and hath its *decora* [seemly qualities] which becomes it, and its *indecora* [unseemly qualities], unseemliness that do blemish and imbase it, antecedent to any law commanding the one or prohibiting the other. *Reverere te ipsum* [respect yourself] is a dictate of the natural law, as well as of that wise philosopher that enjoined it to his disciples.[102]

5. From the consideration of the dignity of the human nature especial and appropriate to itself ariseth that natural law, which requires that the due order and subordination of his faculties be observed; that the regent principle in him, namely his soul and his reason, preside and govern the inferior faculties, and be not commanded or governed by them; that he keep the reins of his passions and sensual appetite in the hands of reason and moderate them according to that law of nature which is the rule of his reason: because otherwise he doth not order himself either according to the dignity or order of his nature, but inverts it, going as it were with his heels upwards. We may observe in the brutal nature many of the same passions that are in man, as anger, revenge, hatred in the irascible part, [and] love, delight [and] joy in the concupiscible part; and in the brutes these are excited and acted in the animal nature by a kind of necessary connection between the object and the passion that they excite; and for the most part they exercise them as fully and as durably, as the object or the phantasm thereof abides before them, for they are [not] under the regiment of the superior faculty, but are but the [33r, 61] various habitudes and motions of the animal appetite which is the supreme imperative faculty in the animal nature. Again [regarding the] sensual motions of the same animal appetite touching eating and drinking and venery,[103] there are two things observable. 1. That they [seem][104] to be carried by a kind of natural necessity towards their objects and therefore have rarely anything of choice or deliberation touching the decency or seasonableness or measure less than what answers the measure of their appetite, because they are under no superior faculty but the appetite or phantasy.[105] 2. That yet the motions or tendency

[102] "But above all things respect thyself." Pythagoras, *The Pythagorean Golden Verses*, ed. Johan C. Thom (Leiden: E. J. Brill, 1995), verse 12.

[103] OED: indulgence of sexual desire.

[104] All MSS: see men.

[105] See note 15.

of the sensual appetite are so limited that they rarely exceed the convenience or exigence of nature. When a brute hath eaten or drank enough, he will take no more; and even in that impetuous motion of the sensual appetite, *in congressus venereus cum appetitus venereus nunquam se exerit inordinate postquam femella impletur, nec mas coitum solicitat, nec femella patitur* [in sexual intercourse he will never inordinately exert himself with sexual desire after the female is sated; he neither incites more intercourse, nor does the female submit]. But in the human nature, the passion and sensual appetite are but inferior faculties, and in their just state and exercise subject to the empire of the will, at least as to the measure, manner, time, season, and other circumstances of its exertion.

And when this subordination and the exercise thereof are but suspended, man is under a double offence against the law of nature that [1.] imbaseth and degradeth himself from the dignity of his nature to a brutal life. 2. And not only so: but [also] the very advantage of his reason, when prostituted to the empire of his lusts and passions, makes him ten times worse than a brute, for the position of nature being thus inverted becomes wild, unruly, and †by so much the more [as] it hath the advantage of reason to assist him in these disorders.†[106] And hence it is that whereas the passions of anger in a beast never ariseth to malice or envy, nor the passion of love in [33v, 62] a brute ever ariseth to frenzy, nor the lusts of the brutal appetite is inordinate, but is satisfied within the bounds and limits proportionate to his nature; a man, on the other side, whose lusts and passions are once out of the regiment and discipline of reason, becomes prodigious in his passions and lusts, improves his passions of anger and hatred into malice and envy, his passion of love into frenzy, invents enormous[107] and unnatural lusts, and becomes insatiable in them. So that it happens with reason displaced and the natural order of the faculties of the reasonable soul inverted, as it happens by the extravasation[108] and displacing of the animal spirits in the body, from whence arise spasms and convulsions and distortions and those terrible symptoms that wholly disorder the operations and beauty of the body and mind.

By this it appears that the keeping up of the regiment of the reasonable soul over the passions and lusts of the animal nature and the subduing of them to the law of dignity is part of that law of nature, which conserves the dignity and order of the human nature.

6. And upon the same account those distempers of the soul that arise from the want of regiment of the passions, like diseases that rise from the putrefaction of humours, are contrary to this natural law: malice, that ariseth from the putrefaction of anger; envy, that ariseth from the putrefaction of anger and self-love; pride, that ariseth from the overvaluing [of] a man's self and from the putrefaction of self-love;

[106] H and BL: by so much the more disorderly but how much the more it hath the advantage of reason to assist him in these disorders.

[107] OED: abnormal, monstrous.

[108] OED: escape [or leaking out] as of an organic fluid.

covetousness, that ariseth from the putrefaction of distrust and self-love; ambition, vainglory, and those other diseases of the soul, that arise principally from the putrefaction of passions, the neglect of the light, law and guidance of reason, and the mistake of the worth and value of things. These are prohibited by the law of nature upon a double account: 1. Because they are not suitable nor convenient to the state of human nature, because they [34r, 63] discompose and disorder it, make it lose its peace and tranquillity, and are directly contrary to the law of self-preservation in respect of the whole composition, for they naturally tend to its dissolution, and in respect of the nobler part of the soul, wherein they are so many ulcers, cancers, and gangrenes. 2. Because they are contrary to the dignity of the human nature, because they depose and degrade reason, and put the human nature below its dignity, nay below the very state of the animal nature.

7. By the same law of nature all those habits and temperaments[109] of the mind that enable and advance the true dignity of the human nature, are commanded by this law of nature, especially such as promote tranquillity of mind, and all those contrary habits or dispositions that interrupt or hinder it [are prohibited].

And though all virtue conduceth to this end, and all vices are enemies to it; yet these are two habits or temperaments of the mind that do most directly and naturally procure it, and their opposites do extremely interrupt and hinder it: namely, [a] contentation[110] with their station and condition of life and those externals, which the divine providence allots; the contrary whereof, namely the murmuring and discontent, like the worm at the root of Jonah's gourd[111] knaws asunder the tranquillity of life. [b] Patience under pains or afflictions; the contrary whereof, impatience and tumult of mind, creates more disorder and trouble than the affliction brings.

The law of nature, though it commands the conservation of the dignity of human nature, yet it commands humility and lowliness of mind and forbids its opposite, namely, pride and haughtiness, and the unreasonableness [34v, 64] of the latter discovers the great congruity and suitableness of the former to the human nature.

For pride is not only one of the greatest enemies to tranquillity of mind that can be; for it is restless, never long pleased, always contending for what it would have, fretting and vexing if disappointed, and not satisfied when it attains. It besides is an unreasonable disease of the mind, since by nature all men are essentially equal, and that, which gives the discrimination and prelation[112] of one man above another, whether it be excellence of parts, honour, wealth, [or] power, are things that we have not from ourselves, but by the gift of God or the collation[113] of others. This one

[109] OED: constitution or natural dispositions, [perhaps involving some balancing or moderating of elements].

[110] OED: acquiescence in or acceptance of. [111] See Jonah 4:5–8.

[112] OED: superiority, pre-eminence.

[113] OED: the bringing together and comparison; in Roman law, bringing together in order to effect an equal division of the whole stock.

question—what hast thou which thou hast not received?[114]—doth render all pride and haughtiness unreasonable.

And thus far concerning those laws that relate to a man's self, which, though in many respects they may in some degree concern others, yet they principally concern a man's self, and come under that common virtue of sobriety.

III

Therefore I come to those laws of nature that concern others which is righteousness or justice and these are of three kinds. [A] Such laws of nature, as exist primitively and antecedently to the institution of civil government and are to be considered abstractively from it. [B] Such laws of nature, as seem to be directed and ordained in order to the establishment of civil or political government. [C] Such laws of nature, as relate to civil government already instituted and settled.

[A] Touching the former of these, it seems most evident that there are certain natural laws antecedent to the institution of civil and political government, which did bind mankind, and do bind it this day, abstractively considered from political or civil constitutions.

And herein I shall suppose as unquestionable and indeed not within the verge of the present question [35r, 65] that all those natural laws that relate to Almighty God or immediately to a man's self, did unquestionably bind mankind without relation to any constitution of civil or political laws or society; for we are not to suppose that the wise lawgiver of the world should be so deficient, as not to institute some laws or rules for human nature suitable to that state wherein he stood; for the human nature was well enough capable of such laws or rules, though political regiment in the world had never been instituted.

Therefore the enquiry must proceed touching those laws which relate from one man to another.

And as to these it seems to me unquestionable that, as to such moral actions relating to others which had in them an intrinsic congruity to the human nature or dissonancy from it, there were and must be necessarily supposed such moral or natural laws as such a state was capable of.

For there is no man that doth acknowledge a deity, and that that deity governs all things by his providence, and that he is a most wise being and orders everything to suitable ends by suitable means, but must needs acknowledge another regiment of the world than that which the laws of man have made; and that though there were no human monarchy, aristocracy, or oligarchy settled in the world, yet there would

[114] You must not "be puffed up for one against another. For who maketh thee to differ from another? and what hast thou that thou didst not receive? now if thou didst receive it, why dost thou glory, as if thou hadst not received it?" (1 Cor. 4: 6–7).

be the divine monarchy or theocracy, to the due administration whereof there would be a necessity of laws for the regiment of the reasonable nature, and that although there were no instituted human government or laws, but men were in that natural state wherein they were propagated into the world, yet even in that state there would be some things *justa*, *honesta*, and *decora* [right, honourable, and proper] and some things *injusta*, *inhonesta*, [35v, 66] and *indecora* [wrongful, dishonourable, and improper]. Everything would not be lawful to every man; and that imaginary state of war, wherein every man might lawfully do what he thinks best without any law or control, is but a phantasy; or if it be admitted, it must not, cannot be supposed as the just state of nature, but as a disease, disorder, and corruption in it.[115]

And I shall instance therefore such natural laws, as are obliging in the state of nature antecedently to any settled government among men by mutual capitulation or consent.

1. That great natural law of *fides est servanda*, keeping faith and pacts, did as forcibly bind, though there were no natural human power settled, as it did after such human government settled. For [a] it included the same congruity to intrinsic natural justice for a man to keep his contract before human government settled, as well as after the institution of coercive laws, which only added an external power of the exacting of the fulfilling of it. [b] Without the supposition of this truth, it were impossible to maintain the obligation either of human laws or government that should be established by such pacts and promises; because such pacts and promises must necessarily antecede the institution of such law or conventional government. And therefore the obligation of such pacts must needs be supposed antecedent to the obligation of government, and to be at first made in that state which those men supposed to be a state of war. [c] If it should be otherwise, there should no obligation arise between supreme princes by their promises or pacts; because neither is under the law or government of the other, but stands as in relation one to the other as men are supposed to stand in the imaginary state of nature, which they call a state of war; and such a doctrine as this would put the world into combustion.

[36r, 67] 2. The consequence whereof is that if in this state of nature A should contract with B that B should have those or these goods, or this or that portion of land, though there were no other external law or government in the world to enforce A *de non contraveniendo huic contractui* [from not breaching this contract], yet by this law of nature A were obliged thereunto.

3. There be some things in the world that, antecedently to any contract or pact, a man hath an undoubted property in, [may][116] not without natural injustice and violation of the law of nature be causelessly invaded by another. As every man hath an unquestionable property in his own life and in his own self. And therefore

[115] MH has in mind Hobbes's account of the state of nature (*Leviathan*, ch. 13).
[116] AL MSS: that may.

if for the purpose A gives himself up to the propriety of B as in matrimonial contracts and contracts of servitude, as A may not contravene his own contract without violation of the law of nature, so neither can C between whom and B there intervenes no contract, divest B of such his possession or property; because it is given up to B by him that had the full dominion or propriety of what he so gave up. And the like is to be said touching the property that a man hath in his children.

4. Consequently, antecedently to any pact or constitution civil, no man may take away the life of another, or do his body any corporal injury without just cause without the violation of this natural law: and upon this stands the natural law against murder. I say without a just cause; for there may be a cause to take away another's life, as in [the] case of self-defence, *cum debito moderamine inculpatae tutelae.*[117] But it is not an imaginary cause that either hath no reality in it or that ariseth not to that height as naturally to justify it, that can make such bodily injury justifiable by the [36v, 68] law of nature; for though there be no terrene[118] judge or governor to punish it, yet that no more makes the thing lawful than the most unjust action under heaven that by the power of the party committing it is rendered *de facto* unpunishable.

5. Upon the same reason the violating of another man's wife, [that is,] adultery, is against the law of nature, though no pact intervened between the adulterer and the husband because the husband hath a propriety in the body of his wife by the matrimonial contract, which was in her power to give up and is well transferred to her husband.[119]

6. And upon the very same reason and by the same law of nature C may not take away the servant of A which is made his by the contract of the servant, who had power to transfer the propriety of himself at least temporally to A.

7. And upon the same reason it is against natural law for C to take away the children of A while they are *sub jure parentum* [within the rightful rule of the parent]; because they are naturally, and *jure natural[e]* [by natural law], the goods of A antecedently to any contract.

8. As touching the right of propriety that any man may have in the state of nature and antecedently to any contract or consent and touching translation or acquisition of particular property, the question seems more difficult; because most of the methods of acquisition of property seem to be by institution.

However, possibly much may be said to maintain a secondary law of nature for the acquest of property by the first possession or occupation; because that in as much as before the institution of the laws of property it is admitted that all have an equal right to all things, the man that hath acquired the first possession hath somewhat

[117] See note 98. [118] OED: earthly.

[119] MH is often said to have established the "marital rape exemption" in his posthumous on English criminal law. See Editor's Introduction, note 12.

superadded to that [37r, 69] primitive right in common that puts him in a better condition than any other, and to his interest in common there is superadded somewhat by his industry that another hath not, namely a prior possession. And the same may be said in reason of such acquisitions that are made by art or industry, whereby the things so acquired are in some kind become his affects; as by planting, semination, culture, artificial manufactures, and the like.

Yet to avoid all disputes of this nature I will suppose that in the state of nature all things are common; and that antecedently to civil institutions, whereby the rules and laws of property are settled, there is no means peculiarly to appropriate anything to any man.[120] This, though it be a difficult supposition, I shall *argumenti gratiâ* [for the sake of argument] at present admit. Yet I say, in that state of community there are certain rights of natural law and justice instituted by Almighty God and obliging every person of mankind.

For I do suppose it unquestionable that the original dominion and propriety of all things is in Almighty God; and that he hath given the profitable use of all things in this lower world to mankind. *Terram vero dedit filiis hominum.* [In truth he gave the earth to the sons of man.][121] And now suppose that he gave it promiscuously to men as they should be born in the world in common without any particular laws of property. Yet certainly in that state no man hath a right totally to exclude another; for if every man hath a right in that state of community, no man can justly be excluded by another from all participation of that right, without the violation of that right that was in that state of community or nature, which was common to all. For instance, if I am justly entitled by the laws of settled property at this day unto a piece of land, and give it to A, B, and C, though [none][122] of them have a distinct or separate propriety in this or that acre; yet it is most certainly a [37v, 70] wrong and against natural justice for A wholly to exclude B and C from any portion of the profits, though the settled laws of England give them not any remedy by action against him that takes the whole profits. So in that state of nature, in as much as every man hath a right, the rule of natural justice forbids any man to usurp the whole; because it takes something from him that is agreed of all hands to have a right as well as himself, though not determined in the particular *quantum*.

[120] MH invokes a premise that initiated the search for a defence of ownership in much of late medieval and early modern political theory. See Aquinas, *Summa Theologiae*, IIaIIae, qu. 66, a. 2 (*Aquinas: Political Works*, ed. and tr. R. W. Dyson (Cambridge: Cambridge University Press, 2002), 208); Duns Scotus, *Ordinatio*, IV, dist. 15, q. 2 (*Duns Scotus: On the Will and Morality*, ed. Allan B. Wolter and tr. William A. Frank (Washington, DC: Catholic University of America Press, 1986), 219–22); William of Ockham, *Works of Ninety Days*, chs 26–7 (*A Letter to the Friars Minor and Other Writings*, ed. Arthur Stephen McGrade, ed. and tr. John Kilcullen (Cambridge: Cambridge University Press, 1995)); Francisco Suarez, *On Laws*, Bk II, chs 14. 2, 14; Hugo Grotius, *The Rights of War and Peace*, Bk II, ch. 2 (ed. Richard Tuck (Indianapolis: Liberty Classics, 2005)). Its roots can be found in Canon Law (*Decretum*, Dist. 1, can. vii, §3), and even earlier in Cicero, *De officiis*, I.21 (*On Duties*, ed. M. T. Griffin and E. M. Atkins (Cambridge: Cambridge University Press, 1991)). Generally, see Brian Tierney, *The Idea of Natural Rights* (Grand Rapids, MI: Eerdmans, 2001), 69–76, 131–69, 329–35.

[121] Ps. 115:16 (Vulgate: Ps. 113:24).

[122] All MSS: neither.

But it is true that even in the reason of nature in that state of community there may be differing reasons of proportion or inequality. He that hath many children, hath reason to have a greater share thereof, than he that hath none. But when in that state of nature antecedent to the institution of property *de facto* there might be and was sufficient for all according to the exigence of their condition (as there was of the manna that fell among the Israelites) it is against natural justice that he that might have and had enough proportionable to his state and condition should wholly exclude another from all, which had at least an equal right to so much as answered his condition.

Again even in that state of nature that law or rule of natural justice obtained and was equally applicable to that condition of indeterminate property as is or might be to a state of civil settlement; namely, not to do to another what a man would not have done to himself.[123] And therefore if in that state of community that man that without any reasonable or just cause invades the whole and excludes another, would not be so served himself, he gives judgment against himself as an invader of that rule of natural justice, which is [38r, 71] applicable even to that state of community.

Again that law of loving a man's neighbour is a law of nature given by God indistinctly to men under any condition, whether of community or separate interests. This our saviour excellently instanceth in the parable of the Jew that fell among thieves, and was relieved by the Samaritan, not only as an act of beneficence but of duty—"Go thou and do likewise"—though there was no intervenient law, nor so much as any common commerce between the Jews and the Samaritans.[124]

And though it be true, the specification of those actings of this command of loving one another be various according to variety of circumstances, and therein receives a great determination even where civil institutions are settled by the secret guidance of the judgment and conscience; yet it is most certain that it is a law of eternal rectitude and righteousness, and given out by the sovereign lawgiver of the world, who did and most justly might equally oblige all men in that state of nature by his natural laws, as well as in a state of civil settlement. For the obligation of his laws, especially those that are natural, respect men as his own subjects, whether under any settled form of †civil† government or in the state of nature antecedent to it: and it had been clearly an evident breach of this law of natural love, even in that state of community, to have deprived another of the whole benefit of those necessaries for his life, wherein he had a common share by the conception of the lord of the whole earth without any just cause for him so to do.

But the objection is made that there may be a just cause for one man in the state of nature to deprive another, not only of his common share in that common [38v, 72] interest that every man hath in the things of this world:[125] and if there may be such a

123 At p. 35, MH cited the golden rule as one of the first principles of natural law.

124 MH refers to the Biblical story of the Good Samaritan in Luke 10:30–36.

125 There is not complementary "but also" clause in H and BL; MH may have meant to add "but also of his life," as suggested by the paragraph to follow.

cause, it must necessarily follow that every man is naturally the judge of that cause and of the reasonableness of it.[126]

I answer, it is true, [a] that there may be just cause in that state of nature for one man to invade the common interest that another may have; yea and to take away the life of another. And so there may be also [such a right] even in a state of civil settlement.[127] And to omit that disputed problem, whether *in casu extremae necessitatis omnia sunt communia* [in the case of extreme necessity all things are common], a man may *cum debito moderamine inculpatae tutelae* [with due moderation (engage in) blameless defence], as in case of necessary defence of his own life, not only temporarily take away those weapons which an enemy hath whereby the other's life is endangered, but may also take away the life of his enemy if he cannot otherwise save his own; and consequently, if that natural law of self-preservation cannot be otherwise observed, nor a man's life preserved, or if another man in that state of nature doth wrongfully invade any possession, then indeed we are in the state of war, and what by the just laws of war may be done may be justified in such a case.

[b] Antecedently to civil government settled there is no external judge, but a man's self, of what is a reasonable cause to invade another man's life or to deprive him of his common interest in the things of this life, because all men as in relation to themselves are equal. But in that case he judgeth at his peril; and if he doth either wilfully and presumptuously or erroneously and mistakenly judge amiss, if he entertain a vain fear or suspicion that unless he invade the other the other will invade him and thereupon judgeth it expedient for his safety to be the aggressor, it doth not truly justify such an action. For [i] the law of nature, by which he is bound not to commit any unjust action, is not therefore dispensed [39r, 73] withal [just] because there is no other temporal judge to punish it, or because a man mistakes in his judgment; for it is an intrinsical obligation. Otherwise it were impossible for an absolute sovereign prince to do anything intrinsically unjust; because he hath no superior power on earth to judge him. [ii] Even in that state of nature there is a sovereign lord and judge, who hath given this law of nature by the most just reason and authority imaginable, and hath authority to give it and power to exact a conformity to it and to vindicate the breach of it. When there were but three men that we read of in the world, and Cain took an offence at his brother and slew him, God Almighty sends him not to the parental government of Adam but [convicts][128] him himself. And though there were no other law in the world that we know of, there was then a discrimination of good and evil, and divine vengeance for the one and reward for the other. "If thou dost well, shall thou not be accepted? And if thou dost not well sin lies at the door" (Gen. 4:7). And it hath been but a pitiful answer for Cain to have said we were both *jure parentis emancipati* [freed from parental rule]; and there was no law intervened

[126] MH has Hobbes in mind again here, as throughout this discussion of property. See Hobbes, *On the Citizen*, ch. 1.8–10 *Leviathan*, ch. 14.1–4.

[127] BL and Harley: government.

[128] All MSS: convents.

between us, but we were in a state of war, and I was a competent judge what was fit for me to do to my brother.

And therefore it is but a mere fancy, a pleasing imagination that some men have taken up and made much of and built goodly and fine consequences upon; that the state of nature antecedent to civil laws or government is a state of war, and that therefore whatsoever a condition of war ^renders^ justifiable is justifiable in the state of nature.[129] The falseness of which supposition appears in what follows. [a] The [39v, 74] state of nature is really and in its nature a state of peace, under the obligation of duty to the great sovereign rector of the world which is a God of peace, under the obligation of the laws of this sovereign implanted in nature, which are laws of love and natural justice. And if they fall into a condition of war one with another, it is not connatural to the state of nature, but accidental, a disease and disorder in the nature of some at least of mankind: and to measure the state of nature by the disorder of it, we may with as much reason conclude that intemperance, cruelty, and villainy is the law of nature, because many are of that distemper. [b] It is plain that, antecedently to any positive institution, the frame of human nature tends naturally to society and the law of society; and 'tis a vain thing to say, this ariseth from fear,[130] for we may see this propension grow up even in children and from them. So that it is rightly observed by the great philosopher that mankind are more sociable than bees, even upon a kind of natural propensions.[131] [c] It is a mistake in fact that there is no *medium* between a state of war and a state of peace so far forth as peace stands established by mutual pact and contract. There is a state of peace established by mutual leagues, contracts, or stipulations, which is varied according to the variety of the capitulation[s]; and some are of mutual defence, some of simple friendship. Again there is a state of war, which sometimes is solemn with a solemn denunciation going before it.[132] Sometimes it hath not that solemnity; but men or people fall into an actual hostility, either by occasion of some damage done by one to the other, or by [40r, 75] some other provocation or jealousy happening between them. But there is a third state, either between man and man or nation and nation, which hath neither the superinduction of a capitulation or contract to make it perfect peace, nor any hostility between them either denounced or begun, which at its best or highest advance is a mutual commerce or intercourse, as there is between the English and the Persian or Indian at this day, or at least is a bare negation of war or hostility according to the ancient Roman law, *si cum gente aliquâ neque amicitiam, neq[ue]*

[129] See Hobbes, *On the Citizen*, ch. 1; *Leviathan*, ch. 13.

[130] Following in the Epicurean tradition, Hobbes argues from this premise in *On the Citizen*, ch. 1. See Epicurus, *Key Doctrines*, 33, 32, in *The Hellenistic Philosophers*, tr. A. A. Long and D. N. Sedley (Cambridge: Cambridge University Press, 1987), and Roderick T. Long, "Hellenistic Philosophers of Law," in Fred D. Miller (ed.), *A History of the Philosophy of Law from the Ancient Greeks to the Scholastics* (Dordrecht: Springer, 2007), 111–31. Against this premise, see *Treatise*, 55–6.

[131] See Aristotle, *Politics*, tr. C. D. C. Reeve (Indianapolis: Hackett Publishing Company, 1998), Bk I, ch. 2.

[132] That is, formal and official declaration of war. See Grotius, *Rights of War and Peace*, Bk I, ch. 3.4–5.

hospitium neq[ue] fides amicitiae causa factum habeatur hi hostes quidem non sunt [if there be any nation with whom there is no friendship, hospitality, or alliance, they are not to be reputed as enemies];[133] and though the corrupt customs of some nations permitted piracies and robberies to be committed between them, yet they were always claimed and styled by the name of *Latrocinia* [robbers]. And this was the true state of man in nature out of the extent of paternal government before the institution of civil society, neither perfect peace settled by contract, nor war, but a state of mutual intercourse and commerce *or at least or worst* a state undetermined to perfect peace or plain hostility and rather tending to the former than to the latter. So that the affirmation that the state of nature is a state of war is but only a pretty phrase taken up and pleasing to the inventors of it, without any thing of truth or reality in it.

9. Again the paternal power over the children, during their minority, and while their dependence is upon the parents, is right settled in the father by the law of nature; and accordingly was in use, till civil and political government was established in the world.

10. Again by the very law of nature there is a secret obligation of gratitude to him, from whom I freely and without reciprocal contract receive a benefit. And this held as well in the state of nature, as after the institution of civil government; neither hath the institution of civil government or any laws induced thereby, altered this obligation; for though the laws of gratitude be most certainly a duty [40v, 76] by the law of nature, yet it stands as it then was, no law that I know of having made it compulsory by any civil action, but it *is as it* stood before merely as a natural law obliging *in fore interior* [one's internal court].

And thus far touching those laws that are natural yet applicable to that natural state which may be supposed antecedent to any political or civil laws or government.

[B] Therefore I descend to those laws of nature which are preparative and in order to the attaining of civil or political society.

And previous to this consideration we must premise that as the frame and order of the greater world was not digested into that comely and useful constitution that is still observed by chance or casualty;[134] so neither did the frame or texture of the lesser world [of] man come together by casualty or chance, but by the most high wisdom of the most wise God.

And as thus the contexture of the human nature was the contrivance of the most sovereign, wise, and intelligent being; so all the propensions, inclinations, and common tendencies of the human nature, and the adaptation of all his faculties to their suitable objects, in order to the well-being of man, were all ordained, disposed, and placed in that nature by the same wise intelligent being, who foresaw all his

[133] MH quotes *Digest*, 49.15.5; Grotius discusses this passage in *Rights of War and Peace*, Bk II, chs 15, 5.2.
[134] OED: casual occurrence, contingency.

works from the beginning, and knew what was most convenient for the human nature in all the various ages and circumstances of his being.

In the first ages of the world, the people were few [and] long lived; and that natural regiment, which was so lodged in the parental power, might possibly have served[135] that infancy of time. But Almighty God, to whom all his works are [41r, 77] known from the beginning, easily foresaw that, as people were multiplied, political external regiment and laws would be necessary for the well-ordering of mankind; and that without it those laws of nature, though sufficiently obliging to the human nature without any positive or human institutions, would be usurped upon by the prevalence[136] and lusts of men. He did therefore, partly by the propensions and inclinations of the human nature, partly by the exhibition of the reasonableness of things to the understanding of men, bend them to coalitions into civil societies and laws, as being admirably congruous and suitable to the well-being of mankind. And there are those natural laws which come now to be considered, as preparatively disposing to civil regiment and society.

1. Therefore there is in the human nature a natural propension and love of society, which is highly improved by the reasonableness and usefulness thereof to man's well-being apparent to his reason and understanding. This the great master of observation and learning in the first [book] of his *Politics* observes to my hand; wherein after some instances to this purpose he concludes. *Ea quo patet sociale animal esse hominem magis quam omnes apes et omne gregarium animal: nihil enim natura frustra facit.*[137] Two things are observable herein namely, [a] that there is a natural propension in man to society even antecedent to any discursive operation of the mind. And [b] that this is no casual incidence in the nature of man, but an instituted character imprinted upon that nature, which appears by this: that by the advantage of speech and instituted signs which no creature besides man is capable of [41v, 78] he is adapted and fitted to that sociability that his nature is inclined to—the ordering of anything to the use of another being the greatest evidence of such an agent that works by intention and intellect. Therefore this natural propension thus accommodated with the faculty of speech so singularly apposite thereunto was the work of the great and wise and intelligent being.

And therefore it is but a narrow and weak conjecture that fear was the *primum movens* [primary motive] of man to the entering into societies; since it is apparent that this natural propension placed in man is antecedent, not only to the actings of the passions, but in some measure antecedent even to any act of deliberation of the mind.

[135] MSS: serve. [136] OED: effective force or power.

[137] This passage from Aristotle's *Politics*, I.2, reads: "by which it is evident that man is a social animal more than all the bees and every gregarious creature: for nature does nothing in vain."

But besides this natural propension, which is the *primum movens* to societies, there is something that seconds and enforceth it; namely that congruity and convenience, which renders it useful and beneficial to the human nature, and is so presented to the judgment of reason. [a] It gives a man security against his fears of injuries from others by the mutual associations, confederacy, and united strength of those of the same society. But this is not all, nor indeed an half of the reason and †reasonableness† of society: and therefore they do look but half way that make fear the only or principal reason of mankind's affecting societies. For [b] there is a further advantage; namely the mutual communication and participation of one man in that good that he wants and another hath, or hath in greater abundance. For nature hath so ordered the several states and conditions of men that one man stands in need of what another hath, and this creates necessitude between one man and another; and by this disposition of the divine regiment of things there is a mutual necessitude and indigence of mutual offices [42r, 79] between man and man. One man hath more wit; another more courage; another is a good naturalist or physician; another is a good orator; one is dexterous in mechanics of one kind, another of another; and the advantage of consociation makes the communication of the good of one to another more ready facile and useful: and by this means one man is as it were mortised[138] into another, and contiguated[139] by the communication of offices and supplying of wants of each other.[140]

2. By the same propension and the consonance also of reason there is distinction of properties: for though the full complement of settling of properties and of the laws for the acquiring and translating was not fully obtained or regulated till government [was] settled; yet it is plain that the distinction of property began early in the world, and that by a kind of natural congruity and propension to which men were inclined, without any great process of ratiocination. And the reason of the thing gave in itself a great suffrage to it. [a] The great inconvenience and disturbance that must necessarily grow upon an indistinction of property. [b] The distinction of property engaged men's industry: for no man would take pains for that, wherein another should be participant that took none; neither would any take pains for that which he might equally enjoy without the derogation of it. And so the habitable world would run to disorder and confusion, and never be improved for the advantage and supply of the increase of mankind; because there would be no necessity, nor encouragement in it, which would be detriment to the beauty and usefulness of the world and would be to the common disadvantage of mankind. Therefore Plato's community [of goods] hath

138 OED: to join with a mortise; i.e., to join securely.

139 Ed: possibly a word of MH's coining meaning "brought into close association".

140 MH here echoes themes prominent in Althusius and Grotius. See Johannes Althusius, *Politica* (3rd edn, 1614), abridged edition ed. and tr. Frederick S. Carney (Indianapolis: Liberty Fund, 1964), 17; Hugo Grotius, *The Free Sea*, ed. David Armitage and tr. Richard Hakluyt (Indianapolis: Liberty Fund, 2004), 10–11.

been deservedly rejected, notwithstanding the reputation of the author,[141] because in the frame of it [it is] pernicious to industry, and consequently to the human [42v, 80] nature, which is advanced and improved by industry and would like a standing water putrefy without motion.

3. By the same preparatory law of nature is the propension to the institution of government in a society. And hence it was that, amongst those *precepta Noachidarum* that *de judiciis* was one,[142] which was no other than a command of institution of government. And this is upon those two grounds formerly delivered: [a] There is a kind of natural propension in the human nature to have some imperative and coercive power lodged in the society and though the various forms of that government are not determinate in nature; yet the generality of mankind have most of all fixed on monarchical government, as most resembling the regiment of Almighty. [b] The reasonableness of government is apparent: for as a society much contributes to the peace and good of mankind, so government is the bond of society that holds it together, without which it would be imperfect to its end, and soon fall in sunder by factions,[143] and the ends of society would fail and the nerves and ligaments which hold it together would be cut asunder.

4. By the same preparatory law of nature the reasonableness of institution of laws for the government of a society is apparent. For [a] there would be no sufficient external terror to keep from evil; because the penalties, which are natural to laws, would not otherwise be known, nor public. [b] Without such laws there would be no certain external rule, whereby the governor or governed should order themselves. Either the government of the governor should be arbitrary and uncertain, or else none at all; and the governed should be at a loss how to walk and order themselves or their actions. But of this hereafter.

And thus for those laws of nature that are [43r, 81] preliminary to the institution of civil government or laws.

[C] Therefore I come to those laws of nature that obtain after political government and laws [have been] established. And herein I shall be very brief; not intending a discourse at large of politics or human government or laws; for that is besides my purpose, and would be too large a subject for this time. And these natural laws that abstractively belong hereunto, are very few; because, notwithstanding the institution of civil or political laws and government, all those laws of nature, whereof before, still obtain and retain their force and obligation, and therefore it were but vain to repeat them over again.

141 See Plato, *Republic*, tr. G. M. A. Grube and C. D. C. Reeve (Indianapolis: Hackett Publishing Company, 2004) at the end of Book III and the beginning of Book IV (416c to 421d).

142 For the injunction in the Noachide laws to establish judicial institutions, see pp. 101–2 and notes 285 and 286.

143 All MSS insert: "and that popular argument of the equality of mankind by nature," but it is not clear how it fits into the sentence.

1. Therefore the great law of nature, upon which all civil or political government and laws are built, and wherein the strength and stability of them among men consist. It is this great law of nature *fides est servanda*. For this, being that law of God, which we call natural, is fixed in nature, obligeth in conscience, and renders all human government laws, contracts, and promises reductively[144] and consequently under the obligation of the divine law of Almighty God.

And this *fides* is either express and verbal, or implicit and by way of reasonable interpretation.

Expressa fides is that which is given expressly: as when people enter into a mutual society or confederacy one with another; when they set up a government and oblige themselves to obey it; when they either make laws by common consent among themselves, or transfer that power to some person or society among them and [43v, 82] oblige themselves to be obedient to them; when one man contracts with another, gives to another his faith or promise to do or not to do this or that thing. There, though the matter of the contract or agreement and the formality of its constitution be human, yet when it is made, the signature of this divine law of Almighty God is set to it: *servabis fidem* [you will keep your agreements]; and consequently, though the breach of such faith as to the matter of it be of some human contract or institution, yet in relation to this signature that superadds unto it the stamp, value, and authority of Almighty God, it is breach of his law.

Tacita or *Implicita fides* is when a man that was not the first party to the contract, but comes in after and lists himself under that society that was at first engaged in this faith or that by succession of new pacts and capitulations hath been bound to it, comes into a city, kingdom, or commonwealth, and participates of the benefits and advantages thereof. Here he is tacitly obliged in the same manner as the rest of the society is obliged; namely, to keep their laws and support the government, and to the common assistance and defence of the society wherein he lives.

And to this head I may refer the matter of veracity or speaking truth and avoiding lying, especially in matters of accusation, testimony, and reports. Certainly veracity or speaking truth from the heart is a dictate of human nature. [a] It is suitable to the honour and dignity of the human nature; and lying is unseemly, base, and an argument of an ignoble and impotent mind. [b] Nature having given to mankind the common use of speech to render themselves useful to and to communicate with each other, there is a kind of common obligation [that] runs through the whole human nature to preserve that power or faculty conformable [44r, 83] to its end and institution.

And certainly the supervenience of contracted civil society superadds a further obligation for men to speak truth one to another, the contrary whereof is lying and deceit; and to speak truth one of another, the contrary whereof is false witness:

[144] OED: by consequence or inference.

both which are extreme violations of civil society and that common faith that everyone either expressly or implicitly gives to the other to speak truth and not to ^testify^[145] or affirm falsely; a lie or false testimony being a breach of faith touching a thing to be known, as a breach of contract or promise is a breach of faith touching things to be done.

2. But since the duty we owe to God as the supreme lord of all things is greater and prior to the duty we owe or can owe to human government, and since the obligation to laws of men or civil societies is subordinate and inferior to that obligation to the laws of God, whether natural or positive; therefore in all that faith [requires] between societies or the governors and governed for the observation of such human laws there is tacitly implied *salvâ fides et ligeantiâ deo debitâ* [preserving the faith and allegiance owed to God]. And therefore a man is not bound to offend God by the active obeying of the commands or laws of men. But then let him look to it at his peril, that he hath a good warrant to justify him in the sight of God; for otherwise his disobedience to the human laws of men is *violatio fidei* [violation of agreements], which is against the law of God.[146]

3. But even in that case, though in the contradiction of the laws and commands of God and of men there the obligation actively to obey the latter is taken away; yet according to the ordinary constitution of government, a man in such case is under the obligation of non-resistance and passive subjection. For though the governor that imposeth a law contrary to the law of [44v, 84] God, and punisheth for not observing it, breaks the duty he owes to God, by commanding things contrary thereunto, yet the subject offends no law of God or man in suffering or not resisting; and as he observes the duty he owes to the supreme sovereign[147] of the world in not yielding an active obedience to the unlawful commands or laws of men, he also observes the duty he owes to this natural law, which is the law of God, *fides est servanda*. For though an *active* obedience in such case be tacitly excepted, yet a passive subjection even in these cases is not excepted but enjoined by virtue of this natural law, *fides est servanda*. And this stands with natural reason and the convenience of human societies, without which confusion and dissolution of government would issue. For every man would thereby be put into a condition, not only to dispute the lawfulness of everything commanded, but also the power and authority of laws in inflicting punishment in whatsoever they should judge not lawful, wherein every man would be a judge of the lawfulness of †the command†, the lawfulness of inflicting the penalty, and consequently the lawfulness of resistance, when and how he please.

145 H: justify.

146 MH held that it is a mistake to legally recognize a right of conscience, because "the supposition of such a condition doth utterly enervate all the power of the magistrate, for it sets up in every particular subject a tribunal superior to that of the magistrate" (Lambeth 3507, 2, quoted in Cromartie, *Hale*, 180–1). An individual may, perhaps must, obey his conscience, but government is still entitled to punish disobedience.

147 Harley: governor.

And thus I have run through some *specimina legis naturalis*. I take not upon me to give an exact catalogue or system of natural laws. I know I have omitted many; as namely charity, compassion, remitting offences upon repentance for injuries, longanimity, clemency, the various partitions and instances of distributive and commutative justice, together with the various temperaments of them. My design was not to pursue all the *capita legis naturalis* but to give such [45r–85] instances to make what I say and shall say touching the laws of nature the more intelligible and applicable.

6

That these Natural Laws Have in their Matter an Intrinsic Moral Goodness and Congruity to Right Reason, and Conveniency to the Condition of Mankind Antecedent to and Abstractive from any Law Enjoining them

By what hath been before said it appears in some measure, what those laws of nature are, and likewise that they have an intrinsical goodness in them. This argument I shall further prosecute in this chapter and I shall shortly give those instances, whereby their intrinsic goodness antecedent to any law and abstractively from it may be shown. This appears:

First, from the author of them who is a God of infinite wisdom and therefore doth everything by the most exact wisdom, ordering everything to most suitable ends, and conducting everything to those ends by most suitable means. It is he that hath drawn these lines and strictures[148] of those natural laws in the human nature.

[148] OED: restrictions.

And if we look into the whole frame of nature and every species and rank of things therein contained, we shall find the instances and footsteps of the divine wisdom in everything. We need go no further in this topic than the instincts of all the animals we see in the world. Every little animal is accommodated, not only with faculties [45v, 86] suitable to his being, but with certain instincts and propensions engrafted in their nature antecedent to any discipline, education, instruction, or imitation, whereby they are *sweetly,* secretly, effectually, and orderly carried to the convenience of their natures and conditions.

And certainly he that sees this in animals cannot but reasonably conclude that in the noble nature of man there are those secret propensions and directions connatural to him that may be answerable to the dignity and use and end of the human nature.

Secondly, from the congruity that appears in the matter of these laws to the convenience and benefit of the human nature and its well-being. This appears by the induction of the particulars, and hath been in some measure opened and applied in the former chapter.

Thirdly, though there be some particulars in the law of nature that are appropriate to man as he is a corporeal and dependent being, and therefore not to be applied to the spiritual and glorious nature of the immortal and glorious God, yet there be many particulars of the law of nature, which are but finite and small transcripts of the perfections of the divine nature, and are so many little rays of that light and beauty and small models of that most perfect and glorious being. Such are those natural laws of justice, goodness, benignity, truth, veracity, and divers others, which are impressions and strictures of the divine exemplar; and from those as well as from the nature and faculties of his soul man is styled the image of God.

Therefore in as much as these attributes are [46r, 87] parts of that essential and sovereign perfection of the divine nature, they must needs have an eternal and intrinsic goodness and beauty in them; and so much the nearer the nature of man arrives[149] to these perfections, so much the more he resembles his maker, and partakes of the irradiation and signature of the divine nature.

Hence it was the compendious method of some of the ancients to attain the greatest advance of perfection, that the nature of that having once attained a true notion of the divine perfection to draw as near as they could to the imitation and resemblance of him in those attributes wherein mankind had a capacity to participate, as namely, his holiness, purity, justice, goodness, benignity, love, truth, and faithfulness, which they shortly digested into this precept *Imitare quem colis* [imitate whom you worship],[150] which differs little in meaning from that of the Apostle [in]

[149] Ed: approximates.

[150] MH may quote here Robert Leighton (1612–94), Archbishop of Glasgow: "*Summa Religionis est imitare quem colis.*" See Leighton, *An Exposition of the Creed, Lord's Prayer and Ten Commandments* (London, 1701), 167. But the phrase can be found earlier in Lancelot Andrewes' sermon preached before Queen Elizabeth, 6 March 1594. Available at <http://anglicanhistory.org/lact/andrewes/v2/lent4.html>.

Eph. 4:24. "Put ye on the new man, which after God is created in righteousness and true holiness."

Therefore, inasmuch as the truest notion of Almighty God is that he is *ens summe perfectum* [the most perfect being]; and that the attributes of the divine nature are but so many essential perfections of the divine nature; and that [they] are such in their own nature eternally and necessarily; and that these excellences of holiness, righteousness, justice, goodness, benignity, truth, and veracity, which are principal parts of the law of nature, are but the little and finite transcripts of the perfect and infinite exemplar of these attributes, which originally and in their highest perfection are in the divine nature *and [that] certain structures and delineations of the divine exemplar drawn by the finger of God, upon the human nature*: it must needs follow that those parts of the natural law have an eternal and [46v, 88] intrinsic beauty and goodness in them abstractively from any positive command or law antecedent to it.

7

Touching the Formal Reason of the Law of Nature and its Obligation

We have seen in the former chapter this position laid and in some measure proved that the matter of the law of nature is intrinsically and simply good, and good for the use and convenience of mankind, and therefore upon the account of the strictest and most natural reason and prudence highly eligible by the reasonable nature.

But the bare goodness, resemblance, or fitness of anything, for a creature endued with understanding and will, doth not therefore presently[151] induce an obligation, unless some superior power will impose it as a law and exhibit it as good. My physician tells me that such a course of diet will preserve my health and a contrary course will shorten my life; and I am convinced in my own reason that life and health are both eligible goods; and I am likewise convinced that the thing he tells me is true and evident to my reason that it cannot be otherwise. Here is a good propounded that is very eligible, and my understanding is satisfied, and yet without the supposition of

[151] Ed: immediately or directly.

a law to bind me to the choice of it, which my physician cannot give me, I am yet under no obligation to follow my physician's direction; not to him, for he cannot give me a law; nor yet to myself, or to my reason, for my reason is indeed myself, and I cannot be obliged to myself, [47r, 89] for as I cannot bind myself at my pleasure, and if I have no obligation but ^to myself^[152] I am presently[153] loose as soon as I go contrary to that supposed obligation, neither can I myself incur any guilt to myself by what I myself do or will.[154]

So that it seems, to the obligation of that which we call the natural law, there must be something else, besides the intrinsical nature of the object, that must have the formal nature of a law and induce an obligation; for it is most certainly true that where there is no law, there can be no transgression.

There seems therefore in this law of nature to be two things.

I. The indication of the object of natural law, discovering the natural goodness and natural evil of moral actions, or the *vis indicativa boni et mali moralis* [power of indicating of moral good and evil]; which doth not singly create any formal obligation, but barely discovers what the thing is, and accordingly presents it to the understanding or the mind. And if it rested here, there were no lawgiver: for though the man, under this indication had reason to follow that which is thus presented as morally good, and to decline that which is morally evil, out of the reasonableness and congruity of such choice or rejection; yet still he is under no law to accept or reject, nor incurs any guilt to any, but is only accountable to himself, either for his folly or loss if he act not suitable to reason or for his advantage and benefit if he act according to it.[155]

Therefore, II. besides this *vis indicativa*, which we find in the law of nature, there is *vis preceptiva* or *imperativa*, that gives to this that we call the law of nature the true formal reason of a law, and thereupon induceth an obligation; namely, Almighty God, the sovereign lord and lawgiver of the world, by this edict or law of nature, commanding some things to be done, other things not to [47v–90] be done, which, though the things abstractively in themselves are natural, such as the law declares, yet there is superadded to them this that gives it the reason of its obligation, namely, the institution of it as a law by the sovereign lawgiver. That excellent text in Micah chap. 6, verse 8[156] excellently discovers both these. "He hath shewn thee, O man,

[152] H: to bind myself. [153] OED: at that moment. [154] See note 23.

[155] Suarez argues similarly; see *Treatise on Laws*, Bk I, ch. 1.7–8, ch. 5, ch. 12.4; Bk II, ch. 6.5–6. But the view has roots deeper in the medieval tradition. For example, Marsilius of Padua clearly argues that it is not sufficient for a rule's being a law that it *indicate* actions as just or right. See Marsilius of Padua, *Defender of the Peace*, ed. and tr. Annabel Brett (Cambridge: Cambridge University Press, 2005), Discourse I, ch. 10.3, Discourse II, ch. 12.3–8. However, in his essay "Of doing as we are done unto," MH expresses a different thought: Although God commands that I not do that which I would not have another do to me, yet "if there were no such express commands . . . the very precept itself includes a most evident conviction of an eternal and indispensable justice in it; for if I judge this action should not be done to me, and that it were unjust and unreasonable if it were so done, why should I go about to do that to him that I would condemn as unjust if done to me?" (Hale, *Works*, I, 413–14).

[156] H: 9.

what is good." There is that *vis indicativa* of the law. "And what doth the lord require at thy hands but to do justly and to love mercy and to walk humbly with thy God." There is that *vis imperativa* or *preceptiva*: "What doth the Lord require at thy hands." Yet both terminated in those natural laws of justice, mercy, and the reverence of Almighty God. The first, the *vis indicativa legis naturalis,* is the effect of Almighty God as the author of nature; for those propensions of the human nature, that adaptation and congruity of his reasonable faculty whereby he discerns and tests the moral good and evil of his actions, are the effect of his wisdom and power as the author of human nature. The *vis preceptiva legis* [*naturalis*] is that which proceeds from the sovereign will of God as the supreme rector and legislator of mankind.

Touching this *vis preceptiva legis*, it is necessary to explain what it doth not in relation to natural laws; and next what it is that is thereby superadded to natural laws.

(1) First, as to the former, this *actus preceptivus* or *imperativus* [preceptive or imperative act] is not that which gives the intrinsic good or evil to the things it commands or forbids; for, antecedently to this *actus preceptivus legis naturalis* [preceptive act of natural law]; the things commanded or prohibited were determined in their natural or moral good or evil. And herein is the true formal difference of a positive or natural law.[157] The latter hath its determination antecedently [48r, 91] to the law that commands or prohibits it, *precipitur quia bonum prohibetur quia malum* [commanding it because it is good and forbidding it because it is evil]. But in positive laws the good or evil of the thing thereby commanded or prohibited depends originally upon the law itself that so commands or prohibits it.

(2) What this *actus preceptivus* that gives the formality of a law superadds to the law of nature. I think it hath these effects.

[a] This *actus preceptivus* is that which gives that effect, which is the most natural and equal effect of a law; namely, obligation to obey it. There is in this law of nature a double obligation: [i] The *obligatio ad officium* [obligation of performing the office or act], which is obedience. [ii] The *obligatio ad poenam* [obligation to (submit to) punishment] in case of disobedience.[158] And the former is a distinct obligation from the latter. If we should conceive no vindicative[159] power in the world, and that all men were in a state of equality and nature; yet if one man should promise another anything upon a just consideration, there would be a natural obligation to perform his promise, though there were no penalty added, nor any external coercion to compel its performance, a certain intrinsic bond of natural justice to do what he promiseth. So the just

157 Ed: between a positive and a natural law.

158 John Locke, in an early essay, similarly identifies a twofold obligation of natural law: *debitum officii* ("a liability to pay dutiful obedience") and *debitum supplicii* ("a liability to [submit to] punishment"). Locke, *Essays on the Law of Nature* (composed 1660/1), ed. W. von Leyden (Oxford: Clarendon Press, 1954), 182–3. MH and Locke may have taken this distinction from a common source in Robert Sanderson's *De Juramenti Promissorii Obligatione* (London, 1655), 25, although MH may have encountered the distinction in Suarez, *On Laws*, Bk II, ch. ix.7, 255.

159 OED: punitive or retributive.

subjection of the reasonable creature to Almighty God, as his creator, preserver, and benefactor, gives a most just and natural imperative power and authority to bind his reasonable creature to observe what he commands, though there were no regard had to that executive power that can exact an obedience by punishment.

And by this means we have two things in this preceptive act of the law that makes this obligation: [48v, 92] [i] the sign of the divine will that he will have his creature obliged, when it is given *per modum legis et precept* [by way of legal precept]. [ii] Hereby there is the *terminus obligatorius*,[160] wherein it is fixed, namely Almighty God, who, by giving a law creates an obligation from the creature, as that person or being to whom the obligation is made; for as we have before observed there can be no obligation, unless the person by whom and to whom be distinct.

[b] This primitive obligation or *obligatio ad officium* rests primarily in the natural conscience. There are two things to be observed touching the obligation of conscience. [i] That the *terminus obligationis conscientiae* is only God. [ii] And consequently no law can primarily and immediately oblige the conscience, but that of God. The laws indeed of men do secondarily and reductively bind the conscience: but it is by virtue of the primitive obligation that is due by the conscience to the law of God commanding the observing of our faith and pacts; for the conscience [is] both the province immediately subject to God and his laws and his vicegerent and substitute in the soul.

And therefore, though it may be truly said that [the] primitive obligation of the natural conscience is by the natural law, yet it must be also said that it [is] by the natural law as it is formally such *ex vi precipientis* [from the preceptive power], namely, Almighty God as the sovereign lawgiver.[161]

[c] That this preceptive act doth superadd to the natural law certain sanctions of rewards and punishments that are *ex instituto* and *arbitrio legislatoris* [by the institution and judgment of the lawmaker].

It is true that such is the congruity of the laws of nature in respect of their matter to the good of the human nature, that by a kind of natural necessity, connection, and consequence in the due observance of them, mankind may attain a very great degree of happiness in this life [49r, 93]—namely, tranquillity of mind, health, and a due state of the body—yea, and for aught any man can reasonably define to the contrary, some measure of happiness in the life to come.

And on the other side, by the very same natural connection and necessity, a habit of violation of these natural laws draws necessarily with it a great perturbation and

160 Ed: the party to whom ultimately the obligation is owed.

161 MH's point seems to be that the conscience not only registers or discovers certain principles of natural law, but also recognizes them *as law*, i.e., as dictates of divine authority.

disorder and unhappiness in the present life, and a great degree of that *poena damni* and *poena sensus*[162] in the life to come.

For as we see in the animal life, if that order and *taxis* of the body be broken, there ensue pain and inconvenience; *and as* animals in the due state and observation of their natural motions and instincts enjoy that felicity that their nature is capable of; and even in all things in nature, everything is beautiful, comely, and obtains its conservation in that place, state, and order, in which by nature it is placed; and when it is out of that place and order, contracts corruption, disorder, and dissolution; [so it][163] is reasonable for any man that considers the great consonance and adaptation of the matter of the laws of the human nature †unto that nature† reasonably to conclude that a life in conformity to that law must needs be the happiness and perfection of the human nature as far as it is naturally capable; and that on the other side a life unconformable to a law so benign and convenient to the human nature must needs be full of breaches and perturbations and inconveniency, even as we see the very sin of an intemperate man by a kind of natural and necessary consequence becomes his punishment by filling him with diseases and bringing him to death.

[49v, 94] I say, though all this be true, yet ^it seems most reasonable to think that^ inasmuch as the preceptive part of natural law superadds something to that natural state of natural laws, and so there is an accession of reward to the obedience of that law more and greater than that which by a natural connection is acquirable by it; so on the other side, it seems reasonable that as the offence against the natural law carries an aggravation of contempt against the sovereign authority of the lawgiver besides that natural *ataxy* [disorder] in the deviation from the rule of nature, there should be an enhancing of the punishment [above][164] that which is naturally consequential upon the *ataxy* itself.

Howsoever, it is apparent that it is most just for the sovereign lawgiver, if he please and as he pleases *ad arbitrium* [according to his will or judgment], to enhance the punishment at his pleasure. Thus even in the laws of men, when they prohibit anything that by the law of nature is prohibited, suppose it to be intemperance, though that sin carries with it *ex congruo* [suitably] a natural punishment; yet by the superaddition of the prohibition thereof by temporal law, there ariseth another obligation to a further punishment either expressed in the law or tacitly reserved to the *arbitrium* of the executive power of the lawgiver or his ^ministers^, the judges. And this superaddition of obligation to obedience and of additional punishment by the preceptive act of Almighty God, relative to the natural law, is necessary to the divine economy in the regiment of the world, to contain men more forcibly within their duties.

And thus far for the explication of this preceptive act of Almighty God, whereby the law of nature is constituted into the due formal reason and nature of a law.

Now to make it appear that the law of nature is thus completed into a formal law by the preceptive act of the [50r, 95] divine legislation it appears,

[162] See notes 37 and 39. [163] H: so that it. [164] All MSS: about.

1. By the common suffrage of the learned among the heathen who style it a law and obliging as a law.
2. By the sacred writers who style it the law of nature, the law inscribed in the heart (Romans Chap 1 and 2).
3. Because without this preceptive act it could never obtain the adequate and natural effect of a law, namely obligation to obedience.
4. It would be a flaw in the divine regiment of mankind, if that which is so necessary for the containing of mankind within their duty and obedience to the material part of natural law should be wanting in the regiment of the most wise and sovereign ^legislator^.
5. The acting of the natural conscience, the sense of its obligation by this natural law, the comfort and contentment and quietness and complacency[165] of the conscience in the due observance of it, the *ictus [et] laniatus conscientiae* [blows and lacerations of the conscience], those terrors and furies and vexations that torture us in the violation of it, whereof all ages have given experience and every man that but attends himself may find it true: these all bear witness to the divine authority that lays hold on the conscience in this natural law, and to that sacred obligation that binds our nature by virtue of this law; none of which could be, if we should remove the preceptive or imperative act of Almighty God, whereby the matter of the natural law is rendered obliging both *ad officium* and *ad poenam*.

8

Concerning the Publication of this Law of Nature under the Manner of the Communication thereof to Mankind

Having considered the matter of this natural law and the formal constitution of it *per vim legis* [by the power of law], I now come [50v, 96] to consider the manner of its communication or publication thereof to mankind.

[165] OED: tranquil pleasure.

The publication of the law of nature is of two kinds; primitive and natural, and supplemental or adventitious. Of the former thereof in this chapter.[166]

Touching the former I do take it that Almighty God did institute a natural communication of this law of nature, from whence it principally borrows its denomination of natural, which is in its extent as universal and comprehensive as the nature of mankind; for it is reasonable to judge that since this law concerns and is to oblige all mankind, the publication or notification thereof should be as comprehensive.

The natural promulgation of this natural law of God to the human nature seems to be of these four kinds viz. I. By a common irradiation. II. By *institution* or implanting. III. By ratiocination or the exercise of the intellectual faculty in man. IV. By that vigorous application of the former *media*, which we ordinarily call conscience.

Touching the *first* of these, namely irradiation, I mean not that special, or extraordinary efflux of the divine grace, which is sometimes communicated to particular persons at least sometimes, which is usually called special grace; but that common irradiation, which, though it proceeds from a supernatural cause, is commonly communicated to all mankind, and so without any improperness of speech may be called natural; that is, as the ever blessed God, by a kind of common efflux of his goodness and power, upholds everything in its being and operations *quasi per modum naturalis effluxus* [as if by way of natural emanation], so he doth some way communicate a certain common [51r, 97] efflux into his intellectual creatures in the exercise of their intellectual faculty *per modum communis effluxus naturalis* [by way of common natural emanation].

And by this common efflux the human intellect is furnished with certain common principles both intellectual and moral, the latter whereof is that which we call the law of nature. Thus, as the sun and its light and heat are a kind of common principle of motion to all sentient and vegetable beings in this lower world; so this common efflux of intellective light is a common principle, assisting all intellective operation, and deriving unto the whole intellective nature those common notions both speculative and moral that are necessary for their intellective life.

Therefore from this common efflux equally communicated to all rational creatures, they do agree in those common principles both speculative and moral, or those notions, which we commonly call the laws of nature.

And it should seem without some one common principle of this kind, equally communicated to all mankind, they could not concenter in those common notions; nor could one man learn of another; nor could they intelligibly understand one another, much less conspire and consent into those sentiments, which we find commonly received by all men. The scholar learns of his master, which yet seems hard to be done, unless they had both as it were one common master that communicated to and with both.

166 MH discusses the "primitive and natural" publication of the natural law in Chapters 8–10—by "common irradiation" in Chapter 8; by "implanting" in Chapter 9; by "reason" and "conscience" in Chapter 10—and the "supplemental or adventitious" modes of publication in Chapter 11.

I dare not affirm that this is a necessary or rigorous consequence; because it is possible the individual souls of every particular person might in their singular [51v, 98] constitutions be so framed, as that they might *convenire in specie* [agree in kind], in certain operations and sentiments specifically consonant one to another, as we find that even in inferior animals of the same species their individual instincts and operations proceeding from them have a kind of parity and suitableness specifically consonant one to another.

But yet, as there are many other motives to entertain the persuasion of such a common principle communicating with and to the individual souls of men; so even this consonancy in the whole nature of mankind in common notions both speculative and moral is best and most naturally resolved into the common supposition of such a common principle; the farther explication whereof I shall therefore pursue in this section.

The principle of intellective light hath been variously styled by those that have considered it. Most ordinarily by the ancients it was called *intellectus agens*, by others *mens* and *natura mentalis*, by others *spiritus Dei*,[167] not that co-essential third person of the blessed Trinity, but a divine efflux or irradiation proceeding from the glorious God as an emanation settled and instituted to be the ordinary means of communicating light and those common principles, which are necessary for the right ordering of the intellective and rational nature.

Touching the doctrine of *intellectus agens* as a common principle of intellective light and intellection, it is certainly very ancient, though somewhat variously explicated [by][168] the philosophers of several sects, by Jews and by Christians.

[52r, 99] The Platonists,[169] at least in some of their writings, seem to think it be Almighty God, and accordingly give those *eulogia* [words in praise] to it that seem proper unto God.

Aristotle and his follower Averroes[170] took it to be an intelligence material [and] impassable,[171] always in act and actual understanding, not Almighty God, but yet

[167] That is, called agent (or active) intellect or mind or mental nature or spirit of God. For an explanation of the idea of *intellectus agens*, see the Editor's Introduction, pp. xliii–xlv.

[168] All MSS: both by.

[169] As in *Primitive Origination*, 322, MH here probably has the Middle Platonists (Neo-Platonists) in mind, specifically Plotinus (204–70 CE), *Enneads*, tr. A. H. Armstrong (Cambridge, MA: Harvard University Press, 1966–8), I.1.8.

[170] Aristotle, *De Anima*, 3.4–5, tr. J. A. Smith, in *The Complete Works of Aristotle*, ed. Jonathan Barnes (Princeton: Princeton University Press, 1884), vol. 1, 682–4. His most influential "followers" include (1) Alexander of Aphrodisias (third century CE); see *Alexander of Aphrodisias: On Aristotle on the Soul*, tr. Victor Caston (London: Duckworth, 2012). Alexander also wrote a treatise of his own on the same topic: *Alexander of Aphrodisias: On the Soul*, tr. Victor Caston (London: Bloomsbury, 2014). (2) Themistius (middle of fourth century CE) was the most important Greek commentator on Aristotle's *De Anima*; see *Themistius, On Aristotle On the Soul*, tr. Robert B. Dodd (London: Bloomsbury, 2014). (3) Avicenna (980–1037), Persian philosopher and physician; see F. Rahman, *Avicenna's Psychology: An English Translation of Kitab al-najat, Book II, Chapter VI* (Westport, CT: Hyperion Press, 1952). (4) Averroes (1126–98), *Averroes (Ibn Rushd) of Cordoba. Long Commentary on the De Anima of Aristotle*, ed. and tr. Richard C. Taylor and Thérèse-Anne Druart (New Haven: Yale University Press, 2009). For a very helpful discussion of these and other related authors, see Herbert A. Davidson, *Alfarabi, Avicenna, and Averroes on Intellect* (New York: Oxford University Press, 1992).

[171] Ed: an unmoved and unmovable substance that moves everything else.

eternal and but one; that it was always *in actu intelligens* [actual understanding or intelligence (as against potential/*in potential*)] in itself, and by a perfect intuition it had the knowledge of all truths both speculative and moral; that it did and doth communicate itself unto all mankind by a kind of contingency[172] to their souls, though the perfection or imperfection of that *intellectus*, which was wrote by it, was according to the due or undue temperament of their souls and exercise of their faculties; that it was not the informing form of any [particular] man, but the assisting form of all men,[173] exciting and giving actual intellection by irradiation of the sensible species in the phantasy,[174] and drawing into the soul those common notions and sentiments wherein mankind do generally agree; that the human intellective faculty could not more actually use the power of intellection without the irradiation and activity of this *intellectus agens*, than the eye can see without the light; that therefore it is *unum et multa* [one and many], one essentially and, as I may say, personally, but many in respect of application, as the light is but one, that yet is participated [in] by several eyes and one seeing what another sees not.

[52v, 100] And therefore, though every man had his own particular and individual unintermitted contingency and application of this *intellectus agens* to acquire the act or habit of understanding, or that which they call the *intellectus adeptus* [acquired intellect],[175] yet [it] were as impossible for the human soul to actually understand

[172] OED: close connection or affinity of nature; close relationship.

[173] MH's use of "informing form vs assisting form" is somewhat uncommon language for this centuries-long debate. It is not clear what he has in mind. Followers of Averroes typically held that the *intellectus agens* was the form of a human being (indeed, of all human beings), but it was not that which made a particular human being (Socrates, for example) who or what he is. Nevertheless, the *intellectus agens* plays an indispensable role in enabling Socrates to be what he essentially is (namely, a rational being). In this sense, perhaps, it can be said that the *intellectus agens* is Socrates' "assisting form." Alternatively, Albert the Great, in the thirteenth century, held that the soul is not the proper form of the body, but rather is the perfection of the body, which can exist apart from the thing it perfects, just as a sailor can exist apart from the ship. (Richard Dales, *The Problem of the Rational Soul in the Thirteenth* Century (Leiden: Brill, 1995), 91). This usage can be found in work of MH's near contemporary, the German natural philosopher, Daniel Sennert. In *Epitome naturalis scientiae* (Wittenberg, 1618) Sennert wrote that "no sane philosopher denies that the rational soul is the form of a human being," but one might regard it as "an assisting form" joined to the body as a sailor is to a ship (VIII.1, p. 513). More specifically with respect to the intellect, Arab commentators (drawing on Alexander) sometimes spoke of the active intellect that penetrates the passive or material intellect of a human being as "acquired intellect" which comes "from without" and "aids the [human] intellect," establishing "the *habitus* [for thought] within the material intellect" (Davidson, *Alfarabi, Avicenna, and Averroes*, 11–12).

[174] MH uses this terms to refer to a primitive faculty (shared with human beings) of forming sensible images but not capable of grasping universals. See note 15 and Editor's Introduction, pp. xliii–xliv, xlvi.

[175] This term was variously used by Arab, Jewish, and later Christian writers in this tradition. On most views it is the disposition of the human intellect to think and reason with intelligible thoughts acquired from without, and so the active exercise of knowledge acquired, as when a grammarian parses a sentence. In some, Al-Kindi and Maimonides, for example, the acquired intellect is the culmination of the development of the human intellect. See Davidson, *Alfarabi, Avicenna, and Averroes*, 11–12, 196, 201–3, 216 and Deborah L. Black, "Psychology: Soul and Intellect," in Peter Adamson and Richard Taylor (eds), *Cambridge Companion to Arabic Philosophy* (Cambridge: Cambridge University Press, 2005), 317–18.

without the pertingency[176] and act of the *intellectus agens* than for †a† man to see without light, or for any matter to move itself without being first moved.

Indeed, without it man would have a more eminent sentient perception than the brutes, because a more noble animal, but still without the interposition of the *intellectus agens* it would be but a sentient perception resting in particular[s]; but as to any motion of universals or argumentation [or] definition, and those acts that are properly of the understanding, he would be different without it,[177] and his knowledge would go no farther than imagination or phantasy.

In short therefore according to those men's learning the *intellectus agens* did these offices in relation to mankind:

1. It wrought up their imaginative or sensible species to be *species intelligibiles* [intelligible forms].[178]
2. It did actually excite and actuate intellection of those *species intelligibiles* and those operations that were consequential upon them as definition, division, argumentation, etc.
3. It did communicate to the human understanding *lumen intellectual* [intellectual light].
4. It did communicate also to the human intellect [many][179] of those first principles both speculative and moral [53r, 101] which they call eternal truths.
5. By being one and the same active principle of intellection unto all men, it did communicate those truths to all men, especially those moral principles which we call the laws of nature, whereby it comes to pass that all human understandings had as it were one common doctor or master and thereby concentered in the same common notions both speculative and moral.

That which was comprehensible in the doctrine of the philosophers touching the *intellectus agens*[180] seems not to be the supposition of a common illuminative principle assisting to the intellective nature of men [and] extrinsical to the human soul, as I shall hereafter show, but [rather] principally this: that they denied an active intellective principle intrinsical to the human [soul] but [recognized] the highest perceptive faculty of the human soul [as] intrinsical and essential to it—[which was] not [mere phantasy but][181] more elevated and advanced than phantasy of brutes—and

176 OED: close connection.

177 Ed: without the assistance of the active intellect a human being would not be able to acquire universals, entertain definitions, participate in argumentation, or engage in any proper acts of understanding.

178 Intelligible species are mental representations graspable by thought ("thinkables") of sensible objects that enable the intellect to think about that which is presented to the senses ("sensibles"). See Leen Spruit, "*Species Intelligibilis*": *From Perception to Knowledge*, 2 vols (Leiden: E. J. Brill, 1994).

179 H: intellect to many.

180 Ed: that which we can distill from this doctrine (i.e., MH is summarizing but not endorsing the doctrine at this point.)

181 All MSS: only than phantasy but.

therefore that in effect a man was but a kind of sentient animal and that his soul was mortal as well as the soul of brutes, only his soul and especially the perceptive faculty thereof, [that is] the phantasy, was of such a make it might hold communion with the *intellectus agens* whereby as by an intrinsical assisting form he was enabled to acquire and appropriate to itself the intellective acts and habits.[182]

And though the great master[183] only speaks of the *intellectus agens* as a common universal principle of intellection in the human nature and speaks obscurely touching that which he calls *possibilis* or *materialis intellectus*,[184] leaving it uncertain whether it be not individuated in every man and so multiplied according to the numbers of men; yet some of his commentators make the *intellectus* [53v, 102] *possibilis* of the same extension and universality as the *intellectus agens*, so that, [as] the latter is but one in all men immaterial, eternal, and unindividuated, so is the former, and of this opinion is Averroes in his commentary of the third [book of Aristotle's] *De Anima*, though as to the unity of the *intellectus possibilis* he seems doubtful in his book *De Beatitudine Animae*.[185]

The learned of latter ages therefore much dissented from the opinion of Aristotle in some things.[186]

First, therefore they asserted the immortality of the human soul and that every man had his individual soul, and that every individual human soul had intrinsically and essentially the faculty of intellect and was essentially and intrinsically intellective. And that the agent and passible intellect were not merely foreign or extrinsical beings but were ^intrinsical^[187] to every individual human soul and they were but several modes of the exertions of intellection in each particular human soul therefore called *intellectus agens* because it did *per modum activi principii* [by way of an active principle] illuminate the phantasms, made them *species intelligibilis*, and united them to that other part of the human intellect which received them and therefore was *per modum principii passivi ad instar materiae* [by means of a passive principle

[182] MSS agree on the text of this paragraph, but it is difficult to make grammatical sense of it as it stands. It appears that MH is saying that the Aristotelian/Averroist doctrine rejected the view that an active intellective principle is intrinsic to the human soul and held, rather, that the only intrinsic faculty was the perceptive faculty ("phantasy"), akin to that of lower animals, except that human perception was of a kind that it could receive the intellective activity of the agent intellect.

[183] Ed: Aristotle.

[184] These are technical terms in a complex discussion extending over centuries. The Latin may be translated literally as "potential or material intellect." Alexander of Aphrodesias coined the term "material intellect" to refer to Aristotle's "potential intellect." Note: "material" does not mean "having to do with matter" in the modern sense, but rather it means "passive and capable of receiving certain properties."

[185] *On the Happiness of the Soul*, attributed to Averroes, was influential in the Renaissance and early modern period. Recently, scholars have argued that it is not a genuine work of Averroes and does not offer an accurate statement of his views. See *La béatitude de l'âme Averroès: éditions, traductions annotées, études doctrinales et historiques d'un traité d' "Averroès,"* ed. and tr. Marc Geoffroy and Carlos Steel (Paris: J. Vrin, 2001).

[186] MH may have in mind Christian thinkers like Albert the Great (1200–80), William of Auvergne (1180/90–1249), Roger Bacon (1214/20–90), and especially Aquinas (1225–74). See note 199.

[187] H: extrinsecal.

like matter]. And so the whole business of intellection was forged and framed as it were within the shape of the human soul by its own intrinsic and essential power and ability without the immediate agency of a foreign extrinsic agent or passible intellect.

And this was thus settled about 400 years since especially in the council[s] of [Vienne][188] and Lateran[189]and hath still obtained against the opinion of some few dissenters [for] the whole history of this matter. See in Selden *De Jure* [*Naturali et*] *Gentium* L.1. cap. [9].[190] [54r, 103] But why the true settling of this point touching the intellective soul of man should wholly exterminate the supposition of some common universal principle concurring towards the †perfecting† of the human intellection I do not see, for they may both stand together as in what follows may seem reasonable.

I do not take here upon me to say that this which I express by the ancient name of *intellectus agens* to be immediately the divine power of Almighty God as some of the Platonists [held],[191] or a created intelligence *destined* to the assistance of the intellective human nature as Aristotle, Themistius, Avicen[na], and Averroes [held]. I shall rather take it to be [the] settled and stable and common emanation from the divine power, wisdom, and goodness which is diffused through the whole universe and communicates itself to everything according to the rise and exigence of its nature established by the God of nature and particularly to the intellective soul of man *per modum lucis seu luminis intellectualis* [by means of light or intellectual illumination].

And therefore under that relation it may not be altogether improper with the ancients to call it *intellectus agens* or rather *divinum lumen intellectual* [divine intellectual light]. So that as in the act of seeing, there is first an intrinsic, sentient, visive power which it exerciseth by the organ of the eye, secondly [a] sensible visible object of that power, and thirdly an external light that illuminates the object and joins itself to that internal light that is in the soul and organ; so in the act of intellection, there is first an intrinsic, essential, individuated, active principle, namely the human soul, which hath radically in itself an active power to exert its act of intellection by that [54v, 104] faculty of understanding which is as the eye of the soul and a kind of

[188] All MSS: Vienna [Vienne was a town in southern France in which the Council of Vienne met in 1311–12.]

[189] In 1277 (nearly 400 years before MH was writing), Étienne Tempier, Bishop of Paris, condemned 219 philosophical and theological theses, among them doctrines associated with Averroist views on the soul and powers of intellect. Although this condemnation was not an act of a full church council, but only the Bishop's act (possibly invited by the Pope), it had great, albeit contested, significance among medieval philosophers and theologians in the fourteenth and fifteenth centuries. The Council of Vienne declared heretical the thesis that "the rational or intellectual soul is not of itself and essentially the form of the human body." The Fifth Lateran Council (1512–17) reiterated the Council of Vienne's condemnation, challenging directly Averroist doctrines of the soul which had attracted renewed interest in the late fifteenth century, especially in Italy.

[190] All MSS: 2.

[191] MH may have in mind Roger Marston (d.1303), John Pecham (1230–92), and Roger Bacon (1214/20–90). See note 199.

internal, intrinsic, luminous, and active power, secondly the intellectual object or *species intelligibilis*, whether it be simple or complexed, and thirdly this *lumen divinum intellectuale* which unites the object to the faculty and joins itself to that internal intellectual light which the father of lights hath radicated[192] in the human soul.

And the reasons that move me to think [thus], they are these which follow.

1. It bears a great analogy with other things in nature: the true, great, active principles that [appear][193] visible in nature next to the intellective power of man are those of heat and light, the former the great producer of vegetable life, the latter having a great concern in the noblest of the external senses namely the sight.

And all those several vital and sentient beings have an active principle of their own appropriate to their kinds and individuals according to their several specifical natures which we usually call their forms thus the vegetables of several kinds have their internal and essential active forms resembling fire and heat whereby they move themselves in their growth and vegetation and whereby they are determined within their several species. Animals also have their several luminous souls and certain intrinsic lights as I may call them, whereby they exercise their own faculties as sight and others, and likewise that internal light of imagination or phantasy which they exercise about the objects of their senses, especially in their luminous faculty of sight.

And yet though all vegetables have that internal principle of fire and heat, and all sentients [have] their [55r, 105] intrinsic and appropriate [principles] not only heat but light, whereby as from an inward principle they exert those vital acts of nutrition and sustentation, the glorious God hath placed a common principle in this inferior world, namely the sun endued both with heat and light, which joins itself with the vital fire of vegetables and the sensual light of animals and promotes and advanceth thereby the operations of both.

It is true the common principle of light and heat would not be effective for the production of life in vegetables unless there were that internal appropriate heat or fire lodged in vegetables or in their seminal principles that are scattered abroad on this lower world, nor would there be vision of phantasy by the bare light of the sun without that intrinsic, specifical light that is in the sentient nature their souls, spirits, and organs. But on the other side, without this common influence of the solar heat and light, those internal powers of fire and light in vegetables and animals would be inactive and quickly finally expire, and therefore as the returning sun gives a kind of additional fire to that specifical fire that is in the souls of vegetables and animals and calls it out in act, so the light of the sun puts the light in the animals into act and discovers the visible object to the soul through the eye and optic nerve, which are as it were the perspective glass of the soul.

192 OED: rooted, deep-seated, firmly established.

193 All MSS: appears.

And therefore it seems highly analogical in the intellective world that, although there be an intrinsic, essential, intellective light in the soul yet there should be such an universal, common, settled, intellective light rendered under the name of the *intellectus agens* that should aid and assist it as the external and common light of the sun aids and assists the luminous power of the sentient faculty and organ to discern the object. [55v, 106] And this is that resemblance that the ancients made, that in the intellective process of man the phantasy hath itself in relation thereunto as the object the human intellect hath itself as the visive organ and faculty and the *intellectus agens per modum luminis* [active intellect by means of light].[194]

2. It hath been always until the last four hundred years the constant opinion of the learned in all ages that there was some such common intellective influence that united itself to the human soul *per modum assistentis* [by way of assisting], generally called by the philosophers *intellectus agens*. The philosophers, as well Platonists as Peripatetics,[195] generally agree in the main in this supposition, though they sometimes differ in the nature of it, some taking it to be the immediate but common influence of Almighty God, others as Aristotle and his ancient commentators Alexander, Themistius, Averroes, Avicen[na], and others taking it to be an eternal intellection in the human soul.

But herein they went too far, that they attributed the whole intellective power unto this *intellectus agens*, stripping the human soul not only of immortality, but of all intellective power further than it was formed in them by the activity of this *intellectus agens*, and so making the highest faculty appropriate and intrinsic to the soul [to be] but only [the] phantasy or imagination which subministered objects to the separate *intellectus agens* to work upon and thereby to create as it were an *intellectus adeptus* or intellectual habits and acts in the human soul; so that they made the human intellect to be but an imaginative power, as that of brutes, only of a [56r, 107] nobler coassistance and activity and capable to be touched with or united to the *intellectus agens* which the souls of imaginative power of brutes were not.

If we come to the Jewish doctrine, though they hold unquestionably the immortality of the human soul and that it had an intrinsical active intellective power and therein differed from many of the philosophers, yet they generally [assert][196] the *intellectus agens* as a kind of modical[197] intelligence between Almighty God and the intellective soul of man. Their doctrine is at large set forth [in] Selden *De Jure [Naturali et] Gentium* L.1.c. 9 insomuch that Maimonides in *ductore dubitant* parte 2. cap: 36 determines that even *veritas et quidditas prophetie nihil aliud est quam*

[194] This sentence is obscure and may be corrupted. We might read it as follows: The analogy that the ancients drew to the intellective process in human beings is that, as the faculty of vision is enabled to see objects by the sun's light, so the human intellect is illuminated by the light of the active intellect.

[195] Ed: followers of Aristotle, [196] All MSS: are generally asserted.

[197] All MSS; MH's meaning is uncertain; perhaps he means "mediating."

influentia a deo optimo maximo mediante intellectu agente super facultatem rationalem primo deinde super facultatem influens.[198]

And as to the doctrine of Christian philosophers it was generally held by the most learned that the *intellectus agens* was an intelligence that assisted the human understanding and was not part of it, as [held by] Robert Bishop of Lincoln, William Bishop of Paris, Adam de Marisco, and Roger Bacon[199] whose opinions are large set down *apud Selden ubi supra.*[200] But from that time downward indeed hitherto the Roman councils and Schoolmen have rejected that opinion of the *intellectus agens* at least as a modical intelligence. But yet they have all agreed in the substitution of that which is equivalent unto all mankind as *gratia communis auxilia communia* [common grace, common aids] and the like.

[56v, 108] 3. [Another reason for accepting the thesis regarding the *intellectus agens* is] the common consent[201] of mankind in all ages and places in common speculative principles as [for example,] the existence of Almighty God, the making of all things by his power and wisdom, the immortality of the human soul, [and] the future state of rewards and punishments, and also in divers moral principles of *iustum [et] decorum* [the just and proper/decent], in benignity, mercy, gratitude, and the like, do fairly intimate at the least some one common tutor or instructor of the human understanding and will, namely, the common one *intellectus agens* or something equivalent thereunto; for these and the like are not always learned by every ratiocination or human instruction, but seem to be taught by one common invisible teacher and therefore [are] called not improperly *communes notiones et anticipationes* [common notions and preconceptions].[202]

I know this is no conclusive evidence of any such common principle; for the wise God may so order the frame of the individual souls of men that they may have and

[198] The quotation reads: "the truth and the essence of prophecy is nothing other than a outflowing [or emanation] from Almighty God, first upon the rational faculty, then upon the imaginative faculty, through the mediation of the agent intellect." Maimonides, *The Guide for the Perplexed*, Part II, ch. 36, ed. Leo Strauss, tr. Shlomo Pines (Chicago: University of Chicago Press, 1963), 369.

[199] MH mentions four thirteenth-century Christian critics of Averroist understanding of the agent intellect: (1) William of Auvergne (1180/90–1249), Bishop of Paris, in *The Soul*, tr. Roland J. Teske (Milwaukee: Marquette University Press, 2000) and *The Universe of Creatures*, tr. Roland J. Teske (Milwaukee: Marquette University Press, 1998), part 2. (2) Robert Grosseteste (*c.*1170–1253), Bishop of Lincoln, best known in philosophical circles for his commentary on Aristotle's *Posterior Analytics.* (3) Adam de Marisco (Marsh) (*c.*1200–59), Franciscan monk and theologian, who collaborated with Grosseteste and taught Roger Bacon. (4) Roger Bacon (1214/20–90), *Distinctio tertia de anima* (esp. chapter 3, "On the Unity and Plurality of the Soul") in *Opera Hactenus Inedita Rogeri Baconi*, ed. Robert Steele and Ferdinand M. Delorme (Oxford: Clarendon Press, 1909–41), vol. iv. Among Christian philosophers, Aquinas's critique was the most influential. See Aquinas, *A Commentary on Aristotle's "De Anima,"* tr. Bob Pasnau (New Haven: Yale University Press, 1999), 364–70; and *Aquinas Against the Averroists: On There Being Only One Intellect*, tr. Ralph McInerny (West Lafayette: Purdue University Press, 1993).

[200] Ed: whose opinions are set down at length, according to Selden as mentioned above (*De jure naturali*, I.9, pp. 113–15).

[201] Ed: agreement or concurrence.

[202] See note 85.

really have these common impressions characterized in their very souls, and we see that the strings of two or more several instruments may be winded up to an unison without any common sound to make them such; as the brutes of several species though they have not one common *sensus agens* [active sense] to tutor them yet agree in their several specifical instincts as exactly as if animated by one common soul. Birds of the same species make their nests alike, feed on the same appropriate food, [and] have their voices and calls appropriate to their several kinds.

Yet this I may say, considering the variety of and [57r, 109] indeterminate motions of the human soul, which consists of a multitude of complicated wheels more than the souls of animals, [and] considering the high variety of intellective operations and intelligible objects, the great liberty and indeterminations of the human will, and the various relations, consents, and oppositions that are between the superior and inferior faculties in man, the supposition of one such common active principle as it were naturally destined to be the assisting form of the human soul in its intellective and volitive[203] operations seems a more ready and facile solution of that congruity and consonancy among men in common notions both speculative and moral [than any denial of it].

And therefore those that have laid aside the supposition of a common *intellectus agens* as unnecessary in the operations of the human soul [regard it] as snares, and others do not take them[selves] to determine it an heresy to be of that opinion and therefore lead a favourable eye to Aristotle and those others which cannot be fairly denied to have maintained it.

4. It seems to me there are several passages in the sacred scriptures that seem strangely to import that there is a certain common emanation from the glorious God destined as a common intellectual light, assistant and auxiliary unto, and influencing upon, the intellective souls of all men.

And although the name of *intellectus agens* is not to be found in that holy book, nay it may be it is not so fit a name to express what is there intended by it, and those philosophers which called it an intelligence or angel possibly were too adventurous in that appellation, much more [so were] they that tell us with Averroes of what rank or order it is, namely, *ultima intelligentia in specie intelligentiarum* [the highest intelligence among all intelligences]; yet there are names by which the same thing in substance is described and named, namely, that emanation of a common [57v, 110] spirit or grace from the glorious God communicating an intellectual light, activity, and common direction to all the children of men, to guide them in the important notions and sentiments of the understanding and moral principles of their will.

And therefore, as the sun is appointed by the glorious God as a common principle of life and light to the vegetable and sensible provinces of this lower world, so this

[203] Ed: having to do with volition.

common efflux, irradiation, spirit, or intellectual light, or by any what other name I shall call it, is terminated by the glorious God to preside and assist in the intellectual province of the human nature.

The texts of holy scripture that seem to express this thing are these that follow.

Gen. 6:3: "And the Lord said my spirit shall not always strive with man for that also he is flesh." By the spirit of God I do not think †is† meant the essential spirit or third person in the sacred Trinity, but this common illuminative[204] emanation or influx upon the human soul, as that spirit of God that moved upon the face of the waters (Gen. 1:2) is not to be intended of the essential spirit of God, but that common efflux or emanation from God which in subordination to him did form, cherish, and quicken the common mass of confused matter.

Job 28:19:[205] When Job had made a strict scrutiny [whence][206] cometh wisdom and [what][207] is the way of understanding, he tells in our ears that when God created the world, then he saw it and prepared it and tells us what the direction of this prepared understanding was, that in relation to man. And to man he said behold, the fear of the Lord, that is wisdom, and to depart from [58r, 111] evil is understanding, which is that common notion of piety and righteousness that this prepared wisdom teacheth the children of men; and therefore the Lord owneth the putting of wisdom or understanding into the heart of man to be his †own† work. Job 38:36: "who hath put wisdom into the inward parts and who hath given understanding to the heart."

Ps. 4:6: "Lift up the light of thy countenance upon us" and Ps. [36:9]: "In thy light shall we see light," which, though some expound to be meant of the light of reason and discerning in us, seems rather to be meant that common emanative intellectual light communicated indifferently to all mankind.

Prov. 8:2:[208] Solomon describes both the essential wisdom of God (vers. 20, etc.). But vers. 31 seems to describe this emanation [as] wisdom or understanding resulting in the habitable parts of the earth and delighting with the sons of men.

John 1:9: "This was that true light that lighteneth every man that cometh into the world." As he was the true God, so he had in him an essential incommunicable light, but as the sun besides that essential light that is in it derives[209] a common emanative light to the universe whereof all that are capable of light participate, so the Son of God had not only that essential light which was radically in him, rather *lux* than *lumen*,[210] [but also][211] there emanates from him effectively that light that enlighteneth—*lumen*, or the effect of *lux*. And although our blessed Lord in relation to his office of mediator styles himself oftentimes light, and the kingdom of the gospel, †called† the gospel of light and the kingdom of light in a most restrained sense, namely, in relation to the

[204] BL and Harley insert: persuasive. [205] See the entire chapter, Job 28.
[206] All MSS: where whence. [207] All MSS: where.
[208] The whole chapter would serve MH's purpose.
[209] OED: convey down a course or through a channel.
[210] Ed: source of light rather than reflected light. [211] All MSS: So.

church of Christ and believers, yet this place must [58v, 112] needs be intended of that common and as I may call it natural illumination of all mankind: "Every man that cometh into the world."

And although those passages Job 35:11 ("which teacheth us more than the beasts of the field") and [Isa. 28:26][212] ("for his God doth instruct him to discretion and doth teach him") may be applicable to the original endowment of the soul of man with the intellective power, yet it may be true also of this divine common intellectual influence which the ancients called *intellectus agens*.

Now concerning the energy of this divine emanation and influence which the ancients called *intellectus agens* it may be of two kinds: extraordinary or singular and common or ordinary.

[a] The extraordinary or singular is varied according to the divine *placitum* [decree or will] both in its kinds and in its degrees and I choose to speak not of that divine illumination in matters spiritual but in matters of civil government; thus [Bezaleel and Aholiab][213] had from this influence a special skill and dexterity for the forming of the vessels and ornaments of the tabernacle (Ex. 36:2). It is said God put wisdom into their hearts to perform these works and [in] 1 Sam. 10:9, when Saul was anointed king, it is said God gave him another heart, namely, an influence fitted for the politic regiment of the kingdom wherein he was perfected, and afterwards (1 Sam. 16:14) this spirit of wisdom and regiment departed from him. And possibly of this kind was the prophetical spirit that fell even upon evil men whereby they were enabled to prophecy and predict future events, as Balaam (Num. 24) [and] Caiaphas (John 11:49).[214] Yea and I do not know whether the strange predictions of Nostradamus[215] and others that pretend merely astrology for their conduct may not be by some irradiation of [59r, 113] their appropriate understanding, for surely the events they foretell could never be within the verge of ordinary or more natural causes. And yet I think these men [were] not endued with the same spirit which enlightens the holy prophets of God.

[b] The ordinary energy of this divine influence upon the human understanding is of two kinds, viz., illuminative and objective.

[212] All MSS: Esa 28:16. [213] H and BL: Beualiel and Hohal.

[214] According to the story in Numbers 22–24, Balak, king of Moab, sent Balaam to curse Israel. Balaam tried to do so three times, but each time God allowed only blessings of Israel to come out of his mouth. In chapter 24, Balaam has a vision of Israel's flourishing. John 11:45–52 tells the story of the religious authorities who sought to stem the growing influence of Jesus among the people. The Roman-appointed high priest, Caiaphas 'prophesied' [King James Bible] that Jesus would be sacrificed, saying that "it is expedient for us, that one man should die for the people."

[215] Nostradamus (1503–66), an astrologist, was believed to have predicted several major world events in a collection of prophesies (*Proféties*, Lyon, 1555). See Nostradamus, *The Prophecies*, tr. Richard Sieburth (New York: Penguin Books, 2012).

[i] The illuminative energy is as the light of the sun to the eye; for as the visive faculty is intrinsical and essential to the sensitive soul and yet without that external light it cannot, or at least not so well, exert it in perception of the object, but by *it, it* exerciseth its act of vision. Yet the eye may close itself and shut out that external light; so though the soul hath an intellective faculty intrinsical and essential to it, yet without the help of this intellective light it is not able so well to govern and discern and exercise itself upon the objects in the phantasy. And therefore if it shut it out, it is in darkness, and the more it takes it into itself the greater and better is its intellective perception, and that not only about divine objects but even [about][216] natural or moral objects. And therefore Isa. 28:28–29: The very skill of the husbandman in threshing of corn with the flail and the raine[217] with a rod is carried up to the divine influence, not only in relation to the animal faculty of the soul, but also as it seems in relation to this common intellective light.[218] "This also cometh forth from the Lord who is wonderful in counsel and excellent in working."

[ii] The objective energy of this intellective light seems to be not only by illumination, but also by bringing or conveying into the human intellects those *communes notiones* of intellective and moral truth, which seem to be lodged in this universal common influence, and are derived and communicated into the human understanding. [59v, 114] And of this kind are those common sentiments of [the] existence of a God, the perfection of his wisdom, power and goodness, and those moral sentiments of piety, moderation, gratitude, and reverence to him, and those common moral instructions of justice, beneficence, sobriety, and all other heads of the natural righteousness or law.

And that which seems to persuade that this comes †from†[219] one common, effective principle is [1] that generally the common nature of all mankind concur and agree in these common sentiments and inclination[s], unless they are strangely corrupted with ill customs and education; 2 that although these sentiments be highly reasonable as might be easily evidenced by a strict examination of particulars, yet the assent and submission unto them seems to be antecedent to the exercise of any long rational process and to be common anticipations that do *antevertere exercitium actualis ratiocinationis* [precede the exercise of ratiocination], and therefore are rather brought into the mind by a certain common instruction, as the rudiments of arts are taught the scholar as it were by rote before he exactly finds them out by the reasons of the things themselves.

And this common objective residence of common principles in this *intellectus agens* as they call it, and the secret delivery of them over to the mind might render the opinion of Plato the more explicable who thought all knowledge to be but a kind of

216 All MSS: without.

217 So read all MSS. It is not clear what word MH has in mind.

218 Isaiah 28:27 reads: "For the fitches [dill] are not threshed with a threshing instrument, neither is a cart wheel turned about upon the cumin; but the fitches are beaten out with a staff, and the cumin with a rod."

219 H and BL: from such.

reminiscence,[220] and may also explicate the reason given by some of the ancients how it comes to pass that at least in these common notions all men agree, how one man understands the reasons [60r, 115] given by another, and the scholar learns from his master, namely, because there is one common maker and instructor, both this *intellectus agens* or as I call it the common efflux from Almighty God to all human understandings.

And thus we have one instance of the publication of moral law namely by this divine efflux. But because this opinion touching a common intellect is under some prejudice in these latter ages, I rest not here but proceed farther.

9

Concerning the Second Kind of Publication of the Moral or Natural Law by the Institution or Engraving of it by the Finger of God in the Crasis of the Human Soul

I now proceed to a second method whereby we may [explain that][221] this natural law of piety and righteousness is implanted in the human soul.

Whether the human soul be a spiritual substance immediately created and infused by Almighty God into every man or whether the soul being at first created by God in the first man with a power to traduce[222] the like to his posterity by generation is a great question and not fit here to be discussed.[223] But be it the one way or the other, [the question of] the conveying of moral principles into the human soul and inscribing them there may be sufficiently salved[224] only because the former opinion

[220] In Plato's *Meno*, Socrates tries to show that some knowledge, especially knowledge of virtue, is innate, recovered by a kind of recollection (*anamnesis*). See Plato, *Meno*, tr. G. M. A. Grube (Indianapolis: Hackett Publishing Company, 1976).

[221] All MSS: contain. [222] OED: pass on.

[223] MH discusses this matter at length in *The Primitive Origination of Mankind*.

[224] OED: solved, answered.

touching the origination of the human soul hath generally obtained, namely, that it is an immaterial spiritual substance created by God and [60v, 116] endowed with understanding and will and immediately united to the body after it hath obtained a complete organical structure.

I shall take this to be the method for my application of my second supposition touching the second method of publication of the natural law. And in order to [offer] my explication thereof I shall suppose as followeth.

[1] That this immaterial substance is not a bare simple substance as it comes out of the hands of the glorious God but hath superadded to it by the divine wisdom and will certain powers and faculties which it is enabled actually to exercise in that state of conjunction and union to which it is designed and ordered namely those specifical powers of understanding and will.

[2] That besides these powers or faculties there are superadded to this incorporeal substance, certain strictures or imprinted characters of some of those important principles of truth and moral righteousness that are suitable and necessary to the well-being of the reasonable nature and certain secret tendencies or propensions to close with moral good and to fly from and avoid the contrary.

[3] That these principles and tendencies are not produced *per modum discursus* or *ratiocinationis* [by way of discourse or reasoning] nor is this tendency or propension distinctly elicited from the connatural implanted principles, but they are indistinctly bound up together, and though when they are settled and fixed there they are principles upon and by which the soul actively moves itself, yet in their primitive impression the soul is passive in them and receives [them] from the hand and will of his maker. And in this [61r, 117] respect these principles and propensions of the reasonable nature [bear][225] a great analogy with the instincts of the animal nature, though in some other respects they much differ as shall be further shown.

And as we may every day observe in the instincts of the animal yea and vegetable nature, though the first rudiments or foundations thereof are laid in the first foundation of every individual, yet they are in the beginning and infancy of their being not altogether so complete and conspicuous, at least in all their operations. But as the animal nature expands and dilates itself, as they are more conspicuous and operative, so it is with the exertions of these instincts of the rational nature. Though they are radicated in the basis of the reasonable soul, yet inasmuch as the exertions—not only of the very faculties of the reasonable soul, but [of] all these connatural principles and tendencies—are in the state of union with the body [and] depend much upon the state of the body and the degrees of its maturation and ripeness, they are therefore suspended in their operations in a perfect infancy and weak and confused in youth; and as the soul and reasonable faculties thereof do involve and

[225] All MSS: bears.

expand themselves together with the maturation of the body in their exertions and the gradual perfection of their operations, so do these moral primitive and implanted principles and tendencies of the reasonable soul.

And hence it is that as on the one hand the tender usage of these primitive instincts of the reasonable soul and †the† diligent attendance to them and exercise of them by man as he grows in years, they are highly improved and rendered of singular use and advantage to the perfecting of human nature—as he that diligently trades upon any stock improves and increases it—so on the other hand [61v, 118] these tender and delicate primordial instincts in the reasonable soul like the tender bud of some curious flower may be weakened, checked, and discouraged by giving the reins to the sensual appetite by idleness [and] by ill *customs and education,* especially in the time of youth when the actings of these principles and instincts are but green and feeble.

For these instincts of the reasonable soul, though they are a kind of bias bending and including the reasonable nature to moral goodness, and being duly attended unto and cherished are of great force to conform the life of man to the true state and standard of a rational life, yet they are not wholly irresistible by contrary motions, habits, or customs, neither are they wholly exempted from the dominion of the will and are daily opposed by the impetuousness and violence of the sensual appetite, from whence ariseth that continual strife in the human nature of the spirit and flesh—or the reasonable and sensual appetite, the law of the members and the law of the mind—so fully described by the apostle (Rom. 7:18 *et sequentibus* [and following]). And as that faculty of empire in the soul takes part with the one law or the other, [so that][226] individual act that is controverted between those two laws fall[s] to the sensual or rational appetite.

And by this means of these engrafted and engraved principles and instincts, the soul of man that is sent to manage that little but important province of the human nature is not only fitted with those faculties of understanding and will for the due management of its regiment of that province, but is also furnished with a necessary stock of connatural principles and propensions as a viaticum[227] and common instructions for the management of its government, which it may improve and trade upon with singular advantage to itself and that [62r, 119] province whereunto it is designed, namely, the human nature.

This therefore is the sum of my supposition; it remains that I should give my reasons that induce me thereunto. And the things inducing me to be fully of this persuasion are principally these.

1. The doctrine of the holy scriptures [does][228] seem either clearly to assert or at least strongly to imply it. The holy text tells us that man was created after the image of

[226] All MSS: in that. [227] OED: provisions for a journey. [228] All MSS: do.

God (Gen. 1:[27][229]). It is true there are some excellences of the divine nature that it is impossible that any created being can partake [of], as namely eternity, infinitude of power, wisdom, goodness, and existence, and a plentitude of all imaginable perfection. And there are some perfections in Almighty God that possibly the glorious angels are capable [of] in respect of their frame and make, [which][230] the human nature consisting partly of a corporeal nature—nay possibly the very incorporeal soul of man—is not capable of in respect of the degree or allay[231] of that rank of being wherein it is constituted; yet when he finds Almighty God himself affirm that man was made according to the image of God, as much of that resemblance that was possibly communicable to a being of that frame and constitution, such are those that of all hands ^attributed^ to man, viz. the incorporeity of the soul, the power of intellection, and the freedom and dominion of the will. But besides all this there is *in* Almighty God a primitive essential rectitude and perfection of his nature antecedent to any act of his will, which, though it be impossible that the [62v, 120] sovereign God can be subject to any law properly so called, yet is by a kind of analogy called the law of his nature, the essential natural perfection of his being, such as are his holiness, purity, goodness, beneficence, mercy, justice, righteousness, and truth.

And therefore although the consistence of the human nature or human soul is not capable of an adequate measure *of such perfections, yet it is certain he was capable of them in some measure,* viz. a natural propension of the soul of man to those moral excellencies. And that in this also man was made after the image of God appears by that often mentioned text Eph. 4:24. "Put ye on the new man which after God is created in righteousness and true holiness."

And as to the objection that may be offered that it is true that man in his first formation might have [had] this antecedent intrinsic natural rectitude, but it was lost by the fall and consequently is not to be supposed in the state of man fallen, I answer [that] it is plain that Adam had a twofold perfection, one that was redundant and superadded to his nature wherein he was created, as greatness of knowledge, glory and splendour of his body, immortality, and very high participations of moral righteousness beyond the bare rate of this natural constitution; these he lost by his fall. But that natural and essential perfection of his soul he lost not, neither for himself nor for his posterity, and this was that created image of God in which he was constituted. And this essential image was not lost by the fall, for it is apparent [that] Almighty God took notice of this image of his in man as a thing continuing after the fall of man and thereupon made it the great reason of his renewed [63r, 121] law against murder (Gen. 9:6), which is also affirmed by the apostle to be continuing (1. Cor. 11:7). So that man lost not by his fall that image of God that was concreated with him, but that which was superadded and adventitious by the further beneficence of his maker.

[229] All MSS: Gen. 1:17. [230] All MSS: with. [231] OED: quality.

And certainly if we shall grant that first constitution of the soul of man had those impressed notices and inclinations of natural righteousness, we have no reason to think that the souls of men that are created by God should be created by him in a less degree of natural perfection. It is neither agreeable to the excellence of the divine operation nor the uniformity of his working in the things he creates for the sin of the first man to make the new created souls of men below the essential dignity of the first man's soul. The souls of all men therefore are pieces of the making of the great God all whose works are done in perfection; they are pieces that come out of the same mind, stamped with the image and superscription of the great God of heaven, the monarch of heaven and Earth; and [if][232] the first man's soul had the strictures of the divine image drawn upon him in its first creation concreated with him, so hath the soul of every child of Adam.

Again that singular dispute of the Apostle (Rom. [1:]2) proves this natural law to be something [that is not acquired][233] by ratiocination and discourse (though that be also mentioned); [for] what else can be meant by "the doing †by† nature the things contained in the law" (ver. 14) [and] "The law written in their hearts" (ver. 15)? [And] what else can be reasonably meant by "that law of the mind in opposition to the law of the members"? 'Tis true that these texts may be evaded by saying the law acquired by ratiocination or discursive act of reason may answer these expressions, but let any man but be [63v, 122] impartial to himself, his own reading will tell him the scope of the Apostle is touching a law connatural and not acquired, though as I shall show this natural law is communicated by the light of reason also, as I shall further show in the next chapter.

2. The opinion of most of the ancient philosophers subscribes also to this [thesis of the] connatural or concreated rudiments of natural law in the soul.

Aristotle [in][234] some places will have the soul to be merely *rasa tabula* [blank slate] in its first production, yet elsewhere is forced to acknowledge that the principles of moral justice are connatural to the mind or soul or nature (Rhet.1.cap.14) *est enim aliquid quod tanto intellectu augurantur omnes natura communi justum et injustum etiam se nulla societas inter ipsos intecesserit nulla pactio.*[235]

Again the general doctrine of the Stoical philosophers agreed that there were planted and engraven in the mind certain principles of morality antecedent to any discursive act which they call *prolepses* and *anticipationes* [and] *communes notitiae*;[236] and therefore their great precept was *sequere naturam* [follow nature]. *Vide congesta sententiarum stoicarum Lipsii manuductio* (lib.2.cap.11).[237]

[232] All MSS: of. [233] All MSS: that which is acquired. [234] All MSS: that in.

[235] See note 73. MH's quotation here differs slightly from that quoted earlier on p. 29. The correct citation is *Rhetoric* I.13 (1373b).

[236] See note 85.

[237] MH refers to the influential *Manuductionis ad Stoicam philosophiam libri tres* (*Guide to Stoic Philosophy*) (1604) by Lipsius (1547–1606).

Again the Pythagoreans, whereof Hierocles upon the verse of Pythagoras: *A Deo ostensa multi non vident quod communibus notitiis non recto utantur quas ad sui cognitionum opifex ipse in nasei voluit.*[238]

The Platonists were so far transported with this persuasion that they taught that all the knowledge men had was nothing else but *reminiscentia*[239] of those principles and conclusion both of truth and morality that lay primitively in the soul before its union to the body.

[64r, 123] And therefore we are not without such a suffrage as may give attestation to our supposition and vindicate it from pure novelty or invention.

I shall now subjoin therefore those reasons that make this supposition highly probable if not fully evident.

1. Therefore, a great convenience and suitableness to the good of human nature ariseth by this supposition. And although it is *not convincing* in things disputed to say it is very suitable and convenient it should be so and the contrary imports much inconvenience, yet certainly even this argument is not without its use and contributes a great force and strength to small evidences or reasons that contribute to the proof of this supposition. For since the manner of the divine working is in all things full of incomparable wisdom, we have reason *in dubiis* [in doubtful circumstances] to suppose that to be done by him which is most consonant to the best wisdom and most conducing to the end [proportionable][240] to the thing about which the question is.

It is certain the wise God who always works to a most wise end and by excellent means both in his creation of mankind and their preservation had an end to the glory of his own name and to communicate his goodness to them in a way and by a means proportionable and suitable to the condition and state of human nature.

It is also most clear that the continuing of mankind in that state of moral goodness and righteousness conformable to the divine will as is most pleasing and acceptable to God, most suitable to his will and most conducible to his honour, [and] most for the beauty, dignity, and happiness of the human nature. It is also most certain that there could not be a more [64v, 124] suitable means to this end, suitable and congruous to the human nature, than to exercise the immediate regency of the

[238] Hierocles was a fifth-century CE Greek philosopher; see "Commentary of Hierocles the Philosopher on the Pythagorean Verses," in *Hierocles of Alexandria*, tr. Hermann S. Schibli (Oxford: Oxford University Press, 2002). The passage quoted above, embedded in its larger context, is translated by Schibli as follows: "This would be the turning around, motivated by sacred philosophy, to the things revealed by god, which the majority do not see because they do not correctly use the common conceptions that the creator has implanted in the rational class for recognition of himself." ("Commentary," XXV, 12, p. 306). Earlier in the same work (XII, 6, p. 242), Hierocles writes, "Man's nature is a bearer of all sorts of twisted opinions whenever it does not correctly follow common conceptions." As Schibli notes, Hierocles here uses the Stoic technical term, "common conceptions," in a general way to refer to notions accessible to all human beings insofar as their thought is not distorted by passion.

[239] Ed: recollection from memory; see note 220.

[240] All MSS: propoundable.

human nature by the uniting of the intellectual and free principle of the soul to the human nature whereby he might become a noble and free agent.

But now [for God] to send out a soul destitute of all kind of principles and inclinations that might conduce to the due management of this province, without any manner of previous instructions to direct or incline it or to be assisting to it to the due management of his regiment, which is full of difficulties and must meet with great opposition from the sensual appetite with the lusts and passions of the sensitive nature, if with humility and submission we may speak, it seems not so suitable to that excellent wisdom and goodness which we observe in all his other works.

But on the other side to suppose that this little particle of divine fire being thus designed to this difficult province should have concreated with it certain instructions that might to this her subordinate regiment as sovereign use to give their legates and viceroys in their deputation;[241] that it should be supplied with propensions and instincts that might balance at least the contrary motions of the sensual appetite if it be not wanting to itself and its own dignity and perfecture;[242] that it should have a stock of principles delivered to it to trade upon in the province and regiment whereunto it is designed, a viaticum for its end and talent to exercise for the honour of his Lord and the good of human nature—[all this] seems to be very agreeable to the divine goodness, justice, and benignity, and to the common good and benefit of the human nature, and for the high improvement of this noble particle the soul of man.

[65r, 125] And if any man shall say that I may as well conclude that this soul of man should be endued with such a condition of strength and perfection and immutability that it should infallibly attain his end—namely, the conforming of every particular man to the constant obedience and conformity to the divine will—and because this is best therefore to conclude it is so, I answer that, first, the argument is not propounded as necessary or concludent,[243] but only so far as it concurs with other probabilities or presumptions. [Second] that the supposition which is made in the objection is not compatible to the condition of mankind which at his best estate is mutable and in the hands of his own will according to the rank and state of his being, but our supposition stands with the rank and state of his nature. [Third] the supposition in the objection is crossed by the common appearances in the human state which is evidently subject to mutation as appears by daily experiences, but our supposition is no way crossed but favoured by the common appearance in human nature.

2. But to come a little nearer in the contemplation of the works of nature, we may generally observe that the natures of the next inferior rank have somewhat of resemblance and analogy to that which is the next superior nature: minerals seem to have somewhat in them analogical to a life of vegetation, vegetables besides that which is proper to their nature, viz. vegetation, have some kind of dark resemblance of the life of

[241] So read all MSS; it is not obvious how to make grammatical sense of this clause.
[242] OED: perfection, maturity. [243] OED: conclusive.

sense, a kind of election or choice in their food and aversation to that which is inconvenient or unsuitable to them. Again animals have not only a life of sense but that life partakes of a kind of shadow analogy of the reasonable nature, their phantasy carrying some analogy to intellection and discursive reason, their appetite some analogy to the will, their spontaneity some analogy to liberty. [65v, 126] Again we find nothing in the inferior nature which is not contained more perfectly in the superior: the life of vegetation is more perfect in the animal nature, and the life of sense or the animal life more perfect in the reasonable nature, so that by a due observation of the inferior nature somewhat is to be gathered which is in the superior and universe.

Now we may observe in the vegetable and sensible nature and especially in the latter, besides those distinct faculties which reside in them, there are certain regent instincts which are distinct from their other faculties, neither gathered from any choice, election, or imitation, which are of as great moment to direct and govern them in their animal life as their other faculties are. And those instincts are various both in relation to the several conveniences of the animal life and likewise variously appropriate to every species, and most singularly suitable both to the common exigence of their animal nature and to the specifical exigencies and conveniences of every species.

Every animal according to his kind hath instincts different from other kinds, yet common to his whole kind in the nature of their food, in the acquest of it, in the kind of his defence against injuries, in the seasons of their act of generation, in the care and order of their young as might be instanced in [a] multitude of particulars which I have elsewhere done. And touching these instincts of animals there are these things very observable.

[a] That they learn not these instincts by imitation or instruction, but they bring them with them into the world and regularly and uniformly exercise them upon the occasions given to them.

[b] Though every animal hath its common sense, phantasy, memory, and appetite, yet those instincts are [66r, 127] distinct from these faculties, neither are they the production of *these* faculties primarily but antecedent to any operation of them. And though it be true that these faculties are the means or instruments whereby these instincts are put into execution, yet the instincts themselves are antecedent and previous to the exercise of these faculties and do determine them to their operations consonant to these instances. And this appears beyond all contradiction by this that the instincts peculiar to the several species are regular and consonant to themselves and to their whole kind, neither the particular instincts of one species acted by another—this appears in every species of animals, especially in the various artificial nidifications[244] of the several species of birds and in infinite more instances.

[244] OED: pertaining to nest building.

[c] That therefore these instincts are purely natural, woven into the texture[245] of the several natures of animals, to be the regent principles of their communications and the determiners of the indifferency and multiplicity and variety of their other faculties, namely, the phantasy and the appetite which by these instincts are harnessed and determined to the operations suitable to their natures.

[d] That these instincts are highly necessary to the direction and order of their animal life without which they would be irregular and confused and the operation of their specifical nature very much disordered. And these connatural instincts are so excellently contrived and ordered in their constitution and are so firmly bound to their several natures and kinds that it contains them within that beauty, harmony, convenience, and order that is most suitable to their several natures.

[e] That therefore this designation and determination [66v, 128] of the several instincts of animals in their several ranks and ranges is the work and institution of the most wise lord and institutor of nature.

And the scope of this labour is to show but these things. 1. That there may be something in the nature of spontaneous agents that may be distinct from their faculties of phantasy and appetite, namely, this that I call the animal instinct. And 2. that these instincts do add a great complement and degree of perfection to the animal nature.

And certainly of what importance and use the animal instinct is to the animal life, of the same importance and use [is] this rational instinct, which I call the engrafted law of nature, to the rational life; and as in the animal life those animal instincts have their antecedence to any act of the phantasy or appetite, so this internal radical natural law hath a kind of inclination or tendency to their proper ends and in the proper motions antecedently to the actual exercise of the ratiocination or will. And that since we see in the nature of the inferior animals such an excellent and useful principle settled in their nature and adding so great an advantage and perfection and order to the animal life, so we have just reason to suppose that the most wise God would not deny to his nobler creature called man that privilege by a †rational†[246] instinct which he communicates to the animal nature by the implanted and connatural animal instincts. And inasmuch as in the animal nature we see a kind of adumbration of the powers and faculties of the reasonable nature—we see a phantasy carrying a shadow and [67r, 129] resemblance of our intellective ^faculty, a sensitive memory carrying a shadow and resemblance of our intellective memory, and^ an appetite carrying a shadow and resemblance of the will—so the animal instinct of the animal nature carries a resemblance of the rational instinct in man which we call the law of nature. And by the prospect of the animal nature which contains a dark image of the reasonable nature in its degree as we see in the former, the animal instinct, so we may collect that there is in the latter that more noble and rational instinct which

[245] See note 91. [246] H: natural.

we call the law of nature; and, as those animal instincts though in their first plantation are radical and connatural not *owing* their being barely to the phantasy are yet in process of time perfected and improved by use and experience in the animal nature, so this radical rational instinct in the rational nature is perfected and improved by the exercise of the rational or intellective faculty upon it.

The difference nevertheless between these stands in these particulars.

[a] That the animal instincts are of an inferior allay and nature and so specifically differ from the rational instincts in man: the one being only a power of the animal soul, the other [a] habit or force of the intellectual soul; the one a sensitive or animal instinct, the other a rational and moral instinct.

[b] That the animal instincts are only exercised about sensible objects, [while] the rational instinct is exercised or terminated in intellectual and moral objects.

[c] That the animal instincts are implanted only [67v, 130] to the well-being and convenience of an animal life or a life of sense, but the rational instincts are in order and direction to a life of morality and reason.

[d] That these animal instincts are only analogically and improperly laws because given to beings that are not endued with understanding and will *and so not capable of a law*, but the rational instincts have in them *formalem rationem legis* [formal aspects of law], being implanted in a creature endued with understanding and will and therefore capable of a law.

[e] That the animal instincts are in their kind necessary and do for the most part absolutely determine the phantasy and appetite to act conformable to them, but this rational instinct is still under the dominion of the will in man, and though it incline, persuade, and move the will to a conformity to it, it doth not necessitate or compel it, for the will is essentially free and renders a man free to act or not; and therefore †his conformity thereunto is truly and formally obedience and† his disconformity thereunto is sin, the consequence whereof is guilt.

[f] [Consequently, the][247] actings of the animal instincts in brutes and animals do appear more distinct from the seminal actings of the phantasy and the spontaneous actings of the rational instincts of men, partly because the former do in a manner determine the actings of the †sensitive† appetite and are more regnant and uncontrollable by it, whereas the rational instincts of the human nature, though they persuade and incline the will, yet are under the dominion of it, and partly because the animal nature is an automaton consisting of fewer wheels and motions; and therefore [68r, 131] the distinction of their motions are more perceptible and distinguishable. But the human nature is like an automaton consisting of various[248] wheels and motions, and therefore the distinct application of every motion to its several principles is more difficult and perplexed.

[247] All MSS: The consequently. [248] Ed: many and varied.

And thus far of my second reason.

3. My third reason is this: because upon a due consideration of the inclinations and dispositions and actings of the children of men, we ^shall^ find that thousands of men in the world [never][249] know the connection[s] of consequence, nor how to form them, nor so much as ever thought of any discursive reason inducing them to believe or assent unto the principle[s] or laws of nature, yet firmly [assent][250] to them, and upon no other reason but by their mind is persuaded of the truth or fitness of what they thus believe or assent to. It is demonstrable by the strongest evidence of reason that there is a God and that he is to be worshipped, feared, and obeyed; that perjury, breach of faith, injuring an innocent person, cruelty, ingratitude, and doing to another what a man would not have done to him, are not only against natural reason in themselves but inconvenient and prejudicial to the safety of that man that declares it; yet the generality of mankind that never knew how to frame a consequence or never practised [rational demonstration][251] doth carry a secret detestation and abhorrence against atheism and contempt of God and the sins above mentioned. Nay, let any man whatsoever whether he be learned or unlearned he will find his heart rise against these [68v, 132] and the like villainies, even *primo intuit* [immediately intuitively] without drawing of consequences or framing any process of internal discourse concerning it, all which are many evidences to me that antecedently to the exercise of the discursive act of reason, there is a primitive, connatural, implanted principle in the soul that anteverts[252] the reason and by the vigour of this connatural law riseth against it.

And that as in the animal instinct there are secret, primitive, and connatural sympathies with some things and antipathies against other things even *primo intuitu*, so by the primitive energy of this instinct of the law of nature implanted in the soul there are some things of that moral beauty and conformableness to [it] that it secretly and *per saltum* [at once] closeth with and embraceth, so on the other side there are certain moral obliquities that this natural law connaturally planted in the soul doth *quasi per saltum* [as if all at once] and antecedently *ad aliquem processum rationale* [to any rational process] doth abhor and detest and fly from or disapprove.

And if any man shall object that the approbation or disapprobation may be by reason of some common tradition that men in process of time have taken in and not by connaturality of these acts to this internal principle, I answer, first, that in many instances of this nature it will be hard to suppose any tradition of moral good and evil hath come to all mankind in all ages, and yet this general sympathy and antipathy in morals of this kind hath been always found. [Second, we can] admit that [there is something] which[253] gives some occasion of that approbation and aversation, yet it

[249] All MSS: that never. [250] All MSS: assenting.
[251] Harley: it; H and BL: practised doth. [252] OED: anticipates.
[253] All MSS: that that which.

is reasonable to think that *oportet* [69r, 133] *esse alquid intus* [necessarily there is something else within] that so universally accepts of these traditions and [is] close with it. But [third] and principally, though it be true that traditions commonly received have a great prevalence[254] in forming the judgment, yet this may be observed: that the motions of acceptation and aversation that arise from the inward disposition and rational instinct are more violent, intense, and vigorous than those that arise simply upon the account of instruction or bare tradition, though this hath a great effect upon the judgment; yet the acts especially of aversation that arise upon judgment are more moderate, but those that arise from nature are more earnest and *become* abominations; and this a man may easily discover that observes himself. And therefore though tradition oftentimes fixeth men in certain schemes and distinctions of religion and from thence ariseth great aversation and animosity against a contrary religion and the practisers and professors thereof, yet that abomination ariseth from an internal principle, namely, that the opposite religion is false and untrue and so contrary to the natural sentiment that all falsity in religion is contrary to the will of God and prejudicial to the good and felicity of mankind. Tradition indeed forms the determination of religion in such a man, but it is the common substratum of religion itself that gives the abomination of that which a man thinks to be false religion and consequently no religion.

Now to give an account of the particular heads of those connatural sentiments or this engrafted instinct of the reasonable nature which I call natural law, all I shall say is this: that it seems [69v, 134] to contain in it the rudiments and first draughts of all moral righteousness, though indistinctly and as it were in the ore,[255] though the rudiments of some seem more distinct and involved than others. And it seems also to me that those great and important *notitiae communes* of the existence of a God and of the immortality of the soul have some impression in the soul antecedent to the discursive faculty, and [that] these common notions, propensions, and inclinations to the laws we call natural are like the first strokes in limning,[256] which are fitted up and perfected by exercise of the reasoning faculty in a man, or like those *idee formatrices*[257] in the seeds of plants or animals which are wrapped up together confusedly and indistinctly at first and do gradually expand and involve themselves into more distinctness and regularity by the adventitious supplies of nourishment.

And thus much concerning that which is the first[258] kind or degree of the natural publication of the natural law, namely the first and primitive engraving thereof by the finger of God in the texture and frame of the soul of man, namely certain

[254] Ed: influence. [255] Ed: in its unrefined state.

[256] Ed: the image seems to be that of the initial outline of an illumination on a manuscript page.

[257] Ed: formative germs.

[258] This seems to overlook the discussion of the "first method of publication" in Chapter 8; again in Chapter 10 MH refers in the text to the next method as "second" although in the chapter title he refers to it as "third." It is possible that Chapter 8 was added later to fill out MH's discussion.

common notices and propensions of the soul towards the moral rectitude of the human nature.

[70r, 135]

10

Touching the Third and Fourth Methods of the Natural Publication of the Natural Law; Namely of the Intellective Faculty and the Natural Conscience and the Actings thereof in the Reasonable Nature

In the former chapter I have given an account of my thoughts touching that natural impress or engraving of the law of nature in the reasonable soul, wherein I have said that though the rudiments of the law of nature are thus imprinted upon the soul in these common [notions][259] of moral good and evil inclinations suitable to it, yet these first rudiments of natural law have not their full distinctions and delineations and are tender and delicate twigs and as on the one [hand] they are capable of improvement so [on the other hand] they are subject to be greatly checked and discouraged by evil, education, customs, or neglect of exercise.

And therefore Almighty God, who is wonderful in counsel and excellent in working, and all his works [are] full of incomparable wisdom and goodness, as a farther subsidiary, supply and discovery and advancement of the energy of the natural law in man, hath added certain other powers to the human nature, namely, the reasonable and reasoning faculty of the understanding, and that which we call conscience in man and the actings of [both][260] which I shall handle briefly in this chapter and first concerning the former, namely reason.

[259] All MSS: notices. [260] All MSS: it both.

By reason, I understand that rule or method of the intellective faculty whereby it discerns between truth and falsehood and good and evil whether moral or natural; so that, as the understanding [70v, 136] is the eye of the soul, so this reasoning power is like the visive faculty by which it sees and perceives and judgeth concerning truth and falsehood [and] good and evil.

Now in relation to this law of nature or moral law in man this reasoning power hath two principal subjects or objects upon which it is exercised.

First this reasoning faculty is exercised upon those connatural and engraven principles of truth and morality that as before I have shown are lodged in the mind by the finger of God, and upon these principles this reasoning faculty trades as upon a natural stock or talent[261] committed to its charge and employment; wherein reason seems to act principally these parts. First, it separates and distinguisheth them. These principles as I said before lie in the soul together and reason considers those *communes notitiae* that are speculative [and] those that are practical, and reduceth them into several series, ranks, and orders. [Second] reason compares, examines, and illustrates these principles themselves; considers what may be thought of farther to prove or evidence the reasonableness, truth, and regularity of them; brings together what it can find to give a suffrage[262] to them or †what† may be opposed against them; and when upon the whole account it finds them reasonable, witnessed to by many other suffrages, convenient and suitable to the well-being of the human nature, and answering the dignity and worth thereof, it approves and pronounceth them good, true, just, and reasonable. Third, reason thereupon proceeds to a further act, namely, it draws consequences and conclusions from these natural principles and by several connections and ^chains^ of consequences draws out those several [71r, 137] particular ramifications of the more general notion into more special or determinate species of action, applies them to particular actions and their several circumstances, compares one part of these natural laws with another, and considers them under various comparisons one with another in their several values and preferences, when in particular actions they come in competition one with another, and so husbands these general and natural principles that it draws [them] into the various extents and ramifications of [them],[263] as the veins or arteries or nerves in the body branch themselves out into several branches till at last they divide themselves into those innate and capillary veins, arteries, and nerves that we see in the body.

Secondly, the reasoning faculty exerciseth itself upon those external or intelligible objects that are abroad in the world. Now these intelligible objects are of various sorts, some are purely speculative [and] some [are] practical, among all these [are those] that we call moral good or moral evil of moral actions.

261 Ed: accumulated wealth. 262 OED: support, assistance.
263 All MSS: draws it into the various extents and ramifications of it.

Now as in things that are purely speculative wherein the inquiry is whether they are or are not, there is an objective truth or falsehood in the thing supposed antecedent to the power or faculty that judgeth them such. And as in the objects of sense, the object is really of this or that figure or colour antecedent to the act of my sight and my common sense whereby I perceive and judge it to be such, so in all moral actions of human nature or that can be supposed to be done by a rational nature that are not purely indifferent there is an intrinsic eternal good or evil antecedent to any perception or judgment that can be made of them. And they are not made such by the perception or judging [71v, 138] faculty; [for moral][264] good or evil, though they be in the concrete but modes or qualities of actions, yet they have an eternal, abstract nature. That which is morally good is eternally and intrinsically so, and that which is morally evil is eternally and intrinsically evil, and therefore the matter of this natural law is in that which is eternally or intrinsically good or evil, though there were no law superadded commanding or prohibiting it.

The first act therefore of the reasoning power of man which in reference to morals as to speculative is the perception of this objective good or evil that is in moral actions.

And the reason of this active perceptibility in reason, as of objects speculative so of objects moral, is that admirable, wise disposal of Almighty God that hath fitted and accommodated and adapted the faculties in the human nature their several objects. The eye discerns colour, figure, [and] distance in objects, for the visive faculty is fitted to those kinds of objects, but †it† discerns not sounds, because the visive power is not accommodated or fitted to an object of that nature; and upon the same reason, the ear discerns sounds, but not colour or figure. The touch discerns the roughness, smoothness, and other tangible qualities of bodies but perceives not the sweetness, bitterness, or sourness of them, because the receptivity of the power of touch is accommodated to the former but not to the latter.

Now as the divine goodness hath accommodated the animal nature with these faculties of sense that is convenient for the perception of all things and objects necessary for the animal life by fitting and [72r, 139] accommodating and adapting those powers to their objects, so it hath accommodated the reasonable nature with this perceptive faculty or power of reason whereby it is fitted for the perception of all such things or objects that are necessary for a rational life, namely, by adapting and fitting that faculty to objects of that congruity to the reasonable life.

And because the moral good or evil of the moral actions of the reasonable nature are of great importance to the conduct of a rational nature to his perfection and end, the same divine goodness hath instituted a certain aptitude and cognition between the reasoning faculty in man and those ^moral^[265] objects whereby it discerns and tastes them.

[264] All MSS: for though moral. [265] H: natural.

And this perception of reason touching common notions and common rules of moral actions is of two kinds.

1. That which though it may be rationally evinced to be morally good or evil, yet it is done *quasi per saltum* [nearly all at once] and by a kind of intuition *tota simul* [all at the same time]. For there are many truths, which though they be evincible by a rational process and rightly concluded from undeniable premises, that yet have that clear evidence in them that reason by a compendious method takes them up and assents to them, and the transition between the antecedent and consequent is so swift and evident that, though it be to itself a consequent or conclusion, yet it is assented to without any such way of procedure, as that God is to be honoured [or] that we are not to hurt him that is innocent.

And the truth is [that] those *communes notitiae* and *anticipationes* which we have before mentioned as the first stock and object of our reason saves the rational faculty [72v, 140] much labour in forming a process of probation for the eliciting of many *dictamina juris naturalis* [dictates of natural law], because [they are] compendiously there exhibited and presented.

2. The second and ordinary method of concluding the moral good or evil of actions and consequently eliciting the law of nature is that which we call ratiocination, discourse, or the rational process, namely, by inferring of one thing upon another by drawing conclusions from evident premises [and] by comparing one thing with another; and by this method of rational process there is no one precept of the law of nature but it is discovered to be highly reasonable, nor no one thing that the laws of nature prohibited but will appear highly reasonable to be avoided, and all the precepts of the law of nature by the just rule of reason and a rational process be discovered and reduced into a system of morals. For instance, if the thing in question were whether drunkenness were consonant to the law of nature or not, reason easily considers that[266] in the excellency of the human nature [lies][267] that which gives him power to judge what is fit for him, that a decent and handsome deportment is agreeable to the dignity of human nature, that health and integrity of body is greatly convenient for the human nature. Therefore that which deprives or suspends the use of all these must needs be against the convenience and beauty and good of human nature and consequently against the law of nature. Then it considers what drunkenness doth in reference to all those and rightly frames its conclusion that drunkenness is against the law of nature. But [on this matter][268] and the like we have in the [fifth] chapter given some account.[269]

The next act of †the† reasoning power after it hath [73r, 141] discovered the *capita legis naturalis* [is that] it proceeds to improve them to their uttermost ramifications, it applies them to the several and particular circumstances,[270] and as it did improve

[266] H: it is reason[able] that. [267] H: it is. [268] All MSS: as this.
[269] See p. 43. [270] All MSS add: factions.

the stock of congenite and connatural instincts, so it improves and advanceth this acquired knowledge gained upon the perception of these objects of moral good and evil.

And this [is] the [third][271] instance or degree of the natural publication of this law of nature, namely the reasoning act of the intellective faculty.

The [fourth] instance of the natural publication of the law of nature is that of conscience.

Now this faculty of conscience doth not really add anything to the discovery of the matter of the laws of nature more than what is discovered by those two before mentioned, namely congenite and engrafted principles and that of reason. But that which it seems to superadd in this point of natural publication is this, namely, there is in the natural conscience a secret powerful persuasion that these that are thus discovered by the two former instances are really and truly the law of God.

Concerning man and his actions and that he is under an obligation unto Almighty God to observe and conform to [the laws of God][272] and [who] thereupon institutes a comparison between the particular act that is done or to be [done] and thereupon makes the conclusion that this is well or ill done or this ought to be done or not to be done, [the following may be said]:

First the natural implanted law and the dictate of right reason frames a general proposition that this or that action is against that rule of moral rectitude which is evident to both those lights. [73v, 142] Then the conscience adds: surely this rule of rectitude that I find *thus* inscribed in my very soul and dictated to me by the clearest reason is the law of the sovereign of my being, and that these are but so many manifestations of this law *and* of his will to have it observed. And from hence ariseth the obligation of conscience and those judicial acts that it exerciseth over the man of condemnation and absolution, by comparing the particular actions of his life with this law by such syllogism as this: It is the law and will of God that no man should do to another what he would not have another do to him. But in such an act I did that which I would not have had done to me. And therefore I have offended the law of Almighty God, have incurred his displeasure, and am obnoxious to[273] his judgment.

There is nothing that can primarily oblige the conscience but the law of Almighty God, therefore if the conscience find itself under an obligation by that which we call the law of nature it doth necessarily give its suffrage[274] that it is the law of God, *and consequently the natural law is not only published in its matter, but even under the true and formal nature of a law, and of a law of God.* And that there is this suffrage of the natural conscience to these *dictamina* as *the* law of God appears by the great energy of the natural conscience in relation to moral actions done or to be done, in

[271] MSS: second. The chapter title indicates it as the third. See note 258.

[272] All MSS: them. [273] OED: liable to the condemnation of.

[274] OED: approval or sanction; in this case: announced recognition.

the latter by a great and powerful direction, in the former by that sentence of approbation or condemnation pronounced and indeed executed by their conscience. It is that which the apostle observes (Rom. 2:15) which show[s] the law written in their hearts, their conscience also bearing witness, and their thoughts the meanwhile accusing or excusing one another.

And from this conviction of the conscience that this [74r, 143] natural law is the law of God, and from the sense of the conformity of the life to the law, arose the best hypothesis of happiness that the learned heathens [thought attainable][275] at least in this life, namely, tranquillity of mind, and on the other side that which really is and was ever thought the greatest hell of this life did and doth arise from [the conscience's conviction of] the violation of this natural law.

Juvenal [writes]:

Exemplo quodcumque malo committerit[,] ipsi
displicit authori[.] prima haec est ultio[,] quod se
Iudice nemo nocens absoluitur,[276]

Again:

Cur tamen hos tu
Evasisse putes[,] quos dira conscia facti
Mens habet attonitos et surdo verbere caedit
occultum quatiente animo tortore flagellum
poena autem vehemens et multo savior illis
Quas et [Caedicius][277] gravis invenit et Rhadamanthus
Nocte dieque suum gestare in pectore testem.[278]

And ^that^ this energy of the conscience ariseth from the sense of the offence of the great God upon the conviction that this natural law is really the law of God is evident upon these considerations. 1. That these *stimuli conscientiae* [goads of the conscience] have fastened upon those that know no other law of God than this of nature as generally [was true in] the heathen world. 2. That always the most importunate[279] and execrable torments of conscience have followed more upon the violation of the great *capita legis naturalis* as [for example] tyranny and murder more than upon the violation of positive laws, as being committed against the primitive law of God given

[275] All MSS: tho'.

[276] Ed: "A deed that sets a bad example never brings joy | to the doer. The first effect is this: no guilty party | is acquitted by his own conscience..." Juvenal, *The Satires*, ll.1–3, tr. Niall Rudd (Oxford: Oxford University Press, 1991), 112.

[277] All MSS: et sedit vis.

[278] Ed: "In any case, what makes you think | that they have got away, when the consciousness of their terrible crime | holds them in fear, flogging them raw with a soundless whip | and the mind is a torturer laying on an invisible lash? | It is, indeed a savage punishment, far more cruel | then any devised by the fiendish Caedicius or Rhadamanthus, | to carry within you, night and day, an accusing witness" (Satire 13, ll. 192–8; ibid., 117–18).

[279] OED: burdensome, grievous, grave.

to the human nature. 3. That these *laniatus conscientiae* [lacerations of conscience] have followed the violation of [74v, 144] these natural laws in those persons who by reason of their power and greatness or by reason of the secrecy of their offences were privileged from the fear of the tribunal of men; therefore certainly it must needs be the sense and conscience of the violation of the law of the supreme judge of heaven and earth whose justice, power, and omniscience are unavoidable that tortures the conscience of such offenders.

Conscience therefore hath its part in this publication of the law of nature to be the law of the glorious God.

And thus I have done with that natural subjection of the divine law of nature; and as that law concerns and obligeth the universal nature of mankind, so is the publication thereof as universal as the law itself [is] common to all mankind.

And though this publication be not such as that, with which the same law was republished from Sinai with the voice of thunder and of the trumpet of Almighty God; yet it is as real, though not so loud, a publication as the other, even by this still voice of nature, reason, and conscience. And God is in that voice.[280] †I now descend to that adventitious and providential publications of the law.†

11

Concerning those Other External or Adventitious Publications of the Law of Nature

I have before set down my thoughts touching the divine methods of the natural publication of this law of nature, which, though it were of itself a true, real, and sufficient publication thereof not only in regard of the matter of them but also of them *sub ratione legis divinae* [with the force of divine law] and of [75r, 145] that obligation that necessarily ensued thereupon obliging mankind to the obedience thereof; yet there did arise in mankind many things that did not only obscure the matter of these laws, *but* also the evidence of its obligation—such were the

[280] MH alludes to the story of Elijah (1 Kings 19:11–12) in which God appears to Elijah, not in the wind, earthquake, or fire, but in a still, small voice.

prevalence of the lusts of the sensual appetite, sloth and neglect of the improvement of the natural light, the prevalence of evil customs, and ill education, and many other impediments. Almighty God was pleased out of his abundant goodness and love to mankind to give out unto mankind several repetitions and restorations of this natural law and thereby to wipe off that rust that was contracted by mankind obscuring these laws of nature and those *false and corrupt glosses* and superstructions that evil men and evil customs had brought in, and at once to revive and discover the principal heads of the law of nature and to discover his will that mankind should obey and observe them.

We may observe four principal periods from the creation of the world unto this time, in every one of which the Lord was pleased to use this method. [A] From the creation of man to the general deluge. [B] From thence to the giving of the law from Sinai. [C] From thence unto the coming of Christ the Messiah. [D] From thence unto this age wherein we live.

[A] Touching the first of these whether Almighty God did give unto the first man any vocal or audible publication of the laws of nature as he did of that positive command touching the eating of the tree of the knowledge of good and evil we have no evidence to assure us, neither is it at all necessary to be supposed.

[75v, 146] For besides that original and natural impression of the rudiments of the laws of nature upon his soul common to the first man and all the rest of mankind, there was doubtless an extraordinary and supernatural irradiation of his understanding with a greater measure of divine light then ever happened to any of his posterity, Christ only excepted, and by virtue of this supernatural irradiation he had a more distinct and clear comprehension of this natural law than ever any mere man had, which was as effectual a discovery thereof as if he had had delivered unto him an exact system or pandect[281] in writing by God himself of all the laws of nature in their full extent and perfection.

And although by the fall of man this extraordinary irradiation left him and he stood simply in the state of his essential constitution, yet no man can reasonably suppose that in that moment he lost the remembrance of everything that he knew before by the virtue of that irradiation, but retained if not all yet a great part of those distinct discoveries which that extraordinary light that [had once lent][282] and afforded him. And this ^remembrance^ afforded him a more large and distinct prospect and knowledge of the natural law than could be acquired by the greatest industry of any of his posterity.

And therefore besides that natural publication of the law of nature above spoken †of† there were in that period between the creation of man and the flood these adventitious publications thereof:

[281] Ed: compendium of law akin to the Roman *Code of Civil Law*.
[282] All MSS: had now lent him once lent.

1. This tradition of this law of nature [was] delivered over by Adam to his descendants, and hence it was that early in the world the use and practice of sacrifices and other [76r, 147] religious worship was practised in that interval.

And this tradition had two notable means whereby it was propagated and conserved. [a] The long life of the primitive fathers whereby the tradition might be handed easily from one to another with the greater purity and certainty, for Noah the last of those ancient patriarchs was coexistent with those of his progenitors that were coexistent to Adam, so the tradition might be conveyed from Adam to Noah by the help of one single intervenient person. [b] Again it seems that in the line of Seth there was a stricter and more regular observance of this tradition than there was in the rest of the posterity of Adam, so that the family of Seth was segregated as a kind of peculiar[283] church of God for the conservation of these traditional oracles, though it seems that the greatest part of this line also degenerated into disorder and confusion, so that the tradition was in effect kept alive in the patriarchs and most of their descendants [but] swept away in the common deluge.

2. Besides this tradition of his natural law Almighty God in this interval raised up prophets and persons specially inspired that did inculcate this natural law to the men of the old world, as Seth, Enoch, and Noah, who were preachers of righteousness [2 Pet. 5] that is publishers of this natural law.

But for all these helps the generality of mankind corrupted their ways (Gen. 6:12) and the wickedness of man was great upon it and the whole earth was filled with violence (Gen. 6:11–12) which brought on that common judgment of the universal deluge.

[B] The second period from the flood unto the giving of the law at Mount Sinai, in which period there *were* [76v, 148] these means for the more distinct discoveries and propagation of the natural law:

1. The †evident†[284] delivery of those *septem precepta Noachidarum* [seven Noachide laws], which contained the principal heads of the natural law and by some signal way expressly notified to the children of Noah the heads whereof:

> [i] *de cultu extraneo* or against idolatry; [ii] *de maledictione nominis sanctissimi*; [iii] *de effusione sanguinis sive homicide*; [iv] *de turpitudine ex concubitu*; [v] *de furto et rapina*; [vi] *de judiciis seu regimine forensi et civili obedientia*; [vii] *de membro animalis viventis non comedendo.*[285]

[283] Ed: special or set aside. [284] H and BL: eminent.

[285] MH here cites the Noachide laws, the seven minimal duties which, according to the Rabbinic tradition (Babylonian Talmud, Sanhedrin 56–60), were given by God to "the sons of Noah" (i.e., all humanity). Rabbis derived them exegetically from divine commands addressed to Adam and Noah recorded in Genesis. The Noachide code includes prohibitions of (i) idolatry, (ii) blasphemy, (iii) bloodshed and murder, (iv) sexual immorality, and (v) theft; (vi) mandating the establishment of a judicial

Those with their several explications and extensions made up a kind of *corpus juris naturalis* [body of natural law] (*explicati de quibus vide apud Selden*).[286]

2. The tradition of the natural law with which Noah was well acquainted, and doubtless communicated it orally to his descendants and family, and their tradition had these two advantages also for its propagation and preservation, viz. [a] the long life of Noah and his sons, Shem himself being according to the Jewish chronology contemporary with Abraham. [b] The more strict and severe discipline in the line and family of Shem and Heber over what was to be found in the residue of the descendants from Noah. And yet we find that idolatrous worship notwithstanding this crept into the family of Heber (Joshua 24:2).[287]

[3] Therefore there ensued this further supply: God Almighty separated Abraham from his father's family, instituted him in a reformed worship, confirmed that worship by a solemn contract or covenant made with him, and sealed [it] by a solemn sign. And this reformation was by Abraham settled [77r, 149] in ^his^ family and traduced[288] over to his descendants Isaac, Jacob, and the twelve Patriarchs, but this was but a particular publication communicated immediately to the single family of Abraham.

But notwithstanding this single manifestation of the law of nature to Abraham and from him derived to his posterity by their stay in Egypt somewhat above 200 years they began to gather a corruption of their principles and manners and this leads into the third period.

[C] Therefore the next period was from the time of their migration out of Egypt till the coming of Christ the Messiah.

In the beginning of this period the principal heads of the law of nature were promulgated and published from Mount Sinai more explicitly than formerly in those ten words or commandments in that wonderful, terrible, and stupendous manner that never any law either before or since had the like promulgation.[289] And though Almighty God did about the same time give other laws as well judicial as ritual, yet they were not promulgated with the same circumstances of terror and majesty as those moral or natural laws were given or promulgated thereby designing great difference in the value and importance of this above the former.

institution, and (vii) prohibiting eating from a living animal. See Michael Berenbaum and Fred Skolnik (eds), *Encyclopedia Judaica*, 2nd edn (Detroit: Macmillan Reference USA, 2007), vol. 15, 284–7.

286 MH again directs attention to Selden's *De jure naturali*. MH quotes directly Selden's Latin tags and their order (Bk I, ch. 10, pp. 118–19). (Traditionally, the injunction to establish a judicial system is regarded as the seventh.)

287 Heber was the great-grandson of Shem, Noah's son. MH understands Joshua to refer to this lineage when he refers to "Teher and his sons Abraham and Nahor" in Joshua 24:2.

288 OED: passed on to offspring.

289 MH has the Biblical story of the giving of the law in Exodus 19–20 in mind.

First, those ten words were given with visible and sensible demonstration of the special presence, majesty, and glory of Almighty God affecting all the senses, the Mount Sinai trembled and shook, it burned with fire to the midst of heaven and the voice of thunder like a trumpet that sounded louder and louder and was heard to the uttermost confines of the camp of the Israelites. Second, the very laws of the Decalogue were [77v, 150] distinctly and articulately and vocally delivered in the voice of thunder, viz. none of the other ritual or judicial laws were thus audibly delivered to the people. Third, these laws [were written] by the finger of God in two tables of stone but the other laws were wrote in a book by Moses.

It is true that this promulgation of the Decalogue was primarily and especially intended for the children of Israel. But yet by the whole economy of Almighty God to that people, it seems evident that it was intended that *actus judicativus legis *naturalis** [right-judging or -determining act of the natural law] from Mount Sinai was *mediately* intended for the generality of mankind, though the *actus *preceptivus** [the preceptive, law-imposing act] was particularly applied to that people.

For [i] Egypt at that time and long before and after was the most famous country in the world for commerce and trade [and] for the reputation of wisdom, and thereby attracted the access[290] of most people. Again [ii] the Phoenicians that were conterminous to Canaan were the greatest traders in the world famous for their navigation and emission[291] of colonies. [iii] The passage of such a numerous body from Egypt into another country could not choose but be a thing of great note and discourse in all the adjacent parts of the world. [iv] The admirable miracles that ushered in this migration, the miraculousness of their passage through the red sea, and the miraculous defeat of the great army of the Egyptians in their pursuit could not but be publicly known and discoursed of in all Egypt and all the countries adjacent and amongst all that had commerce with them. Again [v] the very manner of the delivery of the law in the presence of above 600,000 men besides women and children at Sinai could not be concealed from the neighbour nations. [vi] [The same is true of] the admirable [78r, 151] miracles that attended their passage through the wilderness—manna, quails, water out of the rock, the prodigious judgments upon the contemners of this law, Corah and his company, the miraculous cure of those that were bitten with fiery serpents, the wonderful and miraculous victories and successes of Joshua upon Canaan, the flourishing condition of the kingdom under David and Solomon, that stupendous work of the temple for the rituals of that people, the situation of their dominion in *umbelico orbio* [the centre of the world], namely Palestine. These and many other circumstances could not choose but make the state of this people and all that concerned them especially their laws very observable and notable to the greatest part of the then inhabited world, and make men very inquisitive touching them and their laws, and by this means those *capita legis naturalis* contained especially in the

[290] OED: going or coming to or into a place.

[291] OED: sending forth.

Decalogue must needs at the second hand be intimated and published to the greatest part of mankind.

So that as I have formerly said this judicial state and people were by the divine providence set up as a glorious pillar in the middle of earth upon which he hanged the tables of the law and exposed them to the view of the greatest part of mankind.

This is that which Moses tells the people (Deut. 4:33–34). "Did ever people hear the voice of God speaking out of the midst of the fire as thou hast heard, and live, or hath God assayed to go and take to him a nation from the midst of another nation by temptations, by signs, and by wonders and by war and by a mighty [78v, 152] hand and by great terrors according to all that the Lord your God did for them in Egypt before their eyes and ours." "I have taught them statutes and judgments even as the Lord my God commanded me that ye should do so in the land whither ye go to possess it. Keep therefore and do them for this is the wisdom and the understanding in the sight of the nations which shall hear all these statutes and say surely this great nation is a wise and understanding people etc."[292] And though this be true even concerning their rituals and judicials, many of which were but explications of the Decalogue and conclusion[s] drawn from them, yet it was principally †and primarily† applied to the laws of the Decalogue which contain the explicit and principal heads of the laws of nature.

To this I might add the commentaries upon the law of nature by the writings of the prophets, which though immediately given to the people of Israel, yet these together with the whole body of the Old Testament was mediately derived to the gentiles, especially in that signal translation thereof into the Greek tongue under Ptolemyus Philadelphus, commonly called the translation of the Septuagint, whereby it became known to the generality of those that used the Greek tongue, which were the greatest part of the then civilized world.[293]

And thus much touching the third period.

[D] The fourth period is from Christ Jesus beginning of his ministry unto this day. I shall not spend not much time in this, for all the time of my life would be too little to give a full account of this publication of the law of nature in this period. [79r, 153] The sum thereof of all I shall say is this: that the doctrine of Christ Jesus commonly called the gospel doth give the most universal, perfect, effectual, [and] explicit publication and †explication† of the law of nature that ever was or can be given. I shall therefore set down those few observables concerning it.

1. This publication is universal not as the publication of the moral law intended to the Jews only but to every nation and every person in the world; the grace of God bringing salvation hath appeared unto all men.

[292] The second passage is actually taken from Deuteronomy 4:5.

[293] According to legend, the Greek King of Egypt, Ptolemy II, in the third century BCE, commissioned seventy Jewish scholars to translate the Hebrew Scriptures into koine Greek for use by Alexandrian Jews who were not fluent in Hebrew. The Torah was translated at that time and the remaining books of the Hebrew Bible were translated over the next few centuries.

2. It gives us the most clear discovery of those prime noetical[294] principles that are naturally necessary to be known by the children of men and which are the great principles of nature, as [for example] the existence and attributes of God, his providence, general and special, his will concerning the manner of his worship, his intentions touching the children of men and their everlasting state of happiness or misery, the means to attain the one and avoid the other, the immortality and value of the soul, the resurrection of the body, the last judgment; so that these principles or conclusions, which were more darkly, obscurely, and confusedly perceived by the light of nature, reason, or conscience, like the man newly cured of his blindness that saw men walking like trees, here are more particularly, distinctly and expressly delivered. [God][295] hath brought life and immortality to light by the gospel.

3. It gives us a full, perfect, distinct and adequate account of all the precepts of natural righteousness, both in relation to God, [to] ourselves, and [to] others; [it] vindicates them from these corrupt glosses and superstructions that either ill men or ill customs had added thereunto; [79v, 154] it gives them full latitude and extent carrying their obligations not [only][296] to external actions but to the very thoughts, intentions, and motions of the mind.

4. It discovers those to be duties of the law of nature which were never before thought of or at least little practised among many moralists of the gentiles, as [for example] humility and lowliness of mind—which by the mistake of heathen moralists was thought a kind of pusillanimity—self-denial and mortification of the passions and lusts of the sensual appetite—which many of the heathen moralists thought to be scarce agreeable to the law of self-preservation—abstinence from revenge, love and beneficence to enemies, and charity, contempt of the honours and wealth of the world, abstinence from vain glory and divers other eminent, advanced moral virtues, all which he showed not only to be counsels, but to come under the divine precepts of natural law.

5. It shows the original and ground of the obligation of these laws of nature carrying it up to the command and will of Almighty God *and Christ himself by authority of* himself, among his preceptive acts unto them: "But I say unto you, love your enemies. Do good to them that hate you" (Matt. 5:[44]).[297]

6. It shows the example of Christ himself as well living or commanding the duties of piety, morality, righteousness, and justice, exhibiting in and by himself a noble exemplar of all those duties that he required of others.

7. It gives the highest motives imaginable to urge mankind for the observance of the natural law: [a] by discovering the placability of Almighty God towards repenting and returning offenders; [b] by discovering that [80r, 155] clear means of appeasing and reconciling Almighty God to fallen and returning offenders by the sacrifice of Christ and thereby removing the great obstacle of repentance and obedience, namely,

[294] OED: purely intellectual. [295] All MSS: he.
[296] All MSS: out. [297] MH's quote better fits Luke 6:27.

the despair and despondence of reconciliation with God after offences committed; [c] by showing forth to the [light][298] the love of God to mankind, thereby obliging them to love and obey him by that incomparable instance of giving his own son to die for the sins of men to expiate their guilt and to procure their happiness; [d] by discovering to the [light] explicitly, clearly, and [distinctly the][299] state of everlasting rewards of obedience and the everlasting punishments of disobedience in that life.

8. It gives us the most full and clear and demonstrable evidence of the truth of the mission of Christ by the eternal God and the truth and reality of all that he taught that could possibly be desirable to convince the most inquisitive and scrupulous hearer as namely [a] the accomplishment in him of all those prophecies that were to be fulfilled in the Messiah; [b] His miraculous conception; [c] the powerful and convicting delivery of his doctrine; [d] the many miracles he performed to confirm and attest it; [e] his laying down his life in the witness and confirmation of it; [f] in that miracle of miracles his resurrection further to seal and obsignate[300] the truth of it; [g] in that admirable ^self-evidence^ and intrinsic testimony that his doctrine and every part give to itself, the purity and holiness and rectitude of it, that singular congruity that it did bear in every particular to the exactest reason of the human nature and to the perfecting and advancing of it to its due perfection and rectitude and to carry it on to the end of its primitive creation. [80v, 156] And therefore the great duty of faith in Christ and the belief of the evangelical doctrine which is the great instrument operative[301] and effectual upon the lives of men is not only required as a great duty of the gospel, but is required upon the fullest and most convincing evidence in the world.

9. And all this evangelical doctrine [is] proposed and delivered plainly [and] perspicuously, whereby the meanest capacity may understand and know it and needs not that choiceness of ratiocination and rational process to discover it which every man hath not the capacity or dexterity to practise or exercise, so that it exhibits the natural *law* *quasi per saltum* and evidently and in an entire system, and delivers mankind from these difficulties that it before had in *eruenda lege naturalis* [drawing out (conclusions) from the law of nature], namely, the generality and obscurity of it in its natural delineation [and][302] the difficulty of the exercise of the rational process about it, [and] the prejudices that evil customs, private interest, and self-love had brought upon the dictates of it.

So that the doctrine of the gospel is not only the unveiling and unriddling of it given by Moses, but also the unveiling of the true law of nature, and the distinct explication and exposition of it, and the most efficacious and powerful application of it to the human nature, for the reforming, perfecting, and advancing of it. And the

[298] All MSS: life. [299] All MSS: distinctly the life to God and the.
[300] OED: to seal; to mark as with a seal; to ratify.
[301] Harley: instrument to render it operative. [302] All MSS: of.

sun of righteousness which had been thus long rising higher †and higher† from the first fall of man in the gradual discovery of the dictates of primitive natural righteousness and truth came to its meridian [81r, 157] in the exhibition of Christ to the world in the fullness of time, who brought life and immortality to light by the gospel; and being the express image of the father of lights came into the world to reimpress that divine image of God upon the souls of men which by the corruption of the human nature through sin and evil customs and the subtlety of the prince of darkness had been much defaced and injured.

And thus far for this four-fold *superinducted* publication of the natural law.

12

Concerning Human Laws and their Use in Relation to the Law of Nature

Having hitherto considered the law of nature and the various publication[s] thereof, it will be necessary, partly for the further explication of this law of nature and partly to prevent or answer a tacit objection that may arise, to subjoin something concerning human laws and their necessity and use.

The objection stands thus: if the law of nature be of that perfection, extent, and amplitude that it accommodates to the great end of the human [being] and to direct him in all the moral actions of life and is not only a rule or direction, but bound upon the children of men by the supreme obligation of the empire and command of Almighty God and under the greatest penalty imaginable, eternal death; and if this law hath so many effectual publications of it, as well by instinct of nature as by the manuduction[303] of reason, and not only †by that† but by that plenary and powerful [81v, 158] publication of it by Christ in the gospel; what need is there of human laws? Can they add anything to that which is already perfect? Or is their authority or obligation equal to the authority of Almighty God, or that obligation that ariseth from a law given by him.

To give an answer to this objection some things must first be premised.

[303] OED: guidance, direction (leading by the hand).

We must observe that besides †the† law of nature which consists in the command and prohibition of certain moral actions there is that which they call *lex permissiva* [permissive law]. And this imports these things:

1. That there are certain moral actions or things that in themselves fall neither under the command or prohibition of the natural law but were left indifferent to be done or to be omitted.

And though perchance it may be difficult in the concrete to find any moral actions but by the various opposition of circumstances they may lose their indifference, yea and perchance there *neither* is nor can be possibly found any moral action in the concrete so purely and simply indifferent but that there may be [in] the circumstances considered a greater preponderation of reason to the one part than the other; yet we are not thereupon presently to conclude that all these are under the precise command or prohibition of the law of nature. I am now writing. It is perchance more reasonable for me to write now than tomorrow, because some accident or other may probably fall out that may make it more reasonable for me to write today than tomorrow, yet I cannot say that I am under an affirmative command of the law of nature to write now, or under a prohibition of that law to defer it till tomorrow. There are thousands, [an] infinite [number,] of actions in the world that may *be more* or less reasonable to be done and yet the[304] more reasonable may not therefore fall under the command, or the less reasonable under [82r, 159] the prohibition of the law of nature, [which] fixeth [only] upon things of the great[est] importance to human nature.

And therefore some things there are that are in a state of indifferency in themselves as in relation to the preceptive or prohibitory acts of that law.

2. Again there be certain things that though they may fall under the precipient[305] part of the law of nature, yet for [the][306] circumstances of their performance—as [for example] for the time, place, manner etc.—are not particularly determined by the law of nature. For instance had there been no particular prescription by the fourth commandment of the time of God's solemn worship, there had been the obligation of the natural law to have set apart some time to his solemn and public worship, though the particular quantum[307] of the time had not been limited, and so for place and other circumstances.

3. Again in external punishments of things prohibited by the natural law, as [for example] theft, adultery, [and] drunkenness. The external punishments are not determined by the law of nature but left either to the *arbitrium judicis* [will or judgment of the judge], which is to proportion his punishment according to the proportion, nature, or example of the offence, or is to be determined by positive constitutions.

[304] All MSS: yet not the.
[305] Ed: the preceptive or mandatory.
[306] All MSS: that yet for their.
[307] All MSS: quotum.

And therefore according to the various laws and usages of several nations, or of the same nation at several times, offences that are prohibited even by the laws of nature have yet various punishments inflicted according to the constitutions and laws of several countries; and as to the penalties being the principal end of them is example according to the exigence and convenience of public examples, so penalties are intramixed, abused,[308] and sometimes remitted.[309]

This being thus stated, I say touching this *lex* [82v, 160] *permissiva* [that] it is that law of Almighty God whereby things not determined by the law of nature are left to the determination of human laws.

In this *lex permissiva*, these [points] are considerable: 1. The proper matter of the law, [and] 2. wherein the formality of it as a law consists.

[First, regarding the matter of human law:]

1. No human law can derogate from the law of nature. It cannot forbid what the law of nature enjoins, nor command what the law of nature prohibits; but *it could forbid* how far a passive obedience may be exacted to commands contradictory to natural law.[310]
2. Human laws may enact what the [natural] law enacts and forbid what it forbids; for though this gives not the original obligation to those laws, yet it serves as a further manifestation of it, and may add a civil sanction or penalty to a law that is simply natural.
3. The proper and natural matter of human laws or this *lex permissiva* are those moral actions that are left indifferent and unprohibited or uncommanded by the law of nature (for I do not in this speak of the divine positive law which is of a distinct consideration), such as are those of the three ranks before mentioned: things simply neither forbidden, nor commanded by the law of nature, circumstances not determined by the law of nature, and penalties even of those things that are not prohibited by the law of nature.

Secondly, as to the formality of this that I call *lex permissiva*, it consists in these three acts of the divine will manifested in the law of nature viz.

1. In the leaving of some things out of the command or prohibition of any law of God whether natural or positive.
2. In subjecting those things thus left undetermined [83r, 161] to the power of the civil magistrate to determine and specificate.

308 OED: disused or neglected.

309 The text of the second half of this sentence may be corrupted. Its point seems to be that since the principal end of punishment is to set an example, the penalties may vary according to circumstances and convenience of the enforcing agency.

310 Ed: law could determine the extent to which a citizen might be bound passively to obey (i.e., bound not to resist actively) laws that derogate from the law of nature.

3. In obliging of the subjects of such *magistrates* to the obedience of those laws by the very law of nature. And this obligation to the obedience of the laws of the civil magistrate ariseth from these two *capita legis naturalis*, namely, [a] that law of nature which is in order to[311] civil government whereof before,[312] or that *caput juris Noachidarum de judiciis* which enjoins the direction of magistracy and human laws and judicatories,[313] the commentary upon which laws is that of Deut. 16:18: "Judges and officers shalt thou make thee in all thy gates which the Lord thy God giveth thee throughout thy tribes and they shall judge the people with just judgment" and Deut. 17:12: "And the man that will do presumptuously and will not hearken to the priest that standeth to minister there before the lord thy God, or unto the judge, even that man shall die." [b] That law which obligeth a man *fidem servare*, which as before is shown is that law of nature, which obligeth the conscience to obey that authority and those laws that are made by his express or tacit consent or by those whom he hath virtually and implicitly at least trusted with that power.

And though it is true there is a great difference as in many respects between a lawgiver or governor and a judge, between government and laws that proceed from it, [and] between a law and a judgment, yet these two laws of nature are equally applicable to government, governors, judges, laws, and judgments, as to their obliging to power and the laws of nature that [give][314] them their institution and obligation.

Now as to the answer of the object[ion], I say that although the laws of nature are of that great virtue and efficacy for directing mankind in their moral actions and containing them in their duty, yet civil government [83v, 162] and laws are very necessary for the well-being of mankind.

1. They are institutions that are commanded by the general laws of nature as hath been shown, although the special and particular forms and governments and laws receive their determinations from human or positive institutions.

2. There are very many things that are most wisely and necessarily left without any determination by the law of nature, as hath been shown, and yet the circumstances of them and the accidental junctures that they have are of that importance, that they are necessary to have a determination, and that determination to be given them by the governors and laws of the state or kingdom, who reasonably must have the best estimate of them that concern them. What a confusion would there be in the world if the particular laws and rules of property were not settled and governed by some established laws or rules, if all punishments should be equal or none at all, if there were no compulsory [agency] for the enforcing of every man to perform his promise or make retribution in damages.

[311] Ed: which directs us to establish. [312] See Chapter 11.

[313] Ed: the seventh of the Noachide law mandating the establishment of a judicial institution. See pp. 101–2 and notes 285 and 286.

[314] All MSS: gives.

These and infinite more are left undetermined by the laws of nature and it was necessary they should [be], because of their great variety and the great diversity that ariseth by the exigencies and conveniences of several people[s], and[315] therefore they are by the wise disposal of the divine providence left to the guidance and laws and customs of people.

3. The corruption of manners and educations [is][316] or may be so great, and the blindness and prejudice that men are under by their love to themselves and [84r, 163] their own interest [may be so serious], that the laws of nature are very much obscured to men under these circumstances, and therefore there is a great necessity of human laws and judicatories that may be indifferent between man and man and not under the prejudice of the love that either party hath to himself or his interest, [and] may give to each his due and be an equal standard between the interests, proprieties, and concerns of every party; for in controversies between man and man, each party is so addicted to himself and his interest that everyone would judge for himself, and that would cause confusion in the world. Therefore, by the common consent of nations judges are appointed to decide controversies and laws to govern judges.

4. Although the violation of the laws of nature is under the danger of a punishment from the hands of the glorious God of infinite more severity than can be inflicted by human governors or laws, and although the rewards reserved for the obedient to the divine law be of far greater moment than the temporal rewards of men, and although there seems in the very light of nature a presensation[317] of these rewards and punishments, which are great motives in the state of nature, to a due conformity to the laws thereof, and do certainly prevail with them that are truly sensible thereof to carry and keep them in a due conformity to this law; yet the worst of men and those [that] are like to do most mischief in the world are a sort of people that rarely think of it, or at least do not believe it, whose very minds and consciences by corrupted educations or customs are corrupted and now are below no other rewards than the wealth and pleasure of this life, and therefore will venture the uttermost for them, nor no other punishments but †gaols† and whips and gibbets stand more in fear of those than of hell itself; and were [84v, 164] it not for those they would be as wolves and bears and lions in the world. Therefore, to coerce those that are of most danger to mankind laws and severities and punishments suitable to their fears must be instituted to deter them from that evil that they would otherwise commit.

5. Even in the more moral sort of men there is a great prevalence of sense and sensual appetite, and present and sensible objects have a more strong impression upon their passions than those that are remote and at a distance, though possibly their judgment upon consideration and deliberation would be convinced of the truth of them. And hence it is the rewards and punishments that immediately strike upon the sense and that are within our views [that] have a [more] sudden and secret impression upon men's

315 All MSS: people require and. 316 All MSS: are.

317 OED: perception of something before it occurs.

hopes and fears than these rewards or punishments that seem more remote and out of sight, and those are such as are inflicted or exercised by civil laws and governors.

For although it be true that Almighty God could exercise the regiment of mankind immediately and from heaven inflict temporal punishments and give temporal rewards as well as eternal, and sometimes for the vindication of his justice and regiment doth so, yet the ordinary and constant administration of the world in such a manner would neither be suitable to his wisdom or providence.

And therefore as in the regiment of the natural effects in the world, God Almighty rarely interposeth an immediate or miraculous administration, but governs natural effects by an ordinary connection of natural cause and according to that perpetual order and law that he hath instituted for things of nature, so in the [85r, 165] ordinary regiment of mankind he doth it by a certain scheme and settled method suitable and proportionable to the just state and order of the human nature, namely, by the wise institution of laws and government, so that by this means the several wheels of the great engine of the human nature are orderly set at work and everything acts its part regularly and orderly. The laws of nature have their rise and motion in inclining and directing the general nature of mankind, the law of reason perfects and improves this natural law and carries up their obligation to the sovereign ^lord^[318] of nature, inclines men to societies and laws, the Christian religion gives more clear and explicit instruction, the particular laws of nature, and stronger and more effectual motives for its observance and civil government. Societies and laws are like those outworks and *sepimenta legis naturae*[319] and for the better ordering of the laws of man in a state of civil society.

13

Concerning the End of the Laws of Nature

I am now come to the conclusion and winding up of this whole discourse concerning the laws of nature and now shall make some enquiry touching the end intended in this law and what is attainable by it.

[318] H: law. [319] See note 33.

First, therefore it is certain that Almighty God who is not only an intellective being but a being of infinite wisdom, goodness, and power in all his works hath a most wise and excellent end, an end exquisitely [85v, 166] suitable to the value of this work he makes, an end carried on by most excellent and suitable means.

Secondly, that as well the nature of man as the incision and engraving of this law of nature in the soul of man and all the accessions provided and ordained for the advance and perfecting of this law of nature in the soul and nature of mankind is the work and institution of that most wise God, and therefore ordered to an end answerable to the wisdom and goodness of such an efficient [cause] and no way inferior to the work and dignity of such a nature and such a law.

Thirdly, that inasmuch as in the operations of an intelligent agent we may reasonably make some estimate of the end of what he designs in any work by the value and nature of the work itself, and inasmuch as the human nature is in a rank of being above the animal nature and hath connatural to him a certain law or rule of operations above the animal instincts; therefore, mankind and this law of nature was directed and designed to our end nobler and higher than the animal nature and the animal life, namely, to a reasonable life and a life answering the dignity and value of the reasonable nature.

Fourthly, that next to the glory of Almighty God, the greatest good attainable on this side [of] death by the means of this natural law, and the strict and due observance [of it], and the highest happiness that may be compatible to a reasonable life in this world, is the common benefit of mankind by goodness and beneficence and a full enjoyment of tranquillity of mind.

[86r, 167] Fifthly, that, although, if the soul of man be mortal and die with his body, this happiness last before mentioned seems fully commensurate to the expectation and end of an animal life, yet if the soul of man survive his body this tranquillity of mind is not a commensurate good or end to the human nature [rests] upon two great and evident reasons. 1. Because such a tranquillity is but temporary and partial and not fitted to the extent of the soul's duration. 2. And besides as long as a man is ignorant or unacquainted with the condition of that which is most valuable [in him][320] and yet must survive him, it creates unquietness, anxiousness, and solicitousness, and checks and disorders and discomposeth the present state of the mind and spoils that tranquillity which it enjoys here; for how can that mind be in quietness and free from care and trouble that knows it must survive his body and knows not whether that tranquillity it might possibly enjoy here shall be then held.

Sixthly, therefore that this law of nature was primarily and originally designed as an apt and fit means to perfect the soul of man and [bring][321] it into an everlasting state of blessedness and to give a man a happiness commensurate to the extent of his being and duration.

[320] All MSS: in him unto him. [321] All MSS: state.

But because *de facto* no man can constantly, universally, and indefinitely at all times or in its full measure and amplitude perform exactly this law of nature, but sometimes or other fails, no man barely upon the account of his own natural righteousness can *ex condigno* [by his own merit] challenge that happiness that was at first annexed to the fulfilling of that law, for any one offence in strictness of justice doth *obicem ponere* [place an obstacle] to that claim.

[86v, 168] Seventhly, and therefore *de facto*, as the case stands with him, [no one] can make any pretension to the claim of happiness without the mercy and bounty of God forgiving his sin and admitting him into a state of everlasting felicity.

Eighthly, that inasmuch as the whole economy of the distribution and communication of mercy to the children of men is in and through Christ and that price and satisfaction he laid down for the sins of men and the purchase of their admission into everlasting glory, therefore no man upon any account whatsoever can be actual partaker of that everlasting happiness by all the righteousness he can perform without the application and actual communication of the redemption by Christ. As to those that have or had the doctrine communicated to them and are of capacity to understand and believe, it is to be done by a true faith and belief of him to be the Messiah and that all that doctrine of the gospel is true, and upon the strength of that faith and belief conforms his life according to it. For since he hath this grace given to him to hear the gospel, he receives it in vain if he doth not believe and practise it.

Ninthly, that as in the pains of the damned there are degrees of punishment proportionable to the degrees of their sins and contempts in this life, so in that happiness that shall be enjoyed in the world to come there shall be degrees of glory and happiness to some a greater to some a lesser as one star exceeds another in glory.

[87r, 169] Thus far there will be little controversy; all the question will be whether by virtue of the divine goodness and benignity in and through Christ the efficacy of the redemption wrought by him be not by the divine ordination applicable to such as having never had the explicit knowledge of Christ yet have lived up in a very great measure and proportionable to the means of natural light unto the directions of the law of nature. This is no curious nor unprofitable speculation, neither are [we] without sufficient manuduction in the holy scriptures and by great and evident reason to establish ourselves in this truth as will appear by what follows. And though as to the degrees of that happiness which those men may partake of in the life to come 'tis not possible to determine, yet as to the main question itself it seems more than probable that the affirmative of this question is true and the contrary thereof not only untrue but greatly derogatory to the glory, perfection, and amplitude of the divine beneficence, mercy, goodness, justice, and providence. My reasons are these:

1. Though the characters of the divine natural law be engraven in every man's soul and conscience and though the reasonable faculty be that visive power of the soul whereby it is enabled to discriminate moral good and evil, yet Christ, the wisdom of God, is that universal light which enlighteneth every man that comes into the world (John 1), that true *intellectus agens*, which the ancients resembled to the sun that gives

the universal light to the works of nature, [87v, 170] without which the eye of reason were in the dark and the characters of natural righteousness not so clearly legible.

He therefore that exhibits himself as universal light to all men to render the rudiments of natural justice the more conspicuous and legible will not probably deny some benefits of his redemption to those that make a diligent use and improvement of that light which he gives them.

2. The philanthropy and beneficence of Almighty God is so great and his wisdom so unspeakable that it finds ways to communicate the efficacy of redemption wrought by this son according to the variety of the means that [human beings][322] are capable of. Infants cannot actually believe—they are under an invincible impotency thereunto—yet none dares to say that they are incapable of the benefit of Christ's redemption, nay though they die before baptism, which is not in their power to assume.

The ancient patriarchs and generally the whole Jewish church were for the greatest part ignorant of Christ to come, and those which had the greatest perspicuity[323] among them saw him but obscurely afar off, nay his own very disciples were in *their* lifetime ignorant of the true spiritual design of the redemption of the world, but expected an external worldly kingdom, and yet it would be great rashness to say they were not within the benefit of his redemption in that state of their darkness and ignorance.

And if it be said that the church of the Jews were under a covenant [but] the gentiles [were] not, I answer: [a] It is true they were under a covenant, but it was a covenant of works—do this and live—not under an express covenant of grace such as was made in Christ. This is the whole scope of the apostle in his [88r, 171] epistle[s] to the Romans, Colossians, [and] Hebrews, wherein he discourses [on] the impotence of that covenant; so that that covenant made little to their advantage, but only this that the divine goodness chose and instituted in that means even the obedience to the moral, ceremonial, and judicial law to be the external means whereby to apply to them the efficacy of that redemption wrought by Christ. [b] And if it be said they were within the extent of the special covenant made with Abraham, I say [that] though the gentiles were not within the external symbol of that covenant, yet they were within the efficacy of that promise. "In thy seed shall all the nations of the earth be blessed" [Gen. 22.18].

Therefore if Almighty God could make the death of Christ which was not till 2000 years after effectual to the church of the Jews by making their obedience to the Mosaical law the means of the application of that energy, why should we think it incongruous that the industrious observance of the law of nature by the gentiles should be the instrument of the like application?

3. The covenant of God in Christ was given to all mankind [and] his death sufficient for the sins of all mankind, the exhibition thereof as a covenant was to all mankind; he stood as perfectly an universal representative of mankind as Adam was

[322] H and BL: they. [323] OED: mental penetration, insight.

(Rom. 5:19, etc.). And though the ordinary condition of that covenant was faith as well as repentance to as many as were capable of it, yet 'tis without warrant to exclude all from that general benefit which were invincibly incapable of performing it; for how could they believe unless they had heard? And therefore it seems to stand with the wisdom and goodness and intention of God that [he provided] some other method of communicating that benefit and now more probable than the [88v, 172] sincere and industrious walking according to the natural law.

4. This supposition magnifies the divine mercy and philanthropy towards all mankind *in giving them a means to escape everlasting misery and to participate of that common salvation, which was universally procured for all mankind* that according to the means exhibited was communicable to them, which was in their power by the common aids of divine grace to perform and attain, and the contrary opinion unnecessarily shrinks up the divine benignity to a small portion of mankind and leaves the rest of the world under an invincible necessity of being eternally lost.

5. This supposition justifies the justice of Almighty God, which is as dear to him as any attribute and upon the clearness whereof he frequently exposeth the exactness of his justice even to the scrutiny of his creatures (Ezek. 18:*25*, 26), that when he shall come to the general judgment of the world every mouth may be stopped [Rom. 3:19]; and this is the method by which he will proceed at the last day even to the condemnation of the sinners of the world to judge them according to the means he gave them (Rom. 2:12). They that have sinned without law shall also perish without law and ^as many as^ have sinned in the law shall be judged by the law, which is no more than if he had said they that have sinned against the unwritten law of nature shall be judged by the law of nature not by the written law, and they that have sinned in the law, that is against the express command of the written law, shall be judged by the law (again 2 Thess. 1:8): ["]in flaming fire and render vengeance on them that know not God and obey not the gospel of our Lord Jesus Christ.["] There are two subjects of the divine vengeance, viz. first, such as know not God, [89r, 173] who by the light of nature they might have known, and [second] them which obey not the gospel, which having received the message of the gospel yet presumptuously disobey it. Now if we should for instance sake suppose a heathen such a one as Socrates or Zeno should *at the last day be called* before the tribunal of the divine justice and demanded what he could say for himself and he should thereupon plead for his life as once Hezekiah did—"I have walked before thee in all piety and sobriety and righteousness. I improved that natural light thou didst lend me with as much integrity and sincerity as was possible and if I did at any time offend I did with all sorrow of heart and resolution of amendment repent of it and ordered my life according to the strictness of such a resolution"[324]—can we reasonably think it should be replied to him that for all this he must everlastingly die because he did not believe in Christ of

[324] MH freely adapts the deathbed prayer of Hezekiah recorded in 2 Kings 20:3.

whom he never heard or could have [heard][325] being then not come into the world? On the other side, if some vicious heathen that yet never heard of Christ should be called to the bar of the divine justice and should take up this defence, "Lord it is true I am a great offender but I never heard of Christ; if I had I had believed on him and my sins had been purged, but it was impossible I could ever hear of him and so I am condemned by a kind of inevitable and invincible necessity." Must not the mouth of all contradiction be stopped if it should be replied to him, "Thou hadst the law of nature and if thou hadst lived up to that law that was in thy power and of which thou couldst not be ignorant thou mightest have had some share in that common redemption, but thou hast totally rejected that righteousness which was in thy power at least in a great measure to fulfil"? This reply [89v, 174] necessarily vindicates the divine justice from the imputation of condemning men for that which was impossible for them to do otherwise.

And therefore though I find that natural death was the effect that Adam's sin brought upon his posterity, yet we never yet read that any man should be condemned to everlasting death merely upon the account of Adam's sin, for this is directly contrary to that rule that God Almighty gives of his own justice: the soul that sinneth it shall die.

The supposition highly asserts and vindicates the divine providence and the care that he hath of all mankind and every particular person thereof when I consider that every man hath within him an immortal soul that is more valuable than his body and all his concernments in the world. And when I behold the admirable economy of the divine providence in providing all things necessary and convenient for the life of man in this world, it easily assures me that he that takes such care for the case of the [body],[326] the carcass, that must by the necessity of his nature in a few years return to his dust, it mightily assures me that the care of the glorious God is much more for the souls of men that are the jewels of his casket. Yet when I consider how many thousands, how many millions of men now are in the world, how many more there have been in the world in this great period of 6000 years [who] never heard of that common salvation by Christ Jesus, that were and are invincibly ignorant of him, and yet I am satisfied that that blessed name is that only name under heaven by which men must be saved [Acts 4:12], that no [90r, 175] man ever was or ever shall *be made* partaker of eternal life without it, I am at a stand and begin to stagger whether there be any such providence governing the affairs of mankind or at least to call in question whether immortality be an essential privilege of the soul of man or only a special privilege purchased by the redemption of Christ for these that actually believe in him.

But again when I do consider that this law of nature is as universal and as universally published as the amplitude of mankind and that every man hath his stock put into his hands to trade upon and that it is his own fault if he doth not; that the divine goodness and beneficence hath received a price from the hands of his son

[325] All MSS: hear. [326] All MSS: soul.

for the forgiveness of sins and the everlasting happiness of all mankind; and though his providence hath not given the explicit means of the knowledge and faith of Christ, yet he hath instituted another that may be in its degree effectual for the application of that redemption, namely, the industrious exercise of that talent of natural light and natural law and they are to live according to it in a very great measure; [and] that *agenti quantum in se est non denegatur gratia* [grace is not denied to one who does all that is in him (in his power?)]—it clears my doubtings as clear as the noon day and [renders][327] the providence, goodness, and justice of Almighty God to all mankind evident and conspicuous, exhibiting to all mankind a means suitable to their condition for the application of that great redemption and the fruit thereof to their everlasting good, and leaves them without excuse that neglect the use of that means, which by the divine beneficence [was] communicated to them in the due use of the light and love of nature, so that as the apostle excellently concludes (Rom. 1:[20])[328] [90v, 176] "They are without excuse."

6. The wisdom and goodness of Almighty God is *so* abundant that it seldom or never gives any faculty, power or inclination into any creature in vain, but it is still or most commonly answered with a suitable object really existing and expletive[329] of that faculty, power, or inclination.

Now we see in the generality of mankind not only the common rudiments and propensions towards moral goodness lodged in their nature and rational connection. But they have a common sentiment of the immortality of the soul and a future estate of rewards and punishments according as they have behaved themselves in this world, and though this sentiment be less distinct and vigorous in some than in others, yet there are very few in the world that have not some glimpses of the future judgment or that are not under some invincible jealousies or suspicions thereof. And as they are under this persuasion, at least suspicion of a future state of rewards and punishments, so this very persuasion, nay the very bare doubt and suspicion thereof, hath very great efficacy upon mankind to keep and contain them within the bounds of those laws of nature and the observation of those rules of natural devotion, honesty, and righteousness that these laws of nature suggest and require.

And certainly these sentiments [that] are very suspicious of the future state of rewards and punishments have not their radications[330] in the minds of men [91r, 177] without the will and institution of the great God of heaven and earth who doth all his works with infinite wisdom and to ends becoming it. Sentiments of this nature and importance for keeping of mankind in a state of congruity in some [degree] to the dignity and worth of his nature came not unto him by chance, neither are [they] lodged there merely to deceive or impose upon it with vain hopes and vain fears.

327 All MSS: renders both. 328 All MSS: Rom. 1:10.
329 OED: filling out, supplying a deficiency. 330 OED: rootedness.

And therefore since I find [that] these hopes and fears of future rewards and punishments are lodged in the minds of the generality of mankind and that by the divine providence, wisdom, and goodness of Almighty God; and since I find these hopes and fears are the instruments of the greatest importance even in the state of _____[331] to bring and hold men to a conformity to the natural law; and since I am well assured that it is the efficacy of the redemption wrought for mankind by Christ Jesus [that] is the great and only means to communicate to the children of men the actual fruition[332] of the happiness [for which] they hope and to avoid that misery after death which they fear—I cannot deliver myself from this persuasion that the divine philanthropy hath instituted a sincere endeavour of obedience to the law of nature to be the means of application of that purchased redemption in relation to those heathen that had never [had] Christ revealed to them, nor any other means of attaining that happiness which he purchased but by walking conformably and suitably to that law of nature, which they knew or without their supine yea wilful neglect that they might easily know and discern. Neither can I bring myself to believe that all the differences between the future state of [on the one hand] Socrates, Zeno Citicus, Aristides, [91v, 178] Antonius Pius, and other heathens, admirable for the exercise of all kind of virtue,[333] [and] on the other side, an Heliogabalus, Nero, and other monsters of human nature [notorious] for their prodigious lusts and cruelties[334] should be only this that the former should be less miserable in the life to come, but yet miserable still, and all the reward of their excellent laws and virtues should be only this that though their punishments should be more easy but yet punished they should be, and their virtues never rewarded, which yet did exceed most of the lives of many professors of Christianity and perchance the disproportion of the means considered equalled the lives of the best. Therefore those positions of some men that all the virtues of heathens were but *splendida peccata* [magnificent sins], that there is no more reward for a virtuous heathen than for a vicious and debauched heathen, that all the virtues of heathens *in eventu* [in the event] and *de facto* obtained no more from the divine goodness than to be beaten with fewer stripes, yet to be beaten, are not only uncharitable theories but unsound [and] unwarrantable and damp all the endeavours of goodness and virtue and render men either desperately wicked or very faintly and feebly virtuous being stripped of all possibilities of reward.

[331] All MSS leave a blank here. [332] OED: pleasurable possession, enjoyment.

[333] Socrates (469–399 BCE) was the philosopher of Athens, protagonist in most of Plato's dialogues, who taught it was better to suffer injustice than to do it. Zeno of Citium (334–*c*.262 BCE) was a Greek of Phoenician descent, founder of the Stoicism, and honoured for his moral influence on the youth. Aristides (530–468 BCE) was an Athenian statesman nicknamed "the just." Antonius Pius (86–161 CE, Roman Emperor 138–161) was called "pious" (perhaps in part) because, out of filial piety, he convinced the Senate to grant divine status to his adoptive father, Hadrian.

[334] Heliogabalus, (203–22), Roman Emperor from 218 to 222, was infamous for impiety and sexual impropriety. Nero (37–68 CE, Roman Emperor 54–69 CE), infamous for his extravagance, tyranny, and cruelty, was said to have burned Christians in his garden for light in the evening.

It is true there is no proportion between the merit of virtue and the state of everlasting happiness, nay the most excellent Christians that ever were can never upon the account of their own virtue and goodness make a challenge to heaven. No, it is the liberality and bounty and goodness and beneficence of the glorious God that hath instituted rewards of so great a value for these virtues and that goodness that at the utmost is but our duty.

[92r, 179] All that I contend for is that that goodness and beneficence of God may have its due glory and extent according to the true compass and amplitude thereof; and [that] our eye may not be evil because he is good; and that because he hath given us Christians a more clear and free access with that happiness purchased by his son [and] an easier and more infallible and indisputable way to attain it and reason to expect a greater measure and degree of it, we should not shrink up the immensity of the divine goodness so much as to deny them any means or degree of participation of the divine bounty through Christ, who though they have not explicitly known him have in sincerity according to the light of nature lived up as near to the end of his coming into the world as that means and the common *auxilia divinae gratia* [aid to divine grace] enabled them.

[7.][335] The testimony of the word of Almighty God gives a great attestation to it, what shall we think of Job and his four friends, who were not for aught appears within the covenant of circumcision made with Abraham but were [unacquainted with it][336]—for surely they would in some of their discourses have mentioned Abraham or the circumcision—and yet all the testimony that Almighty God gives him and upon the account whereof he so highly commends him is the strict observation of this natural law. (Job 1:1; Job 2:3:) "there is none like him in all the earth an upright man, one that feareth God and escheweth evil." Again in the excellent instance of Cornelius (Acts 10). He was a Centurion of the Italian land and it seems a Roman but however a gentile and yet wholly unacquainted with the faith of Christ, yet a devout man and one that feared God, and yet in that state his prayers and alms [were] accepted before God (Acts 10:4). And for a further testimony of the divine acceptance, God is pleased to give him a farther mercy [and] sends [92v, 180] him to Peter. Peter startles at it and is convicted by a vision of going to him. And what was the conclusion that he makes thereupon? (Acts 10:34[–35]:) "Of a truth I perceive that God is no respecter of persons but in every nation he that feareth him and worketh †righteousness† is accepted with him."

The Jews were the most supercilious people towards gentiles that could be and stood highly upon their own privileges and peculiarity of favour with God, yet this secure people ever held that the gentiles who strictly observed the seven *precepta Noachidarum* had a share in the happiness of the life to come. *Piis ex gentibus mundi sors est in futuro seculo* [Pious gentiles have a share in the world to come] (v. Selden, *De Jure Naturali* L.*7*, cap. 10).

[335] All MSS: 8. [336] All MSS: acquainted with it for aught we know.

Men that consider things by halves are apt to take up a prejudice against this supposition as if it did some prejudice to the dignity of the Christian religion, as if it countenanced that indifferency of religion which is too apt to be entertained in the world. What need of the knowledge of Christian religion [they might ask] if heathens and pagans may be saved without it? But the answer is so plain that I suppose the objection will not be twice made.

[1.] The supposition which I have made asserts the necessity of the sacrifice of Christ and excludes all †hope† of salvation without it; and though it asserts the means of application thereof to be according to the condition of the subject, yet it no way derogates from the dignity of the gospel but advanceth and magnifieth it and the good intended in it by God to the amplitude of the human nature.

2. He that saith that a man that is [as] invincibly ignorant of the gospel as infants and heathens that never [93r, 181] heard of it [might] have [in mind] some other means of the conveyance and application of it by the goodness of God than the distinct knowledge and belief of it, [however] so far from asserting any other means of salvation by it than by faith and belief of it as the first instrument of the reception of it, [he][337] plainly supposeth and asserts it. For the means of application is asserted to be suitable to that exigence, state, or condition that the party hath. He that never heard of Christ or the gospel or the written word of God, the means of application of this salvation is the living up to the light and means he hath, namely, natural light and natural law, but he that hath a better means of application must use it, otherwise he is wanting to his duty. Therefore to him that hath been acquainted with the doctrine of Christianity there is required faith and obedience as unto the law enacted by Christ, and a clearer and more explicit knowledge and more perfect fulfilling of the law of righteousness. The bare living up to the light of nature is not sufficient, because he hath a greater means. The light of nature and the law thereof lends a man but one talent to trade upon and yet upon that he must trade; the light of the gospel is as ten talents which requires a return of a greater proceed to the Lord that commits both.[338]

3. Though the mercy of God hath not left the state of nature totally destitute of a means to participate of the benefit of the redemption of Christ, yet it is no way equal to that means of participation thereof by the light of the gospel. [a] This hath been declared already and need not much repetition. The means of salvation is rendered by the gospel far more easy, clear, and evident. [b] It is rendered far more efficacious, safe, and indeficient to its end. The lights of nature are like the *tabulae post naufragium* [planks after a shipwreck], which may bring men to the shore though not without great difficulty and hazard. But the light and means of the gospel is like the passage in a safe [93v, 182] and strong ship which is better fitted to chide storms and dangers of the sea. [c] The glory attainable by the knowledge, faith, and

337 All MSS: that it.

338 MH alludes to the parable of the ten talents found in Matthew 25:14–30 and Luke 19:12–27.

obedience of the gospel far surpasseth the degrees of glory attainable by natural light. So that it were as great a madness for a man that is acquainted with the Christian doctrine to say, "It is all one to me what religion I am of for I can be saved under paganism and I can be but saved under Christianity," as for a man that is in a sound ship passing the seas to say, "I see yonder a plank floating, I will cast myself into the sea and get upon that plank, because I see another that hath safely come to land upon the like"; for it was his necessity and therefore his wisdom to use the best means he had, but it would be madness and the extremity of folly in [him] to reject a safe and sure means of [his][339] safety and make choice of that which is less perfect, less safe, and more hazardous in a manner especially of that importance as is [his] everlasting happiness or misery. It is the goodness and mercy of God that lends a heathen any means of application of Christ's redemption to him. But it is God's superabounding mercy that lends a Christian a far greater, safer, [and more] powerful and effectual means, and as the greatness of this mercy is not at all diminished by the former, so it renders a Christian infinitely more obliged to the bounty and goodness of God in a due and thankful use of it and obedience to it.

Appendix: Law in the Natural Order

[Democritus, Epicurus, and the Atomists claim that the order of the universe is not the product of God's creation, but merely the operation of "Nature" or some "Rule" or "Law".[340] They] suppose it is a *norma*, rule, or law of a most excellent frame and order (and indeed in so conceiving, they conceive truly that nature is such a law or rule), but still this doth not explicate the *phenomena* of nature, without supposing somewhat more. A law or rule is not in itself effective or active, neither can it subsist or exist without an agent that either gave it, or works by or according to it. The laws of a state are the rules of its government, but this law must be given by some power, and some power must be that must act according to it, otherwise a law is a stupid, dead, unactive, and unconceivable thing. And therefore a law or rule singly explicates not any the *phenomena* of nature without a being that gives this law to things, or acts, or makes things act according to it; and then we are in a great measure where *Moses* brings us, only with this difference. the law by which this great world was made, was no other but the determination and *beneplacitum* [decree] of the divine will, determined or qualified (if we may use that improper word) with the highest and most sovereign wisdom and power;[341] and the law, by

[339] All MSS: folly in me to reject a safe and sure means of my safety.

[340] This selection is drawn from Hale's *Primitive Origination*, 344–7.

[341] It is improper to speak of God's will qualified by God's wisdom or power, because, in Hale's view, God's nature is radically *simple*. We, with our imperfect reason, distinguish distinct properties of will, wisdom, justice and the like. See Hale, *Discourse*, 12–13.

which things thus made were for the future to be governed, was that instituted rule and order which this sovereign lord contrived and placed in created beings; and thus indeed, *Opus naturae est opus intelligentiae* [the work of nature is the work of intelligence]. Nature therefore may have these various acceptations, viz.

1. As it signifies that *Principium activum* [active first principle] that gave everything its being; and thus it imports no other than Almighty God, that supreme intelligent being, though improperly called Nature; viz. *natura naturans* [creating nature].

2. As it imports the things or effects principated or effected by this intelligent active principle, or the effects or creatures of God, or *natura naturata* [created nature], and this hath a double import, viz. 1. for the first and immediate productions of that principle, namely, not only created matter, which was the *Productum primo primum* [first-made fundamental thing], but also the things first produced in their several kinds or natures, or *Producta seconda prima* [second-made fundamental things], as the first vegetable, animal, and human individuals; or 2. for those mixtions and productions which afterwards had their productions in the world by successive mixtions and generations, which include all productions, which though in relation to their dependence and first production of their kind, are still the creatures of God; yet in relation to their immediate causes, are productions of second causes.

3. As it imports the law and rule and method and order, of the production and government and process of created beings; and this of two kinds, 1. The law and rule of the first creation or production of beings; as the production of the first individuals of animals, vegetables, and men: and herein though almighty God proceeds with admirable wisdom and order, yet he used no other law or rule than the immediate determination of his own most wise and perfect will, suitable to the business he had in hand, wherein there was necessary and fit another kind of regiment and order than was afterwards instituted. 2. The laws or rules instituted and appointed by the same most wise God to things already constituted; this is the common and ordinary and regular law of instituted nature. And these two laws or rules were different, and necessary that they should be so. In the first constitutions of beings God Almighty proceeded by a law suitable to that work, namely, according to the wise counsel of his own will, that was best and fittest for that work; he proceeded more suddenly, and by the immediate interposition of his own power, the vegetables constituted in a moment or very speedily, and within the compass of a day came to their full and perfect maturation and growth; so also did the fowls, and fishes, and brutes, and man, without any considerable *mora* [delay, pause] between their first formation and complement or individual perfection. But the law instituted for things already formed and settled was of another kind: vegetables, animals, and men are in the laws of their future existence to pass through those gradations and steps and methods which we see now in use, for the formation, production, increase, and perfection thereof. Again, in the first production of things, though sometimes the wise God used in some measure the order of second or instrumental or effective causes, yet he bound not himself to that rule; though, as we have formerly observed, the instrumentality of heat might be used in separating the *Expansum* [extended (but undifferentiated) world], and the arefaction[342] of the earth, and the production of vegetables. And though the instrumentality of the perfected celestial bodies might be some way instrumental towards the maturation of nature, [e.g.,] towards the production of animals, and though he used the matter which he had created to be the *substratum* of the corporeal natures, even of man himself; yet the great energy and power

[342] OED: the action or process of drying.

whereby he completed all things, was above and beyond the activity of second causes. Yea when he used the instrumentality of second causes, his own powerful and omnipotent hand was engaged in the advancing of efficacy of the second causes, which he used beyond their natural strength and efficacy, there was much that was supernatural and miraculous, as well in the first separation, distribution, and formation of things, as in the first creation of the corporeal matter out of nothing. But in the succeeding process and procedure of created nature he fixed and established certain powers and activities in things, and a certain order and connection between them and their effects, and governed and regulated the motions and productions of things according to those implanted powers and connections; and this we call the instituted law of nature, namely, the activities and powers placed in created beings, and the mutual connections and concatenations of things to such activities and powers: which law was at first instituted by the God of nature to be the common and standing ordinary rule for things, settled and fixed in their created station. And therefore we are far from denying a law of nature or calling in the immediate efficacy of the great God, or a miraculous interposition in all the ordinary procedures of things already fully settled and statuminated[343] by the first divine efficiency. That which we only say in relations to nature already settled is but this, that 1. The primitive and fundamental powers and activities of things were placed in them by the immediate will and efficiency of God. It is this that gives the power to heat and fire to dissolve, dissipate, rarify, and consume; to cold to condense; to heavy bodies to descend; to all the celestial bodies their motions, influences, and positions; [and] that gave the generative faculty to men, to brutes, to fishes; the productive faculty to the earth and waters; the receptivity to semen and intellection, &c. 2. That he by a continuing influx[344] doth support and preserve all things in their being, order, and activity. 3. That this which we call the law of instituted or statuminated nature is his law and his institution, and the connection of natural effects to their natural causes is his institution, his law, his order.

And therefore we do neither deny a law of nature, or a connection between natural causes and effects, but that which we justly blame in these men that pretend themselves to be the great priests of nature, and admirers and adorers of it, is, 1. That they do not sufficiently consider and observe, that this which they and we call nature, and the law of nature, and the power of nature, is no other but the wise instituted law of the most wise, powerful, and intelligent being, as really and truly as an edict of *Trajan* or *Justinian*[345] was a law of *Trajan* or *Justinian*; *Sic parvis magna* [as the greater follows the lesser part]; and 2. That they do not warily distinguish between that first law, *in rebus constituendis* [regarding things being made]; and this second law of nature, *in rebus constitutis* [regarding things made]: but inconsiderably misapply that law and rule and method which is ordinary and regular, constituted, and fitted, and accommodate to nature already settled; as if the same were and ought to be necessarily the rule and law in the first formation and settling of things: which is an error that proceeds from the over-much fixing of our minds to that which in the present course of things is obvious to sense, and not adverting, that the first constitution and order of things is not in reason or nature manageable by such a law, which is most excellently adequated and proportioned to things fully settled.

343 OED: supported, sustained; established. 344 OED: immaterial influence.

345 Trajan was Emperor of Rome (53–117 CE); Justinian was Byzantine (East Roman) Emperor (527–65 CE).

Therefore, besides that law which the divine wisdom, power, and goodness hath fixed in nature fully statuminated, we must also suppose a law and order of the divine wisdom, not rigorously bound either to second causes or present stated methods in the first production of things. And this the due consideration of the different nature of the state of things *in fieri* [coming into being] and *in facto esse* [existing in fact], will easily persuade, that the most wise God that hath established a fixed, regular, ordinary law in things already settled, which he rarely departs from; yet used another kind of order, namely, the regiment of his own will and wisdom, and if I may with humility speak it, a dictatorian power, more accommodate to the first production of things.

PART II

The History of the Common Law of England

Introductory Note

Hale's *History of the Common Law of England* is a Restoration work, although the exact date of composition is not known. It was published posthumously in 1713, with later editions in 1716 and 1739. Charles Gray edited the modern edition for University of Chicago Press in 1971. Hale's autograph manuscripts for this work (Clark Library, Los Angeles Selden-Hale Add. 1) have been followed, consulting published editions when transcription questions arose. Hale's extended references to cases, statutes, and other materials have been omitted. All notes are the current editor's.

In the selection from the *History* presented here, Hale offers not so much a history of English law as a theoretical account of the nature and grounds of common law from a deeply historical perspective. English laws fall into two types, he observes: *leges scriptae* and *leges non scriptae*. These are distinguished not in terms of their current form or content, nor their origin, but rather in terms of their force as law, that is, their mode of standing, validity, or institution as law and the (proximate) root of their legally binding force. *Leges scriptae* have their current legal standing *as enacted* by recognized lawmaking authority and typically are committed to writing. Their proximate force lies in the current authority of parliament. *Leges non scriptae*, by contrast, have legal standing *as practised*, grown into use, acquiring "binding power or force of law" by immemorial usage and by strength of custom and reception in the kingdom (134). This category includes laws that have emerged through custom (popular or judicial) and those which began their life as enacted laws but which over time have been "engrafted into the common law and made part thereof" (130). While enacted law can exist, for a time, on its own, it gets more deeply rooted when it is incorporated into the body of common law. Common law, "the great substratum" (148), binds both together; its principles ground the authority of court, crown, and parliament.

Over its long history, common law has changed greatly, but like the Argonauts' ship it retains its essential identity by virtue of its continuity over time. The "formal nature of a law"—its validity and force—lies not in the origin of its component rules, but in their "being received and approved" in the kingdom (145). Such custom may be rooted in custom of the people, but more often it is custom of the courts. This custom, and the enacted laws grafted onto it, succeeds in governing prince and people by virtue of the fact that over time it is accommodated to the frame of English government and incorporated into the complexion and constitution of the English commonwealth.

Judicial decisions, within this framework, do not themselves make law, but they are taken as best evidence of the law, due to the judges' great learning, their commitment to the law, and their mode of deliberating and deciding together as a tribunal. It is their practice to ground their decisions directly on the laws and customs of the kingdom, or principles derived from them or from past decisions in like cases. When these materials leave matters indeterminate, judges look to "the common reason of the thing," but when they do so, their reason is guided and disciplined by long experience in the law and the ordinary business of life (see also "Preface to Rolle's Abridgement" and "Reflections," Chapter 1).

Chapter 5 of this selection argues for the continuity of the common law against those who maintain that the "conquest" of William I marked a radical break in the history of English law and introduced a foreign mode of law into the kingdom (the "Norman Yoke"). Hale begins with a general discussion of the conditions under which conquest may generate legitimate title to rule. As in *Prerogatives of the King*, he argues that the conqueror is typically forced to seek consenting submission from the people, making concessions to secure their allegiance. Their consent may emerge only in their practice of conforming to the conqueror's rule over time. However, only conquest of the people that is complete (*victoria in regem et populum*) gives the right to replace old law with a new system. In contrast, *victoria in regem* only wins the crown from a rival and installs a new king on the throne. It does not bring with it any radical change in law. The victor assumes the title, subject to all the legal limits on it already in existence. William I, Hale argues, was only victor *in regem*.

1

Concerning the Distribution of the Law of England into Common Law and Statute Law. And First, Concerning the Statute Law, or Acts of Parliament

The laws of England may aptly enough be divided into two kinds, viz., *lex scripta*, the written law: and *lex non scripta*, the unwritten law. For although (as shall be shewn hereafter) all the laws of this kingdom have some monuments or memorials thereof in writing, yet all of them have not their original in writing; for some of those laws have obtained their force by immemorial usage or custom, and such laws are properly called *leges non scriptae*, or unwritten laws or customs.

Those laws therefore, that I call *leges scriptae*, or written laws, are such as are usually called statute laws, or acts of parliament, which are originally reduced into writing before they are enacted, or receive any binding power, every such law being in the first instance formally drawn up in writing, and made, as it were, a tripartite indenture,[1] between the king, the lords, and the commons; for without the concurrent consent of all those three parts of the legislature, no such law is, or can be made. But the kings of this realm, with the advice and consent of both houses of parliament, have power to make new laws, or to alter, repeal, or enforce the old. And this has been done in all succession of ages.

Now, statute laws, or acts of parliament, are of two kinds, viz., first, those statutes which were made before time of memory; and, secondly, those statutes which were made within or since time of memory; wherein observe, that according to a juridical account and legal signification, time within memory is the time of limitation in a writ of right, which by the Statute of Westminster 1. cap. 38[2] was settled, and reduced to the beginning of the reign of King Richard I or *Ex prima Coronatione Regis Richardi*

[1] OED: A deed or sealed agreement or contract between two or more parties.

[2] In real property law, a writ of right was an action by which a person could recover land in fee simple that was unjustly withheld from him. MH's reference should be Statute of Westminster 3 Edw. I, c. 39 (1275) (St. Realm I, 36).

Primi, who began his reign the 6th of July 1189, and was crowned the 3d of September following. So that whatsoever was before that time is *before* time of memory; and what is since that time is, in a legal sense, said to be *within* or since the time of memory.

And therefore it is, that those statutes or acts of parliament that were made before the beginning of the reign of King Richard I and have not since been repealed or altered, either by contrary usage, or by subsequent acts of parliament, are now accounted part of the *lex non scripta*, being as it were incorporated thereinto, and become a part of the common law; and in truth, such statutes are not now pleadable as acts of parliament (because what is before time of memory is supposed without a beginning, or at least such a beginning as the law takes notice of), but they obtain their strength by mere immemorial usage or custom.

And doubtless, many of those things that now obtain as common law had their original by parliamentary acts or constitutions, made in writing by the king, lords, and commons; though those acts are now either not extant, or if extant, were made before time of memory; and the evidence of the truth hereof will easily appear, for that in many of those old acts of parliament that were made before time of memory, and are yet extant, we [may] find many of those laws enacted which now obtain merely as common law, or the general custom of the realm. And were the rest of those laws extant, probably the footsteps of the original institution of many more laws that now obtain merely as common law, or customary laws, by immemorial usage, would appear to have been at first statute laws or acts of parliament.

Those ancient acts of parliament which are ranged under the head of *leges non scriptae*, or customary laws, as being made before time of memory, are to be considered under two periods: viz., first, such as were made before the coming in of King William I commonly called, The Conqueror;[3] or, secondly, such as intervened between his coming in, and the beginning of the reign of Richard I which is the legal limitation of time of memory.[4]

[Of those written laws made before time of memory] we have no authentical records, but only transcripts, either in our ancient historians, or other books and manuscripts; so they being things done before time of memory, obtain at this day no further than as by usage and custom they are, as it were, engrafted into the body of the common law and made a part thereof.

[3] In 1066, William of Normandy invaded England, claiming for the Normans the English crown, which was contested after the death of the Anglo-Saxon king, Edward the Confessor (1042–66). Edward ("Saint Edward") had gradually established a relatively unified rule in England and compiled a substantial body of laws and customs, which in the seventeenth century came to be seen as England's "ancient constitution." William believed he was entitled to the crown, but Edward, on his deathbed, named Harold Godwin as his successor. In October 1066, William defeated Harold at the Battle of Hastings. After the Conquest, William further centralized rule over all of England and consolidated laws. These laws, especially those brought together by King Edward I (1272–1307), formed the core of the emerging common law. William I reigned from 1066 to 1087.

[4] Ed: Extended examples from ancient collections omitted.

And now I come to those *leges scriptae*, or acts of parliament, which were made since or within the time of memory, viz., since the beginning of the reign of Richard I and those I shall divide into two general heads, viz., those we usually call the old statutes, and those we usually call the new or later statutes. And because I would prefix some certain time or boundary between them, I shall call those the old statutes which end with the reign of King Edward II (1307–27) and those I shall call the new or later statutes which begin with the reign of King Edward III (1327–77) and so are derived[5] through a succession of kings and queens down to this day, by a continued and orderly series.

Touching these later sort I shall say nothing, for they all keep an orderly and regular series of time, and are extant upon record, either in the parliament rolls, or in the statute rolls of King Edward III and those kings that follow; for excepting some few years in the beginning of K. Edward III, i.e. 2, 3, 7, 8 & 9 Edw. III,[6] all the parliament rolls that ever were since that time have been preserved, and are extant; and for the most part, the petitions upon which the acts were drawn up, or the very acts themselves.

Now therefore touching the elder acts of parliament, viz., those that were made between the first year of the reign of K. Richard I and the last year of K. Edward II we have little extant in any authentical history; and nothing in any authentical record touching acts made in the time of K. Rich. I unless we take in those constitutions and assizes mentioned by Hoveden[7] as aforesaid.

Neither is there any great evidence [of] what acts of parliament passed in the time of King John, though doubtless many there were both in his time, and in the time of K. Rich. I. But there is no record extant of them, and the English histories of those times give us but little account of those laws; only Matthew Paris[8] gives us an historical account of the Magna Charta and Charta de Foresta granted by King John at Running Mead the 15th of June, in the seventeenth year of his reign.[9]

[5] OED: transmitted. [6] Ed: Years 2–3, 7–9 of the reign of Edward III (1328–30, 1333–6).

[7] The reports by Roger of Hoveden (d.1201) covering the years 1148–70 were regarded as an authentic record of the laws of that period.

[8] Matthew Paris (1200–59) was a Benedictine monk, artist of illuminated manuscripts, and English chronicler working in St Albans Abbey. His *Chronica Majora* appeared in print in H. R. Luard (ed.), Rolls Series 57, 7 vols (London: Longman & Co., 1872–83).

[9] After a struggle with his powerful barons, King John (1199–1216) agreed to terms of a kind of treaty in June 1215, which came to be called "Magna Carta." The Charter mainly established the feudal rights of the barons against the king, but among the sixty-three clauses addressing specific grievances there are a few that articulate what over time came to be understood as fundamental liberties of the English people and limits on the exercise of ruling power. (Notably, section 39: "No freemen shall be taken or imprisoned or disseised [dispossessed] or exiled or in any way destroyed, nor will we go upon him nor send upon him, except by the lawful judgment of his peers or by the law of the land." See also section 61, which established a committee of twenty-five barons who could at any time meet and overrule the will of the king if he defied the provisions of the Charter.) The agreement immediately collapsed, abandoned by John and annulled by Pope Innocent III soon after it was signed. However, John died in 1216, and in 1217 the young King Henry III affirmed the Great Charter along with a smaller Charter of the Forests, dealing with governance of royal forests. He reaffirmed them upon reaching majority in 1225, at which time the Magna Carta was given definitive form. It was confirmed notably by Edward I in 1297, when it entered the statute books of English law, a defining document of the English constitution. See Anthony Arlidge and Igor Judge, *Magna Carta Uncovered* (Oxford: Hart Publishing, 2014).

And it seems that the concession of these Charters was in a parliamentary way. You may see the transcripts of both Charters verbatim in Mat. Paris, and in the Red Book of the Exchequer.[10] There were seven pair of these Charters sent to some of the great monasteries under the seal of King John, one part whereof sent to the Abbey of Tewkesbury I have seen under the seal of that king; the substance thereof differs something from the Magna Charta, and Charta de Foresta, granted by King Henry III but not very much, as may appear by comparing them.

But though these Charters of King John seem to have been passed in a kind of parliament, yet it was in a time of great confusion between that king and his nobles; and therefore they obtained not a full settlement till the time of King Henry III (1216–72) when the substance of them was enacted by a full and solemn parliament.

I therefore come down to the times of those succeeding kings, Henry III, Edw. I (1272–1307), and Edw. II (1307–27) and the statutes made in the times of those kings, [which] I call the old statutes, partly because many of them were made but in affirmance of the common law, and partly because the rest of them, that made a change in the common law, are yet so ancient that they now seem to have been as it were a part of the common law, especially considering the many expositions that have been made of them in the several successions of times, whereby as they became the great subject of judicial resolutions and decisions; so those expositions and decisions, together also with those old statutes themselves, are as it were incorporated into[11] the very common law, and become a part of it.

In the times of those three kings last mentioned, as likewise in the times of their predecessors, there were doubtless many more acts of parliament made than are now extant of record, or otherwise, which might be a means of the change of the common law in the times of those kings from what it was before, though all the records of memorials of those acts of parliament introducing such a change, are not at this day extant. But of those that are extant, I shall give you a brief account, not intending a large or accurate treatise touching that matter.[12]

Now those statutes that ensue, though most of them are unquestionable acts of parliament, yet are not of record that I know of, but only their memorials preserved in ancient printed and manuscript books of statutes; yet they are at this day for the most part generally accepted and taken as acts of parliament, though some of them are now antiquated[13] and of little use.[14]

From whence we may collect these two observations, viz.

[10] The Red Book is a collection of official documents including charters and writs for use of the Court of Exchequer. First compiled by Alexander of Swerford, the MS dates from 1230, but was supplemented with new material into the seventeenth century. See *The Red Book*, ed. Hubert Hall, 3 vols (London: Eyre and Spottiswoode, 1896).

[11] Ed: made part of the body.

[12] Ed: MH's list of extant sources of statutes from *c.*1216–1377 omitted.

[13] OED: made obsolete.

[14] Ed: Reference to approximately forty such statutes omitted.

First, that although the record itself be not extant, yet general statutes made within time of memory, namely, since 1 Richardi Primi,[15] do not lose their strength, if any authentical memorials thereof are in books, and seconded with a general received tradition attesting and approving the same.

Secondly, that many records, even of acts of parliament, have in long process of time been lost, and possibly the things themselves forgotten at this day, which yet in or near the times wherein they were made might cause many of those authoritative alterations in some things touching the proceedings and decisions in law, the original cause of which change being otherwise at this day hid and unknown to us; and indeed, histories (and annals) give us an account of the suffrages[16] of many parliaments, whereof we at this time have none, or few footsteps extant in records or acts of parliament. The instance of the great parliament at Oxford, about 40th [year] of Henry III, may, among many others of like nature, be a concurrent evidence of this;[17] for though we have mention made in our histories of many constitutions made in the said parliament at Oxford, and which occasioned much trouble in the kingdom, yet we have no monuments of record concerning that parliament, or what those constitutions were.

And thus much shall serve touching those old statutes or *leges scriptae*, or acts of parliament made in the times of those three kings, Henry III, Edw. I, and Edw. II. Those that follow in the times of Edw. III and the succeeding kings are drawn down in a continued series of time and are extant of record in the parliament rolls and in the statute rolls, without any remarkable omission, and therefore I shall say nothing of them.

2

Concerning the *Lex non Scripta*, i.e., the Common or Municipal Laws of this Kingdom

In the former chapter, I have given you a short account of that part of the laws of England which is called *lex scripta*, namely, statutes or acts of parliament, which in their original formation are reduced into writing, and are so preserved in their

[15] Ed: the first year of Richard I's reign. [16] OED: votes.

[17] At Oxford in 1258, barons forced Henry III to agree that a committee of twenty-four barons (half royal and half baronial nominees) should rule the kingdom. The reforms were embodied in the Provisions of Oxford.

original form and in the same style and words wherein they were first made. I now come to that part of our laws called *lex non scripta* under which I include not only general customs, or the common law properly so called, but even those more particular laws and customs applicable to certain courts and persons, whereof more hereafter.

And when I call those parts of our laws *leges non scriptae*, I do not mean as if all those laws were only oral, or communicated from the former ages to the later, merely by word. For all those laws have their several monuments in writing, whereby they are transferred from one age to another, and without which they would soon lose all kind of certainty; for as the civil and canon laws have their *responsa prudentum, consilia* & *decision[e]s*,[18] i.e. their canons, decrees, and decretal determinations extant in writing; so [also] those laws of England which are not comprised under the title of acts of parliament are for the most part extant in records of pleas, proceedings, and judgments, in books of reports and judicial decisions, in tractates of learned men's arguments and opinions, [all of which are] preserved from ancient times, and still extant in writing.

But I therefore style those parts of the law, *leges non scriptae*, because their authoritative and original institutions are not set down in writing in that manner or with that authority that acts of parliament are, but they are grown into use and have acquired their binding power and the force of laws by a long and immemorial usage, and by the strength of custom and reception in this kingdom. The matters indeed, and the substance of those laws, are in writing, but the formal and obliging force and power of them grows by long custom and use, as will fully appear in the ensuing discourse.

For the municipal laws[19] of this kingdom, which I thus call *leges non scriptae*, are of a vast extent, and indeed include in their generality all those several laws which are allowed, as the rule and direction of justice and judicial proceedings, and which are applicable to all those various subjects, about which justice is conversant. I shall, for more order, and the better to guide my reader, distinguish them into two kinds, viz.

First, the common law, as it is taken in its proper and usual acceptation.

Secondly, those particular laws applicable to particular subjects, matters, or courts.

1. Touching the former, viz., the common law in its usual and proper acceptation. This is that law by which proceedings and determinations in the king's ordinary courts of justice are directed and guided. This directs the course of descents of lands,[20] and the kinds, the natures, and the extents and qualifications of estates;

[18] In Roman law and canon law, *responsa prudentum* were authoritative answers of learned jurists to difficult legal questions, advising litigants, judges, and the praetor; *consilia* were advisory opinions to which judges turned to decide doubtful points of law; *decisiones* were opinions of judges who had taken part in cases, explaining reasoning of the court.

[19] OED: laws pertaining to the internal affairs of a state.

[20] OED: transmission of property by inheritance.

therein also the manner, forms, ceremonies, and solemnities of transferring estates from one to another; the rules of settling, acquiring, and transferring of properties; the forms, solemnities, and obligation of contracts; the rules and directions for the exposition of wills, deeds, and acts of parliament; the process, proceedings, judgments, and executions of the king's ordinary courts of justice; the limits, bounds, and extents of courts, and their jurisdictions; the several kinds of temporal offences, and punishments at common law; and the manner of the application of the several kinds of punishments, and infinite more particulars which extend themselves as large as the many exigencies in the distribution of the king's ordinary justice requires.

And besides these more common and ordinary matters to which the common law extends, it likewise includes the laws applicable to divers matters of very great moment; and though by reason of that application, the said common law assumes divers denominations,[21] yet they are but branches and parts of it, like as the same ocean, though it many times receives a different name from the province, shire, island, or country to which it is contiguous, yet these are but parts of the same ocean.

Thus the common law includes *lex prerogativa*, as 'tis applied with certain rules to that great business of the king's prerogative;[22] so 'tis called *lex forestae*, as it is applied under its special and proper rules to the business of forests; so it is called *lex mercatoria*, as it is applied under its proper rules to the business of trade and commerce; and many more instances of like nature may be given. Nay, the various and particular customs of cities, towns, and manors are thus far parts of the common law, as they are applicable to those particular places, which will appear from these observations, viz.

First, the common law does determine what of those customs are good and reasonable, and what are unreasonable and void. Secondly, the common law gives to those customs, that it adjudges reasonable, the force and efficacy of their obligation. Thirdly, the common law determines what is that continuance of time that is sufficient to make such a custom. Fourthly, the common law does interpose and authoritatively decide the exposition, limits, and extension of such customs.

This common law, though the usage, practice, and decisions of the king's courts of justice may expound and evidence it, and be of great use to illustrate and explain it; yet it cannot be authoritatively altered or changed but by act of parliament. But of this common law, and the reason of its denomination,[23] more at large hereafter.

[2.] Now, secondly, as to those particular laws I before mentioned, which are applicable to particular matters, subjects, or courts: these make up the second branch of the laws of England, which I include under the general term of *leges non scriptae*, and by those particular laws I mean the laws ecclesiastical, and the civil law, so far

[21] OED: classes or kinds distinguishable by specific names.

[22] The law of royal prerogative defines the special rights, powers, and privileges (and their limits) of the king, especially those pertaining to the exercise of ruling power. See Part VI, *Prerogatives*.

[23] Ed: being named in this way.

forth as they are admitted in certain courts, and certain matters allowed to the decision of those courts, whereof hereafter.

It is true that those civil and ecclesiastical laws are indeed written laws, the civil law being contained in their pandects, and the institutions of Justinian, &c.[24] (their imperial constitutions or codes answering to our *leges scriptae*, or statutes). And the canon or ecclesiastical laws contained for the most part in the canons and constitutions of councils and popes, collected in their *decretum gratiani*, and the decretal epistles of popes, which make up the body of their *corpus juris canonici*,[25] together with huge volumes of councils and expositions, decisions, and tractates of learned civilians and canonists, relating to both laws; so that it may seem at first view very improper to rank these under the branch of *leges non scriptae*, or unwritten laws.

But I have for the following reason ranged these laws among the unwritten laws of England, viz., because it is most plain, that neither the canon law nor the civil law have any obligation as laws within this kingdom, upon any account that the popes or emperors made those laws, canons, rescripts, or determinations, or because Justinian compiled their *corpus juris civilis*, and by his edicts confirmed and published the same as authentical, or because this or that council or pope made those or these canons or degrees, or because Gratian, or Gregory, or Boniface, or Clement did, as much as in them lie, authenticate this or that body of canons or constitutions; for the king of England does not recognize any foreign authority as superior or equal to him in this kingdom, neither do any laws of the Pope or Emperor, as they are such, bind here. But all the strength that either the papal or imperial laws have obtained in this kingdom is only because they have been received and admitted either by the consent of parliament, and so are part of the statute laws of the kingdom, or else by immemorial usage and custom in some particular cases and courts, and no otherwise. And therefore so far as such laws are received and allowed of here, so far they obtain and no farther. And the authority and force they have here is not founded on, or derived from themselves, for so they bind no more with us than our laws bind in Rome or Italy. But their authority is founded merely on their being admitted and received by us, which alone gives them their authoritative essence, and qualifies their obligation.

[24] The *Digest* (or *Pandects*) and *Institutes*, two of the main components of the *Corpus Juris Civilis* (the body of Roman civil law), were compiled by scholars as directed by the Roman emperor, Justinian, in 529 to 534.

[25] *Decretum* of Gratian (*Concordantia discordantium canonum—Concordance of discordant canons*) is a compilation and conciliation of principles, rules, and decisions of ecclesiastical law dating from the mid-twelfth century. It compiled materials from earlier collections of canon law. *Decretals* were papal letters clarifying matters of canon law collected in various editions in the twelfth century. In 1230, Raymond Pennafort was commissioned by Pope Gregory IX (1227–41) to compile an authoritative collection of papal decretals. Later decretals of Pope Boniface VIII (1294–1303) and the constitutions of Clement V (1305–14) were added. Together with the *Liber Sextus*, the *Decretum* and *Decretals* made up the *Corpus Juris Canonici* or "body of canon law."

And hence it is, that even in those courts where the use of those laws is indulged according to that reception which has been allowed them, if they exceed the bounds of that reception by extending themselves to other matters than has been allowed them, or if those courts proceed according to that law when it is controlled by the common law of the kingdom, the common law does and may prohibit and punish them. And it will not be a sufficient answer, for them to tell the king's courts that Justinian or Pope Gregory have decreed otherwise, for we are not bound by their decrees further or otherwise than as the kingdom here has as it were transposed the same into the common and municipal laws of the realm, either by admission of, or by enacting the same, which is that alone which can make them of any force in England. I need not give particular instances herein, the truth thereof is plain and evident, and we need go no further than the statutes of 24 H. 8. cap. 12 and 25 H. 8. c. 19, 20, 21,[26] and the learned notes of Selden upon *Fleta*,[27] and the records there cited. Nor shall I spend much time touching the use of those laws in the several courts of this kingdom, but will only briefly mention some few things concerning them.

There are three courts of note, wherein the civil, and in one of them the canon or ecclesiastical law, has been with certain restrictions allowed in this kingdom, viz., 1st. the Courts Ecclesiastical of the Bishops and their derivative officers; 2dly, the Admiralty Court; 3dly, the *Curia Militaris*, or Court of the Constable and Marshal, or persons commissioned to exercise that jurisdiction. I shall touch a little upon each of these.[28]

... And thus I have given a brief prospect of these courts and matters, wherein the canon and civil law has been in some measure allowed, as the rule or direction of proceedings or decisions. But although in these courts and matters the laws of England, upon the reasons and account before expressed, have admitted the use and rule of the canon and civil law, yet even herein also, the common law of England has retained those *signa superioritatis* [marks of superior authority], and the preference and superintendence in relation to those courts: namely,

1st. As the laws and statutes of the realm have prescribed to those courts their bounds and limits, so the courts of common law have the superintendency over those

[26] MH cites Reformation era statutes. Statute 24 H 8 c. 12 (1532) (St. Realm III, 427) forbade appeals to Rome; Statute 25 H 8 cc. 19–21 (1533) (St. Realm III, 460–71) dealt with other issues central to establishing the independence of the English Church from Rome.

[27] John Selden, *Ad Fletam Dissertatio* (1647), ed. David Ogg (Cambridge: Cambridge University Press, 1925).

[28] Hereafter, in material omitted, MH offers an extended description of the issues, civil and criminal, over which ecclesiastical courts (and in them canon law and civil law) and admiralty and military courts (and in them civil law) have jurisdiction, as recognized by the common law. He makes clear that ecclesiastical jurisdiction is derived from the crown. Similarly, he argues, the admiralty court "is not bottom'd or founded upon the authority of the civil law, but hath both its power and jurisdiction by the law and custom of the realm, in such matters as are proper for its cognizance."

courts, to keep them within the limits and bounds of their several jurisdictions, and to judge and determine whether they have exceeded those bounds, or not. And in case they do exceed their bounds, the courts at common law issue their prohibitions to restrain them, directed either to the judge or party, or both. And also, in case they exceed their jurisdiction, the officer that executes the sentence, and in some cases the judge that gives it, are punishable in the courts at common law, sometimes at the suit of the king, sometimes at the suit of the party, and sometimes at the suit of both, according to the variety and circumstances of the case.

2dly. The common law, and the judges of the courts of common law, have the [exclusive right of] exposition of such statutes or acts of parliament as concern either the extent of the jurisdiction of those courts (whether ecclesiastical, maritime, or military) or the matters depending before them. And therefore, if those courts either refuse to allow these acts of parliament, or expound them in any other sense than is truly and properly the exposition of them, the king's great courts of the common law (who next under the king and his parliament have the [right of] exposition of those laws) may prohibit and control[29] them.

And thus much touching those courts wherein the civil and canon laws are allowed as rules and directions under the restrictions above-mentioned; touching which, the sum of the whole is this:

First, that the jurisdiction exercised in those courts is derived from the crown of England, and that the last devolution is to the king, by way of appeal.

Secondly, that although the canon or civil law be respectively allowed as the direction or rule of their proceedings, yet that is not as if either of those laws had any original obligation in England, either as they are the laws of emperors, popes, or general councils, but only by virtue of their admission here, which is evident, for that those canons or imperial constitutions which have not been received here do not bind. And also, for that by several contrary customs and styles used here many of those civil and canon laws are controlled and derogated.[30]

Thirdly, that although those laws are admitted in some cases in those courts, yet they are but *leges sub graviori lege* [laws subject to weightier (higher) law]; and the common laws of this kingdom have ever obtained and retained the superintendency over them, and those *signa superioritatis* before-mentioned, for the honour of the king and the common laws of England.[31]

[29] Ed: call them to account, censure. [30] OED: curtailed or restricted.

[31] In his disquisition on admiralty jurisdiction, MH offers another reason for keeping civil law within limits defined by the common law: "it is a position generally received in the Civil Law *quod principi placuit legis habet vigorem* [whatever pleases the prince has the force of law]" (*Digest*, I.4.1). And English law rejects this absolutist doctrine and insists that the monarch's lawmaking power is qualified, requiring the assent of both houses of parliament for enactment of laws. See *Hale and Fleetwood on Admiralty Jurisdiction*, ed. M. J. Pritchard and D. E. C. Yale (London: Selden Society, 1993), 7.

3

Concerning the Common Law of England, its Use and Excellence, and the Reason of its Denomination

I come now to that other branch of our laws, the common municipal law of this kingdom, which has the superintendency of all those other particular laws used in the before-mentioned courts, and is the common rule for the administration of common justice in this great kingdom, of which it has been always tender. And there is great reason for it; for it is not only a very just and excellent law in itself, but it is singularly accommodated to the frame of the English government, and to the disposition of the English nation, and such as by a long experience and use is as it were incorporated into their very temperament,[32] and, in a manner, become the complexion[33] and constitution of the English commonwealth.

Insomuch, that even as in the natural body the due temperament and constitution does by degrees work out those accidental diseases which sometimes happen, and do reduce the body to its just state and constitution, so when at any time through the errors, distempers, or iniquities of men or times, the peace of the kingdom, and right order of government, have received interruption, the common law has wasted[34] and wrought out those distempers, and reduced the kingdom to its just state and temperament, as our present (and former) times can easily witness.

This law is that which asserts, maintains, and, with all imaginable care, provides for the safety of the king's royal person, his crown and dignity, and all his just rights, revenues, powers, prerogatives, and government, as the great foundation (under God) of the peace, happiness, honour, and justice of this kingdom. And this law is also that which declares and asserts the rights and liberties, and the properties of the subject, and is the just, known, and common rule of justice and right between man and man, within this kingdom.

[32] Ed: a medical metaphor: balanced mixture of elements in a compound.

[33] OED: in medieval natural philosophy: the combination in certain proportion of qualities that determine the nature of something.

[34] OED: put an end to.

And from hence it is, that the wisdom of the kings of England, and their great council, the honourable house of parliament, have always been jealous and vigilant for the reformation of what has been at any time found defective in it, and so to remove all such obstacles as might obstruct the free course of it, and to support, countenance, and encourage the use of it, as the best, safest, and truest rule of justice in all matters, as well criminal as civil.[35]

Now the reason why 'tis called the common law, or what was the occasion that first gave that determination to it, is variously assigned, viz.

First, some have thought it to be so called by way of contradistinction to those other laws that have obtained within this kingdom; as, 1st, by way of contradistinction to the statute law, thus a writ of entry *ad communem legem* is so called in contradistinction to writs of entry *in casu consimili*, and *casu proviso*,[36] which are given by act of parliament. 2dly, ["common law" is used] by way of contradistinction to particular customary laws. Thus descents at common law, dower at common law, are in contradistinction to such dowers and descents as are directed by particular customs.[37] And 3dly, ["common law" is used] in contradistinction to the civil, canon, martial, and military laws, which are in some particular cases and courts admitted, as the rule of their proceedings.

Secondly, some have conceived, that the reason of this appellation was this, viz., in the beginning of the reign of Edward III (1042–66) before the conquest, commonly called Edward the Confessor, there were several laws, and of several natures, which obtained in several parts of this kingdom, viz., the Mercian laws, in the counties of Gloucester, Worcester, Hereford, Warwick, Oxon, Chester, Salop, and Stafford; the Danish laws, in the counties of York, Derby, Nottingham, Leicester, Lincoln, Northampton, Bedford, Bucks, Hertford, Essex, Middlesex, Norfolk, Suffolk, Cambridge, and Huntington; the West-Saxon laws, in the counties of Kent, Sussex, Surrey, Berks, Southampton, Wilts, Somerset, Dorset, and Devon.[38]

35 Ed: MH's examples of civil and criminal laws protecting the rights and liberties of the English people omitted.

36 From the end of the twelfth century, writs of entry were used to recover land from someone who had defective title. Different forms of this writ developed in the thirteenth century. The standard writ of entry had a common-law origin (*ad communem legem*), but in 1278, the Statute of Gloucester (6 Ed. I, c. 7; St. Realm I, 48) provided a writ of entry for the heir if it was alienated by a widow holding the land in dower. The writ based on this statutory provision was called a writ of entry *in casu proviso*. And in 1285, the Statute of Westminster II (13 Edw. I, c. 24; St. Realm I, 83) empowered the Chancery to issue a writ in cases similar to ones for which a writ was already provided (*in casu consimili*). A writ of entry *in casu consimili* was based on the statute that was followed.

37 Dower concerned rights of a widow to inherit (a portion of) her husband's land; descent concerned rights of inheritance of other kin. "Descent by particular customs" refers to the customs of gavelkind (dividing a man's property equally among his sons) and ultimogeniture (right of inheritance pertaining to the youngest of the family). These were customs of inheritance in specific counties or regions of medieval England.

38 In the Anglo-Saxon era (from around the sixth to the eleventh century), seven kingdoms (Heptarchy) took hold in England: Kent, three Saxon kingdoms (Sussex, Essex, and Wessex) and three Angle kingdoms (Mercia, East Anglia, and Northumbria). Mercia was dominant for some time, but later Wessex established dominance. In the ninth century, Danes invaded and established law in some parts of the island. MH

This king [Edward the Confessor], to reduce the kingdom as well under one law, as it then was under one monarchical government, extracted out of all those provincial laws, one law to be observed through the whole kingdom.[39]

Thirdly, others say, and that most truly, that it is called the common law, because it is the common municipal law or rule of justice in this kingdom: so that *lex communis*, or *jus communis*, is all one and the same with *lex patriae*, or *jus patrium* [i.e., common law or common right . . . law or right of the land (i.e., the whole kingdom)]. For although there are divers particular laws, some by custom applied to particular places, and some to particular causes, yet that law which is common to the generality of all persons, things, and causes, and has a superintendency over those particular laws that are admitted in relation to particular places or matters, is *lex communis angliae*, as the municipal laws of other countries may be, and are sometimes called, the common law of that country—as *lex communis norrica, lex communis burgundica, lex communis lombardica*, &c.[40] So that although all the former reasons have their share in this appellation, yet the principal cause thereof seems to be the latter. And hence some of the ancients called it *lex communis*, others *lex patriae*; and so they were called in their confirmation by King William I, whereof hereafter.

4

Touching the Original of the Common Law of England

The kingdom of England being a very ancient kingdom has had many vicissitudes and changes (especially before the coming in of King William I) under several either conquests or accessions of foreign nations. For though the Britons were, as is supposed, the most ancient inhabitants, yet there were mingled with them, or brought in upon them, the Romans, the Picts, the Saxons, the Danes, and lastly, the Normans. And many of those foreigners were as it were incorporated together, and made one common people and nation. And hence arises the difficulty, and

maintains that by the tenth century three centres of power and three kinds of law existed side by side. In the eleventh century, Saxon kings, especially Edward the Confessor, did much to unify ruling power and the law.

39 Ed: Support for this claim in a variety of historical and other writings omitted.

40 Ed: common law of Noricum, common law of Burgundy, common law of Lombardy [i.e., the laws indigenous to various areas of medieval continental Europe].

indeed moral[41] impossibility, of giving any satisfactory or so much as probable conjecture, touching the original[42] of the laws, for the following reasons, viz.

First, [the difficulty arises] from the nature of laws themselves in general, which being to be accommodated to the conditions, exigencies,[43] and conveniencies[44] of the people, for or by whom they are appointed, as those exigencies and conveniencies do insensibly grow upon the people, so many times there grows insensibly a variation of laws, especially in a long tract of time. And hence it is that, though for the purpose in some particular part of the common law of England we may easily say that the common law, as it is now taken, is otherwise than it was in that particular part or point in the time of Hen. II when Glanville wrote, or than it was in the time of Hen. III when Bracton wrote,[45] yet it is not possible to assign the certain time when the change began. Nor have we all the monuments or memorials, either of acts of parliament or of judicial resolutions, which might induce or occasion such alterations; for we have no authentic records of any acts of parliament before 9 Hen. III [1225] and those we have of that king's time are but few. Nor have we any reports of judicial decisions in any constant series of time before the reign of Edw. I though we have the plea rolls[46] of the times of Hen. III [1327–77] and King John [1199–1216], in some remarkable order. So that use and custom, and judicial decisions and resolutions, and acts of parliament, though not now extant, might introduce some new laws, and alter some old, which we now take to be the very common law itself, though the times and precise periods of such alterations are not explicitly or clearly known. But though those particular variations and accessions have happened in the laws, yet they being only partial and successive, we may with just reason say they are the same English laws now, that they were 600 years since in the general, as the Argonauts' ship was the same when it returned home, as it was when it went out, though in that long voyage it had successive amendments, and scarce came back with any of its former materials.[47] And as Titius is the same man he was forty years since, though

[41] Ed: practical. [42] Ed: origin. [43] OED: needs, requirements.

[44] OED: aptitudes, matters consistent with their nature.

[45] MH refers to the earliest classic works on English law: *The Treatise on the Laws and Customs of the Realm of England Commonly Called Glanvill* (*c.*1187/9), ed. G. D. G. Hall (Oxford: Oxford University Press, 2002); *De Legibus et Consuetudinibus Angliae* (*c.*1250–59), attributed to "Bracton" (Henry of Bratton (1210–68)), but probably written by a number of royal justices, 4 vols, ed. George E. Woodbine, tr. Samuel E. Thorne (Cambridge, MA: Belnap Press, Harvard University Press, 1968–77).

[46] Ed: records of pleas heard before common law courts.

[47] In Greek mythology, Jason and his band spent many years on the high seas in search of the Golden Fleece in their ship called the "Argo." (See Jason Colavito, *Jason and the Argonauts through the Ages* (Jefferson, NC: McFarland & Company, 2014).) Some traditions regarded Theseus as an Argonaut; hence, MH may have confused the story of the Argonauts with the story of the ship of Theseus. Plutarch (CE 46–120) told the latter story in its canonical version: "The ship wherein Theseus and the youth of Athens returned had thirty oars, and was preserved by the Athenians down even to the time of Demetrius Phalereus, for they took away the old planks as they decayed, putting in new and stronger timber in their place, insomuch that this ship became a standing example among the philosophers... one side holding that the ship remained the same, and the other contending that it was not the same." *The Life of Theseus*, tr. John Dryden (New York: Modern Library, 1979), 14. The story posed for ancient and medieval

physicians tell us, that in a tract of seven years, the body has scarce any of the same material substance it had before.[48]

Secondly, the 2[d] difficulty in the search of the antiquity of laws and their original is in relation to that people unto whom the laws are applied, which in the case of England will render many observables to shew it hard to be traced. For, 1st, it is an ancient kingdom, and in such cases, though the people and government had continued the same *ab origine* [from the beginning] (as they say the Chinese did, till the late incursion of the Tartars) without the mixture of other people or laws, yet it were an impossible thing to give any certain account of the original of the laws of such a people, unless we had as certain monuments thereof as the Jews had of theirs by the hand of Moses, and that upon the following accounts, viz.

First, we have not any clear and certain monuments of the original foundation of the English kingdom or state, when, and by whom, and how it came to be planted. That which we have concerning it, is uncertain and traditional.[49] And since we cannot know the original of the planting of this kingdom, we cannot certainly know the original of the laws thereof, which may be well presumed to be very near as ancient as the kingdom itself. Again, 2[dly], though tradition might be a competent discoverer of the original of a kingdom or state, I mean oral tradition, yet such a tradition were incompetent without written monuments to derive to us, at so long a distance, the original laws and constitutions of the kingdom, because they are of a complex nature, and therefore not orally traducible[50] to so great a distance of ages, unless we had the original or authentic transcript of those laws as the people the Jews had of their law, or as the Romans had of their laws of the Twelve Tables engraven in brass.[51] But yet further, 3[dly], it is very evident to every day's experience, that laws, the further they go from their original institution, grow the larger and the more numerous. In the first coalition of a people, their prospect is not great; they provide laws for their present exigence and convenience. But in process of time possibly their first laws are changed, altered, or antiquated, as some of the laws of the Twelve Tables among the Romans were. But whatsoever be done touching their old laws,

philosophers the question of identity through change over time; it also found its way into jurisprudence via glosses by Accursius (1182–1263) and Baldus (1327–1400) on *Digest*, 5.1.76, discussing whether a court whose members changed over time retained its identity. (See Ernst Kantorowicz, *The King's Two Bodies: A Study in Medieval Political Theology* (Princeton: Princeton University Press, 1957), 295.) Selden uses the trope in his *Notes on Sir John Fortescue, De Laudibus Legum Anglicae,* in John Selden, *Works* (London: T. Wood, 1726), vol. 3, at col. 1892; and mentions the ship of Theseus explicitly in his *The Dominion or Ownership of the Sea* (London, 1652), 133.

48 Alan Cromartie reports that MH, in his work on principles of life ("*animae*") in nature, "showed an interest in identity, stressing that organisms could persist when all of their constituents were in perpetual flux." (Cromartie, *Sir Matthew Hale: 1609–1676* (Cambridge: Cambridge University Press, 1995), 222, citing unpublished manuscripts: Lambeth 3500, 38 and 3509, 41.)

49 Ed: asserted or handed down by tradition.

50 Ed: capable of being handed down.

51 The Twelve Tables, the foundation of Roman law, were composed in 451–450 BCE. Tradition has it that the laws were engraved in metal and displayed publicly.

there must of necessity be a provision of new and other laws successively answering to the multitude of successive exigencies and emergencies[52] that in a long tract of time will offer themselves. So that if a man could at this day have the prospects of all the laws of the Britons before any invasion upon them, it would yet be impossible to say which of them were new and which were old, and the several seasons and periods of time wherein every law took its rise and original, especially since it appears that in those elder times the Britons were not reduced to that civilized estate as to keep the annals and memorials of their laws and government, as the Romans and other civilized parts of the world have done.

It is true, when the conquest of a country appears, we can tell when the laws of conquering people came to be given to the conquered. Thus we can tell that in the time of Hen. II when the conquest of Ireland had obtained a good progress, and in the time of K. John, when it was completed, the English laws were settled in Ireland.[53] But if we were upon this inquiry: what were the original of those English laws that were thus settled there? we are still under the same quest and difficulty that we are now, viz., what is the original of the English laws. For they that begin new colonies, plantations,[54] and conquests, if they settle new laws, and which the places had not before, yet for the most part (I don't say altogether) they are the old laws which obtained in those countries from whence the conquerors or planters came.

Secondly, the 2^{d} difficulty of the discovery of the original of the English laws is this, that this kingdom has had many and great vicissitudes of people that inhabited it, and that in their several times prevailed and obtained a great hand in the government of this kingdom, whereby it came to pass, that there arose a great mixture and variety of laws. In some places the laws of the Saxons, in some places the laws of the Danes, in some places the laws of the ancient Britons, in some places the laws of the Mercians, and in some places, or among some people (perhaps) the laws of the Normans. For although, as I shall shew hereafter, the Normans never obtained this kingdom by such a right of conquest as did or might alter the established laws of the kingdom, yet considering that K. Will. I brought with him a great multitude of that nation, and many persons of great power and eminence, which were planted generally over this kingdom, especially in the possessions of such as had opposed his coming in, it must needs be supposed that those occurrences might easily have a great influence upon the laws of this kingdom, and secretly and insensibly introduce new laws, customs, and usages; so that although the body and gross[55] of the law might continue the same, and so continue the ancient denomination that it first had, yet it must needs receive diverse accessions from the laws of those people that were thus intermingled with the

[52] OED: unexpected occurrences.

[53] Henry II established a degree of control in Ireland in the 1170s, and in John's reign the Norman barons controlled much of Ireland.

[54] OED: settlement of a people in a dominated country.

[55] OED: entire, total, whole.

ancient Britons or Saxons, as the rivers of Severn, Thames, Trent, &c. though they continue the same denomination which their first stream had, yet have the accession of divers other streams added to them in the tracts of their passage which enlarge and augment them. And hence grew those several denominations of the Saxon, Mercian, and Danish laws, out of which (as before is shewn) [Edward] the Confessor extracted his body of the common law. And therefore among all those various ingredients and mixtures of laws, it is almost an impossible piece of chemistry to reduce every *caput legis* [head or principle of law] to its true original, as to say, this is a piece of the Danish, this of the Norman, or this of the Saxon or British law. Neither was it, or indeed is it much material which of these is their original. For 'tis very plain, the strength and obligation, and the formal nature of a law, is not upon account that the Danes, or the Saxons, or the Normans brought it in with them, but they became laws, and binding in this kingdom, by virtue only of their being received and approved here.

Thirdly, a third difficulty arises from those accidental emergencies that happened, either in the alteration of laws, or communicating or conveying of them to this kingdom. For first, the subdivision of the kingdom into small kingdoms under the Heptarchy did most necessarily introduce a variation of laws, because the several parts of the kingdom, were not under one common standard. And so it will soon be in any kingdoms that are cantonized and not under one common method of dispensation of laws, though under one and the same king. Again, the intercourse and traffic with other nations, as it grew more or greater, did gradually make a communication and transmigration of laws from us to them, and from them to us. Again, the growth of Christianity in this kingdom, and the reception of learned men from other parts, especially from Rome, and the credit that they obtained here, might reasonably introduce some new laws, and antiquate or abrogate some old ones that seemed less consistent with the Christian doctrines. And by this means, not only some of the judicial laws of the Jews,[56] but also some points relating to, or bordering upon, or derived from the canon or civil laws, as may be seen in those laws of the ancient kings Ina, Alphred, Canutus, &c. collected by Mr Lambard.[57]

Having thus far premised, it seems, upon the whole matter, an endless and insuperable business to carry up the English laws to their several springs and heads, and to find out their first original. Neither would it be of any moment or use if it were done. For whenever the laws of England, or the several *capita* thereof began, or from whence or whomsoever derived, or what laws of other countries contributed to the matter of our laws, yet most certainly their obligation arises not from their matter, but from their admission and reception and authorization in this

[56] That part of the Mosaic Law concerning political, social, and interpersonal matters.

[57] King Ina of Wessex (688–726); King Alfred of Wessex (849–99); King Cnut of England (1016–35). William Lambarde (1536–1601) was an Elizabethan antiquarian. MH refers to Lambarde's *Archeonomia* (1568), a collection of Anglo-Saxon laws.

kingdom. And those laws, if convenient and useful for the kingdom, were never the worse, though they were desumed[58] and taken from the laws of other countries, so as they had their stamp of obligation and authority from the reception and approbation of this kingdom by virtue of the common law, of which this kingdom has been always jealous, especially in relation to the canon, civil, and Norman law, for the reasons hereafter shewn.

Passing therefore from this unsearchable inquiry, I shall descend to that which gives the authority, viz., the formal constituents, as I may call them, of the common law. And they seem to be principally, if not only, those three, viz., 1st. the common usage, or custom, and practice of this kingdom, in such parts thereof as lie in usage or custom; 2dly, the authority of parliament, introducing such laws; and, 3dly, the judicial decisions of courts of justice, consonant to one another in the series and successions of time.

1. As to the first of these, usage and custom generally received, do *obtinere vim legis* [acquire the force of law], and is that which gives power sometimes to the canon law, as in the ecclesiastical courts, sometimes to the civil law, as in the admiralty courts; and again, controls both, when they cross other customs that are generally received in the kingdom. This is that which directs descents, has settled some ancient ceremonies and solemnities in conveyances, wills, and deeds, and in many more particulars. And if it be enquired, what is the evidence of this custom, or wherein it consists, or is to be found? I answer, it is not simply an unwritten custom, not barely orally derived down from one age to another, but it is a custom that is derived down in writing, and transmitted from age to age, especially since the beginning of Edw. I, to whose wisdom the laws of England owe almost as much as the laws of Rome to Justinian.[59]

2. Acts of parliament. And here it must not be wondered at, that I make acts of parliament one of the authoritative constituents of the common law, though I had before contradistinguished the one from the other. For we are to know, that although the original or authentic transcripts of acts of parliament are not before the time of Hen. III and many that were in his time are perished and lost; yet certainly such there were, and many of those things that we now take for common law were undoubtedly acts of parliament, though now not to be found of record. And if in the next age, the statutes made in the time of Hen. III and Edw. I were lost, yet even those would pass for parts of the common law. And indeed, by long usage and the many resolutions

[58] OED: to take from a mass, pick out, cull.

[59] During the reign of Edward I (1277–1307) some of the most significant statutes of the medieval period were enacted. Many were omnibus bills covering a number of issues, many clarifying, modifying, and codifying doctrines of existing law, some introducing new law. For his efforts, he was called, already in the medieval period, "The English Justinian." See MH's "Preface to Rolle's Abridgement," 162. The great Roman *Corpus Juris Civilis* was compiled by scholars as directed by the Roman emperor, Justinian, in the sixth century. Hume added a sober note to this conventional encomium. Edward, he wrote, was "no enemy to arbitrary power." David Hume, *History of England* (1788 edition), ed. William B. Todd (Indianapolis: Liberty Classics, 1883), II, 141–3.

grounded upon them, and by their great antiquity, they seem even already to be incorporated with the very common law. And that this is so, may appear, though not by records, for we have none so ancient, yet by an authentical and unquestionable history, wherein a man may, without much difficulty, find that many of those *capitala legum* [leading principles of law] that are now used and taken for common law, were things enacted in parliaments or great councils under William I and his predecessors, kings of England, as may be made [to] appear hereafter. But yet, those constitutions and laws being made before time of memory, do now obtain and are taken as part of the common law and immemorial customs of the kingdom. And so they ought now to be esteemed though in their first original they were acts of parliament.

3. Judicial decisions. It is true, the decisions of courts of justice, though by virtue of the laws of this realm they do bind, as a law between the parties thereto, as to the particular case in question, 'till reversed by error or attaint,[60] yet they do not make a law properly so called (for that only the king and parliament can do). Yet they have a great weight and authority in expounding, declaring, and publishing what the law of this kingdom is, especially when such decisions hold a consonancy and congruity with resolutions and decisions of former times. And though such decisions are less than a law, yet they are a greater evidence thereof than the opinion of any private persons, as such, whatsoever.

1st, because the persons who pronounce those decisions are men chosen by the king for that employment, as being of greater learning, knowledge, and experience in the laws than others. 2[dly], because they are upon their oaths to judge according to the laws of the kingdom. 3[dly], because they have the best helps to inform their judgments. 4th[ly], because they do *sedere pro tribunali* [sit together as a tribunal], and their judgments are strengthened and upheld by the laws of this kingdom, till they are by the same law reversed or avoided.[61]

Now judicial decisions, as far as they refer to the laws of this kingdom, are for the matter of them of three kinds:

First, they are either such as have their reasons singly in the laws and customs of this kingdom, as, who shall succeed as heir to the ancestor, what is the ceremony requisite for passing a freehold, what estate and how much shall the wife have for her dower? and many such matters wherein the ancient and express laws of the kingdom give an express decision, and the judge seems only the instrument to pronounce it. And in these things, the law or custom of the realm is the only rule and measure to judge by, and in reference to those matters, the decisions of courts are the conservatories[62] and evidences of those laws.

Secondly, or they are such decisions as by way of deduction and illation[63] upon those laws are framed or deduced. As for the purpose, whether of an estate thus or

[60] Ed: by reversal of false jury verdict.
[61] Ed: invalidated or nullified.
[62] OED: storehouse, repository.
[63] OED: inference.

thus limited the wife shall be endowed; whether if thus or thus limited the heir may be barred; and infinite more of the like complicated questions.[64] And herein the rule of decision is, first, the common law and custom of the realm, which is the great substratum that is to be maintained, and then authorities or decisions of former times in the same or the like cases, and then the reason of the thing itself.

Thirdly, or they are such as seem to have no other guide but the common reason of the thing, unless the same point has been formally decided, as in the exposition of the intention of clauses in deeds, wills, covenants, &c. where the very sense of the words, and their positions and relations, give a rational account of the meaning of the parties. And in such cases the judge does much better herein, than what a bare grave grammarian or logician, or other prudent men could do. For in many cases there have been former resolutions, either in point or agreeing in reason or analogy with the case in question; or perhaps also, the clause to be expounded is mingled with some terms or clauses that require the knowledge of the law to help out with the construction or exposition. Both which do often happen in the same case, and therefore it requires the knowledge of the law to render and expound such clauses and sentences: and doubtless a good common lawyer is the best expositor of such clauses, &c. vide Plowden 122, to 130, 140, etc.[65]

5

How the Common Law of England Stood at and for Some Time after the Coming in of King William I

It is the honour and safety,[66] and therefore the just desire, of kingdoms that recognize no superior but God that their laws have those two qualifications, viz., 1st, that they be not dependent upon any foreign power; for a dependency in laws derogates from

[64] MH here mentions as examples of contested questions of law two issues regarding the inheritance of landed property.

[65] MH cites Buckley v Rice Thomas (1373) in Edmund Plowden (1518–85), *Les Commentaries ou Reportes*, ed. Richardo Tottelli (1571). For further discussion of the theme of this paragraph, see "Reflections," Chapter 1.

[66] MH has in mind a wide notion of "safety," including "well-being" or "welfare" (as in the Latin motto he often quotes: *salus populi suprema lex esto*—the welfare of the people is the supreme law).

the honour and integrity of the kingdom and from the power and sovereignty of the prince thereof. Secondly, that they taste not of bondage or servitude; for that derogates from the dignity of the kingdom, and from the liberties of the people thereof.

In relation to the former consideration, the kings of this realm, and their great councils, have always been jealous and careful, that they admitted not any foreign power, (especially such as pretended authority to impose laws upon other free kingdoms or states) nor to countenance the admission of such laws here as were derived from such a power.

Rome, as well ancient as modern, pretended a kind of universal power and interest; the former by their victories, which were large and extended even to Britain itself, and the later upon the pretence of being universal bishop or vicar-general in all matters ecclesiastical. So that upon pretence of the former, the civil law, and upon pretence of the later, the canon law, was introduced or pretended to some kind of right in the territories of some absolute[67] princes, and among others here in England. But this kingdom has been always very jealous of giving too much countenance to either of those laws, and has always shewn a just indignation and resentment against any encroachments of this kind, either by the one law or the other. It is true, as before is shewn, that in the admiralty and military courts, the civil law has been admitted, and in the ecclesiastical courts, the canon law has been in some particulars admitted. But still they carry such marks and evidences about them whereby it may be known that they bind not, nor have the authority of laws from themselves, but from the authoritative admission of this kingdom.

And, as thus the kingdom, for the reasons before given, never admitted the civil or the canon law to be the rule of the administration of common justice in this kingdom, so neither has it endured any laws to be imposed upon the people by any right of conquest, as being unsuitable to the honour or liberty of the English kingdom, to recognize their laws as given them at the will and pleasure of a conqueror. And hence it was that although the people unjustly assisted King Hen. IV in his usurpation of the crown, yet he was not admitted thereunto until he had declared that he claimed not as a conqueror, but as a successor; only he reserved to himself the liberty of extending a pretence of conquest against the Scropes that were slain in battle against him, which yet he durst not rest upon without a confirmation in parliament. Vide Rot. Parl. 1 H.4. No. 56. & Pars 2. Ibid. No. 17.[68]

[67] Ed: could mean having unlimited authority, but here probably meaning autonomous, independent.

[68] In 1399, Richard II surrendered in battle to Henry Bolingbroke and agreed to abdicate his throne. Henry initially laid claim to the crown by conquest, but in a speech to parliament he put forward a largely specious claim to rule by descent. Nevertheless, parliament accepted his claim and received him as King Henry IV. In 1405, Richard Scrope, Archbishop of York helped lead an armed rebellion against King Henry IV. He was defeated and executed by the king's order after a summary trial. Public outcry against the execution throughout England and other difficulties forced the king in 1406 to submit to parliament-imposed constitutional constraints. MH cites Parliament Rolls (RP iii, 423, 453).

And upon the like reason it was that King William I though he be called the Conqueror, and his attaining the crown here is often in history and in some records called *Conquestus Angliae*, yet in truth it was not such a conquest as did or could alter the laws of this Kingdom, or impose laws upon the people *per modum conquestus*, or *jure belli* [by means of conquest or by right of war]. And therefore, to wipe off that false imputation upon our laws, as if they were the fruit or effect of a conquest, or carried in them the badge of servitude to the will of the conqueror, which notion some ignorant and prejudiced persons have entertained, I shall rip up and lay open this whole business from the bottom, and to that end enquire into the following Particulars, viz.

1. Of the thing called conquest, what it is, when attained, and the rights thereof.
2. Of the several kinds of conquest, and their effects, as to the alteration of laws by the victor.
3. How the English laws stood at the entry of King William the First.
4. By what title he entered, and whether by such a right of conquest as did, or could, alter the English laws.
5. Whether de facto there was any alteration of the said laws, and by what means after his coming in.[69]

First, touching the first of these, viz., conquest, what it is, when attained, and the rights thereof. It is true, that it seems to be admitted as a kind of law among all nations, that in case of a solemn war between supreme princes, the conqueror acquires a right of dominion, as well as a property over the things and persons that are fully conquered. And the reasons assigned are principally these, viz.

1st, because both parties have appealed to the highest tribunal that can be, viz., the trial by war, wherein the great judge and sovereign of the world, the Lord of Hosts, seems in a more especial manner than in other cases to decide the controversy.[70] 2dly, because unless this should be a final decision, mankind would be destroyed by endless broils,[71] wars, and contentions; therefore, for the preservation of mankind, this great decision ought to be final, and the conquered ought to acquiesce in it. 3dly, because if this should not be admitted, and be by, as it were, the tacit consent of mankind accounted a lawful acquisition, there would not be any security or peace under any government. For by the various revolutions of dominion acquired by this means, have been, and are to this day, the successions of kingdoms and states preserved. What was once the Romans, was before that the Graecians, and before them the Persians, and before the Persians, the Assyrians. And if this just victory were not allowed to be a firm acquest of dominion, the present possessors would be

[69] Ed: MH's extended discussion of third, fourth, and fifth topics has been omitted.

[70] MH expresses here the common view that war, the "appeal to heaven," acknowledges God's judgment as the only possible resolution of disputes between sovereign parties.

[71] OED: a confused disturbance, tumult, or turmoil; a quarrel.

still obnoxious to the claim of the former proprietors, and so they would be in a restless state of doubts, difficulties, and changes upon the pretention of former claims. Therefore, to cut off this instability and unsettledness in dominion and property, it would seem that the common consent of all nations has tacitly submitted that acquisition by right of conquest, in a solemn war between persons not subjects of each other by bonds of allegiance or fidelity, should be allowed as one of the lawful titles of acquiring dominion over the persons, places, and things so conquered.

But whatever be the real truth or justice of this position, yet we are much at a loss touching the things *in hypothesi*, viz., whether this be the effect of every kind of conquest? Whether the war be just or unjust? What are the requisites to the constituting of a just war? Who are the persons that may acquire? And what are the solemnities requisite for that acquest? But above all, the greatest difficulty is, when there shall be said such a victory as acquires this right? Indeed, if there be a total deletion of every person of the opposing party or country, then the victory is complete, because none remains to call it in question. But suppose they are beaten in one battle, may they not rally again? Or if the greater part be subdued, may not the lesser keep their ground? Or if they do not at the present, may they not in the next age regain their liberty? Or if they be quiet for a time, may they not as they have opportunity, renew their pretentions? and although the victor, by his power, be able to quell and suppress them, yet he is beholden to his sword for it, and the right that he got by his victory before, would not be sufficient without a power and force to establish and secure him against new troubles. And on the other side, if those few subdued persons can by force regain what they once had a pretence to, a former victory will be but a weak defence. And if it would, they would have the like pretence to a claim of acquest by victory over him, as he had over them.

It seems therefore a difficult thing to determine in what indivisible moment this victory is so complete, that *jure belli* [by the laws of war] the acquest of dominion is fully gotten; and therefore victors use to secure themselves against disputes of that kind, and as it were to underpin their acquest *jure belli*, that they might not be lost by the same means whereby they were gained by the continuation of eternal forces of standing armies, castles, garrisons, munitions, and other acts of power and force, so as thereby to overbear and prevent an ordinary possibility of the prevailing of the conquered or subdued people, against the conqueror or victor. He that lays the weight of his title upon victory or conquest rarely rests in it as a complete conquest till he has added to it somewhat of consent or faith of the conquered, submitting voluntarily to him, and then, and not till then, he thinks his title secure and his conquest complete. And indeed, he has no reason to think his title can be otherwise secure; for where the title is merely force or power, his title will fail, if the conquered can with like force or power overmatch his, and to regain their former interest or dominion.

Now this consent is of two kinds, either expressed, or implied. An express consent is, when after a victory the party conquered do expressly submit themselves to the victors, either simply or absolutely, by dedition,[72] yielding themselves, giving him their faith and their allegiance; or else under certain pacts, conventions, agreements, or capitulations, as when the subdued party, either by themselves, or by substitutes, or delegates by them chosen, do yield their faith and their allegiance to the victor upon certain pacts or agreements between them, as [for example,] for holding or continuing their religion, their laws, their form of civil administration, &c.

And thus, though force were perhaps the occasion of this consent, yet in truth 'tis consent only that is the true proximate and fixed foundation of the victor's right, which now no longer rests barely upon external force, but upon the express consent and pact of the subdued people. And consequently this pact or convention is that which is to be the immediate foundation of that dominion. And upon a diligent observation of most acquests gotten by conquest, or so called, we shall find this to be the conclusion of almost all victories: they end in deditions and capitulations, and faith given to the conqueror, whereby oftentimes the former laws, privileges, and possessions are confirmed to the subdued, without which the victors seldom continue long or quiet in their new acquests, without extreme expense, force, severity, and hazard.

An implied consent is, when the subdued do continue for a long time quiet and peaceable under the government of the victor, accepting his government, submitting to his laws, taking upon them the offices and employments under him, and obeying and owning him as their governor, without opposing him or claiming their former right. This seems to be a tacit acceptance of and assent to him. And though this is gradual and possibly no determinate time is stinted[73] wherein a man can say this year, or this month, or this day such a tacit consent was completed and concluded, for circumstances may make great variations in the sufficiency of the evidence of such an assent; yet by a long and quiet tract of peaceable submission to the laws and government of the victor, men may reasonably conjecture that the conquered have relinquished their purpose of regaining by force what by force they lost.

But still all this is intended of a lawful conquest by a foreign prince or state, and not an usurpation by a subject, either upon his prince or fellow subject; for several ages and descents do not purge the unlawfulness of such an usurpation.

Secondly, concerning the several kinds of conquests, and their effects, as to the alteration of laws by the victor. There seems to be a double kind of conquest, which induces a various consideration touching the change of laws, viz., [1] *victoria in regem & populum*, & [2] *victoria in regem tantum.*[74] [First,] the conquest over the people or country is when the war is denounced[75] by a prince or state foreign, and no subject, and when the intention and denunciation of the war is against the king and

[72] OED: surrender. [73] OED: appointed definitely.

[74] That is, conquest over king and people and conquest over the king only. See MH's discussion in "Reflections," 196 and *Prerogatives*, 211, 216–17.

[75] OED: proclaimed, announced, declared.

people or country, and the pretention of title is by the sword, or *jure belli*. Such were most of the conquests of ancient monarchs, viz., the Assyrian, Persian, Graecian, and Roman conquests. And in such cases, the acquisitions of the victor were absolute and universal. He gained the interest and property of the very soil of the country subdued, which the victor might, at his pleasure, give, sell, or arrent.[76] He gained a power of abolishing or changing their laws and customs, and of giving new [law], or of imposing the law of the victor's country. But although this the conqueror might do, yet a change of the laws of the conquered country was rarely universally made, especially by the Romans, who, though in their own particular colonies planted in conquered countries they observed the Roman Law, which possibly might by degrees, without any rigorous imposition, gain and insinuate themselves into the conquered people, and so gradually obtain, and insensibly conform them, at least so many of them as were conterminous[77] to the colonies and garrisons to the Roman Laws, yet they rarely made a rigorous and universal change of the laws of the conquered country, unless they were such as were foreign and barbarous, or altogether inconsistent with the victor's government. But in other things, they commonly indulged unto the conquered, the laws and religion of their country upon a double account, viz.

First, on account of humanity, thinking it a hard and over-severe thing to impose presently upon the conquered a change of their customs, which long use had made dear to them. And, 2dly, upon the account of prudence; for the Romans being a wise and experienced people, found that those indulgences made their conquests the more easy, and their enjoyments thereof the more firm, when as a rigorous change of the laws and religion of the people would render them in a restless and unquiet condition, and ready to lay hold of any opportunity of defection or rebellion to regain their ancient laws and religion, which ordinary people count most dear to them. (Though at this day the indulgence of a paganish religion is not used to be allowed by any Christian victor, as is observed in Calvin's Case in the seventh report.[78]) And to give one instance for all, it was upon this account that though the Romans had wholly subdued Syria and Palestina, yet they allowed to the inhabitants the Jews, &c. the use of their religion and laws, so far forth as consisted with the safety and security of the victor's interest. And therefore, though they reserved to themselves the cognizance of such causes as concerned themselves, their officers or revenues, and such cases as might otherwise disturb the security of their empire, as treasons, insurrections, and the like, yet 'tis evident they indulged the people of the Jews, &c. to judge by their own law, not only of some criminal proceedings, but even of capital in some cases, as appears by the history of the gospels, and acts of the apostles.

[76] Ed: to let at a fixed rent. [77] OED: bordering on each other.

[78] Edward Coke, "Calvin's Case" (1608), *Seventh Reports*, 17b; *Selected Writings of Sir Edward Coke*, ed. Steve Sheppard (Indianapolis: Liberty Fund, 2003), 207.

But still this was but an indulgence, and therefore was resumable by the victor, unless [first] there intervened any capitulation between the conqueror and the conquered to the contrary, which was frequent, especially in those cases, when it was not a complete conquest, but rather a dedition upon terms and capitulations, agreed between the conqueror and the conquered, wherein usually the yielding party secured to themselves, by the articles of their dedition, the enjoyment of their laws and religion; and then by the laws of nature and of nations, both which oblige in the observation of faith and promises, those terms and capitulations were to be observed. Again, 2dly, when after a full conquest, the conquered people resumed so much courage and power as began to put them into a capacity of regaining their former laws and liberties. This commonly was the occasion of terms and capitulations between the conquerors and conquered. Again, 3dly, when by long succession of time, the conquered had either been incorporated with the conquering people, whereby they had worn out the very marks and discriminations between the conquerors and conquered; and if they continued distinct, yet by a long prescription, usage and custom, the laws and rights of the conquered people were in a manner settled and the long permission of the conquerors amounted to a tacit concession or capitulation for the enjoyment of their laws and liberties.

But of this more than enough is said, because it will appear in what follows that William I never made any such conquest of England.

Secondly, therefore I come to the second kind of conquest, viz., that which is only *victoria in regem*. And this is where the conqueror either has a real right to the crown or chief government of a kingdom, or at least has, or makes some pretence of claim thereunto. And, in pursuance of such claim, raises war, and by his forces obtains what he so pretends[79] a title to. Now this kind of conquest does only instate the victor in those rights of government, which the conquered prince, or that prince to whom the conqueror pretends a right of succession, had whereby he becomes only a successor *jure belli*, but not a victor or conqueror upon the people, and therefore has no more right of altering their laws or taking away their liberties or possessions, than the conquered prince, or the prince to whom he pretends a right of succession, had. For the intention, scope, and effect of his victory extends no further than the succession, and does not at all affect the rights of the people. The conqueror is, as it were, the plaintiff, and the conquered prince is the defendant, and the claim is a claim of title to the crown. And because each of them pretends a right to the sovereignty, and there is no other competent trial of the title between them, they put themselves upon the great trial by battle, wherein there is nothing in question touching the rights of the people, but only touching the right of the crown. And that being decided by the victory, the victor comes in as a successor, and not *jure victoriae*, as in relation to the people's rights, the most sacred whereof are their laws and religion.

[79] Ed: claims.

Indeed, those that do voluntarily assist the conquered prince, commonly undergo the same hazard with him, and do, as it were, put their interest upon the hazard and issue of the same trial, and therefore commonly fall under the same severity with the conquered, at least *de facto*, because, perchance, the victor thinks he cannot be secure without it. But yet usage, and indeed common prudence, makes the conquerors use great moderation and discrimination in relation to the assistants of the conquered prince, and to extend this severity only to the eminent and busy[80] assistants of the conquered, and not to the *gregarii* [the common people], or such as either by constraint or by necessity were enforced to serve against him. And as to those also, on whom they exercise their power, it has been rarely done *jure belli aut victoriae*, but by a judiciary proceeding, as in cases of treason, because now the great title by battle has pronounced for the right of the conqueror, and at best no man must dare to say otherwise now, whatsoever debility was in his pretension or claim.[81]

[80] Ed: engrossed, preoccupied (meant pejoratively).

[81] In the remainder of the chapter here omitted, MH argues that William I was only *victor in regem*. See *Prerogatives*, 216–17.

PART III

Hale's Preface to Rolle's Abridgement of the Cases and Resolutions of the Common Law

Introductory Note

Sir Henry Rolle (1589–1656) was a highly regarded advocate and judge in the generation preceding Matthew Hale. He served as Chief Justice of King's Bench from 1648–55. His *Abridgement* collected and topically arranged a number of cases, opinions and resolutions of the common-law courts. A kind of legal commonplace book, it was intended as a model for students preparing themselves for a legal career at the Inns of Court. Hale's Preface, explicitly directed to students, calls attention to what Hale took to be the distinctive features and merits of common-law practice.

This Preface sounds themes also found in "Amendment" and the first part of "Reflections." The common law, Hale observes, is the product of the wisdom and experience of many judges over a long period of time who have mastered a common discipline of practical reasoning, contributing their experience and judgments to "a common stock by mutual communication" (159–60), and becoming participants in each other's learning. Common-law practice focuses on resolving concrete problems of daily life, preferring detailed, particular determinations to broad, general principles. It attends carefully to the vast diversity of particular circumstances and fashions solutions that prove their value over time. It settles disputed practical matters neither by fiat, nor by reliance on evident first principles, but by allowing their resolutions to settle in the judgments and practices of the courts and ultimately of the people governed by them. This, he argues, lends the law both a degree of certainty and a supple flexibility. It effectively constrains judicial discretion and prevents arbitrariness of judgment.

This selection is drawn from the original (1668) edition of Hale's preface to *Un Abridgement des plusieurs Cases et Resolutions del Common Ley per Henry Rolle, Serjeant del Ley*. Footnotes are the current editor's.

Preface

This ensuing book is a collection of divers cases, opinions, and resolutions of the common law, digested[1] under alphabetical titles, and those titles subdivided into heads and paragraphs. The author of this book intended it only for his own private use; and the publishing of it was intended principally for the benefit of the students of the common law, though it may be also useful for the professors and practisers thereof. By way of preface or introduction some observation shall be delivered touching these particulars following, viz. (1.) Touching the collector or author of this book. (2.) Touching the subject matter of it. (3.) Touching the method of it. (4.) Touching the use of it. (5.) Touching some cautions to be observed concerning it.[2]

1. Touching the collector or author of this book[:] . . . He was a man of very great natural abilities, of a ready and clear understanding, strong memory, sound, deliberate, and steady judgment, of a fixed intention of mind to all business that came before him; of great freedom from passions and perturbations, of great temperance and moderation, of a strong and healthy constitution of body, which rendered him fit for study and business, and indefatigable in it.

He spent his time under the bar, and for some years after in diligent study of the common law, neglecting no opportunity to improve his knowledge therein; and he had this happiness in relation thereunto, that from his first admission to the society of the Inner Temple, which was 1 *Feb. 6 Jas* [1 February 1609] and till his call to be a Sergeant, he had contemporaries of the same society of great parts,[3] learning, and eminence; as namely Sir Edward Littleton, afterwards Chief Justice of the Common Pleas, and Lord Keeper of the Great Seal of England; Sir Edward Herbert, afterwards Attorney General; Sir Tho. Gardyner, afterwards Recorder of London; and that treasury of all kind of learning, Mr John Selden: with these he kept a long, constant, and familiar converse and acquaintance, and thereby greatly improved both his own learning and theirs, especially in the common law, which he principally intended: For it was the constant and almost daily course for many years together of these great traders in learning, to bring in their several acquests therein as it were into a common

[1] Ed: collected and ordered in some fashion.
[2] Ed: MH's discussion of the fourth and fifth titles is not included in this selection.
[3] OED: personal qualities or attributes, especially of an intellectual kind.

stock by mutual communication, whereby each of them became in a great measure the participant and common possessor of the other's learning and knowledge...

2. Touching the subject matter of the book, I shall say something in general, something more particular.[4] In general, the subject matter of this book consists of divers opinions, cases, and choice resolutions applicable unto, and digested under the most considerable titles of the common law. It were superfluous to spend much time in the commendations of the common law of England, it carries in itself and with itself a sufficient commendation of itself: and hath had the suffrage of the whole kingdom in all ages for these many hundreds of years; for according to it the public justice of this kingdom hath been administered in all time with great success and contentment: yet some few things I shall observe concerning it.

1. The common laws of England are not the product of the wisdom of some one man, or society of men in any one age; but of the wisdom, counsel, experience, and observation of many ages of wise and observing men: where the subject of any law is single, the prudence of one age may go far at one essay[5] to provide a fit law, and yet even in the wisest provisions of that kind, experience shows us that new and unthought of emergencies[6] often happen, that necessarily require new supplements, abatements, or explanations, but the body of laws, that concern the common justice applicable to a great kingdom, is vast and comprehensive, consists of infinite particulars, and must meet with various emergencies, and therefore requires much time and much experience, as well as much wisdom and prudence successively to discover defects and inconveniences,[7] and to apply apt supplements and remedies for them; and such are the common laws of England, namely the productions of much wisdom, time, and experience.

2. The common laws of England are settled and known; every entire new model of laws labours under two great difficulties and inconveniences, viz. First, that though they seem specious[8] in the theory, yet when they come to be put in practice, they are found extremely defective; either too strait or too loose, or too narrow, or too wide, and new occurrences, that neither were or well could be at first in prospect, discover themselves, that either disjoint or disorder the fabric; and therefore such new models continually stand in need of many supplies,[9] and abatements, and alterations, to accommodate them to common use and convenience, whereby in a little time the original is either wholly laid aside, or in a great measure lost in its amendments, and become the least part of the law. Again, were such new entire models of laws never so good, yet it is a long time before they come to be well known or understood, even to

[4] Ed: The latter topic is omitted. [5] OED: attempt or endeavour.
[6] OED: unexpected occurrences.
[7] OED: incongruities, inconsistencies with reason or rule.
[8] OED: fair or pleasing to the eye.
[9] OED: actions making up for a deficiency.

those whose business it must be to advise or judge according to them; so that even a more imperfect body of laws well known, at least to those that are to advise or judge, is more of use and convenience to the good of society, than a more perfect and complete body of laws newly settled, and therefore to be newly learned.

3. The common laws of England are more particular than other laws, and this, though it render them more numerous, less methodical, and takes up longer time for their study, yet it recompenceth with greater advantages, namely it prevents arbitrariness in the judge, and makes the law more certain and better applicable to the business that comes to be judged by it. General laws are indeed very comprehensive, soon learned, and easily digested into method; but when they come to particular application, they are of little service, and leave a great latitude to partiality, interest, and variety of apprehensions to misapply them; not unlike the common notions in the moralist, which when both the contesting Grecian Captains most perfectly agreed, yet from them each deduced conclusions in the particular case in controversy, suitable to their several desires and ends, though extremely contradictory each to other.[10] It hath therefore always been the wisdom and happiness of the English government not to rest in generals, but to prevent arbitrariness and uncertainty by particular laws, fitted almost to all particular occasions.

If any man shall object that if there be that excellency in the English laws, what is the reason there have been many changes therein in succession of times? I answer in general, that it cannot be supposed that human laws can be wholly exempt from the common fate of human things, which must needs be subject to particular defects and mutabilities, time and experience, as it hath given it the perfection it hath, so it must and will advance and improve it. But more particularly, the mutations that have been in this kind, hath not been so much in the law, as in the subject matter of it; the great wisdom of parliaments have taken off, or abridged many of the titles about which it was conversant: usage and disusage hath antiquated[11] others, and the various accesses[12] and alternations in point of commerce and dealing hath rendered some proceedings, that were anciently less in use, to be no more useful; and some that were anciently useful to be now less useful: and it shall not be altogether impertinent to give some instances herein of several great titles in the law, which, upon these occasions are at this day in a great measure antiquated; and some that are much abridged, and reduced into a very narrow compass and use.[13]

The ancient Romans, who gloried no less in their laws than in their military discipline, found this to be true, namely, that in tract of time some of their laws grew contradictory, some obsolete, some unpractical, some obscure, and the whole

[10] MH here refers to the two "captains," Agamemnon and Achilles, who, according to Epictetus (*Discourses*, I.22), agreed on very general moral notions but came to contrary conclusions regarding particular applications. See *Treatise*, 35 and note 85.

[11] OED: made obsolete. [12] OED: augmentations, increases. [13] Ed: Examples omitted.

bulk of them too voluminous; so that in Justinian's time there were an incredible number of versicles[14] and volumes of their laws; whereupon that excellent prince by the advice of a great council or college of learned men (as once our English Justinian King Edward the First did by the laws of Wales[15]) reduced them unto a better compendium, which makes up now the body of civil laws. And truly considering to how great a bulk the volumes and books of the common law have in process of time arisen; how many printed resolutions of the same cases or points; how many disagreeing reports there are touching the same matter; how many seeming contradictory opinions that would be explained or settled; how many titles are disused. It would be wished that some complete *corpus juris communis*[16] were extracted out of the many books of our English laws, for the public use, and for the contracting of the laws into a narrower compass and method, at least for ordinary study. But this is a work of time, and requires many industrious and judicious hands and heads to assist in it.[17]

3. The third consideration is the method of this collection, which will give me an occasion to write something upon these three matters, viz. (1) touching the method of the common law in general; (2) touching the method of the study of the common law; and (3) touching the particular method of the collection.[18]

Touching the former of these, I have many times observed that men not much acquainted with the study of the common laws of England, though otherwise of good parts and possibly well acquainted with university learning, pretend[19] two great prejudices and exceptions against the study of the common law, viz. 1. That it wants clear evidence of reason, and that the conclusions and resolutions of it are not deducible by such evident rational consequence as is or may be done in other sciences; that it is obscure and perplexed, so that they that think themselves great masters of reason, yea, and many that are much conversant in subtleties of logic, philosophy, and the schoolmen,[20] are at a loss in it, and can make little of it. 2. That it wants method, order, and apt distributions, and this hath bred some prejudice against it, not only in men much addicted to subtle learning, but also in the professors of the civil law, who think that law much more methodical and orderly than the common law.

To the first of these I say,[21] [(1.)] that it is certainly true, that reason is the common faculty and instrument of mankind for the acquest, application, and exercise of any

[14] OED: short clauses or sentences.

[15] See *History*, 146 and note 59. MH suggests Edward consolidated and codified Welsh law, although it would be fair to say that he imposed English law on the Welsh.

[16] Ed: body of common law, compare *corpus juris civilis*—body of (Roman) civil law.

[17] Ed: A paragraph briefly describing particular features of the abridgement omitted.

[18] Ed: The second and third topics omitted. [19] Ed: claim.

[20] Ed: practitioners of scholastic philosophy and theology.

[21] MH discusses the ensuing three points at length in "Reflections," Chapter 1.

knowledge or art, and they that have the clearest exercise thereof are ordinarily the best proficients in them. It is the same power of reason, that with exercise, study, and experience renders a man a good logician, a good mathematician, a good physician, a good lawyer; but yet the same man that is a good logician, is not therefore presently[22] a good lawyer, mathematician, or physician. Take a man of the choicest natural parts, and turn him upon a piece of Euclid, or upon some parts of the physics or metaphysics or logic of Aristotle (that great master of reason), he will be to seek to make anything of it,[23] till by study and time he hath accommodated his reason to those subjects. And although the reason of some parts of the common law be obvious at the first view to every capacity, yet to get a mastery of the full knowledge of it, requires not only reason but study and industry to understand it. And then his reason will trade upon that stock, and make deductions and inferences upon it in the same manner as the mathematician doth upon a proposition of Euclid. But (2.) in matters moral and civil (the common subject of laws) though possibly the general and common notions of them, or whereupon they are founded, are in a great measure common to all men of understanding, yet the applications and particular deductions and conclusions thereof are not so clear, constant, and determinate, as consequences and conclusions of logic or mathematics are; for as the natures of moral actions are in themselves much more indeterminate than the subjects of those arts and sciences, so they most commonly are strangely diversified by infinite circumstances; and therefore men agreeing in the same common notions of justice and morality, oftentimes deduce different conclusions from them, and applications of them, even although interest and partiality of mind (which are very incident to mankind) do not interpose. It was the complaint of the moralist anciently, *notiones communes omnibus hominibus sunt & notioni notio non repugnat quis enim nostrum non statuit bonum esse utile & expetendum, & quavis ratione consectandum & persequendum? quis non statuit justum esse honestum & decorum? Quando igitur pugna oritur? in notionum accommodatione ad res singulas.*[24] And therefore the wisdom of laws, especially of England, is to determine[25] the general notions of [that which is] just and honest by particular rules, applications, & constitutions found out and continued by great wisdom, experience and time, and thereby to settle that variety and inconstancy of particular applications and conclusions, which without some established rule would be found in most men, though of excellent parts and reason, and agreeing in common notions. (3.) In things that have their original much by institution, men

[22] OED: quickly, soon (i.e., just by that fact).

[23] Ed: perhaps MH means, "he will be unable to make anything of it".

[24] This quotation from Epictetus, *Discourses*, I.22, can be translated as follows: "There are notions common to all men, and a notion does not conflict with a notion; for who of us has not determined that good is right and ought to be sought after, and ought to be accomplished and pursued by any means? Who has not determined that justice is honourable and proper? When, then, does the conflict arise: in the application of notions to separate matters." See *Treatise*, 35 and note 85.

[25] Ed: make specific, concrete.

cannot easily or ordinarily by rational deduction find them out, but only by instruction and education, and yet those things are of as great necessity and use to mankind as other matters more obviously deducible by argumentation: as for instance, in the significance of speech, why such a composition of articulate sounds and syllables and words should signify such a subject, or such an intelligible proposition; and why one kind of composition in France, and another kind of composition in England should signify the same thing; why in grammar the various terminations of words should render them of several imports and significations: no immediate reason can be justly given or required, but institution or custom, which is a tacit institution. And something analogical to this is to be found not only in the English laws, but in all the laws of the world, wherein though the first institution thereof was not without great and profound reason, and the same is continued with great advantage to society, and prevention of uncertainty in things; yet it were a vain thing to conclude it is irrational, because not to be demonstrated or deduced by syllogisms. Thus in our law, the word *Dedi* creates a warranty, the word *Concessi* creates a covenant; the word *Heyres*, required to pass a fee-simple in grants and feoffments; lands in fee-simple descend to the uncle and not immediately to the father, and to the eldest son, not to all the sons;[26] though in some other countries their laws direct descents otherwise; and infinite other instances of like nature may be given, which have their force principally by virtue of institution, or of the common usage of this kingdom, which is a tacit institution, and are of great use to prevent uncertainty; therefore as all the reason imaginable will not render a man a good grammarian, or skilled in any one language, unless he learn it by education, study, or discipline; so a man, though otherwise of pregnant[27] reason, must not be offended if he be not born a common lawyer, nor be master of the knowledge of it without study and experience.

As to the second [objection], concerning the immethodicalness of the common law: I shall say this; (1.) That the common law is reducible into a competent method, as to the general heads thereof, and every student doth, or may easily form unto himself a general digestion of the law, accommodate to his memory and use. (2.) But it is true, that all the particulars in respect of their multitude and variety, are not easily reducible into a Scholastic method, but they recompense that inconvenience by their particularity and useful application to particular occasions, as is before shown. It is true, the body of the civil law is digested into general heads, which are like common boxes in which many particulars are placed; but the particulars themselves, their tractates, responses, counsels, and decisions, have little other method than our common law books have, or easily may have: thus much in general for the method of common law.

[26] MH here gives examples of legal formalities used to create various legal relationships or to transfer property and examples of formal rules of descent of landed property. ("*Dedi*" = "I have given"; "*concessi*" = "I have granted.") MH insists that these formalities and rules are artificial and could have been different. On the use of "heirs" in transfer of property, see J. H. Baker, *An Introduction to English Legal History*, 3rd edn (London: Butterworths, 1990), 324–5.

[27] Ed: richly productive.

PART IV

Considerations Touching the Amendment or Alteration of Laws

Introductory Note

Hale wrote this selection probably in the mid-1660s. In the early 1650s, the "Hale Commission" (see Editor's Introduction, p. xvi) was charged with considering systematic reform of English law, but little came of it and Hale's experience appears to have been frustrating to him. Parliamentary reform efforts began anew early in the Restoration period. Little is known of the occasion for Hale's writing "Amendment," but he may have been moved by his awareness of the need for reform tempered by his experience on the Commission.

Hale articulates in this selection an approving but cautious attitude towards revision of the law. He warns equally against "superstitious veneration" (178) of the law and heedless efforts at its reform. Change must be admitted, he argues, because laws are rarely perfect from the outset and are vulnerable to corruption. Even initially sound and just laws can become obsolete or work injustice when social and political circumstances change materially. Yet, reform of law must be cautious, gradual, and piecemeal, he argues. Lawmaking and law-remaking must always be mindful of the following features of law. (1) Laws are made to govern a diverse and changing multitude or public that extends over time. (2) Law functions well only when it takes root in the community it seeks to govern and shapes the practice of its members. (3) The test of law's value—its claim to "reason"—is not whether its provisions can be derived from general, first principles, but rather whether, as instituted, it meets the practical needs of the community over time. (4) Laws are systematically connected ("contiguous"), each provision "mortised" into another, such that change in any one is likely to affect many others in the body of law. Thus, the best perspective from which change should be deliberated and pursued is not that of the abstract reason of the philosopher, or the "advanced [natural] reason" of the disengaged observer (or sovereign), but rather that of persons fully engaged in and intimately familiar with the law in its quotidian operation. They are able and willing to allow time and experience to shape their judgments of law's merits and proposals for improvement. Hale echoes here his views in "Preface" and "Reflections" regarding the special character of common-law reasoning.

The text for this selection follows Hale's autograph manuscript (Lambeth Palace, Fairhurst Papers MS 3479, which also includes manuscripts of Hale's "Reflections" and his "Draught" of the latter work). The larger work from which this selection of three chapters is taken was published by Francis Hargrave in *A Collection of Tracts Relating to the Law of England* (Dublin, 1787), 253–89. All footnotes are the current editor's.

1

Concerning the Several Extremes Relating to the Amendment and Alteration of Laws; and therein Touching the Extreme in the Excess of Overhastiness and Forwardness to Alterations in Laws

The business of amendment or alteration of laws is a choice[1] and tender business, neither wholly to be omitted when the necessity requires, and yet very cautiously and warily to be undertaken, though the necessity may, or, at least, may seem to require it.

And that I may the more evenly guide myself in this discourse, I shall begin with the consideration of both those extremes, viz.

I. The error in the excess, the over-busy and hasty and violent attempt in mutation of laws under pretence of reformation. And, II, the error in the defect, a wilful and over-strict adhering in every particular to the continuance of the laws in the state we find them, though the reformation of them be never so necessary, safe, and easy.

Touching the first of these, the offence or error in the excess: and therein I will first consider the dangerousness of this temper in men to be over-facile in the change or alteration of the laws; and then I will examine upon what reasons or pretences, or indeed infirmities, men are usually carried to this fickleness and unsteadiness in relation to laws.

Touching the danger and inconvenience of overmuch hastiness in changing of old laws, and introducing of new, there be these considerations that render such dispositions and such attempts very dangerous.[2]

[1] Ed: a matter for careful judgment.

[2] In his work on admiralty jurisdiction, MH wrote: "Inasmuch as all laws that are made or chosen are to be accommodated to those ages and countries wherein they are to be used, and inasmuch as that law which possibly may be convenient and useful for one age or place is not convenient for another, and inasmuch as laws, where they have been long used and are well known, and have been by long practice and experience accommodated to the country whose laws they are, even upon that very account are more eligible and to be

1. Every law that is old hath this advantage over any new law, in that it is better known already to the people who are concerned in it, than any new law possibly can be without some length of time; by means whereof it must needs come to pass that though a new law possibly be as good, and it may be in some degree better than the old, yet many great inconveniences happen in that interval, which will occur between the promulgation of the new law and the full and perfect knowledge thereof in those who are concerned in that law; and if there were no other advantage of the continuance of old laws above the introducing of new but this, yet it should make people very shy and careful in changes, and most perfectly to demonstrate that the advantage of the change would be so great that it would preponderate[3] this very single consideration, viz. the notoriety of the old and the novelty of the new.

2. It is most certain that time and long experience is much more ingenious, subtle, and judicious than all the wisest and acutest wits of the world coexisting can be. It discovers such varieties of emergencies[4] and cases that no man could ever otherwise have imagined. It discovers such inconveniences in things that no man would otherwise have imagined. And on the other side, in everything that is new, or at least in most things especially relating to laws there are thousands of new occurrences and entanglements, and coincidences, and complications that would not possibly be at first foreseen. And the reason is apparent: because laws concern such multitudes, and those of various dispositions, passions, wits, interests, concerns, that it is not possible for any human foresight to discover at once, or to provide expedients against, in the first constitution of a law. Now a law that hath abidden the test of time, hath met with most of these varieties and complications, and experience hath in all that process of time discovered these complications and

preferred as more conducible to the good of that people (the true adequate end of the laws), than a strange law, though perchance in notion and speculation more methodical and polite [refined, elegant] and literate; hence it is prudent people are not ever hasty in changing their laws or admitting super-induction of a body of other laws touching matters determinable by the rules, laws and customs of their own country. Neither indeed have they reason, for it is certain that in process and length of time every nation that is civilized forms and moulds its own municipal laws with the greatest ease, accommodation and convenience to itself (as every shell fish moulds and fashions its shell best for its own constitution, use, defence and convenience)... That law is best that is best for that people whose law it is, as the shell of an oyster is better for an oyster than the shell of periwinkle or scallop, though this may look finer and fitter for that fish whose shell it is.... [W]here a people hath been long civilized, settled under a due government, and governed by known laws, it is most certain that the introduction of a body of new laws upon never so goodly a pretence of the preference of them before the ancient and known laws is a most imprudent and pernicious thing. For though it were granted that the laws imposed might be better in themselves, yea and possibly if they had been long received better for them; yet because they are new and unknown, and must take up a long time before they can be so perfectly known to the people whereby they may conform themselves and their dealings to them, even such laws though it may be in their fabric better, yet in event are more pernicious to a people than their old, which in the theory might not perchance be so good.... [W]here a law is known, the inconveniences thereof, as well as its usefulness, are also known and avoidable; and it is many times more convenient for a people than a new law whereunto they are strangers and unacquainted." *Hale and Fleetwood on Admiralty Jurisdiction*, ed. M. J. Pritchard and D. E. C. Yale (London: Selden Society, 1993), 4–5.

[3] Ed: outweigh. [4] OED: unexpected occurrences.

emergencies, and so [has] applied suitable remedies and cures for these various emergencies. So that in truth ancient laws, especially, that have a common concern, are not the issues of the prudence of this or that council or senate, but are the production of the various experiences and applications of the wisest thing in the inferior world: to wit, time, which as it discovers day after day new inconveniences, so it doth successively apply new remedies; and indeed it is a kind of aggregation of the discoveries, results, and applications of ages and events; so that it is a great adventure to go about to alter it without very great necessity and under the greatest demonstration of safety and convenience imaginable.

3. An over-busy meddling with the alteration of laws, though under the plausible name and pretence of reformation, doth necessarily introduce a great fluidness, lubricity,[5] and unsteadiness in the laws, and renders it upon every little occasion subject to perpetual fluxes, vicissitudes, and mutations. When once this law is changed, why may not that which is introduced be changed, and so onward in perpetual motion? So that possibly in the period of an age or two, the law of a kingdom, and with it its government, may have as many shapes as a silkworm hath in the period of a year; so that they that now live cannot project under what laws their children shall live, nor the child or grandchild understand by what laws the kingdom was governed in the time of the father or grandfather; and thereby the constitution of the government, the rules of property, and all things that are concerned to have the greatest fixedness that may be shall become as lax and unstable, as if every age underwent a conquest from a foreign state. And therefore in all times, the wisest lawgivers and counsellors have been ever careful to keep the settled laws of a kingdom as steady and fast as might be; and hence it was that, not so much to gain observance as firmness to their laws, they were always styled sacred, and the people induced into a venerable esteem of them by a pretence that their laws were given from heaven, and therefore not to be changed by any inferior authority.

4. Overmuch tampering with and changing of laws, which have obtained by long use and custom, is commonly very ungrateful and unacceptable to the people, into whom their ancient laws and customs are twisted and woven as a part of their nature, and introduceth jealousies and suspicions of designs upon them, and gives a handle to busy and turbulent spirits to insinuate unto them the bad consequences that may ensue upon such change, and oftentimes begets seditious rebellions and tumults, and prepares people's minds for distempers. And though possibly at the first changes may be ushered in with plausible pretences and quiet and possibly please the multitude with wonderful expectations of good and benefit thereby; yet, when they find themselves disappointed, and possibly some unexpected inconvenience emergeth upon the change, then

[5] OED: slipperiness, elusiveness.

presently the mouths of people are opened against innovation, and the higher their expectation is raised upon the pretence and promise of benefit, the more they are enraged by any though inconsiderable disappointment therein.

Upon these and many more weighty considerations, the wisest men in all times have been very tender and jealous of changes of laws. And upon this account, though when William the first came in, he introduced here in England many parts of the Norman customs and laws, yet when things began to settle, he found it not only convenient but necessary to restore unto the people their old laws, especially those that obtained upon the account and reverence of Edward the Confessor. And when in the time of Henry III, the clergy endeavoured, but in one point, viz. that of bastardy, to introduce the ecclesiastical laws, the nobility stoutly and resolutely answered, *Nolumus leges Angliæ mutari*.[6]

Therefore, it is of great importance upon any alteration of the laws to be sure,

1. That the change be demonstrable to be for the better, and such as cannot introduce any considerable inconvenience in the other end of the wallet.[7]
2. That the change, though most clearly for the better, be not in foundations or principles, but in such things as may consist with[8] the general frame and basis of the government or law.[9]
3. That the changes be gradual, and not too much at once, or at least more than the exigence of things requires.

[6] English law in the thirteenth century held that children born before their parents married were not entitled to inherit, but civil and canon law held that such children were as legitimate as children born in marriage. Thus, common-law courts and ecclesiastical courts were opposed on this issue. In 1236, bishops, including Robert Grosseteste, eminent philosopher, theologian, and Bishop of Lincoln, sought to change common law to conform to canon law. The barons refused to permit the change, asserting "*Nolumus leges Angliæ mutari*" [we will not change the laws of England]. See Statute 20 Hen. III c. 9; St. Realm I, 4.

[7] According to the fable recounted by Gaius Julius Phaedrus (*c.*15 BC–*c.*50 AD), book IV, fable 10, Jupiter gave to every man two bags, one containing his own faults to hang at his back and the other containing faults of his fellows to hang in front. The OED quotes the following from a sermon by R. Sanderson: "Neither of both . . . were willing enough to look into the other end of the wallet, and to examine thoroughly their own spirits." Sanderson, *Twenty Sermons* (London, 1656), 167.

[8] Ed: may be consistent with.

[9] In Chapter 4 of "Amendment" (not included in this selection), MH insists (1) "that nothing tend to the alteration of the government in any measure; for that were to introduce ruin and confusion, not reformation" and (2) "that nothing be altered that is a foundation or principal integral of the law; for these are very sound, and ought not to be touched, lest the whole fabric be endangered. We must do herein as a wise builder doth with an house that hath some inconveniences or is under some decays. Possibly here or there a door or a window may be altered, or a partition made. But as long as the foundations or principals of the house be sound, they must not be tampered with. The inconveniences in the law are of such a nature, as may be easily remedied without unsettling the frame itself; and such amendments, though they seem small and inconsiderable, will render the whole fabric much more safe and useful." Hale, *A Collection of Tracts Relative to the Law of England*, ed. Francis Hargrave (Dublin, 1787), 272.

2

Touching the Reasons and Grounds that Ordinarily Move Men to this Excess, and Itching after Changes in Laws

I have in the precedent chapter considered the first extreme and the danger and inconvenience of it. I shall now examine what are those humours in men that commonly breed this disease and instability in men in relation to the change of laws. And upon a due consideration thereof, we shall the better see what persons, what tempers and dispositions, and what times are at least unseasonable and unfit for such proposals; and gather thereby a prudent jealousy when we see changes ushered in by such persons or dispositions, or at such seasons or times, though the pretensions may be plausible.

(1) As the nature of man generally is affected with novelty, so there are some persons and dispositions that are wonderfully fond of it, and rather than want [for] it will have it even in those things which are most ordinarily perniciously hurt by it. Such are the form of government and ancient municipal laws. The very same itch of novelty and innovation that carries some dispositions to novelty in garbs and gestures, or to new fashions in clothes, carries such when they happen to be in place to innovations and new fashion in laws; a certain restlessness and nauseousness in what they have, and a giddy humour after somewhat which is new, and possibly upon no other account but because it is new, or possibly upon some over expectations of the benefit of such change, though they have no full nor perfect notion of what is to be introduced in the place of what they nauseate.

(2) A second ground of it is possibly some personal mischief that they in their own particular[10] have received by the present constitution of laws. For there is in mankind a passionate self-law, which makes men think that whatsoever crosseth them in their interest or concern is unjust and fit to be altered. And upon this account it will be impossible for any law to be stable; for laws are not fitted for persons, but for things, and must of necessity displease or prejudice the interest of one party. That which may

[10] Ed: as an individual.

be preserves the right and property of one man, may and must of necessity cross and thwart that which another man mistakenly thinks or calls his right; and if upon a peevish, discontented humour, every man that is crossed by a law must be studying of alterations, there must be no law at all; for possibly that very new law that such a discontented person would introduce will one time or other do him mischief; or if it do not, yet it may do another man a mischief in his concern, and will as much justify him in a new innovation as it could the other in the last.

(3) A third ground of precipitate and inconsiderate innovation in laws is the want of a due consideration of the true state and nature of all human affairs, especially in that of laws and government, viz. a conceit of a possibility of framing such laws and constitutions as might be faultless and exquisitely accommodate to the concerns of the whole community and of every member of it. And hence if there once occur any inconvenience in a law, presently away with it, and a new frame or model must be excogitated and introduced, and then all will be well. But this is a great error; for it is most certain that when all the wisdom and prudence and forecast in the world is used, all human things will still be imperfect. There is no wisdom or counsel perfect, but the wisdom and counsel of Almighty God, who hath infinite knowledge to foresee all possible emergencies, and hath infinite wisdom to accommodate and fit everything according to its necessity and conveniency, and infinite power to bow and bend everything to the determination of his own most wise counsel and will. And if it could be supposed that any human contrivance could be perfect and faultless (as possibly some may be very accurate, as we see in mechanical works); yet it is not possible that any human law can be perfect and faultless. No. Time itself, that as we have said is wiser than all the coexisting wits in the world, is not able to foresee a perfect law that will be absolutely faultless. And the reason is apparent; because it concerns the manners of many men, which are so various, uncertain, and complicated, both in themselves and the circumstances adhering to them, that they are not possibly to be exactly fitted. We see in the concerns of one man, how various his actions, his passions, his concerns are; how they change every moment; what new circumstances adhere to them today that did not yesterday. And if the state of things be so various and complicated in one man, how various, intricated,[11] and perplexed will they be with a multitude of men! And if they are various in respect of a multitude of men, how various will they be with a multitude in various successions of ages, and the occurrences or emergencies thereof! And laws are made in relation to such multitudes in such successions, to which it is impossible that it should perfectly be fit and accommodate. If it be squared so that it fit *ut plurimum* [for the most part] and doth more good, though it possibly *pro hic et nunc* [for here and now] do some harm, yet it is a good law. And besides, according to new emergencies, if they are of moment and importance, there may be some new appendications[12] put to it without

[11] OED: made obscure, complicated.

[12] OED: addition by way of appendix.

a total alteration of the law; such alterations as do not so much constitute a new law as amend the old; so that it still morally continues the same law, notwithstanding these appendications, as the Argonauts'[13] ship was the same ship at the end of their voyage as it was at the beginning, though there remained little of the old materials but the chine and ribs[14] of it.

And now possibly some may say that since all human laws are imperfect and only the counsels and determinations of Almighty God are perfect, why then may we not take a short compendious course, and take in the judicials given by God by the hand of Moses,[15] and so avoid that inconvenience of the imperfection of human laws, the positive judicial law of Almighty God being substituted in the place of all other human laws, and all human laws abrogated and exterminated?

To this I say that most certainly the judicial law given by Moses was the law of God, and consequently a most perfect law, according to the use and end for which it was designed; a law of perfect wisdom, as being the production of an infinite wisdom. But yet this must be observed in relation to the perfection of things of this kind. That is in truth perfect that is perfect in relation to its use and end, *cui nihil deest* [for which nothing is lacking] that may be useful and apposite to that end. And if a man were to fit anything to the use of any other particular thing, and for a certain determinate time, that is said to be perfect, that is perfectly fitted to that use and duration, though it be not fitted to another thing or a longer duration; for that were a kind of imperfection, because it would be redundant and superfluous.

This being premised, I say,

1. Although the moral law, or the law of the two tables, were materially universal both in respect of extent and duration, and therefore, the use being of that amplitude, the divine wisdom fitted it according to the use and extent thereof, both in respect of all people and ages; yet the judicial laws, as likewise the ritual or ceremonial, were never in the design of Almighty God intended farther than that people to whom they were given, and no longer possibly to that people than the state of that republic continued. It was indeed exactly accommodate to the state of that people to which it was given; and therein the wisdom of God is not only justified, but manifested and exalted; for it was exactly suitable to the end it was designed. But we cannot say it was fitted, or that there was any need it should be fitted for another people; for that was not within the design of Almighty God. And this indeed is a circumstance that ought to be an ingredient in the due constitution of all laws, that they should be accommodate to the condition, constitution, and exigence of the people to whom they are given. Consequently, inasmuch as there be things peculiar and proper to the state and condition of one people that are not common to the state of another, nay not of the

[13] See *History*, 142 and note 47. [14] Ed: the structural parts of the hull.

[15] Ed: that part of the Mosaic Law concerning political, social, and interpersonal matters, rather than matters dealing with ritual and worship.

same people at another time, hence it is scarce possible to frame one judicial law for all people; or if it were possible, yet it were not prudent, because inconvenient. Let any man but consider the judicials given to the Hebrews, he will find them in a special manner accommodated and attempered to the state of that people, which would not be apposite to the state of another people; as some of their judicials that referred to the distributions of their possessions, to their discrimination from the rest of mankind, to the redemption of their possessions and keeping them within their tribes, to their late state of captivity amongst the Egyptians, and the extermination of their practices used in Egypt. And diverse other particular reasons, purely concerning that state and inapplicable to another, were the most wise and just foundations of diverse of their laws. But yet these judicials that were given to them that were not upon an appropriate reason delivered to them, and that are consistent with the frame of the constitutions of other nations, have been as far as may be transcribed into, as it were, the judicials of other people, at least since the Christian religion obtained, as the laws touching the degrees of marriage,[16] touching murder, and other things.

2. But yet farther it is to be observed that even in that very people, although the text of the judicial law was that which was the basis and rule of their government and polity, yet the wisdom of Almighty God, even in the very giving of that law, and diverse times after upon variety of emergencies, instituted a clause for the accommodation of things in the same state, according to the exigence of things and emergencies, viz. the great council of that people, their Sanhedrin, and the governors of that people, their kings, which were authorized by Almighty God, as the exigence of things required, in the civil or political administration, though not to change the judicials given by God by the hand of Moses, yet to discriminate, supply, and provide for new cases and emergencies. So that Almighty God in his infinite wisdom did find that there was a necessity of supplementals even in his own state, according as succession of time and various emergencies might occur, and even during the consistency of that policy or republic.

3. Upon the whole therefore, I conclude that that law was contrived with most perfect wisdom for that people, and during that state; and therein consisted in a great measure the wisdom of it in that accommodation. But to translate that law to another people, to whom it was not accommodate, were a wrong to the divine wisdom. It is most certain, the specifical natural law that is given to birds is most wisely accommodate to them by the divine wisdom. But for any man to say, because it is a most wise law, therefore it were fit to be used by beasts or fishes, were to distort and wrong the divine wisdom, by misapplying it to such a use, and such animals, for whom it was never intended to be a rule or law. And though the specifical nature of Jews and Gentiles, and all nations be the same, yet it is certain that there ever were, and ever will be, great variety in the states, dispositions, and concerns of several people; so that

[16] Ed: degrees of consanguinity, i.e., laws prohibiting marriage between persons closely related.

that law, which would be a most wise, apt, and suitable constitution to one people, would be utterly improper and inconvenient for another.

[(4)] A fourth ground of, or rather temptation to, a precipitate alteration of laws already made is the ignorance of the laws that are so intended to be altered, in these that are fond of such alteration; and this ignorance of the laws provokes an alteration upon these occasions.

1. It irritates and provokes men to be angry against that which they do not know, nor possibly cannot without the expense of so much pains and time as men are not willing to spare for the acquest of that knowledge. And this temptation commonly befalls men of parts and advanced reason, or such as think themselves so, and therefore impatient of and angry with that they do not know. They think either [that] the laws are foolish, because if they were reasonable things, they must understand them without study, as they do the force of an argument, or the fallacy or strength of a syllogism or a mathematical demonstration, or other. And they think their reason is much undervalued, if it be told them, the law is reason, and the law is thus; and they are presently apt to say, they understand reason, and blame the law, because they understand it not, when they think it is below them to be ignorant of anything. And upon this account they will become Solons and Lycurgi[17] and legislators, and frame a law that they themselves may know and approve because they make it. And as the Israelites in the wilderness they would have gods that they may see, that may go before them. And this is a great piece of pride, peevishness, and inconsiderateness, yet such as the pregnant wits of the late times, and indeed of most times, labour under. For it is apparent that things that are *ex instituto* [by institution; i.e., made or posited], though framed with the greatest wisdom, cannot be known by the light of reason till they are first learned and studied; and if those men should compile a body of laws according to their own fancies or judgment, they possibly might understand them that make them, but others cannot till they have studied and learned them, though they be never so much masters of reason.

2. Ignorance of the law prompts men to a readiness and forwardness to alter it, because they have not a full comprehension, and thereby many times conceive that to be a default[18] in the law which is not so, but only in the ministers and officers that judicially or ministerially exercise or execute it; and they take that for an error in the law which is only a defect or excess in the administration or execution of it.

Again, possibly they may espy something that may in truth be mischievous in some particular case, but weigh not how many inconveniences are on the other side prevented or remedied by that which is the supposed vicious strictness of the law; and he that purchases a reformation of a law, with the introduction of greater

[17] Solon (638–*c*.558 BCE): archon and legendary lawgiver of Athens; Lycurgus (800–730 BCE): legendary lawgiver of Sparta.

[18] OED: failure, want, defect.

inconveniences by the amotion[19] of a mischief, makes an ill bargain. As I have before said, no human law can be absolutely perfect. It is sufficient that it be best *ut plurimum*; and as to the mischiefs that it occasions, as they are accidental and casual, so they may be oftentimes by due care prevented without an alteration of the main.

And besides this, there is that contiguation,[20] as I may say, of most laws with others that it may be of great importance that whilst men over-hastily and unwarily go to make an alteration in that which they conceive amiss in a small matter, they may endanger a great part of the main fabric. As he that will for every small matter be altering of his house, as he will ever be meddling and never be at rest, so he may before he is aware endanger the whole fabric, while out of an over-curious nicety he is impatient of every little defect. The best crisis[21] of any alteration is this that, though it may procure some inconvenience, yet if it produce an equal convenience, or an inconvenience, but probably, yea or disputably, greater or equal to what it remedies, such an attempt is without more ado to be rejected. Therefore if in anything a full comprehension and circumspection of all things that are or that may be is requisite in any action, it is an alteration in the laws. As the philosopher tells us, *Qui ad pauca respicit facile pronunciat.*[22] They that are but half-sighted in business of the law are more ready with speed and peremptoriness to pronounce for its alteration, than they that look about them and see their whole business before them.

(5) A fifth occasion or temptation to be changing of the laws is somewhat akin to the former, viz. an overweening esteem and valuation that a man many times hath of some pretty new expedient that his own fancy or the fancy of others hath suggested for the reformation of something perchance at least seemingly amiss in the law, without a due deep attentive consideration of what inconveniencies would attend such substitution. Indeed, oftentimes men are in love with the product of their own heads; and as they have not the patience or impartiality to examine it, so they are not willing to hear of anything that might interrupt the pleasure of their fancy or contradict or disparage it, though upon never so clear and pregnant a reason and evidence. And by this means men, having their minds intent upon what they would be at in this kind, seldom discover the inconveniencies till they feel them; like boys that blow a bubble out of a walnut-shell, which when it is up, run after it with their eyes fixed only upon their bubble, and never consider what ditches they fall into or what breaches[23] they run into in their pursuit, till they feel the damage which they had not prudence or patience to foresee. The truth is, if upon the discovery of some

[19] OED: removal. [20] Ed: not just contiguity, but systematic interconnection.

[21] OED: a point by which to judge, a criterion.

[22] Francis Bacon attributes this quote to Aristotle (*De generatione et corruptione*, I.2, 316a10): "But of these conceits *Aristotle* speaketh seriously and wisely, when he sayth: *Qui respiciunt ad pauca de facili pronuntiant.*" ("He who considers [only] a few things may easily pronounce judgment.") Francis Bacon, *Advancement of Learning*, Bk I, in *The Oxford Francis Bacon*, ed. Michael Kiernan (Oxford: Oxford University Press, 2000), vol. 4, p. 31.

[23] OED: a gap, fissure, or break.

inconvenience in laws the business were only to provide a plaster for that sore, the reformation of any law were very easy. But the great business of a reformer is not only to see that his remedy be apposite, but that it doth not introduce some other considerable inconvenience, or at least with the inconvenience that it remedies takes not away some other considerable convenience, which the former constitution before the alteration brought with it. For as I before said, the estimate that is to be made is to be made not upon those single inconveniencies that are remedied, but upon the whole account of profit and loss, upon the whole cargo, not upon this or that particular commodity; for still we must remember that the wisdom and prudence of a long tract of time and experience hath made a kind of aggregation and contiguation in the fabric of laws. One piece is for the most part subservient unto and mortised in another, as the frame of a ship or house is, at least when principals are concerned. And therefore there must be a great knowledge and a vast circumspection in every considerable alteration of the law.

(6) A sixth occasion or temptation to alter the law [is] certain passions in men; and because they are of several kinds, but yet all reducible to the same head, I shall enumerate the most considerable, and so conclude this chapter.

1. Vain glory—Men are fond to be enrolled in the number of legislators with Solon, Lycurgus, Numa,[24] and others; and would be tampering upon that account to get a name.
2. Ambition—Commonly the first step of ambitious men, and one of the most popular and taking to lift themselves up to place and power, is with Absalom[25] to be reforming the constitution or administration of the laws.
3. Fear—When men have achieved great power by usurpations or other undue means, the first thing they ordinarily attempt is reformation of laws; partly *ad faciendum populum* [to subjugate the populace]; partly to remove such laws as fit too hard and uneasy upon their usurped power; but principally to engage the generality of men in acting under new laws, and holding their interest and properties under them, and thereby they may be engaged in a common defence against the true and just power, left upon return of things into their ancient channel the repeal of such acts and interests derived under such laws may ensue.
4. Envy and malice at the professors and profession of the law; and that upon these accounts, upon the account of their wealth, power, number, wisdom, and the necessary use of them. Men hate those either they fear or that have a great advantage either of esteem for wisdom and knowledge above themselves; and this very envy at the professors many times discover[s] itself against the law

[24] Numa Pompilius was an early king of Rome (715–673 BCE). Livy wrote of Numa: "He was as conversant as anyone in that age could be with all divine and human law." Livy, *The History of Rome*, ed. E. Rhys, tr. Roberts (New York: Dutton, 1912), vol. I, Bk 1, ch. 18.

[25] Absalom, son of David, King of Israel, sought to usurp David's throne and replace David's law and judgment with his own; see 2 Samuel 15.

they profess, in contriving new systems and models to put their hands out that they think at present in; though this attempt commonly succeeds to the authors with the like disadvantage, as the conspiracy of the limbs against the stomach: they weaken and sometimes destroy themselves in the attempt.

3

Touching the Other Extreme, the Over-Tenacious Holding of Laws, Notwithstanding Apparent Necessity for and Safety in the Change; the Danger and Occasions thereof

By what hath been said in the two preceding chapters, a man would suppose that all alterations, amendments, or reformations of municipal laws were wholly to be interdicted, and no room left for it with safety or prudence, but what hath been once settled for law must stand everlastingly without any reformation or alteration, and that men were better to live under the inconveniencies of an old law, than undergo that hazard and inconvenience, which may incur by any amendment or superinduction[26] of any new laws.

And accordingly many wise and excellent men have laboured, and still do labour under this extreme; and the motives, reasons, or temptations to this extreme seem to be such as these:

1. By long use and custom men, especially [those] that are aged and have been long educated in the profession and practice of the law, contract a kind of superstitious veneration of it beyond what is just and reasonable. And it happens to them as it doth to the Romanists in point of religion in relation to ancient rites and ceremonies transmitted to them from their ancestors, that though they become overburdensome

[26] OED: instituting or appointing in the place of.

by their multitude, or ridiculous by their vanity or impertinency, or antiquated[27] by the alteration of the ends and uses for which they were at first instituted or introduced, yet they are zealously retained, though to the apparent detriment and oppression of religion itself. And accordingly it happens to these men in point of laws. They tenaciously and rigorously maintain these very forms and proceedings and practices, which though possibly at first they were seasonable and useful, yet by the very change of matters they become not only useless and impertinent, but burdensome and inconvenient and prejudicial to the common justice and the common good of mankind, not considering [that] the forms and prescripts of laws were not introduced for their own sakes, but for the use of public justice, and therefore, when they become insipid, useless, impertinent, and possibly derogatory to the end, they may and must be removed.

2. An over-jealous fear that it may be possible that some unthought-of inconvenience may emerge, which may introduce some unexpected mischief to the community, and with it a disparagement to the judgment of those that are undertakers in it. And this lion in the way[28] chokes all industrious application to this most necessary business. Indeed, this very fear must make men that have to do in this important affair the more considerate and circumspect, the more advising and deliberating, the more solicitous and careful, and the more mature and to take the longer time in their results, but must not wholly obstruct the work itself when the public necessity and good calls for it.

3. A timorousness to displease and disoblige great officers and ministers of justice, especially such as have paid dear for places of this nature (one of the greatest banes to justice and necessary reformation); for it must needs follow upon a due reformation of what is amiss that some offices must be laid aside as needless, others pared from their redundancy. And it is true, those that are concerned in point of interest in such reformation will be sprightfully[29] watchful to see if anything of inconvenience may emerge upon such alterations; and they will be ready to inculcate it with disadvantage enough to such as shall be instrumental therein. And if they find the least imaginable default (as it is impossible but some such thing may evene[30]) they will industriously magnify and aggravate it beyond the bounds of truth or prudence. It is a little petty revenge they please themselves withall. But I shall not need to decry such a pitiful pusillanimity or narrowness of mind that will neglect a public important good, either because it may create some advantage to themselves in point of profit, or to those who hold places of advantage in courts of justice or relating thereunto.

4. A jealousy, lest anything offered for the amendment of what is amiss in the law may give a handle to others to ravell[31] into the whole frame of it, and to be tampering

[27] OED: made obsolete.
[28] OED: a danger or obstacle, esp. an imaginary one (after Proverbs 26:13).
[29] OED: full of spirit; animated, lively. [30] OED: happen.
[31] OED: to introduce confusion.

with it to the public detriment; and so that which is intended to perfect and advance the law shall be used like a little wedge put into a great piece of timber, which shall give opportunity to violent persons to drive greater after them and cleave the whole in pieces.

And indeed this often falls out in great assemblies, especially if times be not very sedate when anything of this nature is offered. Perchance one grafts upon it something else, and a second a second thing, and a third a third; whereby the sole design at first is lost, and something, or it may be many things, produced, pernicious both to the law and government. But this may be with care and vigilance prevented, especially as our legislative constitution is established. There be several halts and stops before a law of this nature be perfected, whereby at any of which such an inundation, if it should happen, may be obstructed; and that which is good and necessary be carried on, as I shall have occasion to mention hereafter.

5. Exemplary miscarriages, in the late times, of such as have undertaken reformation both in matters civil and ecclesiastical, hath brought a disrepute upon the undertaking of any reformation in either, so that the very name of reformation and a reformer begins to be a style or name of contempt and obloquy; so that men are as fearful to be under the imputation of a reformer of the law, as they would be of the name of knave or fool, or hypocrite.

And upon these and the like accounts it fares with the law, and the sages thereof, as to the point of reformation of the law, as it did with the present age and the *virtuosi* of Parnassus in Bocaline.[32] They dare not meddle with it, but let it live as long and as well as it can in the state they find it. Only to save their credits upon such occasions, they meddle with some little inconsiderable things, as they set the price upon turnips and carrot seed, but nothing is dared to be done of use and importance.

But notwithstanding all these difficulties and obstructions, I think good and wise men may and ought to make some prudent essay[33] even in this great business, and with very good success both to their own reputation and the public benefit. And in order to the encouragement therein, I shall propound these considerations:

1. We are not without excellent and happy examples of reformation in this kind to the general good and advantage of mankind; yea, and for the very preservation of the laws themselves, which without due husbandry of them will die of themselves, like trees that want pruning....[34]

[32] MH refers to Triano Boccalini's *Ragguagli di Parnaso* (1612–13), a satire on contemporary life and letters. Boccalini "reports" the discussions of a counsel of wise men of all ages, presided over by Apollo concerning politics, literature, and art. The English translation by Henry Carey, *Advertisements from Parnassus, in Two Centuries with the Politick Touch-stone* (London, 1656) influenced Jonathan Swift and other English writers.

[33] OED: attempt or endeavour.

[34] MH here offers several examples from Roman, ecclesiastical, and English legal history, singling out Justinian (Roman civil law), Gratian (canon law), and Edward I ("our English Justinian") and Elizabeth (common law) for special mention.

[2] The second consideration is this, as all sublunary things are subject to corruption and putrefaction, to diseases and rust, so even laws themselves, by long tract of time gather certain diseases and excrescences; certain abuses and corruptions grow into the law, as close as the ivy unto the tree, or the rust to the iron, and in a little tract of time gain the reputation of being part of the law. So that a great and considerable part of that reformation that is pleaded for is not so much of the law, as of abuses and corruptions, and wens[35] and excrescences, and delays and formalities and exactions,[36] that do adhere to the law and will in time strangle and stifle it with its close adherence to it. And when these dear and profitable exuberances and ulcers are looked after, presently those that are concerned in the profit thereof, or do not duly distinguish between the law and its abuses and diseases, cry out upon destroying the law and altering of the law, when in truth it is the rescuing of the law from those encroachments or abuses that are made upon it or brought into it.

3. But yet farther, I do not think that the only things fit to be reformed in the law are the abuses and corruptions of it, but there are some things that are really and truly parts of the law as necessary to be reformed as the errors or abuses of it.

And we must remember that laws were not made for their own sakes, but for the sake of those who were to be guided by them; and though it is true they are and ought to be sacred, yet if they be or are become unuseful for their end, they must either be amended if it may be, or new laws be substituted and the old repealed, so it be done regularly, deliberately, and so far forth only as the exigence or convenience justly demands it.—And in this respect the saying is true, *salus populi suprema lex esto* [the safety or well-being of the people is the supreme law].[37] Now laws become or are unuseful to their end upon two accounts. 1. When in their very constitution and fabric they are rotten and faulty and unjust, and impossible to be borne without remarkable and common inconvenience. I shall not apply this part to the thing in question.—But 2dly, when a law, though never so good in its first institution, yet by reason of some accidental emergencies that do most usually happen in tract of time, either becomes obsolete and out of use, or weak and unprofitable to its end, or inconsistent with some new superinduction that time and variety of occasions have introduced. And as this is most clear in all laws, so in our English laws we shall find, what was in use, and possibly very effectual in its time, is now deserted and antiquated, and utterly inapplicable to the present state of administration in England. Glanville wrote a system of our English laws in the time of H[enry] 2, Bracton in the time of H[enry] 3, Britton in the time of E[dward] I.[38] Let any man read them, and

[35] OED: a protuberance or wart. [36] OED: demands of payment.

[37] This principle was deeply embedded in medieval legal and political theory. It has roots in Roman civil law and further back in Cicero's *De Legibus*, Bk III, ch. III.8 (in Cicero, *On the Republic* and *On the Laws*, tr. Clinton Walker Keyes (Cambridge, MA: Harvard University Press, 1928), 466. It expressed the overriding principle by which princely rule was to be governed.

[38] Regarding Glanville and Bracton see *History*, 142 and note 45. Britton (possibly John de Breton) wrote an early book on English common law around 1290, in the reign of Edward I (1272–1307).

see whether he can by any means accommodate that administration to the present state of things, or the present regiment or order of things to that. Nay, if we come to the year-books of the time of E[dward] 3, any man that knows anything in this kind will most certainly find that it cannot fit us; for where is there now one assize or real action[39] brought, unless where they have no other remedy? So that the stream of things have, as it were, left that channel, and taken a new one; and he that thinks a state can be exactly steered by the same laws in every kind, as it was two or three hundred years since, may as well imagine that the clothes that fitted him when he was a child should serve him when he is grown a man. The matter changeth the custom; the contracts the commerce; the dispositions, educations, and tempers of men and societies change in a long tract of time; and so must their laws in some measure be changed, or they will not be useful for their state and condition. And besides all this, as I before said, time is the wisest thing under heaven. These very laws, which at first seemed the wisest contribution under heaven, have some flaws and defects discovered in them by time. As manufactures, mercantile arts, architecture and building, and philosophy itself, receive new advantages and discoveries by time and experience; so much more do laws, which concern the manners and customs of men.

All that which I contend for in the first and second chapter is not to render laws of men like laws of nature fixed and unalterable, but that it be done with great prudence, advice, care, and upon a full and clear prospect of the whole business.

4. But yet further, by length of time and continuance laws are so multiplied and grown to that excessive variety that there is a necessity of reduction of them, or otherwise it is not manageable; as we have before observed touching the Roman laws, which in a tract of 1,300 years grew to 2,000 great volumes. And the reason is, because this age for the purpose received from the last a body of laws, and they add more and transmit the whole to the next age, and they add to what they had received and transmit the whole stock to the next age. Thus as the rolling of a snow-ball, it increaseth in bulk in every age, till it becomes utterly unmanageable. And hence it is that even in the laws of England we have so many varieties of forms of conveyances, feoffment, fines, release, confirmation, grant, attornment, common recovery, deeds, enrolled, &c.[40] because the use coming in at several times, every age did retain somewhat of what was past, and added somewhat of its own, and so carried over the whole product to the quotient. And this produceth mistakes. A man perchance useth one sort of conveyance, where he should have used another. It breeds uncertainty and contradiction of opinion, and that begets suits and expense. It must necessarily cause ignorance in the professors and profession itself; because the volumes of the law are not easily to be mastered.

[39] Medieval legal actions brought for restitution of property.

[40] MH here mentions various devices in medieval English law by which property, or interests in property, or relations tied to property are established, confirmed, or transferred.

5. There be in the law to this day some things continuing, which, though possibly of ordinary use or occurrence, yet are mischievous when they come to be used and would not at all be missed if taken away, and which I shall in the pursuit of particulars evidence to the satisfaction I believe of every knowing, considering, and unprejudiced mind.

6. I shall add but this one thing more, that it may justly be feared that if something considerable for the reformation of this [that is] amiss in the law be not done by knowing and judicious persons, too much may some time or other be done by some, either out of envy at the professors, or mistaken apprehensions or popular humours. The amendment of things amiss timely,[41] by knowing, able, and judicious men that understand their business, may do very much good, and prevent very much evil that may otherwise ensue; and when the business is begun by such hands, it may possibly be too late to allay it. And although it be true, that as the legislative power is established there be many reserves to prevent or stop such an inundation, yet we know not how high the public necessities of supplies may arise, considering our many great undertakings in the kingdom; and it is no new thing to observe very hard and unreasonable terms granted as the price and purchase of supplies, when they cannot be had upon easier terms. And it will have this plausible pretence that the judges and lawyers will do nothing to the laws and therefore it shall be done by other hands. Such a humour would be more easily prevented by a wise and seasonable undertaking in this kind, which would not be so easily diverted or allayed, if once it should be flying. And thus much shall serve for this chapter.[42]

[41] Ed: the timely amendment of things amiss.

[42] In Chapter 4 of this work, MH insists that, where feasible, reforms "be done by the power and authority of the courts and judges, without troubling a parliament for such things." But, where parliament must be the agent of reform, "let it be particular, and as little left *arbitrio judicis* [to the judgment of judges] as may be," although "some things are of such a nature as much in the particular application or exercise be left to the judges and officers of courts, as the forming and modelling of writs, process, pleadings, and other proceedings, in conformity and subservience of what is to be settled by parliament in this behalf" (Hale, *A Collection of Tracts*, 272).

PART V

Reflections on Mr Hobbs his Dialogue of the Law

Introductory Note

Thomas Hobbes's *Dialogue between a Philosopher and a Student of the Common Laws* circulated in manuscript in the early 1670s. In 1672, a copy reached Hale, who, as Chief Justice of King's Bench, had responsibility for licensing legal works for publication. Aubry reported that "Judge Hales . . . haz read it & much mislikes it, and is his Enemy."[1] We can infer that Hale's "Reflections" was probably written sometime after 1672. Hale first sketched a rough "draught" of his critique and later refined his thoughts, but he never completed this work. It is possible that he wrote "Reflections" at about the same time as his *Treatise.* Several manuscript copies of "Reflections" and of the draft for it exist. Autograph manuscripts of both are available in Lambeth Palace (Fairhurst Papers MS 3479, fos 60–78)[2] and copies made in 1690 can be found in the British Library (BL 18,235 fos 27–40 and 140–59). This selection follows the Lambeth autograph manuscript. Some passages from Hale's draft are included in footnotes. All footnotes are the current editor's. Numbers corresponding to manuscript folios are included in square brackets.

Each chapter of "Reflections" addresses a major theme of Hobbes's *Dialogue*: (1) reason in and of the law and (2) the nature and limits of sovereign power. Hobbes challenged core claims of common-law jurisprudence, taking Sir Edward Coke as its spokesman. Hobbes accepts Coke's claim that "reason is the soul of law," but he insists that this is the *natural reason* of the king, not the alleged artificial reason of common-law judges, as Coke had maintained. In response, Hale offers a nuanced defence of the common-law doctrine. Reason "in us" is a faculty universal among

[1] Letter of 2 February 1673 quoted by Alan Cromartie in his edition of the *Dialogue* in Thomas Hobbes, *Writings on Common Law and Hereditary Right*, ed. A. Cromartie and Q. Skinner (Oxford: Clarendon Press, 2005), xvii.

[2] On the title page of the MS for this work, someone, perhaps MH's grandson, describes the former as "a rough draught" of thoughts "methodically extended, but left imperfect" in the latter. MH's grandson commissioned copies of this and other MSS of his grandfather in 1690.

human beings, he argues, but it can be disciplined in different ways: it can be directed to specific subject matters and habituated by training and experience shared with others also participating in the practice. The reason of law is one such discipline. Training in this discipline is indispensable because the subject matter with which law deals is especially difficult for untutored natural reason to grasp. Although abstract notions of justice and decency are common to all human beings (as we learned in the *Treatise*), they must be applied in circumstances that are vastly varied and difficult to anticipate. Just judgments in matters of law depend on both a firm grasp of general principles and facility with the complexity of human intercourse. Training in common law, through immersion in the vast body of decisions and resolutions arising from the particulars of daily life—"the common staple of human conversation" (190)—uniquely disciplines judicial judgment and avoids the inevitable arbitrariness and uncertainty of appeals to untutored natural reason. (This line of argument is developed also in *History*, "Preface to Rolle's Abridgement," and "Amendment.")

Hale's opposition to the arbitrary exercise of power led him vigorously to challenge Hobbes's claim in the *Dialogue* (and more extensively in *Leviathan*) that unlimited sovereign power rests in the hands of the monarch. Hobbes argued that the king may accept certain limitations on his power in ordinary times, but he is bound only by his obligation to protect the people in times of necessity, and he alone is the judge of necessity and the best means of protection. To set the stage for his response, Hale rehearses briefly his view of the grounds of political authority (elaborated in *Prerogatives*, Chapter 1). All legitimate government rests ultimately in mutual consent between the governor and the governed, he argues. This consent may be explicit, or it may manifest itself only through long usage; it even underwrites rule established by conquest. Political authority is established, and over time altered, through mutual concessions and adjustments. Limits on power are inevitable features of such compacts. This was true of England after the conquest of William I, he insists.

Sovereign power necessarily includes *inter alia* rights to make peace and war, to raise and support a military, to regulate commerce, to make laws, and to administer justice according to those laws. In England, these powers rest ultimately in the monarch, but only in a qualified form. For example, the king can make law and can raise taxes for military purposes only with consent of parliament; moreover, while the king is not subject to the coercive power of the law, he is subject to its directive power and to its nullifying power. Those like Hobbes who reject such limits and put ultimate and final power in the hands of the monarch not only fail to understand the government-constituting law of England and the principles of natural justice on which it rests, but they also imperil both the governors and the governed. Finally, it is a grave mistake, Hale argues, to fashion a constitution for the rare occasions in which decisive action is needed to avert a threat to the nation's security by subjecting it daily to the untrammelled arbitrary judgment of the king.

Hale left his critique unfinished. The arguments sketched in "Reflections" are developed further in *Prerogatives*, *History*, and "Jurisdiction of the Lords House."

[68r]

1

Of Laws in General and the Law of Reason

When we speak of reason we are to consider it under these several notions.

1. It may be justly taken for that subjective reason[3] that is in things that are to be known or understood, which consists in the congruity, connection, and fit dependence of one thing upon another. Such a reason as this may be found in things that are destitute of the faculty of reason and is or may be antecedent to any exercise of any human reasonable faculty: thus, the connection of effects to their causes, the consequences[4] of properties to their forms or essences, the exertions of acts by their powers, the ordination and disposition of natural things in their several places and orders, the connatural tendencies and the motions of things in nature to their preservation and conveniences have a reasonableness that is a decorum, congruity, and consequetion,[5] though there were no man in the world to take notice of it. The proportion between lines and superficies[6] and figures and of their various coincidences and textures and the reasonableness thereof in the mathematics would be antecedent to any operation of a human understanding upon them, which rather finds its conclusions in them than makes them. And in morals, though the objects thereof are more obscure and not so open to a distinct and clear discovery, yet there is a certain reasonableness and congruity and intrinsic connection and consequence of one thing from another, antecedent to any artificial system of morals or institution of laws.

2. It is taken for that faculty of reasonable nature whereby it moves itself to the attainment of things to be known and then it is called judgment, or in things to be done and then it may be called wisdom, prudence, or skill. And although in some things there is that near vicinity between this faculty and the object that it acts *quasi per saltum* [as if at once] as the bodily eye sees; yet for the most part the exertion of

[3] Here MH follows a common medieval practice of using "subjective" to refer to something *in the subject matter* that is potentially observed, or judged of, rather than in the rational, judging subject. However, in his "draught" [fo. 62r], he reverses these terms: "reason in things" he calls "reason considered objectively," and the common "faculty of the reasonable soul" he calls "reason considered subjectively."

[4] Ed: connections or relations.

[5] Ed: proceeding in argument from proposition to proposition; hence, rational or logical relationship.

[6] OED: surfaces.

this faculty is gradual, discursive, and at [least][7] [68v] by an internal deducing of one thing from another, or an illation or inferring of one thing upon another, which is called ratiocination. And thus reason, as it is a faculty in common to all reasonable creatures, is the common engine or instrument whereby all kinds of knowledge or arts are acquired. It is the same faculty of reason [that] serves the naturalist, the physician, the lawyer, the mathematician, the mechanic,[8] [and] the ploughman in all their several ways and prosecutions.

But although this common faculty be common to all mankind, yet it is easily observable that in several men there are various degrees of quickness, activity, and perfection in this reasoning faculty, which may partly proceed from the various temperament of their spirits and humours or from the various exercise, employment, and excitation of this reasoning faculty in them.

And not only so but it is most evident to any observing man that very often times the edge, the direction, the *apex rationis* [summit of reason], as I may call it, in several men are directed several ways.[9] That man's reason that is dextrous and ready in physic[10] is not suited for politics and another man's reason that renders him apt and quick in mathematics doth not suit to the knowledge of physic; yea sometimes men that could not give a tolerable account of ten words of sense yet [are] strangely dextrous in mechanics and sometimes in music. Tully,[11] that was an excellent orator and a good moralist, was but an ordinary statesman and a worse poet. And though possibly some man may be of so happy a reason that it may bid fair for any kind of object, yet it is rare; and commonly those that pretend[12] to an universal knowledge are but superficial and seldom pierce deep into anything.

3. Thirdly, it is taken complexedly when the reasonable faculty is in conjunction with the reasonable subject[13] and habituated to it by use and exercise. And it is this kind of reason, or reason thus taken, that denominates a man a mathematician, a philosopher, a politician, a physician, a lawyer, yea that renders men excellent in their particular arts as a good engineer, a good watchmaker, a good smith, [and] a good surgeon, [69r] all which consists in the application of the faculty of reason to the particular subject, the direction of it in a particular channel and by particular methods. Whence it comes to pass that as the same natural motion and tendency of water according to the various applications and directions in one place waters a meadow, in another place drives a mill, in another place lifts up a hammer or carries a float, or as the same quality of descent in a weight according to the variety of its application makes the clock to strike, the index of the watch to show the hour, or the jack to turn the spit, so the same faculty of reason variously applied and directed

[7] MS: at least an.
[8] OED: person of a manual occupation.
[9] Ed: in different men in different ways.
[10] Ed: medicine.
[11] Ed: Marcus Tullius Cicero (106–43 BCE).
[12] Ed: claim.
[13] MH's draft has "object" here, corresponding to his use in the phrase "reason considered objectively."

renders this man a mathematician, a physician, a lawyer, [or] an artificer according as the reasoning faculty is directed or applied and habituated by use and exercise to the several objects thereof.[14]

And upon this account it comes to pass that, though two or more men of the same perfection of the reasoning faculty that have yet variously exercised and applied that common faculty to their several objects, they are not equally to expect an equal aptitude and perfection in each other's science or art. If one man hath habituated and applied his reason to the science of physic and another man hath habituated and applied his reason in mathematical sciences, this shall not be so good a physician as the other, nor the other so good a mathematician as this: And therefore, though the mathematician cursorily runs over the titles of the books of Galen and Hippocrates, or the physician runs over the titles of the theorems and conclusions of Euclid or Archimedes, or if a man that pretends himself or really be well-exercised in natural philosophy shall run over the titles or indexes of the digest or code,[15] the first shall be but a weak physician, the second a weak mathematician, and the third a weak civilian,[16] though possibly there might be a parity in the perfection or degree of their reasoning faculty abstracted from its habituation to its object.

Of all kinds of subjects whereabout the reasoning faculty is conversant, there is no one of so great a difficulty for the faculty of reason to guide itself and come to any steadiness as that of laws for the regulation and ordering of civil societies and for the measuring of right and wrong when it comes to particulars. And therefore it is not possible for men to come to the same certainty, evidence, and demonstration touching them as may be expected in mathematical sciences. [69v] And they that please themselves with a persuasion that they can with as much evidence and congruity make out an unerring system of laws and politics equally applicable to all states and

[14] "Draught" [fo. 62v]: "And in this consideration reason is as much diversified as anything we can think of according to the variety of its application. In things speculative there is one kind of reason, in the mathematician another, of the naturalist another, of the moralist one kind of reason in things purely speculative, another of things practical. The watchmaker proceeds by a reason accommodate[d] to his art, the shoemaker by the reason accommodat[ed] to his art; and the reason that directs the one will not serve to direct the other. It is true, the reason of both is that subjective intellectual faculty first mentioned, but it is a reason modified, cased, and accommodate[d] to his special object. Again there is one kind of reason in things to be advised or done, another kind of reason touching the innovation or alteration of things to be done. In these and the like instances, it is not the common, universal, or indeterminate reason, or reason at large, but reason reduced under a special determinate direction—reason modified by the objects or business about which it is exercised, reason *intra cancellus determinatus* [within determinate limits]. And therefore in the exercise and actings of reason thus determined the proceeding of the understanding is governed by the special reason of the thing unto which it is thus determined. The shoemaker in making of his shoes proceeds rationally, but it is upon media proper to his art and not upon the reason of the politician or philosopher."

[15] MH refers to the components of the *Corpus Juris Civilis*, the basic text of Roman law comprising the *Codex*, *Digest*, *Institutes*, and *Novellae*.

[16] Ed: expert in civil (Roman) law.

occasions as Euclid demonstrates his conclusions deceive themselves [with] rash notions which prove ineffectual when they come to particular application.

And the reasons of this difficulty are evident, namely:

1. In morals, and especially with relation to laws for a community, though the common notions of [what is] just and fit are common to all men of reason, yet when persons come to particular application of these common notions to particular instances and occasions, we shall rarely find a common consent or agreement between men, though [they be] of great reason and that reason [be] improved by great study and learning. Witness the great disagreement between Plato and Aristotle, men of great reason in the framing of their laws and commonwealth, [and] the great difference in most of the states and kingdoms in the world in their laws, administrations, and measures of right and wrong when they come to particulars. And let any man but examine the writings of those men that pretend to be the greatest masters of reason, and possibly they may be excellent men; yet no persons differ more than they touching things of this nature. And though they perchance have this happnes[17] to shake and weaken one the others' principles or conclusions, yet when they set up their own positions, they are weak and generally displeasing. And upon this account it is that, where men of observation and experience in human affairs and conversation between man and man make many times good judges, yet for the most part those men that have great reason and learning, which they gather up of casuists, schoolmen, moral philosophers, and treatises touching morals in the theory, that soar in high speculations and abstract notions touching justice and right, and as they differ extremely among themselves when they come to particular applications, so [they] are most commonly the worst judges that can be, because they are transported from the [70r] ordinary measures of right and wrong by their overfine speculations, theories, and distinctions above the common staple of human conversations.

And this instability, uncertainty, and variety in the judgments and opinions of men touching right and wrong when they come to particulars, and to avoid that great uncertainty in the application of reason by particular persons to particular instances, and to the end that men might understand by what rule and measure to live and possess, and might not be under the unknown, arbitrary, [and] uncertain judgment of the uncertain reason of particular persons—[this] hath been the principal reason that the wiser sort of the world have agreed upon some certain laws and rules and methods of administration of common justice and these to be as particular and certain as could well be thought of.[18] By this means, they gained these advantages:

[17] Ed: Variation of "happen." OED's second meaning of happen (to) is "to fall to the lot of" or "come the way of," so possibly MH had in mind "though they perchance have/take the opportunity to."

[18] "Draught" [fo. 61v]: "And hence it is that the world, having sufficiently experimented [i.e., experienced] the instability and unfixedness of men's judgments in relation to moral actions, have taken the care of remedying that inconvenience by propounding and establishing certain laws relating to the moral actions and the civil regiment of the societies of mankind. And [they] have always thought and found that

(1) they avoided the great instability of the judgments and reasons of judges and gained somewhat of certainty which might be known to them that were to judge and to be judged. (2) They hereby avoided that great opportunity that judges had (when they had no other rule for their judgments but their own reason) to be corrupt and partial. (3) They in a great measure avoided that jangling and contradiction that would arise upon the unstable reason of men when they once came to particular decisions.

2. Though a certain and determinate law may have some mischiefs in relation to particulars which cannot all by any human prudence at first be foreseen and provided for, yet it [is] preferable before that arbitrary and uncertain rule which men miscall the law of reason. Yet certain it is that that law is best framed that at once hath certainty and yet induceth as few particular mischiefs as may be. And hence it is that it is a thing of greatest difficulty so to contrive and order any law that, while it remedies or provides against one inconvenience, it introduceth not a worse or an equal [one]. A man that hath a prospect [of][19] one or a few things may with ease enough fit a law to that or those things. *Qui ad pauca respicit facile pronuntiat.*[20] But the texture of human affairs [70v] is not unlike the texture of a diseased body labouring under maladies;[21] it may be of so various natures that such physic as may be proper to the cure of one of the maladies may be [destructive in relation][22] to the other and the cure of one of the diseases may be the death of the patient. And this [is] the difficulty of making, interpreting, and applying laws because it requires [(1)] a very large prospect of all the most considerable emergencies that may happen not only in that which is intended to be remedied, but [also] in those other accidental, consequential, or collateral things that may emerge upon the remedy propounded; (2) a great and experienced judgment to weigh and consider whether the convenience of the law propounded may considerably preponderate the inconvenience that it will occasion; (3) a great judgment and skill so to apply the remedy that it may [work] with the least inconvenience that may be.

The inconvenience of an arbitrary law is intolerable, and therefore a certain law, though accompanied with some mischief, is preferable before it. But it is not possible for any human thing to be wholly perfect. A certain law hath this inconvenience attending it that sometimes some persons or causes may suffer by the rigor of a certain law, yet infinite more must suffer by the inconvenience of an arbitrary and uncertain law.

certain and established laws framed with as good a prospect of prudence or experience to the common good of societies as might reasonably occur, though perchance in some particulars it might produce some detriment to some persons at some times, are far more conducible to the good of societies than to leave things to arbitrary decisions of such as do not only pretend to a great use of reason but really have it."

[19] MS: at.

[20] See "Amendment," 176, note 22. The sentence reads: he who considers [just] a few things can easily pronounce judgment.

[21] See *Treatise*, 37 and note 91.

[22] These words are struck out in the MS, but they seem to be needed for the sense of the sentence.

And the same difficulty which in this respect happens in making laws must necessarily happen many times in the expounding of them, when there is room or latitude for exposition. The expounder must look further than the present instance and whether such an exposition may not introduce a greater inconvenience than it remedies.

3. A third thing that renders [difficult] the true determination of moral [actions] and the application of remedies to them is this, that every moral action is or may be diversified from another by circumstances, which are of so great an influence unto the true [71r] nature and determination of moral actions, that they very frequently [specify different][23] actions that are materially the same, and give such allays and abatements or advances and improvements to them that scarce two moral actions in the world are [in] every way commensurate. And these circumstances are so various and their influx into moral actions so different and so difficult to be discerned or adequately estimated that the making of laws touching them, or the application of laws already made to them, is very difficult.

4. There are many things especially in laws and government that mediately, remotely, and consequentially are reasonable to be approved, though the reason of the party [directly affected] doth not presently or immediately or distinctly see its reasonableness. For instance, it is reasonable for me to prefer a law made by a hundred or two hundred persons of age, wisdom, experience, and interest before a law excogitated by myself who may be a simple, inexperienced young man—though I discern better the reason of that law that I have thought of than the reason of the law of those wise men. Again, it is a reason for me to prefer a law by which a kingdom hath been happily governed four or five hundred years than to adventure the happiness and peace of a kingdom upon some new theory of my own, though I am better acquainted with the reasonableness of my own theory than with that law. Again, I have reason to assure myself that long experience makes more discoveries touching conveniences or inconveniences of laws than it is possible for the wisest counsel of men at first to foresee. And that those amendments and supplements that through the various experiences of wise and knowing men [71v] have been applied to any law must needs be better suited to the convenience of laws than the best inventions of the most pregnant wits not aided by such a series and tract of experience. All these things are reasonable, [although] the particular reason of the laws and supplements themselves perchance is not obvious to the most subtle wits or reason. And this adds to the difficulty of a present fathoming of the reason of laws, because they are the production of long and iterated experience which though it be commonly called the mistress of fools yet certainly it is the wisest expedient among mankind and discovers those defects and supplies which no wit of man could either at once foresee or aptly remedy.

[23] MS is partially illegible.

5. The last reason touching the inevidence of laws already made, at least in all things, to every man's reason is this: because laws are certain institutions, and though perchance at first the makers of them saw reason to pitch upon this institution rather than another, yet in things thus settled it is not necessary that the reasons of the institution should be evident unto us. It is sufficient that they are instituted laws that give a certainty to us and it is reasonable for us to observe them, though the particular reason of the institution appear not. And 'tis a foolish and unreasonable thing for any to find fault with an institution because he thinks he could have made a better, or expect a mathematical demonstration to evince the reasonableness of an institution or the self-evidence thereof. [For example,] it is part of the law of England that all the lands descend to the eldest son without a particular custom altering it, that a freehold passeth not without livery and seisin or attornment by an act in pays[24] but where statutes have altered [the law], that an estate made by deed to a man forever passeth only for life without the word "heirs" [included in the deed of transfer] and infinite[ly] more of this kind. Now if any the most refined brain under heaven would go about to inquire by speculation or by reading of Plato or Aristotle, or by considering the laws of [72r] the Jews or other nations, to find out how lands descend in England, or how estates are there transferred or transmitted among us, he would lose his labour and spend his motions in vain till he acquainted himself with the laws of England. And the reason is because they are institutions introduced by the will and consent of others implicitly by custom and usage or explicitly by written laws or acts of parliament.

And upon all this that hath been said it appears that men are not born common lawyers, neither can the bare exercise of the faculty of reason give a man a sufficient knowledge of it, but it must be gained by the habituating and accustoming and exercising of that faculty by reading, study, and observation, to give a man a competent knowledge thereof.

And although a man that hath long and industriously exercised himself in that study cannot pretend either to infallibility in his judgment or to a full attainment of all that is attainable touching the laws of England, yet he will be much better fitted for a right judgment therein than he that hath no other stock to trade upon than the bare exercise of his faculty of reason, or that hath only taken the pains to read over the titles of the statutes or indexes or repertories[25] of some law books.

It were ridiculous to expect that a man that hath either only the advantage of his own natural ingeny[26] or hath spent a month in reading some of the rudiments of geometry should be as good a master in the mathematics as he that hath made it the study of his life, and yet it is apparent that the positions and conclusions in the mathematics have more evidence in them and are more naturally seated in the mind

[24] That is, transfer of full property rights in some piece of land is not accomplished without some formal mark of delivery of possession or expression of acknowledgement by a tenant of the new lord.

[25] OED: list, catalogue.

[26] OED: intellectual capacity, mental ability, ingenuity.

than institution of laws, which in a great measure depend upon the consent and appointment of the first institutors.

Such persons therefore that have had their education in the study of the English laws have these considerable advantages to render them fitter judges and interpreters of the laws of this kingdom than any other whose studies and education have been entirely or principally [72v] applied to the study of philosophy or mathematics or other studies.

(1) It is not impossible but that at least some of those that have applied themselves to the study of the laws have as fair a measure of natural reason as those that have addicted themselves to philosophy or other studies and possibly would have proved as good proficients in them had they applied and habituated their reason to those studies.

(2) If men of parity of reason and intellectuals[27] have gotten the advantage of others that in natural capacities have been their equals by reason of the advantage they have had by their education in this or that kind of learning, then certainly considering how much the nature of the science of law requires much more assiduity and application to it than other studies, that person of equal parts that hath habituated his reason to the study of the law must needs have so much the greater advantage in his knowledge of it above others that have not made it their business, by how much the more the very nature, kind, and condition of that science requires more study and application than the studies of other sciences.

(3) It is one of the things of greatest moment in the profession of the common law to keep as near as may be the certainty of the law and the consonancy of it to itself, [so] that one age and one tribunal may speak the same things and carry on the same thread of the law in one uniform rule as near as is possible; for otherwise, that which all ages and places have contended for in laws, namely certainty and to avoid arbitrariness and that extravagance that would fall out if the reasons of judges and advocates were not kept in their traces, would in half an age be lost.[28]

And this conservation of laws within their bounds and limits could never be, unless men be well-informed by study and reading what were the judgments and resolutions and decisions and interpretations of former ages and of other [73r] courts and tribunals, and thereby to keep a consonancy and consistency of the law to itself which would never be done without much reading and observation and study.

[27] OED: intellectual faculties.

[28] "Draught" [fos 62v–63r]: With regard to "laws that are already made, the lawyer is not to proceed upon a reason at large, but he is, as near as he can, [to] conform his reason to that state and order and rule that is proper in it, and not to say that, because I think this law might be better if it were thus, therefore it is no law, [that since] it is unjust, I must neither judge according to it, but reduce them all to the standard of that which I think reason. For that were to introduce confusion, [63r] for it may be that [the] law which I think unreasonable and that it were better thus, another would as much be in dislike of my reason and propound something that he thinks reasonable which might differ from both [of] the former." [This passage of "Draught" continues in the passage quoted in the next note.]

(4) As to exposition of acts of parliament and written laws, certainly he that hath been educated in the study of the law hath a great advantage over those that have been otherwise exercised, let them pretend to or be masters of never so much reason. For (a) they have not only the preamble and body and provisos of the acts of parliament before them, but they have a clearer evidence of what the practice or mischief was before, which possibly is not so obvious without reading, especially if it be an ancient act. (b) They have the opportunity of the knowledge of the expositions made by judges of former times, which cannot be so well known to others. (c) They have within their view and knowledge the expositions of other acts of parliament that either have the like clauses or analogy of reasons, which are great guides and helps in exposition of laws, which they that have the naked use of their own faculties without the help of study and education are destitute of.[29]

2

Of Sovereign Power

The modifications of government are [various][30] in their kinds, forms, and degrees—some monarchical, some aristocratic, some democratic, and some mixed of all; and

[29] "Draught" [fo. 63r]: "But then suppose a question falls about the exposition of a law already settled, whether it be by custom or other institution, or if a case fall out that hath not been *in terminis* [with finality] decided. How is the judge to govern himself? I answer that first, he must with all imaginable industry inquire and examine what hath been done formerly in such cases, whether there hath been resolutions of former ages and times, and not rashly or hastily to depart from these without very evident and clear and unanswerable reason. Second, if such resolutions of precedent ages cannot be found, yet still he ought to keep his reason as near as may be within the *cancelli* [limits] of the reason of the law and analogy with resolutions of cases and practices of like nature. And the reason [for this] is because it is of great moment to have the law consonant to itself, to keep resolutions as near as may be in an analogy to and parity of reason. For otherwise, by using of reason at large, without containing it within congruity and analogy of itself, the law will run out into an utter uncertainty. And a law that hath some mischief in it if certain is much better than an arbitrary law, because the constitution[s] of most kingdoms, especially of this of England, have a means by act of parliament to rectify the mischiefs of a certain law, but there is no cure of the inconveniences of an arbitrary law. But, third, if there be no former decision, no legal reason, or reason governed by the analogy of law to direct the judgment, or if these analogical reasons be but found weak or strained, then and not till then reason at large must guide and direct their judgment, wherein their experience and observation and reading give a far greater advantage of judgment than the airy speculations and notions and consequences and deductions from certain preconceived systems of politics and laws of some that call themselves philosophers, which though they may please the authors in the contemplation yet, when they come to practice and use, vanish into smoke and nothing." For a similar discussion, see *History*, 147–8.

[30] MS: various both.

those mixtures are or may be infinitely various. In some constitutions, one part of the sovereign power is in one part of the government, another part in another.[31]

These modifications of government are made in several manners. (1) By the original institution of the government when settled at first by the consent of the governors and governed. But this is difficult to be found in ancient governments, first, because the original instrument of that institution is hardly to be found and, secondly, because in process of time new occasions, emergencies, accidents, and capitulations do necessarily occasion alterations from the first institution. (2) By long custom and usage, which carries in itself a tacit consent of the governors and governed, [or is at least][32] an evidence or interpretation of the original [73v] institution of the nature of the government or of the initial pact between the governors and governed. (3) By victory or conquest, which though when it is plenary and universal, it acquires an absolute dominion or sovereignty in the victor; yet such a conquest is rare, but commonly it ends in dedition[33] and capitulation between the conqueror and the conquered. And then the pacts or capitulations upon such dedition may abridge or modify the extent of that sovereignty. And (4) by concessions and mutual agreements between the governors and governed after the primitive institution of the government, whereby it often falls out that the sovereignty of the governor is various[ly] modified according to the tenor and purport of such pacts and concessions subsequent to the institution of the government.

They that think King William the first got this kingdom by such a right of conquest as abrogated all former rights of government or got such a dominion over this kingdom as absolute conquerors obtain are very much mistaken. For[,]

1. The claim of King William was not by right of conquest, but of succession to King Edward and upon that account indeed he conquered Harold that was an usurper.[34] But he conquered not England, but succeeded in those rights that King Edward had and left. It was *victoria in regem* but not *in populum*.[35] And hence it was that, although the rough dispensation of war brought some hardships upon some particular persons, especially such as took part with Harold, yet there was no general alteration of laws or properties or freeholds of English men, for men recovered their possessions after the victory of King William upon the *seisin*[36] they or their ancestors had in the time of King Edward by those processes that were in use before that victory.[37]

2. But if the intention of the claim of King William had been by way of absolute conquest (as most clearly it was not), yet the full and plenary complement of his acquest[38] was not without pact and dedition in which the laws of King Edward were not only granted but granted upon claim and capitulation and confirmed with all

[31] See *History*, Ch. 5, and *Prerogatives*, Ch. 1, for further discussion of the issues raised in this chapter.
[32] MS: or at least is at least. [33] OED: surrender. [34] See *History*, 130 and note 3.
[35] These terms are explained in *History*, 152–5 and *Prerogatives*, 211, 216–17.
[36] Ed: possession of freehold estate in land.
[37] MH also makes this argument at *Prerogatives*, 216. [38] Ed: acquisition.

imaginable solemnity. And it was this [which][39] gave the full establishment and settlement of the throne of King William.

[74r] 3. But besides all this, there were from time to time both in the time of King William I, King William II, King Henry I, and all those that succeeded them, concession not only of the laws of King Edward, but [of] all those liberties and rights which belong to English men as free subjects of the kings of England.[40]

There is a threefold effect of the laws of this or any other kingdom:[41]

(1) *Potestas coerciva* [coercive power]: this extends indeed to all the king's subjects, but doth not extend to the king. He is not under the coercive power of the laws.
(2) *Potestas directiva* [directive power]: and this obliges the king; and we need not go farther for evidence of [this] than that solemn oath which he takes at his coronation; the iterated confirmation of the great charter,[42] and those other laws and statutes that concern the liberties of his subjects.[43]
(3) *Potestas irritans* [invalidating power]: and thus the laws also in many cases bind the king's acts and makes them void if they are against law; as, for instance, the law saith that no grants of lands under other seal than the great seal is good, that grants of monopolies are void, and the like. The law makes such grants void and subjects the instruments acting by them to such punishments as if there were no such grants.[44]

[39] MS: with.

[40] In coronation charters issued by William I (1066), William Rufus (1087), and Henry I (1101), each promised to rule by the ancient laws gathered by and associated with Edward the Confessor, the last Anglo-Saxon king. This confirmation was made part of the coronation oath in 1308. See Jenelle Greenberg, *The Radical Face of the Ancient Constitution* (Cambridge: Cambridge University Press, 2001), 14, 38, 43–4, 225, and *passim*.

[41] MH makes this threefold distinction elsewhere: once in *Prerogatives*, 221, in terms of "powers" of law, once in *Prerogatives*, 230, in terms of both "powers" and "effects" of law, and twice in "Draught," once in terms of "effects" of law, and another time in terms of "obligation." "Draught" [fo. 65v]: "Now laws or statutes may have a threefold effect or obligation: 1. A coercive obligation, and thus without all question the king is exempt from this kind of obligation. His person is sacred and above the reach of any coercive power. 2. A directive obligation. And thus the king, by virtue of his laws so far as they concern him and [by virtue] of the solemn oath at his coronation, is obliged by the directive obligation of those laws. 3. *Potestas vel obligatio irritans* [nullifying power or obligation], and thus also the king is obliged by his own laws for these acts that are done by his command against the laws are void and the instruments therein are not indemnified by such command, because the *virtus legis irritans* [nullifying force of law] makes the command void."

[42] Ed: the Magna Carta (1215); see *History*, 131, note 9.

[43] "Draught" [fo. 64r]: "this effect it hath upon the community even by virtue of that natural obligation that lies upon all men to keep their faith and observe what either expressly by themselves, or virtually by their representatives or supreme magistrates, or tacitly by custom, they have undertaken to observe."

[44] "Draught" [fo. 64r]: Law's power "*Irritans actus contrarios* [invalidating the act contrary (to the law)]: or putting an inefficacy or civil nullity upon those acts that are within the institution or restraint of the law."

No good subject that understands what he says can make any question where the sovereign power of this kingdom resides. The laws of the land and the oath of supremacy teach us that the king is the only supreme governor of this realm.

And as incident to that supreme power he hath among others these great powers of sovereignty [the following].

(1) He hath the only power of making peace and declaring war;
(2) He alone hath the power of giving the value and legitimation to coin;
(3) He alone hath the power of pardoning the punishments of public offences;
(4) From him originally is derived all jurisdiction for the administration of the common justice of the kingdom, whether civil or ecclesiastical, whether ordinary or delegate;
[74v] (5) In him alone is the power of the militia of this kingdom and the raising of forces and arms both by land and sea;
(6) In him resides the power of making laws. The laws are his laws enacted by him.

These are the great *jura summi imperii* [rights of supreme rule][45] that the laws of this kingdom have fixed in the Crown of England. But yet there are certain qualifications of these powers, especially of the two latter:

1. Though the only power of the militia be in the king and him alone, yet it hath these two qualifications.
   (1) That no subject can by virtue of that power be enforced to go out of the kingdom.[46]
   (2) That no aid or common charge can be imposed for the raising or paying or furnishing of soldiers, shipping, or other common charge without consent of parliament,[47] no not [even] in case of common necessity (17 Car. 1 cap. 14[48]). So [it was] adjudged and declared by the king with the advice and assent of lords and commons in parliament, which is a judgment of the greatest weight that can be.
2. Though the legislative power be in the king so that none but he can make laws obliging the subjects of his realm, yet there is a certain solemnity and qualification of that power, namely, the advice and assent of the two houses of parliament, without which no law can be made. And therefore proclamations

[45] See *Prerogatives*, 207–10, 220.

[46] MH offers the following authorities: Statutes 1 E 3 [stat. 2] c. 5 (1326–7) (St. Realm I, 255) and 13 Car. 2^{d} c. 2. The reference of the second is unclear, but relevant provisions can be found at 13 Car. II c. 6, sec. 4 (1661) (St. Realm V, 309) and at 14 Car. II c. 3, sec. 31 (1662) (St. Realm V, 363).

[47] MH offers the following authorities: Statutes 25 E. I c. 6 (St. Realm I, 123, the *Confirmation of Charters* of 1297 in which Edward I reaffirmed the Magna Carta (1215) and the Forest Charter (1217), see *History*, 131, note 9); 34 E. I c. 1 (the apocryphal statute *De tallagio non concedendo*—see "Reflections," note 64); 1 E. III c. 6 (1 Edw. III, st. 2, c. 6, St. Realm I, 255–6); 3 Car. I c. 1, Petition of Right (St. Realm V, 23).

[48] 16 Car. I c. 14, St. Realm V, 116.

cannot make a law. It is true they may declare and publish laws already made and may serve that power which is lodged in the king's person, as [for example,] to proclaim coin, peace [and] war, and in times of public hostility may prohibit supply of enemies with assistances for war, and some things of that nature. Yet generally, the king's proclamations cannot make a law, but laws are to be made in that solemnity and with that advice of parliament.

[75r] Though these things be unquestionably true, yet there are certain speculators that take upon them[selves] to correct all the governments in the world and to govern them by certain notions and fancies of their own, and are transported with so great confidence and opinion of them[selves] that they think all states and kingdoms and governments must presently be conformed to them. And these are some of the notions they vent: That there can be no qualifications or modifications of the power of a sovereign prince, but that he may make, repeal, and alter what laws he please, impose what taxes he pleases, derogate from his subjects' property how and when he please, that he alone is the judge of all public dangers and may appoint such remedies as he please and impose what charges he thinks fit in order thereunto. These wild propositions are (1) utterly false, (2) against all natural justice, (3) pernicious to the government and governor, (4) destructive to the common good and safety of the governed, [and] (5) without any shadow of law or reason to support them.

1. They are utterly false: In things of this nature the best measure[s] of truth or falsehood are not imaginary notions or reasons at large, but the laws and customs of this kingdom, which have determined reason at large and bound it up within the bounds of such laws and usages.[49]

(1) It is certain the king without consent of the lords and commons in parliament—neither by proclamation, nor by ordinance, act of council or ordinance—cannot make a binding law. And this is so known a truth that it needs no instances to confirm it. But some I shall give, and those not of a common nature, but such which have been so declared by the king himself in his court of parliament. [For example,] a restitution in blood cannot be made but by act of parliament.[50] And therefore a special act was made (H. 8[51]) to enable the king to do it by letters patents. The Statute of 31 H 8 cap. 8[52] was specially made to enable the king by the advice of his council to prohibit certain things

[49] "Draught" [fos 64v–65r]: "But the measure and extents of the powers of princes are to be taken from those public concessions and establishments made by the kings themselves with the advice of their great councils in Parliament. And these are not to be infringed to gratify the fancies of any man that, because he hath read Aristotle's *Politics*, or digested some theories of his own, calls himself a philosopher and thinks his own notions to be the only authentic rules of government."

[50] Conviction for treason or felony in common law resulted, *inter alia*, in "corruption of [the offender's] blood"—that is, no property of his could pass to descendants. Restoration of the offender's rights of inheritance was called "restitution in blood." See Hale, *History of the Pleas of the Crown* (London, 1736), 358.

[51] 14 and 15 Hen. VIII c. 21 (St. Realm III, 259).

[52] St. Realm III, 726; this is the so-called Statute of Proclamations.

under penalties, and the Statute of 34 H 8 cap. 23[53] for the putting them in execution. But this power lasted not long, both being repealed by the Statute of 1 E 6 cap. 12.[54] And therefore although the king and lords assent to a law, it binds not unless the commons also assent. And this is determined by the judgment of the king in parliament (Rot. Parlementi 2 H 5 pt 2 num. 20. 10[55]). From henceforth nothing be enacted at the petition of the commons contrary to their asking whereby they [75v] should be bound without their assent, and to the same purpose are very many instances (Rot. Parl. 6 R 2 pt 1 n. 52[56]).

(2) And as he cannot make a law without consent of parliament, so neither can he repeal a law without the like consent. This is a most known truth yet some instances shall be given wherein the king himself hath in effect concurred in such declaration. [For example,] 26 H 8 cap. 10:[57] a special act of parliament enabling the king by proclamation to repeal all laws touching prohibited goods made after 21 H 8,[58] which [was] needed not if the king might repeal without an act enabling him by act of parliament; 34 H 8 cap. 26:[59] a special clause to enable King Henry VIII to repeal and alter the constitution of that statute. This clause in truth died with Henry VIII, yet because it was a clause of great importance it was repealed by the statute of 21 Jacob cap. 10,[60] which power and repeal had signified nothing if the king might repeal these laws without the help of an act of parliament enabling him. The statute of 1 E 6 cap. 11[61] gave power to that king and all the issues of the body of Henry VIII to whom the crown shall come etc. by these letters patents to repeal all acts of parliament assented to by them before their age of 24 years.

It is true that in the last printed book of statutes, there is a formal revocation made by the king by the advice of his council by proclamation of a statute made the same year, which especially concerned exclusion of trial of all peers other than in parliament, which possibly might give some countenance to such kinds of revocations of statutes. But the matter being truly understood doth not only not countenance any such conclusion, but plainly evidences the contrary. For (1) in very truth there was never any full consent of the king to that act, nay so far it was against his will that the chancellor, treasurer, and judges in open parliament protested against it as contrary to law, as appears by the Parliament Roll, 15 E 3 nos 26, 42.[62] Secondly, the king rested not upon this repeal by proclamation, but in the next parliament, viz., Rot. Parl. 17 E 3 23,[63] a special repeal passed by act of the entire parliament of 15 Edward III, with direction that for such things as were usefully passed in that parliament a new law should be penned and passed in this parliament; so that the repeal by proclamation was not thought then [to be] effectual without an act of parliament of repeal.

[53] St. Realm III, 923. [54] St. Realm IV, 19. [55] RP iv, 22.
[56] RP iii, 141 (Richard 2, Pt 1, no. 52 [should be no. 53]). [57] St. Realm III, 506.
[58] Ed: after the 21st year of the reign of Henry VIII. [59] St. Realm III, 926.
[60] St. Realm IV, 1219. [61] St. Realm IV, 17.
[62] RP ii, 129–30, 131. [63] RP ii, 139.

[76r] (3) As to the king's judging of public dangers and imposing of assessment or charges in order thereunto: Those that will not believe the statute *de tallagio non concedendo*[64] doth not extend to such a case or think that it is under a tacit condition to be repealed when the king thinks expedient, let them consult the judgment of the kings themselves in the Petition of Right 3 Car. Primi [c. 1][65] and in the act for the reversal of the judgment given in the case of Ship Money (17 Car. primi cap. 14),[66] where the king by the advice and assent of the lords and commons doth not only enact but declare that that judgment was against the laws and statutes of the realm, the right of property and liberty of the subject, former resolutions of parliament, and the Petition of Right, which is a judgment of the highest and most solemn nature that possibly can be. And yet the judgment in the case of the Ship Money was bottomed upon a supposition of necessity and so declared by the king.

[(4)] And as to the case of the king's power in relation to acts of parliament: (a) It is true as to offences against acts of parliament already committed, where His Majesty is interested in the penalty, the king may unquestionably pardon. (b) In some cases where the interest of the subject is not immediately concerned, he may as to particular persons and cases by a *non obstante*[67] dispense with the breach of a penal law. (c) But where the subject's interest is immediately concerned as in the case of extending the admiral[ty] jurisdiction, he cannot dispense with a *non obstante*. [(d)] But in no case can the king without an act of parliament repeal an act of parliament, whether penal or other.

2. As to the second [point]: these positions are against natural justice and equity. For certainly kings as well as others are bound to keep their faith and promises. And as it is so much the more obliging when such pacts and concessions are not purely gratuitous, as some kinds of grants are, but such as are made upon mutual contracts and stipulations. And thus are for the most part all acts of parliament and parliamentary concessions, wherein the subject grants some things to the king as aides, supplies, subsidies, tenths, or fifteenths,[68] and the king at their request grants them

[64] This is a medieval statute (34 Edw I) restricting the power of the king to tax royal possessions and boroughs (tallage). Although it was often cited as authority (e.g., in the preamble of the Petition of Right), its authenticity was doubted already in the seventeenth century.

[65] A product of the struggle between Charles I and parliament, the Petition of Right (St. Realm V, 23) set out a number of specific rights and liberties as limits on royal power. Passed in 1628, it stands alongside the thirteenth-century charters (e.g., Magna Carta) as a major document of English constitutional law.

[66] In *R v. Hampden* (the Ship Money Case, 3 St. Tr. 825 (1637)) a majority of judges of the Court of Exchequer ruled that the king, without consent of parliament, could exact money from seaport towns needed to supply his navy in defence of the realm. The court argued that the king's power cannot be restricted, particularly in time of emergency, by the need to secure parliamentary approval for necessary taxes. The decision was reversed by the Long Parliament in 1640 (16 Car. I c. 14, St. Realm V, 116).

[67] This is the phrase used in legislation to permit actions notwithstanding [*non obstante*] any law to the contrary; hence, an act of the king dispensing with established law in certain cases. See *Prerogatives*, 230 and note 80.

[68] Various forms of taxation to fund royal activities, especially military expeditions.

laws and liberties. And thus the Great Charter and Charter of the Forest and[69] most of the parliamentary grants were had upon a kind of reciprocal contract and stipulation between the king and his subjects. [76v] But this is not all; most of the important grants in parliament of liberties to the people were not so much new grants of new liberties, but restitutions of those very liberties, which by the primitive and radical constitution of the English government were of right belonging to them. Such were the grants of King William [I] of the laws of Edward the Confessor, the grant of the great charters by King John, Henry III, Edward 1,[70] the statutes *de tallagio non concedendo*, and divers others, which were the original rights and liberties of the subject. And we have as great reason to conclude them to be parts of the original and primitive institution of the English govern[ment], by their long usage and frequent concessions and confirmations of princes in so long and continued a series of time, as if an authentic instrument of the first articles of the English government were extant.

And as the obligation of natural justice binds princes and governors as well as others to stand to their pacts and agreements with their people, so there is superadded to that obligation the great solemnity of the oath which he takes at his coronation to observe and keep those laws and liberties. And though it is true that the king's person is sacred and not under any external coercion, nor to [be] arraigned by his subjects for the violation of that sacred oath, yet no man can make a question whether he be not in the sight of God and by the bond of natural justice obliged to keep it.

3. These positions are the most pernicious and dangerous to the government and governors whom yet such sycophants pretend to gratify by these flatteries. For certainly the great happiness of any government rests principally in this, namely, the mutual confidence that the governors have in the people as to point of duty and obedience and that the governed have in their governors as to point of protection; and to secure this mutual confidence was that ancient and solemn institution of oath of fidelity of the people to the prince and of protection and upholding their just liberties and laws by the prince to the people. And the first breach that happens in this golden knot as by miserable experience we have learned [is] when insinuations of diffidence and distrust and jealousies are secretly nourished [77r] or openly made. And most certainly there is not any one more mischievous and pernicious root of jealousies and diffidence than to tell the world that the prince is bound to keep none of the laws that he or his ancestors have by the advice of his great council established, that he may repeal them when he sees cause, that all his subjects' property depends upon his pleasure, that there is no law so strictly and prudently penned for the securing of his subjects' liberties and properties but they intrinsically have this condition implied though not expressed that when he judgeth it fit he may suspend

[69] MS: and the. [70] See *History*, 131 and note 9.

or abrogate them. Such a man that teacheth such a doctrine as this as much weakens the sovereign power as is imaginable and betrays it with a kiss.

4. And as thus it is mischievous to the governors, so it is as mischievous to the governed, when people are under this apprehension that their properties and estates are no longer theirs than it shall please their governors. It destroys industry and care to enrich themselves by trade or adventure and consequently impoverisheth the kingdom and renders men very slothful and poor spirited.

For though it be a false and invidious collection[71] and consequence that because, according to the doctrine proposed, a prince may take away his subjects' laws, liberties, [and] estate, therefore he will. Nay, though upon a just and true account of what ever the power of the prince be, yet it is his interest to use that power to the benefit and not to the detriment of his subjects, to keep them rich and thereby make them obedient, rather than to impoverish and make them desperate. Yet it is most certain that if once men be under that jealousy that the laws of the land do not sufficiently fix their properties and liberties, men's minds will be pendulous[72] and unquiet and subject to fears and doubts, and thereupon industry and pains will wither and decay, whatsoever orations men of wit and eloquence may otherwise make to secure them.

5. The reasons that those speculators use to inculcate their pernicious doctrine of this kind are very vain and frivolous. [77v] And they are for the most part such as these.

First reason:[73] [it might be argued that] the end and intention of government is common safety, but such occurrences may happen, as upon a sudden invasion or rebellion, that if the prince should be bound to the letter of laws not to raise supplies for an army till a parliament could be convened, the kingdom might be overrun, and the good subjects lose the benefit of that protection that is due to them for the strict observation of a punctilio of a law against raising taxes without consent of parliament. I answer:

(1) That as laws so the method and modelling of governments are to be fitted to what is the common and ordinary state of things *ad plurimum* [in most cases], because mankind have most ordinarily to do with such circumstances of affairs as most usually happen. And it is a madness to think that the model of laws or government is to be framed according to such circumstances as very rarely occur. 'Tis as if a man should make agaric[74] and rhubarb his ordinary diet because it is of use when he is sick, which may be once in 7 years.

(2) It is not possible for any human constitution whatsoever to be so perfect as to answer exactly to every circumstance of affairs. And therefore in the estimate and

[71] OED: inference, conclusion. [72] OED: in suspense, wavering between opinions.

[73] MH's text breaks off after answering this first argument, without taking up any further arguments.

[74] OED: mushrooms, used medicinally.

measure of the goodness or convenience of government we are to weigh which answers most exigencies of human life, and though it answer not all, yet it deserves a preference before another that answers some occasions but not so many or so well as the former. It is better to be governed by certain laws, though they bring some inconvenience at some time, than under arbitrary government which may bring many inconveniences at many times though it answer some inconveniences that the other doth not.

(3) But this is but an imaginary fear, as appears by experience. For this kingdom hath been now these 500 years governed by laws made by parliamentary advice and no time yet affords us an instance wherein a parliament might not be timely enough called for such a supply, unless in those miserable broyles[75] that happened between the king [78r] and parliament, which never would have been if the king had not consented to a bill to make it perpetual.[76] And it is apparent by reason it must needs be so, unless we should imagine that princes should be so improvident as not to foresee an imminent war above six weeks before it breaks out. We must not think princes and their councils and ministers as so supine and so destitute of intelligence both at home and abroad as not to have a prospect of such things or not to understand their own purposes and intentions in matters of so great moment as war and supply.

And therefore they write and speak at random that tell us the two most eminent kings of this realm, Edward III [1327–77] and Henry V [1413–22] took the greatest freedom in impositions upon their subjects; for he that is but little conversant with the Parliament Rolls of histories of those kings will find that, though they did great things, yet [were] their wars and armies maintained by parliamentary supplies, and those kings had the fewest of arbitrary impositions of any that preceded or succeeded them.

(4) But [MS breaks off]

[75] OED: a confused disturbance, tumult, or turmoil; a quarrel.

[76] Charles I and parliament engaged in increasingly violent struggles between 1640 and 1649 when the king was executed. In 1641, Charles I signed a bill agreeing that the parliament could not be dissolved without its consent (16 Car. I c. 7, St. Realm V, 103). This began the era of the Long Parliament which was not formally dissolved until the Restoration in 1660.

PART VI

Prerogatives of the King

Introductory Note

Hale wrote three works on the topic of royal prerogatives. In the 1640s, during the Interregnum, he wrote "Incepta de Juribus Coronae" and "Preparatory Notes touching the Rights of the Crown." He returned to the topic in 1660–1, shortly after the Restoration. With the kind permission of the Selden Society and Professor D. E. C. Yale, this selection follows Yale's edition of *Prerogatives of the King* (London: Selden Society, 1976). I have incorporated in notes to the text below all of Yale's notes including the important passages from "Rights of the Crown" that he added to *Prerogatives*.

Chapter 1 of this selection sketches a general theory of the nature and grounds of political authority (see also his "Jurisdiction of the Lords House," Part VII of this volume). It frames his analysis of the English political constitution—the grounds, structure, and limits of English government—offered in the remainder of the selection (see also *History*, Chapter 5 and "Reflections," Chapter 2). In a manner typical of late medieval and early modern political theory, Hale argues that political authority is rationally necessary—due to the deep natural inclination in human beings to join in communities and the need for individual and collective preservation—but it is not by that fact natural. Rather, by nature human beings are political equals, not subject to the authority of any other except God. Thus, political authority can exist only as instituted by human actions and interactions, rooted ultimately in "compact," the "mutual interposition of faith" (209) between governors and governed and among the governed. This reciprocal *fides publica* "twist[s] governors and governed into one body" (209). This holds true not only of political communities that have their origins in explicit consent, but even of communities that trace their origins to conquest. For the conqueror can hope to rule only if he pledges protection and he trusts the people to obey and the people look to his protection and submit to his authority.

The form of government and the scope and limits of sovereign power are defined by this compact, which can change greatly over time. The actual historical origin of a community's constitution is likely to be obscured by time and subsequent developments in custom and usage. Indeed, custom and usage have power to alter and replace any original arrangement (whether by consent or conquest). Custom has "institutive power" (215). Actual practice and long usage, rather than origin, determine a community's government. That is what gives normative force and content to its compact.

The political constitution of England, Hale argues, is decidedly monarchical. The sovereign power is vested in the king, who is subject to no other power on earth either individual or collective. But royal power is qualified. The king is subject to the constitutional arrangement by which he holds power. He holds ultimate lawmaking power, but he can make law only with consent of parliament. The power to decide and execute law flows ultimately from the king, but through long custom that power has been devolved onto the ordinary courts, which the king can no longer alter. And final decision of cases upon appeal lies with king, but only when he sits judicially together with the parliament (see "Jurisdiction of the Lords House"). Aside from limited power to dispense with the demands of law (e.g., power of pardon), the king is bound by the ordinary law of the land. He is not (personally) subject to its coercive power, but he is bound in conscience by its directive power and by the power of law to make null and void (*potestas irritans*) actions of the king's ministers and agents of his government that are taken in pursuit of royal policies. While the king is immune from civil and criminal prosecution, his ministers may be denied legal cover for their actions contrary to existing law and hence liable to law's coercive power (see "Reflections").

1

Of Government in General; the Original, Alterations, and Trials thereof

I

The kinds of government and subjection are two; viz. natural and civil.

1. The natural government is that of the father, or mother the father being dead, over the children, called therefore natural because the children deriving their being from their parents according to the course of nature owe them a kind of natural subjection.
2. The civil government [is so called] because it hath its original by a civil compact or somewhat equivalent thereunto. And this again is of two kinds.
   (1) Economical,[1] or a government within the confines of a family which is of two kinds, herile, of the master over the servant, or matrimonial, of the husband over the wife.
   (2) Political. And omitting the former kinds of government, this political government is the subject of this present inquiry.

II

Political government is ordinarily divided into three species or kinds, viz. (1) Monarchical, the government by one, (2) Aristocratical, the government by many, but those of the chief sort, the *optimates*, or (3) Democratical, the government by the people, or such to whom they shall delegate.

All these kinds of governments fall under another division, for either they are simply monarchical, or simply aristocratical, or simply democratical, or else they are mixed, when parts of the *jura summi imperii* [rights of supreme rule] possibly

[1] Ed: From the Greek, *oikomene*, having to do with domestic life. See John Selden, "Community of life, and civil society, beginning first in particular families, under oeconomique rule...," *Titles of Honour* (1614), 3rd edn (London, 1672), 2.

may be exercised in a way wherein all three manners of dispensation of government do or ought to concur or act.

III

There are three considerations that are necessary to be taken up before we descend further.

1. The state of mankind before political government instituted or introduced: and this is in itself and naturally considered a State of Equality. No man in such a state so considered hath a political right of governing another, but every man hath duly so much dominion over another as his own force of strength can acquire and hold.

2. The state of mankind in the initiation of government in its institution, or government *in fieri* [in process of becoming]. And herein, though that there should be a form of government settled among men, [and] be not only necessary for the preservation of human society, and therefore there is a natural propension and tendency of mankind to it, but also a very ordinance and appointment of God himself, yet the particular determination of that generality of government to this or that determinate form or species, monarchical, aristocratical, or democratical, or a mixture of all these, either in all parts or in some parts of the *jura summi imperii*, is of human right,[2] and according either to the compacts or interventions of the governors and governed; though all agree that the monarchical government duly regulated at least, is the best of all other political governments, having in it more contributions to establish and perpetuate it, and rendering it beneficial to the governed.[3]

3. The state of mankind under government already settled or government *in facto esse* [existing in fact], for then there are two things that contribute to its establishment and continuance.

> (1) That general state of government which the law and institution of God himself and the propension and exigence of human nature and society doth require, is now as it were fixed and settled in the government thus established and that which before was a divine institution in general, viz. that there should be government not determined to this or that particular form, is now become lodged and settled in the particular and determinate government thus established.

[2] Ed: that is, instituted by human law.

[3] Yale: In *The Rights of the Crown*, ch. 1, MH writes: "Before it is settled, it is clear that no form of government, nor any government at all, can challenge any right but by positive institution. Man, though he be born *subjicibilis* [subject] to man, yet *jure naturae* [by the law of nature] he is subject to none in a politic consideration. It is true the desire to perpetuate and preserve his own being and profit by communion, inclines him to society, and consequently to government and subjection as the bond of that society, but till he subject himself, he is naturally free. Therefore much less can any formal government challenge a natural right. It is true one form of government may be better in itself or in reference to a society than another, yet all are but of positive or introduced original."

(2) There is a mutual interposition of faith as well between the governors and governed, as between the governed one among another, either expressing or implicitly passed, which may not be violated. The governed have an interest in the protection of a governor by his stipulation to them, and the governor hath an interest in the subjection of the governed by their stipulation, and the governed have an interest in the mutual subjection one of another by a mutual stipulation between themselves and the common concernment one of another. And this *fides publica* [public faith or fidelity] hath twisted both governors and governed into one body. And therefore as God hath set to his seal, so natural justice hath set to her seal to this universal and eternal truth, *fides est servanda* [promises or agreements must be kept].

IV

The originals of political government are of three kinds, viz. *ab intrinseco* [from within], viz. consent or agreement, or *ab extrinseco* [from without] by power or force, or mixed. And because we have an aim principally to insist upon monarchical government as most in order to the intended discourse, the instances shall be applied principally to that form of political government.

1. The original *ab intrinseco* is the mutual consent of the governor and governed. And herein the pact[4] between them is that which determines the extent of the dominion or power in the one and the subjection and obedience required of the other, if this pact be extant, and is as capable of as much variety as any other contract is. This agreement may transfer the *universale dominium* in all points without enumeration or exclusion, unto the governor, or it may transfer some points [of the *jura*] *summi imperii* and may reserve others, or it may transfer some points and omit others, or it may transfer some points absolutely, as the power of coin, of war and peace, and some points qualifiedly, as the power of making laws or imposing public charges wherein possibly it may require the consent of the *optimates* or people or both, that it shall be eligible or hereditary, and infinite the like variations.

[4] Yale: In *The Rights of the Crown*, ch. 1, MH writes of this agreement that "naturally, as before, no man is subject to another. And therefore consequently the greater number have not in them naturally the power over the lesser, but it is nothing but consent or agreement that can civilly put any power in another over me. And this agreement of the society may put the power of the whole society in the greater number, and this should seem to be implicitly the condition of every society even in the first convention of it, because without this presupposed it is almost impossible for any company of men to act in the future disposal of itself. Or it may put the government into some to be chosen by the greater number of the society, and so settle an aristocracy. Or it may settle the whole government in one, and so create a monarchy. And it may qualify that monarchy to be perpetual hereditary, temporary elective &c. Or it may create a mixed government of all three, and that mixed in all points of government, or mixed in some points and simple in others, as to put the power of coin in the king, the power of judgment in *optimates*, the power of making laws in the king, in the *optimates* and in the people."

2. *Ab extrinseco*, and this either from God or man.

(1) From God, either mediately or providentially, and thus all the governments of the world, Dan. 4:25: "the most High ruleth in the kingdom of men and giveth it to whomsoever he will," or immediately and signally, thus as in the state of the Jews God reserved to himself the same as his special inheritance, so he did by his own immediate designation oftentimes appoint them kings, as Moses, Joshua, Saul, David, Jeroboam, Jehu, etc.

(2) From Man, and that in several ways. *First*, by election, either popular as in some kingdoms it hath been, or regular and determinate, as that of the Roman empire by the 7 electors, which now is nevertheless reduced to a piece only of formality, or by the army which was sometimes used under the first Roman emperors. But this being reducible to the first head, viz. consent or agreement, I spare further to prosecute it.

Secondly, in investiture or donation, which was anciently used to be done by the Roman emperors or senate in cases of conquered kingdoms, as Herod, or in cases of patrimonial kingdoms which some held as a kind of propriety and might, and oftentimes did, transfer to others.[5] I mean not barely a titular kingdom, as that of Man and Wight in England,[6] but a kingdom joined with *jus summi imperii*.

Thirdly, by conquest by one supreme prince or state upon another. And this by the laws and usages of nations hath been esteemed a legal acquisition out of a kind of necessity, because the princes being supreme, there intervenes between them no other decision but force and strength, and having put themselves upon that trial, they are at least for the time concluded by it. And upon the same reason it is that ordinarily in popular assemblies and decisions, the major part carries the vote. Not that the minor part are naturally and *jure naturae* [by right of nature] included in the major, but because there is no better decision, and it is founded upon a kind of rule of necessity, because the major part is ordinarily stronger in such popular suffrages and able to exact an acquiescence to their suffrage, and therefore ordinarily and regularly it prevails as a right. And upon the same ground the conqueror having had the trial on his side, there is supposed a kind of rightful acquisition by that conquest.

But then the conquest must be by such a prince or power that owes no subjection to the conquered prince, for that enervates the right of his conquest, because it is a violation of that faith which he owed to the conquered, and so it is not a conquest but

[5] Yale: In *The Rights of the Crown*, ch. 1, MH writes of investiture that "the supreme power may be so transferred to the prince or other governor that he cannot transfer wholly over without the express concurrent consent of the persons governed. And thus *prima facie* is all government, because it is a trust not transferable of its own nature. But in the first institution of this power there may be likewise a power absolutely *abdicare se a regno* [to abdicate the rule], and then the subject is by that means made subject to another by reason of that original consent whereby he trusted the prince to transfer this power without concurrent consent of the people".

[6] Ed: MH refers to the English sub-kingdoms or dependencies, the Isle of Man and the Isle of Wight.

a successful rebellion. For the faith that he owed cannot be remitted by himself nor without the consent of him to whom it was given and consequently principally interested in it.[7]

But yet in case a supreme prince of one country be a homager[8] or feudal prince or subject to another prince in respect of some particular territory that he held in the precinct of another kingdom, this doth not hinder him but that he may acquire *jure victoriae* [by right of conquest] upon the prince whose homager he was, because the homage and subjection was in one respect, viz. as tenant or feudatory of that other prince, but the acquest was in another respect and capacity, viz. as he is the supreme prince of another country. As we shall see hereafter in the acquisitions by conquest of the king of England, though he were a feudal prince that owed and performed a kind of feudal homage to the king of France.

This *jus victoriae* or right of conquest is of two kinds, viz. (1) *Victoria in regem* [conquest over a king], when one prince pretends a right to the kingdom that another enjoyeth and upon the ground or at least pretence of that right invades and conquers. Thus did William, duke of Normandy, upon pretence of a title from Edward the Confessor invade and conquer Harold, and thus did king Edward the third upon the title of descent from his mother as heir to the crown of France invade and in a great measure subdue France.[9] And this kind of *Victoria in regem* doth not give the victor *dominium universale* upon the people but puts him in the place and succession of him from whom he claims or pretends his title. (2) *Victoria in populum* [conquest over a people], when the conquering prince doth intentionally and professedly contend against the whole body and in such a case *acquisitio victoris est universalis* [the acquisition of the conqueror is universal or complete]. He may *agros mulctare* [ravage the land] and *leges mutare* [change the laws]. But in such a case the victory must be complete and perfect before such an acquest is made and the evidence of the completeness of such a conquest is either an express dedition of the parties conquered, thus the Romans used in token of such dedition to make the conquered *transire sub hasta*, come under the yoke, or else there must be an implicit dedition, long subjection, or acceptation of laws, or the like, that may evidence the acquiescence of the people in the decision of this fatal trial by battle.

7 Yale: In *The Rights of the Crown*, ch. 1, MH writes of this qualification that "it must be a lawful war and a lawful conquest. A subject cannot acquire by conquest upon his prince, unless in the capacity of a prince, for that were not a just war but a rebellion. Neither can a prince acquire by conquest upon his people or kingdom, because that were a violation of that contract whereunto he is a party. And as it must be a lawful war, so it must be a perfect conquest, which cannot be without an express dedition or, which is equivalent, a tacit [dedition] by continuance of time and subjection, for till *that* it cannot be a complete conquest as to the persons opposing. And thus we see this likewise includes a kind of consent to the translating of the government."

8 OED: In feudal law, one who owes homage for fealty.

9 Ed: Regarding William, see *History*, note 3. Edward III, who reigned from 1327–77, claimed title to the French crown through his mother, Isabella, daughter of Philip IV of France, and undertook a campaign to establish his rule. The Hundred Years' War (1337–1453) ensued.

Fourthly, the fourth manner of transmission of kingdoms or supreme government is by hereditary descent. And this is the most excellent, peaceful, and happy way of transmission of government from man to man. It is without the faction and tumults incident to elections, without the blood, fury, and oppression attending conquests, but quiet, certain, and regular.

Yet there be some kinds of laws directing the descents of supreme government different from those that direct other descents, some almost common to all kingdoms, as in case no sons, then the eldest daughter inherits, unless it be where the constitutions or rather usurpations have introduced the Salic law excluding females and descendants from them.[10]

3. There is another kind of acquisition that is mixed, partly *extrinseca* and by force, partly by consent. And this is principally in case of conquest seconded after by dedition either implied or express, though it be the consequence of force on the one side, or fear on the other, is not thereby avoidable,[11] but the *fides data* [faith given, a commitment] is as obliging as if it were without the attendance of either. And indeed if it should be otherwise it would shake all leagues and treaties between supreme princes among themselves and with their people, for in all there is a mixture of force or fear and possibly of fraud. The faith given to the Gibeonites by the princes of the congregation, though gotten by fraud, was strictly kept, and the breach of it many years after generally punished.[12] The oath of Zedekiah exacted of him by the king of Babylon by force and fear was severely punished by the hand of God when broken by him, and styled the oath of God.[13]

V

Thus far concerning the institution of government. Something will be fit to be said concerning the alteration of government by any of these ways settled, and these alterations are of these kinds.[14]

[10] Ed: Salic law was a compilation of laws and customs of the Frankish people (a large group of Germanic tribes) dating from early sixth century. It influenced early English law through the Norman Conquest.

[11] Ed: void or invalid.

[12] Ed: Joshua 9 tells the story of the fidelity of the leaders of Israel (the "princes of the congregation") to their treaty with duplicitous Canaanite neighbours. During Israel's conquest of Canaan under Joshua, inhabitants of the city of Gibeon made a treaty with Joshua, falsely representing themselves as "from a very far country," hoping for lenient treatment. Soon their lie was exposed, but the Israelite leaders said that because they had sworn to them by God they would not treat them harshly.

[13] Ed: According to the biblical story in Jeremiah 37–40, Nebuchadnezzar besieged Jerusalem, deported King Jehoiachim to Babylonia, and installed Zedekiah as puppet king of Judah. Against Jeremiah's prophetic counsel, Zedekiah rebelled against the Babylonians. Nebuchadnezzar attacked and destroyed Jerusalem and its temple, killed Zedekiah's sons, put out his eyes, and took him bound to Babylon.

[14] Yale: In *The Rights of the Crown*, ch. 1, MH writes of the alterations of government instituted upon simple agreement or compact. "1. By the mutual consent of all interested in the government. Though the supreme power were in the original absolutely and universally transferred unto the prince, yet by consent

1. In the whole form of government as from an Aristocracy to a Monarchy or from a Democracy to an Aristocracy or *e converso*, and this happens either from an external cause or from an internal cause.

(1) From an external cause. And that is most ordinarily by conquest. When a monarch prevails by conquest upon an aristocracy, he doth most ordinarily reduce it to a monarchical government, and many times when a republic, a popular or aristocratical state, conquers a kingdom, they most ordinarily assimilate their government to their own, as the Romans most times did in their conquests, though many times for their grandeur or other ends they continued a tributary monarchy.

(2) From an internal cause. Some defection in any particular state from that government in which they find it constituted. This change cannot be just in its undertaking, because it is against the faith that they owe to the government whereof they are subjects, unless it be done by the free and unconstrained consent of all persons both governing and governed, which is very rarely if possibly to be done, yet *de facto* it hath been done. And some of the masters of politics both ancient and modern, as Aristotle, Bodin, and others, show the causes and signs of such mutations.[15] Thus the Romans from a royal state fell to a popular and thence by the power and greatness of Caesar were after reduced to a regal. But these concussions in governments as they are commonly the product of rebellion and usurpation, so they bring with them very great inconveniences.

2. Thus much briefly for mutations in the whole frame of government. The mutations in the particulars of government are frequent and daily, and sometimes useful being regularly and duly obtained.

(1) By the concessions of the prince without force. Thus many times when the universal and absolute power is put into the prince either by original compact or

of the prince and people the government may be new moulded and framed from a monarchy absolute and simple into another or a mixed government. For although the people cannot resume that with which they have absolutely parted, because contrary to that agreement which they at first made, yet by that consent of all persons interested it may receive an alteration in part or in all. And this consent is produced sometimes by the treaty and conclusion itself of the prince and people, as by acts of parliament, sometimes by the charters of the prince recommunicating some regality back to the people, sometimes by long custom and usage, which binds both prince and people, as well upon the presumption of such an agreement as by introducing a law, by long uninterrupted tacit submission and consent of both. 2. When by the original institution or pact whereby the government was settled, there was reserved unto the people a power to alter or resume the government thus transferred or any part thereof, either upon pleasure or upon breach of some trust *&c.*" Concerning alterations of government instituted *ab externo*, this may be by investiture or donation, or by force and conquest. Where government is established without a complete transfer of power to the prince MH remarks that a further transfer "is not so much an alteration as a perfecting and supplying of *casus omissi* [omitted cases]. If the translation of government from the people be particular and confined, those other points which are not within these bounds remain still in the power of the society, which as they may retain to themselves, so they may transfer under what qualifications or restrictions they please. But if the translation of government were universal this way of addition to government hath no place."

[15] Ed: See Aristotle, *Politics*, Book V and Jean Bodin, *Six Books of the Commonwealth*, Book IV.

by a lawful conquest, he may remit or qualify some parts of that power by his concessions or charters for the good of his people, or when some ample prerogatives are belonging *de jure*, he may by his grant or concession abridge or qualify some of those powers, as for the purpose that he will not make laws or impose taxes without the consent of his council or *optimates* or the procurators of the people.

(2) By the concession of the people, as where there are some rights of government either reserved to the people or not transferred to him by some omission or mistake, that are necessary for the support or exercise of government, then the people *servata juris forma* [having preserved the form of the law] may supplementally add to the powers of the prince.

(3) By long custom or usage whereby there is presumed a tacit consent of prince and people, there may be an interition[16] or remission or qualification of some particular powers of government.

And these small and accidental alterations do not at all destroy the substance and being of government but many times make it more useful for the governor and governed.

VI

And by all that has been said we may be able to guess what is the measure that must be used to make an estimate of the nature and extent of any government in any kingdom or place, for in such cases either the beginning or institution of government appears or appears not.

1. If it appears, then:

(1) If it be by compact or agreement, and that compact appears, that doth determine what the nature and extent of the government is, taking into it such accessions or diminutions or qualifications as subsequent concessions or capitulations of prince and people have added to it.

(2) If it be by conquest *in populum*, then the dominion is universal upon the conquered, taking in such abatements or qualifications nevertheless as subsequent capitulations of prince and people have introduced.

(3) But if it be only a conquest *in regem*, it leaves the rights of government as it found them, and only constitutes the conqueror a successor to the rights of the conquered prince with[out] abrogation or alteration of the rights of the people which before they had.

2. But if the original of government appears not, then we must have recourse to the common custom and usage of the kingdom. That will determine what rights the prince hath absolutely, what ministers, whether it be hereditary or elective, whether it

[16] OED: decay or end.

be in the power of the people to resume any of his rights without his consent or no. For custom and usage hath not only a kind of declarative evidence what the original pact was in case there were any, but if it be constant and immemorial, it hath a kind of introductive or institutive power.

And here by custom and usage I mean not those exorbitances on either side which the practice of former times hath shown to the world. For as on the one side we find sometimes practices of treasons and rebellions against princes, and on the other side sometimes practices of oppression and tyranny by them, as we shall find in all times practices of murder, theft, and other enormities, yet such a usage doth not give them credit nor make them lawful. But I mean such customs as have been allowed by the known laws of the kingdom. And therefore under the word *customs* I take in the traditions and monuments of the municipal laws, law-books, records of judgments and resolutions of judges, treaties and resolutions and capitulations of regular and orderly conventions, authentical histories, concessions of privileges and liberties. And these, and such as these, are the best evidences both *facti* and *juris* [of fact and of law] of the nature and extent of government, by which every rational [and] upright man may easily understand what are the rights both of prince and people without entering into notions and fancies, as if men were now to be making of governments and new models thereof.

2

The Application of the Former Generals to the Government of the Kingdom of England

I

Therefore to apply the former generals to the particular kingdom of England, and in prosecution thereof, we must needs say two things.

1. That the original pact whereby the government of this kingdom was settled appears not, neither have we reason to believe there was any extant, it having been so ancient a kingdom, translated through several successions and changes; and therefore should we make our estimate of the nature and extent of the government by that, we should be at a loss.

2. That the present state of this government doth not stand upon the foot of a conquest *in populum*, but only *in regem*. King William, though he be styled the Conqueror, yet he was only *victor in regem, non in populum*, which appears beyond all questions upon these evidences.

(1) It is most evident by all that write of his attempt upon England that it was upon a pretence of donation by King Edward and that Harold has usurped upon him, and though possibly there was no such gift, or if there were it could not according to the laws of this kingdom entitle him, as will be seen in the sequel of this chapter,[17] yet it was sufficient to direct and guide the consequence of his victory to be only *in regem, non in populum*.

(2) It is most apparent by the book of Doomsday[18] compiled by his command that the former laws were then in force, and that the former owners held their possessions, and those that were ejected from them recovered their possessions by assize of mort d'ancestor[19] and the king contented himself with those demesnes that were *terrae regis Edwardi*.[20] And if it be said that he disposed of men's lands *juxta habitum conquestoris* [according to the manner of a conqueror], as Eadmerus[21] and some others express it, certainly it infers nothing of a conquest upon the people; but possibly they might be of such as were actually opposites to him, and therefore by him reckoned no better than traitors; and if it went farther, yet after so great a concussion by such a war, it is no wonder if there were some acts of violence done by him as a prince or captain, not as a conqueror.

(3) In that his restitution of the laws of Saint Edward[22] was rather a restitution through a new enacting, and done as an act of justice not of power or grace, and through mended some, and possibly inserted and brought in some of his own laws he did not upon the account of conquest, but of sovereignty.[23]

The sum is that it plainly appears (1) That though there were oppressions, rapines and usurpations upon the people after the Norman *Victoria*, which is always the consequence of a victory, yet it was not *Victoria in populum*, but *in regem*, for neither the laws nor lands of the people were taken from them. (2) That if there had been a colour of a conquest upon the people, yet by this great capitulation at Berkhamstead,

[17] Ed: Chapter omitted.

[18] Ed: William I ordered a record of all the lands and holdings in the kingdom; the Doomsday Book was completed in 1086.

[19] Ed: Assize mort d'ancestor (which dates from 1176) was a procedure by which a close heir sought restoration of possession of land unlawfully taken from the decedent. MH may have in mind possessor assizes in general, which restored possession of land to those wrongfully ousted. Possessor assizes developed during the reign of Henry I. (See also "Reflections," 196.)

[20] Ed: the properties or domain (*dominium*) regarded as belonging to the previous king Edward.

[21] Ed: Eadmerus (1060–1126), monk of Canterbury, wrote a history of England after the Conquest (*Historia novorum in Anglia*).

[22] Ed: the last Anglo-Saxon King, Edward the Confessor.

[23] Ed: A list of authorities to support this claim is here omitted.

the pretence of such a claim was wholly laid aside and the ancient laws restored.[24] (3) Though after that restitution of their laws, which seems to be in the beginning of King William's reign about the fourth year, there were some interruptions of the exercise of those laws, yet they were after the 15th year of his reign restored *in integrum* [to its original state], as appears by Ingulphus, the abbot of Crowland.[25]

And in this point I have been the more prolix for these two reasons.

1. To evidence that the original of our English government is not by conquest *in populum* nor the extent of the government to be measured by the right acquirable by such a conquest, but to make it appear that King William both claimed and obtained the crown upon a pretence of investiture and upon a right only of a *victoria in regem*, and therefore was in the nature of a successor to King Edward, and by his conquest gained no larger a right than that king whom he thus succeeded had, and to silence that untrue calumny objected against our government, laws, and liberties as if they were barely of a Norman extraction or the product of a Norman yoke,[26] as some inconsiderable persons have been bold to say, but [by showing that] they were our ancient government, laws, and rights.

2. And consequently that in our disquisitions touching the latitude and extent of our government, we are not so much to inquire what rights a conqueror gains in case of a *victoria in populum* but what rights of government are inherent and concomitant to it by the laws of this kingdom.

3. And consequently inasmuch as the original of that pact or constitution of our government appears not, we must in the inquiry into the same examine and measure it by those sound and authentical evidences of the laws and allowed customs and usages of this kingdom which is the best and only evidence to discover the rights both of the governor and governed, especially where the original constitution appears not.

II

Therefore according to those evidences of law and approved custom we come to examine the state of our English government. And therein we shall proceed to set down some generals, referring the more particular discussions to their several heads.

[24] Ed: After defeating Harold at Hastings (see *History*, note 3) William "came to Berkhampstead; where Archbishop Aldred came to meet him, with child Edgar, and Earls Edwin and Morkar, and all the best men from London; who submitted then for need, when the most harm was done.... And they gave him hostages and took oaths: and he promised them that he would be a faithful lord to them; though in the midst of this they plundered wherever they went. Then on midwinter's day Archbishop Aldred hallowed him to king at Westminster..." *Anglo-Saxon Chronicle*, 1066, <http://avalon.law.yale.edu/medieval/ang11.asp>.

[25] Ed: Ingulphus was one of the most notable abbots of Crowland Abbey in Lincolnshire, serving from 1075 to 1109. A history of the abbey, attributed to him, it is now believed to date from the fifteenth century.

[26] Ed: The idea, with roots in the late thirteenth century, but prevalent and ideologically powerful in the seventeenth, was that William I replaced the institutions of free, self-governing England with oppressive Norman feudal institutions.

1. It is most certain that the English government is monarchical and so hath been time out of mind, as well before the coming in of William the first as since. And this monarchy is of that dignity and antiquity that it gives not place to the crown of France or Spain.[27]

2. That the supreme administration of this monarchy is lodged in the king, and that not only titularly but really.[28]

3. That this supreme administration annexed to the person of this prince or monarch is not subjected to any other power on earth either without the kingdom or within it.

(1) Not to any foreign power either ecclesiastical or civil.

(a) For the ecclesiastical power, the king hath that supreme ecclesiastical power in him. And though *de facto* the pope did before the times of King Henry 8th exercise the ecclesiastical power here upon a pretence of divine investiture, yet in all times the kings of England asserted their own ecclesiastical power, and curbed at their pleasure the pretended power of the pope when it began to be troublesome either to him or his people.[29]

(b) As there is no subjection of the crown to a foreign ecclesiastical power, so neither to a foreign temporal power. And hence it was that though Edward the first were in respect of some territories which he held of the king of France a feudal prince of France, yet when Nicholas de Segrave adjourned a challenge offered by Cromwell in Scotland into the court of France, it was no less than capital, because it was a kind of subjection of the king of England to the crown of France.[30]

The German emperor upon some pretence of succession to the Roman empire did formerly claim some kind of superintendence over all those territories which were under the *imperium orbis Romani*, as to make tabellions[31] and notaries. But he never prevailed either in England or France. And therefore when upon that presumption he created Dudley duke of Northumberland it was looked upon as an idle attempt and fruitless, and the great scholar Covarruvias[32] agrees that prescription hath antiquated[33] that pretence as well in England as in other countries sometimes part of the Roman empire.

[27] Ed: MH cites authorities (omitted) including "doctissimus" Selden's *Titles of Honour*.

[28] Ed: Discussion of titles and authorities for the claim of supremacy of the king omitted.

[29] Ed: Authorities omitted.

[30] Ed: Nicholas Segrave, a Northamptonshire nobleman, joined Edward I's campaign to subdue Scotland in 1303–4. During the campaign, Segrave had a violent quarrel with Sir John de Cromwell and challenged Cromwell to trial by battle. When the king refused to allow the combat, Segrave challenged Cromwell to fight him in France and withdrew to France for the battle. Cromwell did not follow and when Segrave returned he was charged with treason, but was later pardoned. MH seems to hold that in renewing his challenge in France Segrave in effect treated the king of France as the overlord of Edward I.

[31] Ed: official scribes.

[32] Ed: Covarruvias (1512–77), Spanish canon lawyer and jurist of the School of Salamanca.

[33] Ed: made obsolete.

(2) As the monarchical power of our English monarch hath no dependence upon any foreign state or power, so neither is it subject to the power of the people either distributively, collectively, or representatively. *Rex non habet parem in regno suo.*[34] And the reason is because the people have either by express or tacit consent transferred the sovereignty unto the king according to the just extents thereof.

There hath been a great mistake in making the king of England one of the three estates of the kingdom. Whereas in truth he is head of the three estates and not one of them....[35] If the king were one of these estates, it were to make a coordination and a kind of parity between him and them.[36] But the treaty is not so, for he is sovereign and head of these three estates and as every person by his allegiance owes a subjection to the king as his sovereign, so these three estates taken apart as three several bodies or taken collectively as making up one body in parliament, owe their subjection to the king as their head, and accordingly profess it, *1 Eliz.*, *I Jacobi*, before mentioned.

4. Consequently the people or three estates cannot without the concurrence or consent of the king resume the whole regal power or any part thereof, for there will be the same reason of the whole as of part; for it is against that faith they have given to him which they cannot without him abridge or alter. This was easily found in that artificial but intolerable oppression of King Richard 2 whom though they had deposed with all the formality that might be, yet to secure themselves against this rock as well they might, they extorted from him a resignation of the crown and an absolution of his subjects from their homage, though this prevailed not to excuse Henry 4 from an usurpation and so declared by the parliament of 1 Edward 4.[37]

[34] Ed: "The king has no equal within his realm." MH quotes *De Legibus et Consuetudinibus Angliae* attributed to Henry of Bratton (1210–68) ("Bracton"), vol. 2, 33. The remainder of the quoted paragraph is also of interest: "Subjects cannot be the equals of the ruler, because he would thereby lose his rule, since equal can have no authority over equal, not a fortiori a superior, because he would then be subject to those subjected to him. The king must not be under man but under God and under the law, because the law makes the king... for there is no rex where will rules rather than lex."

[35] Ed: Authorities omitted.

[36] Ed: MH has in mind the *Answer to the XIX Propositions* (1642) in which beleaguered King Charles I endorsed the idea that the king is one of the three estates of parliament. See *The Struggle for Sovereignty: Seventeenth-Century English Political Tracts*, ed. Joyce Lee Malcolm (Indianapolis: Liberty Fund, 1999), vol. 1, 145–78.

[37] Ed: In the late 1390s, Richard II's rule was under serious threat, especially from Henry Bolingbroke of the House of Lancaster, who had been dispossessed by Richard. While Richard was on an expedition to Ireland, Bolingbroke rallied nobles against Richard. Upon Richard's return, Bolingbroke forced him to surrender and promise to abdicate the throne in exchange for his life. Henry had initially asserted his right to rule by conquest, but later fabricated a specious claim to the throne which he offered to parliament. On 30 September 1399, parliament accepted Richard's resignation and declared Henry king (Henry IV). Sixty-two years later, the first parliament of Edward IV (November 1461) declared all Lancastrian kings, including Henry IV, usurpers, in order to solidify Edward's hold on the throne.

5. That by the laws of this kingdom the regal government is hereditary and transmitted by descent. This appears not only by the recognition of 1 Jac. and 1 Eliz. [James I and Elizabeth I],[38] but by the constant usage. The heir of the deceased king writes the day of his predecessor's death the first day of the first year, and this before any of the coronation solemnity or suffrage of the people, for that solemnity doth not give the title but only declare it.

6. That this hereditary descent is to a daughter if there be no son or son's issue, and to the eldest daughter if more than one and no male or descendant from him. This was the case of Queen Maud, daughter to Henry 1, Queen Mary, and Queen Elizabeth.[39]

7. Though this government be monarchical, yet it is qualified in some of the *jura summi imperii*, though absolute in others.[40] We shall mention some of these qualified rights.

(1) In reference to laws to be made, though the laws or statutes cannot be made without the king, yet regularly they cannot be made by him without the advice or assent of parliament. Though when those laws are so made, they are in truth the king's laws. And though sometimes the penning of these laws seem to be in a coordinate style, as *be it enacted by the king, lords spiritual and temporal, and commons*, yet most anciently and ordinarily they run in another style, viz. *dominus rex de advisamento concilii* [the Lord King, by the advice of his council], or *by the advice of the lords spiritual and temporal and commons*, attributing, as the truth is, the authoritative part to the king but taking in the assent of the rest as a condition prerequisite to make the act effectual. Vide 8th Reports, *the Prince's case*, and there is the same reason of the repeal of it.[41]

(2) In reference to taxes to be imposed which by the native constitution of the kingdom and by several declarative acts of parliament cannot be done without such assent of both houses of parliament.

[38] Ed: In his first speech to parliament in March 1604, James I asserted his hereditary title to the English crown, which was reaffirmed in the Act of Recognition. 1 Jac. I, c. 1: 'A Moste joyfull and juste Recognition of the immediate lawfull and undoubted Succession Descent and Righte of the Crowne', in St. Realm IV, pt 2, 1017–18.

[39] Ed: After Henry I's death in 1135, his daughter, Maud (Mathilde), claimed the throne, but the claim was resisted by the Norman barons in England and challenged by Stephen of Blois who was crowned king in December, 1135 sparking a civil war that lasted until 1153. Mary Queen of Scots reigned from 1553–8 and Elizabeth I from 1558–1603.

[40] Ed: Later in ch. 20, MH writes, "*Potestas imperii* or *regulis* in England hath two qualifications. (1) That it is not absolute and unlimited, but bounded by rule and law. (2) It is not simple but mixed with jurisdiction, for the contempt or disobedience to his command ought to receive his punishment by that jurisdiction which the king is intrusted with, viz. in his courts of justice" (Yale's edition, 268).

[41] Ed: MH cites Coke, *Eighth Reports*, 1a.

(3) In reference to laws already made. There are three powers in laws, (1) *Potestas coercens* or *coactiva*, (2) *Potestas directiva*, [and (3) *Potestas*] *irritans actus contrarios*.[42]

As to the former it is very certain that the king is not under the coercive power of the law. Though he do things contrary to it, he cannot be sued but by petition, nor arrested, nor imprisoned, much less deposed or executed for any miscarriage in government or otherwise. And those acts that seem to be contrary hereunto were acts of oppression and usurpation, *de quibus infra* [regarding which see below].[43] It is true our yearbook [makes] mention of a *praecipe quod reddat* [demand to render] brought against Henry the third.[44] What the fact might be I cannot say, for that prince was very much kept under and low, both in his infancy and after, by the power of the great lords. But surely as to the right, the practice and book is apocryphal, for no suit lies against the king but by petition of grace or of right. But of this more largely in the proper place.[45]

But as to the directive power of the law, the king is bound by it. (1) By his office. And therefore the preamble in some writs[46] runs *nos qui ratione muneris nostri regii in exhibenda justitia unicuique de regno nostro sumus debitores* [we who are bound (debtors) by reason of our royal duty to show justice to everyone in our kingdom]. (2) By his oath at his coronation, whereby he swears to govern according to the laws, *de quo vide latius infra*.[47] Whereby he is bound in conscience and before God to whom only he is accountable for his misgovernment and breach of that trust and oath.

Yet nevertheless this directive power of the law hath this effect even as to the king's actions, that it doth *irritare actus contrarios legis directioni* [invalidate acts contrary to the requirements of the law] in many cases. And therefore though the king in case of such acts done contrary to the directive power of the law is not subject to the coercive power of the law in respect of the sacredness and sublimity of his person, the instruments and ministers that are the immediate actors of such unlawful things are subject to the coercive power of the law. For the king's act in such case being void doth not justify or defend the instruments. This is one of the

[42] Ed: that is, (1) coercive power; (2) directive power; (3) power of invalidating acts contrary [to the law]. See "Reflections," 197.

[43] Ed: the material referenced is omitted in this selection.

[44] Ed: The writ *praecipe quod reddat* was an order of a court directing a defendant to perform some particular act, usually to return some property, used to begin an action for recovery. MH probably has in mind YB (1350) Trin. 24 Edw III, fo. 55, pl. 40.

[45] Ed: MH refers to Chapter 8, which is not included in this selection.

[46] Ed: Writs were written court orders—conforming to a regimented form and written in Latin—usually commanding something to be done or authorizing the performance of some action. Writs were typically used to initiate court proceedings and shaped the issues brought to court and the remedies sought. But some writs simply commanded people to be brought to court; for example, the writ of *habeas corpus* ordered officials to bring to court persons detained by them to determine whether the detention was lawful.

[47] Ed: MH directs attention to Chapter 5, not included in this selection.

principal reasons of the maxim in law that the king can do no wrong, for if it be wrong and contrary to the law, it is not the act of the king but of the minister or instrument that put it in execution and consequently such minister is liable to the coercion of the law to make satisfaction.

8.[48] Though the government regal be perpetually and irrevocably settled in the king and descendible to his heirs, yet it is not an absolute dominion transferable over by the king to another. It is true he may transfer some regalities, nay, the very title of king of some parts of his dominions to others, as the *jura regalia* [royal rights] of counties palatine[49] and some others....[50] The *jus summi imperii* remained in the king of England. Neither could nor can he part with that right in all or any part of his dominions, but by consent of the people [and] states of the kingdom in parliament, for the relation and bond is reciprocal. As the kingdom cannot resume the allegiance and faith due to the king, so the king cannot *se a regno abdicare* [abdicate the rule] or transfer the *jus summi imperii* of the kingdom or any part thereof without the consent of the kingdom, for they have an interest in his protection as he hath in their subjection. Though it be *regnum hereditarium* yet it is not *regnum patrimoniale*,[51] so as to be transferred by the absolute power of the king to any other without the consent of the kingdom and that in a regular and parliamentary way.[52]

[48] Yale: In *The Rights of the Crown*, ch. 2, MH writes upon this topic that "It is clear that those rights which the king hath are in him absolutely, perpetually and hereditarily, whereby as he or his issues inheritable cannot, upon any pretence whatsoever either of abuse in him or public good of the state, either be deprived of the whole power regal, which is a deposition, or of any spark of that gem, any prerogative or power which he hath in right of his regality, without his consent. The ground I take is that which was before propounded. The constant usage and custom of this kingdom hath inseparably annexed the regality and every parcel thereof to the person of the king, which custom or usage binds under a double obligation, either as evidencing that at the first agreement the power was absolutely, unconditionally transferred, not resumable upon any pretence, or giving by an implied contract, made by a tacit consent of both parties, an absolute, unresumable right, which equally binds both parties to observe it as strictly as if in the very original compact it had been expressed that the power should be absolutely and irresumably in the prince, notwithstanding any mistake in government whatsoever, inasmuch as by this custom interpretively the contract appears so to be. And as the people cannot take away any of the powers thus settled in the crown, so on the other part the king cannot without the consent of the people transfer the regal power or dignity to another. He may grant prerogatives of interest, privileges and franchises, he may delegate a *prorex* or *custos regni* [guardian of the kingdom] in his absence without assent of parliament. But to resign his kingdom or grant the allegiance of his people to another, this he cannot do without consent of his kingdom. The relation is reciprocal. The subject hath an interest in the protection of his prince, which he may not lose without his consent, and that in parliament."

[49] Ed: territories ruled by a nobleman with a significant degree of autonomy from the king, although bound in allegiance to the king.

[50] Ed: Authorities and examples omitted.

[51] Ed: although the crown is hereditary, it is not owned like property.

[52] Ed: Extended examples omitted.

4

Concerning Allegiance; What It Is; What It Binds to; and the Kinds of It

V

And[53] thus much of the persons that owed homage and the various kinds of those homagers. Now concerning the homage or ligeance itself. Wherein it is to be observed that though the oath of allegiance or fidelity of homage be a farther confirmation or assertion of that homage that is either natural or local or acquisite,[54] yet there is a radical and fundamental allegiance due before any oath at all made to observe and keep the same.[55] For there doth intervene an implicit faith between the governor and governed, viz. of the part of the former, protection, on the part of the latter, allegiance or fealty. And this is the foundation of that superadded stipulation or oath of the king at his coronation for the due protection of the subjects, and of the subject for their fidelity to the prince....[56]

There be two kinds of obligations that the kings of England have of their subjects [viz., homage and oath of allegiance].[57] ... The second obligation that the common

[53] Ed: This selection begins with section V of Chapter 4.

[54] OED: acquired.

[55] Ed: In his *History of the Pleas of the Crown*, MH maintains that the allegiance due to the king is of two kinds (a) "original, virtual, and implied" and (b) "expresst, and declared by oaths or promises." Of the former he says, "The virtual or implied allegiance is that, which the subject owes to his sovereign antecedently to any express promise, oath, or engagement... for as the king by the very descent of the crown is fully invested with the right of sovereignty before his coronation... so the subject is bound to his king by an intrinsic allegiance before the superinduction of those express bonds of oath, homage and fealty, which were instituted for the better securing thereof." Formal oaths do not themselves generate the subject's obligation of fidelity, but rather are public "professions attesting and witnessing that allegiance" (vol. I, 61–2).

[56] Ed: Reference to a collection of ancient customs of Normandy omitted.

[57] Ed: MH here distinguishes between homage and allegiance, but in his *History of the Pleas of the Crown*, he makes a twofold distinction: (a) between original and expressed allegiance and (b) between the fealty owed to the king (or lessor lords) due to feudal service and tenure of land and the unique allegiance owed to the king, not only to the office but also to his person (60–7). Homage as discussed in the page omitted is largely feudal fealty expressed in an oath or other similar act. The obligation discussed here is that owed specifically to the king, not in his capacity as feudal lord, which may be expressed in an oath, but exists prior to it.

law did put upon every subject was the oath of *allegiance* or fealty. Which every man above the age of twelve years is to take in that leet or hundred wherein he is commorant,[58] whether he be ecclesiastical or temporal, noble or not, natural subject or an alien that oweth a local subjection. The tenor of this oath is thus. You shall swear that from this day forward you shall be true and faithful to our sovereign lord King Charles and his heirs, and truth and faith shall bear of life and member and terrene honour, and you shall neither know nor hear of any ill or damage intended to him that you shall not defend, etc.[59] And this ought to be taken by every [person] in the leet, except noblemen, and *femmes coverts*[60] are to take this oath in the leet or turn.[61] And though ordinarily ecclesiastical persons are exempt from suit to the leet or turn by the statute of *Marlebridge*, cap. 10,[62] yet they are to take this oath there, for this is *causa specialis* [special case]. These oaths and professions of homage and fealty are the external signs or confirmations of the bond of allegiance that preceded them; they are *tesserae et signa* [tokens and signs]. *Coke, s. 94*[63] attributes the first institution of that oath of allegiance or fidelity to King Arthur. Certain it is that it is very ancient. There are since that time appointed the oaths of supremacy by the statute of *1 Eliz.* [*cap. 1*][64] and that of obedience by the statute of *3 Jac.* [*cap. 4*].[65]

This allegiance is not only due to the office, but to the person of the king; and therefore the position of the Despencers[66] was seditious and justly condemned, that gave out that the allegiance was only due to the kingly office.[67] And this was well

58 Ed: every manorial court or court of the local community in which he resides.

59 Ed: This oath ("true and faithful... defend") dates from the late thirteenth century. MH cites "Calvin's Case," in Coke, *Seventh Reports* 1a, at 7a, (Sheppard, *Coke: Selected Writings*, 180). "Terrene honour" literally means "honour pertaining to this world."

60 Ed: married women whose legal rights and obligations are subsumed under their husbands.

61 OED: a sheriff's circuit court.

62 Yale: 52 Hen III c. 10, St. Realm I, 22 (sheriff's turns).

63 Ed: MH's reference is to Coke's *Institutes* First Part, section 94, p. 68b.

64 Yale: St. Realm IV, 350 (Act of Supremacy).

65 Yale: St. Realm IV, 1071 (popish recusants).

66 Ed: Hugh le Despencer (1263–1326) and his son Hugh (1286–1326) were advisors and favourites of Edward II, but generally hated for their greed, ambition, and oppressive acts. Father and son were exiled and disinherited by parliament in 1321 and later summarily tried for treason and gruesomely executed in 1326. Among the many grounds for their exile was the following declaration by Hugh the younger: "Homage and the Oath of Allegiance is more by reason of the Crown, than by reason of the Person of the King, and it bindeth itself more unto the Crown than unto the Person; and this appears in that before the Estate of the Crown hath descended, no Allegiance is belonging to the Person; wherefore if the King by chance be not guided by reason, in right of the Crown, his liege Subjects are bound by the Oath made to the Crown to guide the King and the Estate of the Crown back again by reason, and otherwise the Oath would not be kept. Now were it to be asked, how they ought to guide the King? Whether by Course of Law, or by Violence? By Course of Law a Man will not be able to get Redress, for he will have no Judges but such as are the King's, in which case if the Will of the King be not according to Reason, he certainly will have only Error maintained and confirmed; Wherefore it behoveth, in order to save the Oath, that when the King will not redress the matter and remove that which is hurtful to the People at large, and prejudicial to the Crown, it is to be determined, that the thing be removed by Violence, for He is bound by his Oath to govern the People and his Liege Subjects, and his Liege Subjects are bound to govern in Aid of Him, and in his Default." Statute 15, Ed II (St. Realm I, 182).

67 Ed: authorities omitted.

known to those rebels that deposed Richard 2, who though the act was most illegal and traitorous, yet they made it as formal as they could.[68] Thus this detestable action was clothed and dressed up in as much formality as might be, but had there not been force to second it, it had been but an ineffectual piece of solemnity to entitle him that drave[69] on his design for himself. For it is most certain that neither the king could resign his crown nor those states in parliament resign their homage. For every particular subject in England had an interest in the protection of the king and in the fidelity one of another whereby the protection was supported. And if the king were in truth no king when he had resigned, then were those that resigned their homage no parliament, but acted this solemn piece of rebellion as private men. And yet there was this proviso added to the king's resignation *salvis successoribus meis juribus competentibus et competituris* [saving for my successors the rights pertaining now and in future].[70] Which though possibly it might seem to be added by the distressed prince, to preserve the right of his lawful successors, yet it seems rather to be added by the policy of him that expected to be his successor though by usurpation, viz. Henry 4, who though he rebelliously had procured the exclusion of King Richard 2 from the kingly dignity, yet was careful to prevent the lapsing of the regal government into an aristocracy or democracy, and to preserve the regality which he aimed to enjoy, though to dispossess the right proprietor thereof.[71]

This obligation of allegiance, whether any oath or homage be made or not, obligeth:

1. Not to attempt or consent to anything against the person of the king. This is treason.
2. Not to conceal anything whereby the person of the king may be hurt or endangered. This is misprision of treason.
3. To defend the king's person and regal office from injuries.[72] The neglect of this is a contempt.
4. To obey the lawful commands of the king, his courts and officers, ministerial and judicial. The very constable or tithingman,[73] in commanding the peace or assistance in the apprehending [of] malefactors, carry in them so much of the king's authority as makes the neglect thereof subject to fine and imprisonment.

[68] Ed: See *Prerogatives*, note 37. (MH's authorities omitted.) [69] Ed: drove.

[70] Ed: this is an abbreviated quotation from the form of abdication signed by Richard II in 1399. See Johannis Capgrave, *Liber de illustribus Henricis*, ed. Francis Charles Hingeston (London: Longman, Brown, Green, Longmans and Roberts, 1858), 105.

[71] Yale: In *The Rights of the Crown*, ch. 6, MH writes of the subject matter of this paragraph: "But inasmuch as every particular subject hath a kind of interest in that allegiance which is due from another subject to his prince, since the right of sovereignty originally grew as well out of mutual contract between the subjects as of that contract they made with their prince, allegiance of any particular natural subject cannot be resigned without common consent both of king and people in parliament.... Thus that which was underhand and behind the curtain, driven on with violence and oppression, was acted in the view with those solemnities requisite and sufficient for a mutual and voluntary determination of the allegiance between king and people...."

[72] Ed: authorities omitted. [73] OED: parish peace-officer, petty constable.

14

The Great Council and Court of Parliament

The parliament [is] the high and supreme court of this kingdom, being a convention of the commons by their proxies, the lords or peers together with the king, by virtue of his Majesty's writ or summons.[74] . . .

Touching the power of parliament, either it respects things done or things to be done.

(1) In respect of things already done. This is the judicative power of parliament which is the supreme judicature wherein the king by the assent of the lords and commons gives his judgment. For though in the subordinate judgment in parliament, viz. that in the lords' house, there is a judicature exercised without the king or commons, yet the supreme judicature of parliament is not without the concurrence of all.[75] And although this supreme judicature hath in some cases proportioned the punishment not according to the strict rules of the law, and although if it exceed or diminish, it binds, yet the ordinary rule whereby even this supreme tribunal proceeds is the known law of the land.

(2) In respect of things to be done, wherein it acts under a double notion, viz. either by way of council or by way of law.

(a) As a great council. Thus it adviseth the king in the disposition of great offices, in the disposal of his revenue, in undertaking of war or making peace &c. And herein observe, first, it is the most high and honourable council in the kingdom, and their advice is without clear reason to the contrary to be followed. Secondly, it is no compulsory council, it doth not inexorably bind the king who is advised by them, in all points to follow that advice, neither is the advice authoritative in itself if not

[74] Ed: In *The Original Institution, Power and Jurisdiction of Parliaments* (London, 1707), MH writes, "of the power and jurisdiction of Parliament for making of laws in proceeding by bill, it is so transcendent and absolute as it cannot be confined either for causes or persons within any bound" (46). And "the Parliament hath sovereign and sacred authority in making, confirming, repealing and expounding laws; in restoring such as be attainted and outlawed to their former estates; in deciding the hardest controversies between private persons, and in all causes which concern either the safety of the estate or any private person whatsoever" (49).

[75] Ed: see "Jurisdiction," Part VII of this volume.

assented unto, for then it were a command, a law, not a council. The best council in the world as a council binds not unless received.

Thirdly, the subject of parliamentary advice may be all matters concerning the state, even those that the king may act without them, as concerning war, peace, coin, &c. their advice in these things disproves not the king's power to act them without that advice.

(b) As touching the legislative power we must call back what hath been before remembered, viz. that by the constitution of this realm the supreme power of the king is limited and qualified that it cannot make a law or impose a charge but by the consent both of lords and commons assembled in parliament. To supply and make up this qualification or limitation of the supreme power in the king is this concurrence requisite. And yet this concurrence without the king's consent makes not a law, and although by the duty of this kingly office he is bound to assent to all such laws as likewise councils which are propounded and conduce to the good of the kingdom, yet is he likewise judge of what is good, wherein if he err, as it is possible he may, yet that council or law propounded wants that which makes it binding, if it wants that consent....

16

The King's Temporal Power in General and of the Power of Making Laws, Proclamations, and Dispensations with Laws

Now we come to consider the king's temporal power, which we shall divide into these two parts, viz. his power of jurisdiction and his power of empire or command.

His power of jurisdiction is divided into two parts, viz.

1. *Jurisdictio* or *potestas legem ferendi* [authority or power of making law], or *jurisdictio nomothetica* [authority of setting down law].
2. *Jurisdictio legem dicendi* or *distribuendi* [jurisdiction of deciding or distributing (determining) law], in which again I shall divide into *jurisdictio contentiosa* [contentious or involuntary jurisdiction] [and] *jurisdictio voluntaria* [voluntary jurisdiction].

His power of empire considered (1) as general over the person, goods, and estate of his subjects, and how far it extends, (2) in particular wherein specially of these three: (a) The power of peace and war. (b) The power of commerce and trade and the regulation thereof. (c) The power of imposing taxes and tributes.

The ecclesiastical law being before touched [upon], in the first place I [shall] consider of the power of making civil laws, wherein before I come to the king's power I shall consider of these four things wherein the power nomothetical or legislative is usually exercised: (1) The power of making of a law. (2) The power of declaring of a law. (3) The power of abrogating of a law. (4) The power of dispensing with a law.

1. In general touching the making of a law, all human laws have their binding power by reason of the consent of the parties bound. This consent is acted in one of these three ways, viz.

(1) Either by the immediate consent of all the persons concerned in the law to be made, as where upon the first coalition of a company of men to institute a commonwealth every man should agree to some certain laws, which should be the rule whereby their intended governor should distribute justice to them. This we cannot affirm concerning our laws. The institution of our commonwealth is too ancient and hath received too many changes to find out any such institution of laws.

(2) By the immediate consent of that person or those persons in whom by the constitution of the commonwealth that power is placed, be the government monarchical, aristocratical, democratical, or mixed. This [is] the original of all positive constitutions made in this or any other commonwealth, which with us are called statutes or ordinances.

(3) By implied consent, when by long and general usage this or that is admitted for a law, which as I have before observed hath a double means to oblige: (a) by the implied consent which long admission evidenceth, (b) by a presumption of the concurrence of all necessary requisites to the establishing of it for a law in the original. *Ex diuturnitate temporis omnia praesumuntur rite acta* [After a length of time all things are presumed to have been done properly]. This with us is the ground of the particular customs appropriated to places, towns and cities, to the special customs appropriated to special societies, as *lex mercatoria* &c., to general customs of the kingdom, though diversified both in use and appellation according to the divers subjects about which conversant, as *lex communis*, *lex ecclesiastica*, *lex coronae*, *lex maritima* &c. Which are all but the results of the application of a long and constant usage to those several subjects.

2. In general touching a declarative law or power to declare a law, no declaration can be binding but upon [one] of these two grounds: (1) Either because the declaration agrees in truth with the thing declared, and this declaration is not of itself binding but in respect of the consonancy it hath with the thing declared, otherwise every man that declares a thing as it is should have an obliging declarative power of

law, (2) Or else the obligation must arise from the strength and power of the declaration itself, which is no more but a law that every man shall take this declaration to be the law and not examine and question the truth of it, and clearly this is nothing but making a law, and regularly it requires the same power thus to declare and to make a law. And herein observe a great difference between a power to make a declarative law and a power to declare a law. The former is an act of power nomothetical; the latter may be an act of the power judicative. As for example, an act of parliament is made *14 Eliz.* [*cap. 14*][76] that all hospitals, maisons de Dieu, are within the act of *13 Eliz.* [*cap. 10*].[77] This is a declarative law. If the king's bench between 13 and 14 Eliz. had in a particular case adjudged accordingly, this had been declaring a law. But the difference is apparent. The former binds all according to the extent of the act. The latter doth not extend *ultra partes litigantes* [beyond the litigating parties]. If all the judges in England deliver their opinion in a point of law, it weighs far as an authority in the like case, but yet it is not binding further than the parties concerned in that case.

3. In general touching the power to abrogate a law, there is a great difference between the expiration of a law, [where] there is no exercise at all of any power to effect it, and the abrogation of a law, which is to revoke or determine a law that otherwise would continue. And this clearly requires the same power at least with the making of a law, for the old law would have continued unless a new law had been made to repeal it.

4. Touching dispensation, this difference is between it and abrogation, that it takes not away the obligation of the law, but only takes away the sanction, penalty, or consequence of a law as to the person and act dispensed with, differing only from a pardon in this that the latter is subsequent to the breach of the law, the former precedent. But of this hereafter.

And as of their own nature an enacting, a declaring, and an abrogating law are in themselves equal, and require equal power in their creation, so they are with us, so that regularly what is said of one is said of all. Now the sum of all that be said concerning this follows in these three positions: (1) The king by the advice and assent of the lords and commons duly assembled in parliament may make any new or declarative law, or repeal and abrogate any old law. (2) The king without any such advice cannot make any new, declarative, or repealing law. (3) No power can make any binding law without the king's express authority, concurrence, and consent.[78]

Now touching the power of dispensation with laws. It is regularly true that the king is bound by his own laws. The reason partly appears before, because he hath not a sole or at least an absolute power of making or altering laws, but a qualified, requiring the consent of others to concur. But touching the king's being bound by his own laws,

[76] Yale: St. Realm IV, 605 (hospitals for the poor).
[77] Yale: St. Realm IV, 544 (ecclesiastical leases).
[78] Ed: Extended discussion of these three propositions, citing authorities for each, omitted.

we must observe a threefold effect of law. (1) The obligation on conscience. (2) The penalty. (3) The irritation or making void of an act done contrary to the direction of the law.[79] The first proceeds from the directive power of the law; the two latter from the coercive power of the law. Now therefore the power of the law may be considered in reference to the acts of the king or the acts of the subject.

1. Under the first briefly we shall consider the power which the law hath over the king or his actions.

(1) Regularly the king is subject to the first power of the laws whereby he is bound in conscience to observe all such laws as either by the common law or statutes extend to him, there being divers laws out of which he is exempted either by usage or a reasonable interpretation and exposition of the general words thereof.[80]

(2) Regularly the king is not subject to the penalty of law, at least where the penalty is personal. So that acts by him done or omitted contrary to the tenor of those laws or customs, which he is bound to observe in conscience, yet make him not liable to any personal loss or damage, in case there be no express clause to that effect annexed to a new law, whereunto, as before, he ought to be party.

(3) Regularly in those laws whereby a contract is made void as being made against the prohibition of a law, then it binds the king in [such a] case, [except where] either by usage or the necessary construction of the law he be not to be construed within it.

2. Now concerning the dispensation with laws, which are of two kinds, viz. that which dispenseth with the penalty, not the obligation, as a pardon, *de quo infra*, and that which dispenseth both with the penalty and obligation of a law and is precedent, whereof here.

(1) In many cases the king alone is concerned he may dispense with some formalities of law without which the act done were merely void. It is a prerogative introduced for his favour that if in his patent he doth misrecite the value, title, or not recite a former lease of record, the patent is void, yet this he may help by a *non obstante* in the same patent.[81] For the king descends thereby from his own prerogative. But in case the fabric of the patent be void, it cannot be helped by a *non obstante*, as if he mistaketh where the land lies ... So the dispensation with the statute of *13 R. 2* [*st. 2, cap. 1*][82] which requires the word *murder* to be expressed in every pardon.

(2) The king may dispense with such an act of parliament which though in consequence the thing thereby prohibited concerns the profit of the public, yet he is immediately trusted in the managing thereof.... [For example,] that upon

[79] Ed: See *Prerogatives*, note 42 and "Reflections," 197.

[80] Ed: Authority omitted.

[81] Ed: With the words *non obstante* (notwithstanding), the king, in exercise of his prerogative powers, can permit certain kinds of actions that would otherwise violate statute law. For another seventeenth-century discussion, see Coke, *Twelfth Reports*, 18 (Sheppard, *Coke: Selected Writings*, 423–5). This power was abolished in the Bill of Rights of 1688.

[82] Yale: St. Realm, II, 68 (pardon of offences).

pardon of malefactors they should give surety of their good behaviour according to the statute of *10 E. 3* [*st. 1, cap. 3*][83] is of public good, yet the king may dispense with it. That sheriffs should not be made for longer than one year [is] of public benefit and prohibited and the dispensation therewith also prohibited by the statute of *23 H. 6* [*cap. 7*],[84] yet because he is the king's immediate officer, he may dispense with the statute by special *non obstante, 2 H. 7, 6*.[85] That wools should be brought only to the staple was of public benefit for the maintenance of the town and the vent of wools, yet dispensations with these laws frequent and good.[86]

17

Concerning the King's Power of Jurisdiction in Distributing Justice according to Law *in Foro Contentioso*

The power of distributing justice according to law comes now to be considered. I shall divide into *jurisdictio contentiosa*[87] where justice is distributed according to the obligation of law, the other *jurisdictio voluntaria* whereof hereafter.

This jurisdiction contentious includes two things: (1) A power to give judgment. (2) A power to compel the parties to come to judgment and to execute the judgment given.

1. Concerning the power of judicature it is clear that all jurisdiction was originally translated into the crown, and because he was not able in person to hear and determine all suits of his people, therefore he distributed the exercise of his jurisdiction to several courts according to the diversity of the matters proper for each jurisdiction.... In ancient times the king used to ride as justice itinerant, yet reserved still some case to his own determination before himself... And this is evident, for that all jurisdictions are by derivation from him either express by charter or commission, or presumed by usage, and therefore are to render an account to him of the

[83] Yale: St. Realm I, 275 (pardons).
[84] Yale: St. Realm II, 332 (sheriffs' tenure of office).
[85] Yale: YB (1486), Mich. 2 Hen. 7, fo. 6, pl. 20.
[86] Ed: further examples omitted.
[87] Ed: compulsory jurisdiction.

title whereby held, in a *quo warranto* at his suit.[88] ... And upon this ground it is that all misdemeanours committed in peace time to persons exercising temporal jurisdiction or being concerned in it, is a contempt punishable at the king's suit and enhanceth the fine, as for striking in the place of the courts of justice or in the time of parliament within the verge,[89] scandalous words or gestures to a judge, to a juror, to an attorney, to a practiser,[90] as being violation of the king's justice exercised by them.

2. Because the last and supreme devolution is to him, though qualified as I shall show, that the last devolution of admiral[ty] causes is to him in his chancery, though they proceed not according to the ordinary course and rule of common law, the last devolution of causes at common law to the king in his bench out of parliament and in parliament to him in parliament.

3. It appears that by the particular consideration of the great courts of this realm and how the power of judicature is there exercised, which though they were first derived from the crown, yet being settled by usage, they may not be altered from their power or course of proceeding, no more than any other part of the laws of the land may without an act of parliament.[91]

Therefore we shall consider the king's power of judicature under these two notions, viz. (1) What points of judicature or decision he himself may personally execute. (2) In what manner he may transfer the exercise of jurisdiction.

For the king's power of judicature there be two kinds of questions that arise in most civil causes, viz. *quaestio facti* and *quaestio juris* [questions of fact and questions of law].... Now we shall examine the king's power to determine either or both of these questions.

1. Touching questions purely of fact, there be some cases wherein the conusance[92] of the fact in question lies purely in the king's conusance. In which case his certificate or affirmation under his great seal is final and not examinable.[93]

2. Now for the question of right I shall not mention those determinations which by special submission to the king's aware were settled.... But of his concurrence in judicature in the ordinary courts of justice:

> (1) For the parliament, that hath a double jurisdiction, viz. a supreme, consisting in the whole parliament, as a subordinate, ordinarily exercised in the house of peers.[94]

[88] Ed: at his initiative, the king can demand of a person acting under colour of law to show by what legal authority (*quo warranto*) they are exercising that power.

[89] OED: within an area subject to the jurisdiction of the Lord High Steward, defined as extending to a distance of twelve miles round the king's court.

[90] OED: legal practitioner, lawyer.

[91] Ed: These courts, MH writes, "are the distributors of the K[in]gs judgment and will according to rule, for he neither speaks or doth anything in the public adm[inistrat]ion, but what he doth by those or some of those." (BL Add MS 14291, 254v, quoted in Michael Lobban, "Common Law and Common Sense," *Ratio Juris*, 21 (2008), 545.).

[92] OED: cognizance.

[93] Ed: Examples omitted.

[94] Ed: See "Jurisdiction," esp. Ch. 34.

The supreme jurisdiction of parliament acts either *deliberative* where it makes laws or *judicative* when it gives judgment. The first respects the future, whereof before. The second respects the past and is not properly *qua tale* [as such] a law but a supreme judgment unexaminable. Now touching the king's judgment person in such a judgment, it is without all question equally necessary as in the case of making a new law.[95]

(2) Touching the chancery I take it that anciently no jurisdiction was there exercised but only in liveries, petitions of right, and writs of privilege,[96] which were but few. Therefore, as there cannot be expected the assession[97] of the king in the latter, so neither in the former, because for the most part it concerns his own interest. Nevertheless thus much of this concurrence is evident, that the petition of right is made to him and by him endorsed, which is the warrant for the judge to whom transmitted to proceed. Touching the jurisdiction of the chancellor in English proceedings, thus much is clear, that a bill of review lies to the king himself from a decree by the chancellor or keeper, as upon great debate hath been agreed, and there the king may decide in person or by commission as in case of appeals. Touching the other part of the chancery, viz. for the seal, that power which is thereby exercised is of two kinds, viz. ordinary, which the chancellor may do *ex officio*, as sealing of some commissions or patents which require not a special warrant, sealing of original writs &c., or extraordinary, those *brevia de praecepto* [writs of precept or obligation] whereby the king exerciseth all his power of empire. This belongeth not properly to jurisdiction but to the *potestas imperii*, for legally the king doth nor saith anything but under this seal.

(3) Touching the king's bench and common pleas, it is certain that in ancient times all pleas both civil and criminal might have been determined in the court now called the king's bench till the common pleas were severed in the time of King John, viz. *communia placita non sequantur curiam nostrum*,[98] since which time it is not evident that ever [the] king did sit when any causes [were] there happening, at least which did not immediately concern his own revenue or interest.[99] And I conceive that in such case if the king had any voice, it was only a single voice,[100] which appears for that his deputy, the chief justice, hath no more, for the law hath fastened a coordinate power in judicature in the rest of the judges, though it be derived to him by his commission....

All jurisdiction is derived from the crown either by commission, charter, or prescription. Concerning the two latter they come properly to be considered as the

[95] Ed: Examples omitted.

[96] Ed: types of legal action which directly concerned the king's interests.

[97] OED: sitting beside or together.

[98] Ed: Yale cites *inter alia* Magna Carta, c. 17 which reads "Ordinary lawsuits shall not follow the royal court around, but shall be held in a fixed place."

[99] Ed: Examples omitted.

[100] Yale: MH notes in margin: "But by the opinion of Sir Edward Coke, *Jurisdictio Curiarum* [4 Inst.] fo. 73, the king had no judicial voice in this court, but only the judges."

acts of his voluntary jurisdiction, as franchises. Therefore no more hereof here particularly. But observe in general concerning the derivation of jurisdiction.

1. That the king cannot erect any new judicatory to proceed in any matter by any other process, trial, or rule than that which by the common law is settled or allowed in the judicatory settled by law.[101]

(1) [As] to the process, if the king should erect any new course to begin with a *capias*[102] in debt, I do conceive it were void, because the law hath settled another kind of process in the like case, viz. summons, attachment, and distress. . . .

(2) The king cannot erect a court to proceed by a trial not suitable to the trial allowed by the law in like cases, as to erect a judicatory for matters at common law giving a trial by witnesses . . .

(3) The king cannot erect a judicatory to proceed by any other rule but by that rule which is properly applicable to the case. He cannot erect an arbitrary judicatory or court of equity.[103] But custom may settle a jurisdiction for matters of equity, as in the case of chancery, and *10 H.6*,[104] the mayor's court of London. For custom growing by a general consent of all hath a greater strength in matters of public concernment than [royal] letters patent for matters *de novo*.[105] And as he cannot erect a jurisdiction either to determine matters of equity or matters of law by a different trial than the common law allows, so neither can he by charter apply the rule of the civil law to a matter determinable by the rule of the common law.[106]

Those courts therefore that proceed by any other rule of trial than the common law must have their original by custom, as the admiral, ecclesiastical, and constable's courts, or by act of parliament, as the commissioners for policies, sewers, charitable uses &c.

2. Regularly all courts and jurisdictions newly created are and ought to be subordinate to the king's bench in one of these two ways.[107]

(1) Either to review and examine their proceedings upon a writ of error. . . .

(2) Or to supersede or prohibit, where they exceed the bounds of their jurisdiction. . . .

3. Observe, the king cannot by charter extend the jurisdiction of a settled court beyond the power which by custom is incident to that court . . .[108]

4. Observe, the king may not erect a new jurisdiction to the nuisance of such a jurisdiction which was before held by a subject. . . .[109]

[101] Ed: Examples omitted.
[102] Ed: a writ commanding a sheriff to take a person into custody.
[103] Ed: Authorities omitted. [104] Yale: YB (1431), Mich. 10 Hen. 6, fo. 14, pl. 48.
[105] Ed: novel matters. [106] Ed: Authorities omitted.
[107] Ed: Authorities for the following two propositions omitted.
[108] Ed: Examples and authorities omitted.
[109] Ed: Authorities and extended discussion of how jurisdictions are derived from the king omitted.

PART VII

Jurisdiction of the Lords House or Parliament

Introductory Note

Hale wrote the long work from which this selection is taken in the last year of his life, although he had addressed its central topic in several works written earlier. It challenges efforts of the House of Lords in the late 1660s to mid-1670s to assume wide powers of jurisdiction. Defenders of this position claimed that the House had inherent powers of adjudication to hear all cases, from cases of first instance (original jurisdiction) through to final appellate jurisdiction ("dernier resort"), and all types of cases, criminal and civil, including appeals from ordinary common-law courts. Common lawyers strenuously opposed this wide definition of the House of Lords' jurisdiction. The controversy prompted Hale forcefully to state what he took to be fundamental principles of English constitutional law and his understanding of the nature and locus of sovereign authority.

The basic argument of this work rests on two constitutional principles: (1) England's qualified monarchical government vests sovereign power in the union of king and the two houses of parliament. This body has "plenitude of power as well legislative as deliberative and executive, or the power of jurisdiction in its full comprehension" (239). (2) All adjudicative authority derives by law from the crown, although ordinary common-law courts exercise independent authority; and final appellate jurisdiction lies with the "supreme court of parliament, consisting of the king as the head and the two houses of parliament, constituting altogether a sovereign court" (243). The House of Lords' claim that it has inherent ("radical") original and appellate jurisdiction was a frontal attack on the constitution of English government, as Hale understood it. Moreover, he argues, according such jurisdiction to the Lords is unwise and fundamentally unjust. Just below the surface of these constitutional arguments lies Hale's conviction that determination of the law must not be assigned to the untrained natural reason of lay persons, that judicial administration and maintenance of instituted law must lie in the hands of common-law judges and the disciplined practice of deliberative reasoning in which they are trained.

Four arguments to these ends can be found in the selection. First, granting original jurisdiction to the House of Lords denies parties the right to judgment by one's peers and the right of appeal, both fundamental to natural justice and English law (rooted in the Magna Carta). Second, if the House of Lords is empowered to sit in judgment on the king's courts, the monarchy is radically compromised and the government is transformed into an aristocracy. Third, members of the House of Lords lack the experience and skills necessary for just and certain judicial determination of contested cases. Moreover, they are liable to bias and partiality and, because of their exalted position, it is especially difficult to hold them accountable for errors and corruption.

Fourth, and most fundamentally, to locate final appellate authority in the House of Lords, Hale argues, is to locate sovereignty in that body alone, for "wherever the dernier resort is, there must needs be the sovereignty" (244). The "supreme decisive power" settles with finality what the law is on any matter and can judge an act of parliament null and void. But then the body that exercises such power necessarily exercises ultimate legislative power as well. Thus, Hale argues, the supreme decisive power must be located in the body with full legislative power, or the legislative power is rendered "idle, vain, and insignificant" (245). If the House of Lords holds final appellate jurisdiction, that House, rather than the union of king, Lords, and Commons, is sovereign.

The manuscript for this work can be found in Lincoln's Inn Library, Hargrave 12. Francis Hargrave published it in 1796, adding a long introduction. All footnotes are the current editor's.

Chapter 1

All jurisdiction[1] in this kingdom, as well in matters ecclesiastical as civil, is originally derived from the crown.

Those jurisdictions in respect of the matter of them are distinguished into these two, ecclesiastical and civil; and both are usually called courts.... I shall direct and apply myself to those that are usually styled civil jurisdictions.

Of these some are universal; not only in respect of limits or bounds, because they extend over the whole kingdom and the dominions thereunto belonging; but also in the subject matter of their jurisdiction. And such only is the high court of parliament, consisting of the king himself, the lords and commons convened in parliament by the king's writ or summons.[2]

Some again, though universal in the extent through the whole kingdom, are yet by custom or acts of parliament limited in respect of the matter of their jurisdiction. Such are the four great courts; the king's bench, chancery, common pleas, and exchequer.

And although law and usage hath established the jurisdiction of these courts; yet the actual exercise of this jurisdiction is conferred upon the judges that exercise it by the king's writ or commission, or somewhat equivalent thereunto, as [for example,] to the chancellor by patent, to the keeper of the great seal by the king's delivery thereof and a record made of it, to the chief justice of the king's bench by writ, to the rest of the judges of that and other courts by commission under the great seal....

So that, upon the whole account, all jurisdiction is derived from the crown, as is above said, though the actual exercise thereof is performed by substitutes mediately or immediately thereunto appointed by the crown.

[1] Ed: adjudicative or judicial authority.

[2] Ed: In *The Original Institution, Power and Jurisdiction of Parliaments* (London, 1707), MH writes, "Of the power and jurisdiction of Parliament for making of laws in proceeding by bill, it is so transcendent and absolute as it cannot be confined either for causes or persons within any bound" (46); adding "the Parliament being the highest and greatest court, over which none other can have jurisdiction in the kingdom, if by any means a misgovernment should any ways fall upon it, the subjects of this kingdom are left without all manner of remedy" (49).

Chapter 2

Monarchical government is of two kinds, viz., [1] simple and absolute and unlimited with any qualifications (and such as this is now rarely to be found in any kingdom, unless with those Eastern princes, where their wills are uncontrollable laws) or [2] qualified at least in some points of government, as in making of laws and imposing of taxes or altering properties.

And those qualifications are sometimes settled by the original compact between the governors and governed, or by settled usage and custom, or by concessions made to the people by the prince or capitulations made between them.

But be the monarchy of what kind soever, it is not possible for the prince, in his own person alone without assistance, to manage all the parts of government, no more than he can be of force alone without the assistance of his subjects or auxiliaries to manage a war.

The two great parts of administration of civil government consist, 1. In the deliberative part thereof, or that of council consultation and advice. 2. In the executive part thereof; which, though it consists of diverse other particulars, yet principally consists in that which I have mentioned in the former chapter, namely, the exercise of jurisdiction. In both which, though the king under God be the supreme governor and fountain; yet it is necessary for him to call in others *in partem sollicitudinis*,[3] and, as to use their assistance in the executive part, so to have their advice and counsel in the deliberative part of his government....

The kings of England, besides some councils of less moment, had especially four kinds of councils. [I. Privy Council (*consilium privatum*), advising on matters of state, made up of "select persons of the nobility and great officers of state specially called and sworn"; II. Ordinary Council (*consilium ordinarium*) advising on a wide range of matters of state and government, made up of members of the privy council and high ministers of government *ex officio* and judges from the four courts; III. Great Council (*magnum consilium*), the house of lords in parliament made up of lords spiritual and temporal (i.e., bishops of the church and major nobles).]

But although in many cases this *magnum consilium*, or the house of lords, either with the *consilium ordinarium*, which was always present with them in parliament, or at least with their advice, did transact and exercise many points of jurisdiction, as in the following chapters will appear; yet they could not make laws without the consent of the king and the house of commons in no age whereof we have any memorials of record extant.

[3] Ed: to share the burden.

IV. There is also the *commune consilium* (Common Council), which consists of both the houses of parliament; which together with the king is the highest and greatest court in England, and hath a plenitude of power as well legislative as deliberative and executive, or the power of jurisdiction in its full comprehension. But without the king's consent the two houses have no legislative power; neither can the king make laws without the consent of both these houses. They are indeed the highest and greatest council of advice and deliberation. But as to making of laws, the king's *le roy le voet*[4] or some word equivalent gives it the complement and perfection of a law.

The two essential parts of this *commune consilium* are the two houses of lords and commons. And the constituent parts thereof are the three estates of the kingdom; though they are not there personally, yet virtually and in point of representation: viz. the nobility or secular lords, the spiritual lords which are the representative of the clergy, and the commonality.

For these three, viz. the nobility, clergy, and commonality, are the three estates of the kingdom. The king comes in upon a higher denomination and title; namely, the head of these three estates....

Chapter 15

...It cannot be denied, but that sometimes, as well anciently as modernly, the *magnum consilium* or lords house in parliament did proceed to decide and determine causes brought before them by original petition. But how far or how justly by the laws of the land this might be done, shall be considered....

Certainly the original cognizance of causes in the lords house was always highly incongruous and prejudicial to the people in many respects: as 1. By reason of the great attendance that it required, in as much as necessarily these causes and their hearing must give way to weightier matters. 2. In respect that parliaments were of no long continuance anciently, and many times prorogued[5] or dissolved before such causes could be heard, and then the suitor and defendant lost their labour and expense in attendance. 3. The ancient course even in parliament was, if a matter were put in issue, that either commissions issued out of chancery to try the point returnable thither, or else the record was sent into the king's bench to try, who also gave judgment; so that they were fain to go through several courts before they could

[4] Ed: or *le roy le vault* = "the king wills it"; the formula indicating that a bill in parliament has the king's assent.

[5] Ed: discontinued or postponed till a later date.

come to a conclusion of the cause.... 4. The modern course of a trial by examination of witnesses, either *viva voce* or by commission, is ten times worst, because the lords are thereby judges of facts as well as of law; and whereas if a jury give a false verdict an attaint lies,[6] here he is remediless if the lords make a wrong collection of conclusion upon witnesses, and the party has lost that trial that the law of the land and *Magna Carta* so much assert, the *legale judicium parium suorum*.[7] 5. But that, which is more than all the rest, the lords are great persons; and if they give judgment against law, there is no appeal to any but themselves. If there be an appeal to the house of commons, the lords will not allow it; if to both houses, the same must pass through the house of lords, who will be doubtless partial to their own judgment once given; if the appeal be to another parliament, it is true the lords may reverse the judgment given by themselves; but who can expect they will do it?

The wisdom of the laws of England is remarkable in these particulars. 1. That although the judges are constituted by the king and chosen out of learned men knowing in the laws; yet they are not nobles, or peers of parliament, or such as would be too great to be called in question for corruption, or their judgments to be examined if there be cause. 2. That the ordinary courts of justice are still under the check of a review by writ of error, if there be cause; the judgments in the common pleas examinable in the king's bench, those for the most part in the exchequer chamber, those in the exchequer before the chancellor and the treasurer, and all them either mediately or immediately in the court of parliament.

But to begin with an original petition in the lords house, which is now simply the court of the last resort for appeals, is preposterous and infinitely prejudicial to the people.

Chapter 17

I come to consider the jurisdiction of the house of lords in civil causes by original petition or in the first instance.... [A]s to petitions between party and party concerning matters of private interest, how far the lords could or could not exercise a decisive or judiciary determination in the first instance, hath of late been a great cause of contention.

To come therefore to some certainty in that case, we must suppose the matters, wherein relief is desired by such petitions, fall necessarily under one of the two

[6] Ed: Legal process by which a false jury verdict is reversed and the jury penalized.
[7] Ed: Lawful judgment of his peers; Magna Carta, clause 39.

heads, viz. first, either they are such as are relievable in the ordinary courts of justice; or secondly, they are not relievable in the ordinary course and courts of justice.

As to the first of these cases, it is certain that the lords had no decisive jurisdiction in such cases, but were only to endorse the petitions with a remission to the ordinary course and courts of justice.... So that upon the whole matter it is apparent,[8] that for matters remediable in the ordinary courts remedy ought not to be given in the lords house; and indeed it is against all reason it should invert the whole economy of the laws of England, as is shown supra Chapter 15.

In the second place therefore I come to consider of cases not relievable in the ordinary course of justice in the king's ordinary courts, and how far forth the house of lords hath jurisdiction or judiciary decision and coercion in such cases.

And touching these there will be this diversity, which will be applicable to this inquiry: 1. Some cases may not be relievable in the king's ordinary courts, because there is no law already established for this relief, though it may be just and reasonable that a law should be provided for the case or cases of like nature. 2. Some cases are not relievable in the ordinary courts of justice by reason of some collateral impediment or accident that obstructs the relief in the ordinary courts, though the law itself be more defective therein.[9]

As to the former of these it is certain, that the house of lords hath no jurisdiction or power of relief in such cases; for that were to give up the whole legislative power unto the house of lords. For it is all one to make a law and to have an authoritative power to judge according to that which the judge thinks fit should be a law, though in truth there be no law extant for it. In such cases, therefore, the whole parliament is to be resorted to, either to make a new general law which may comprehend the case in question, or to give particular relief to the case by the full legislative power and by act of parliament.

Chapter 27

...If a bill or writ of error be made returnable before the lords in parliament according to the usual form of writs of error now in use, the judgment at this day is authoritatively given by the lords house...and this [is] ordinarily done at this day by majority of votes, which notwithstanding hath been found a great inconvenience.[10] For though the lords spiritual be learned men in their way, and though the temporal lords are usually of a noble extraction and generous education, and possibly

[8] Ed: Apparent from the lengthy list of statutory and case-law authorities not included here.
[9] MH's discussion of the second topic is not included in this selection.
[10] Ed: significant mischief or harm.

well-acquainted with the methods of government, yet it is impossible they should be skilled in judicial proceedings and matters of law, which requires great study and experience to fit persons thereunto. And besides many of them are young and unacquainted with business, especially of this nature; many of them may be absent, and commit their proxies to others. So that certainly it is a great inconvenience, that men's estates and interests, and the judgments of learned judges given with great deliberation and advice, should be subject to be shaken, and it may be overthrown, by, it may be, one single content or not content. Whatever the extraction of men be, yet they are not born with the knowledge of the municipal laws of a kingdom, nor can be supposed to be inspired with the knowledge of the law by the acquest or descent of a title of honour....

Chapter 32

...There are reasons of great weight against an original inherent jurisdiction in the house of lords without a special commission or delegation of such authority from the king, either by commission under the great seal, or by endorsement of such petition or bill of reversal first made to the king.

Although that the English monarchy is not in all respects absolute and unlimited, but hath certain qualifications of monarchical power, especially in point of making laws and imposing taxes upon the people; yet certainly, since the denomination of government is *ad plurimum*,[11] the government is monarchical, and not aristocratical or democratical. And hence it is that all jurisdiction in this realm, whether ecclesiastical or civil, is derived from the crown; and that the exercise thereof in the ministers or judges, to whom it is so delegated by the crown, is in right of the crown and by virtue of a delegation from it. And it were a thing scarce consistent with the monarchical government, that those sentences, judgments, or decrees, which are pronounced and given by the king's authority and commission, should be examined by an original jurisdiction lodged in the house of lords without especial authority given by the king by writ commission or endorsement. This were to make the basis of the government aristocratical; since the last devolution of appeals would be, from the king and the judgments given by his authority, unto the lords....

But by the way, though the court of the lords house in parliament be higher than other courts, yet one must not take it to be the supreme court; for such only is the

[11] Ed: the term "government" applies generally, that is, to different kinds.

supreme court of parliament, consisting of the king as the head and the two houses of parliament, constituting altogether a sovereign court....

Chapter 34

It hath been said that the method of reversal of decrees in chancery by the house of lords, upon the account of their own inherent radical jurisdiction and as justices of the last resort, is most safe and convenient for the people.... [However, in fact] we shall find it highly inconvenient that there should be such a radical jurisdiction in the house of lords, especially in relation to decrees in equity.

1. It is true, the lords are of noble extraction and education; they may be experienced in politics, in military affairs. Yet no one will say that *eo nomine* that they are lords[12] they are all competent judges of cases of law or equity. How many young lords are there that are not thirty years old? How many are unacquainted utterly with the proceedings or rules of law or equity? Yet one of these may have the odd casting voice, which shall overturn judgments or decrees made with greatest deliberation of most learned chancellors or judges.

2. Again, as to matters of equity, they are governed in great measure by circumstances, and are not under such exact rules, as the common law courts or causes are. And therefore, without a very great advertence and attention, the true equity of a cause is not so easily discerned; that therefore it is that there daily happens great diversity of opinions among learned men, when they come to particular cases of equity. What kind of uncertainty shall we then find, when an hundred or more unexperienced men shall be judges of causes of equity? The ancient rule is a certain truth: better a mischief in a particular case, than a common inconvenience. It were far better, there were no relief at all in causes of equity, than to have every cause under the various sentiments of a hundred judges.

3. Again, we daily observe that in particular cases, when they come before a multitude of judges, especially that are great men and therefore not easily controllable, persons concerned in suits meet with some that are their kindred, friends, favourers, landlords, tenants, or relations. And it is grown a fashion in the lords house, for lords to patronize petitions; a course that, if it were used by judges of Westminster-hall, would be looked upon, even by the parliament itself, as undecent, and carrying a probable imputation or temptation at least to partiality. Such addresses as these are undecent and unsafe, and indeed intolerable to be found

[12] Ed: that merely by the fact that they are called lords.

among judges, who must not know persons in judgment, nor be sweetened by such kind applications. Yet I leave it to any observing person to consider whether he think it possible, or at least probably, that these applications can be avoided to so many and so great persons and of such extensive relationship....

For a conclusion of this discourse, I must needs take notice of some extravagant assertions that have been used by some in their asserting the lords' jurisdiction.

They tell us, [the house of lords] is the supreme court; a court, from which no appeal lies; that it hath a primitive inherent jurisdiction; that it is the place or jurisdiction unto which is the last appeal, the dernier resort:—which expressions, as they are very untrue, so they are very unwarily used by them; and I dare say, they either do not understand, or do not consider the consequence of them.

The regiment of England is monarchical, and the king is the supreme head thereof. This is the chief article of the oath of supremacy.

But it is true, that in some points of supreme government this monarchical regiment is qualified. The king cannot make laws, nor impose taxes, without the advice or assent of both his houses of parliament. But when laws are so made, yet they are the king's laws, though not to be altered or abrogated without the like consent by which they are made.

And the supreme court of this kingdom is neither the house of lords alone, nor the house of commons alone; no, nor both houses without the king. The high court of parliament, consisting of the king and both houses, is the supreme and only supreme court of this kingdom, from which there is no appeal. Wherever the dernier resort is, there must needs be the sovereignty; and so this word is constantly used and joined with it....

And now let any man consider the rashness of the before mentioned assertion, that the dernier resort in all cases is radically in the house of lords; which certainly is one of the greatest points of sovereignty that can be and is coincident with it.

Again, if this should be, that the supreme jurisdiction without appeal, the dernier resort, were to the house of lords, then is the legislative power virtually and consequently there also; or at least that power lodged in the king and both houses were insignificant. For what if the lords will give judgment against an act of parliament, or declare it null and void? If they have the dernier resort, this declaration or judgment must be observed and obeyed and submitted unto irremediably; for no appeal lies from their judgment, if they be the supreme court. And if it be said, this shall not be presumed they will do: I say, if this position were true, they may if they will; and the laws of this kingdom have better provided for the preservation both of the king's rights and the people's, than to put them and all the laws of the kingdom into the power of the lords, though otherwise their justice should be unquestionable.

The truth is, it is utterly inconsistent with the very frame of a government, that the supreme power of making of laws should be in the king with the advice of both his houses of parliament, and judgment should be in one of the houses without the king and the other. A supreme power of making laws should be thus in the king, and monarchical; and the supreme decisive power or jurisdiction and dernier resort should be radically in the lords, and so aristocratical. Therefore it is not only *de facto* true in our government, but it is most necessary, that the supreme decisive power or jurisdiction and the dernier resort must be where the legislative power is. And it is impossible it should be otherwise, unless we wholly dissolve the legislative power of the whole body of the parliament, king, lords, and commons, and put it into the house of lords; who, by their supreme decisive power without appeal, and as the dernier resort originally radicated[13] in them, may at their pleasure render the legislative power idle, vain, and insignificant.

And by this, which has been said, any man with half an eye may see the great inconvenience of lodging any judicatory at all in the house of lords singly, except touching their privileges; and upon what great reason this jurisdiction came to be disused by their noble ancestors, whose sense of the common good of the king and kingdom, yea and of their own posterity, did at last relinquish the exercise of jurisdiction singly for some hundreds of years. And it is this.

The high court of parliament consisting of the king and both houses of parliament are certainly the only supreme court of this kingdom, to whom the devolution of the last appeal or dernier resort doth belong. And the lords are a constituent part of this supreme court, without which as no law can be made, so no final unappealable judgment can be given. Though it cannot finally and without appeal be given by them, so it cannot be given without them. If therefore the lords should have a power of jurisdiction, an appeal must necessarily be to the whole parliament: king, lords, and commons. And yet the lords, without whom such judgments cannot be repealed, should, if they should have or exercise such a judicial jurisdiction, be prejudicated[14] necessarily by their own judgment, and an anticipation of that determination, which (as parts of the true supreme power) they must now reverse. And so the true interest of the subject to have his last appeal, his dernier resort, to the true supreme, the high court of parliament consisting of king, lords, and commons, is lost, or must necessarily be fruitless; because the lords, who as part of the parliament must have voice in that appeal, are already prejudicated by their own judgment and anticipated by it.

And all this inconvenience would be remedied, if, according to the ancient course of writs of error, and according to the method propounded as well in writs of error from decrees, a certain select number of lords with the judges were commissionated by the king to examine, hear, and determine errors in judgments and decrees. For that would not engage the whole house; but they would be free to give their judgment upon appeals to the whole parliament.

[13] OED: rooted, deep-seated, firmly established.

[14] Ed: prejudiced.

Select Bibliography

Works by Sir Matthew Hale

The Analysis of the Law (1713), 3rd edition (London, 1739).

"Considerations Touching the Amendment or Alteration of Laws," in *A Collection of Tracts Relative to the Law of England*, ed. Francis Hargrave, vol. 1 (Dublin, 1787), 253–89.

Contemplations Moral and Divine (London, 1676).

Discourse of the Knowledge of God and of our Selves (London, 1688).

Hale and Fleetwood on Admiralty Jurisdiction, ed. M. J. Pritchard and D. E. C. Yale (London: Selden Society, 1993).

History of the Common Law of England (1713), ed. Charles Gray (Chicago: University of Chicago Press, 1971).

History of the Pleas of the Crown, ed. Sollom Emlyn (London, 1736).

On the Primitive Origination of Mankind (London, 1677).

The Original Institution, Power and Jurisdiction of Parliaments (London, 1707).

Prerogatives of the King, ed. D. E. C. Yale (London: Selden Society, 1976).

Works, Moral and Religious, of Sir Matthew Hale, ed. T. Thirwall (London, 1805).

Secondary Sources

Burgess, Glenn. *The Politics of the Ancient Constitution* (University Park, PA: Pennsylvania State University Press, 1992).

Cromartie, Alan. *Sir Matthew Hale: 1609–1676* (Cambridge: Cambridge University Press, 1995).

Cromartie, Alan. "Hale, Sir Matthew," *Oxford Dictionary of National Biography* [online edition] (Oxford: Oxford University Press, 2004–14).

Cromartie, Alan. *The Constitutionalist Revolution* (Cambridge: Cambridge University Press, 2006).

Dales, Richard C. *The Problem of the Rational Soul in the Thirteenth Century* (Leiden: Brill, 1995).

Davidson, Herbert A. *Alfarabi, Avicenna, and Averroes on Intellect* (New York: Oxford University Press, 1992).

Gray, Charles. "Introduction," in Matthew Hale, *History of the Common Law of England* (Chicago: University of Chicago Press, 1971), pp. xi–xxxviii.

Heward, Edmund. *Matthew Hale* (London: Robert Hale, 1972).

Jansson, Maija. "Matthew Hale on Judges and Judging," *Journal of Legal History*, 9 (1988), 204–13.

Lobban, Michael. *The Common Law and English Jurisprudence: 1760–1850* (Oxford: Clarendon Press, 1991).

Lobban, Michael. *A History of the Philosophy of Law in the Common Law World, 1600–1900* (Dordrecht: Springer, 2007).

Oakley, Francis. "Jacobean Political Theology: The Absolute and Ordinary Powers of the King," *Journal of the History of Ideas*, 29 (1968), 323–46.

Pocock, J. G. A. *The Ancient Constitution and the Feudal Law: A Reissue with a Retrospect* (Cambridge: Cambridge University Press, 1985).

Postema, Gerald J. "Classical Common Law Jurisprudence, Part I," *Oxford University Journal of Commonwealth Law*, 2 (2002), 155–80.

Postema, Gerald J. "Classical Common Law Jurisprudence, Part II," *Oxford University Journal of Commonwealth Law*, 3 (2003), 1–28.

Roelker, Edward. "The Concept of Invalidating Laws," *The Jurist*, 3 (1943), 32–63.

Roelker, Edward. "The Interpretation of Invalidating Laws," *The Jurist*, 3 (1943), 364–403.

Sommerville, Johann P. *Royalists and Patriots*, 2nd edition (London: Longman, 1999).

Tierney, Brian. *The Idea of Natural Rights* (Grand Rapids, MI: Eerdmans, 2001).

Tuck, Richard. *Natural Rights Theories* (Cambridge: Cambridge University Press, 1979).

Tuck, Richard. *Philosophy and Government 1572–1651* (Cambridge: Cambridge University Press, 1993).

Van Caenegem, R. C. *The Birth of the English Common Law*, 2nd edition (Cambridge: Cambridge University Press, 1988).

Williams, J. B. *Memoirs of the Life, Character and Writings of Sir Matthew Hale* (London: Jackson and Walford, 1835).

Yale, D. E. C. "Hale and Hobbes on Law, Legislation and the Sovereign," *Cambridge Law Journal*, 31 (1972), 121–56.

Yale, D. E. C. "Hale as Legal Historian" (London: Selden Society Lecture, 1976).

Name Index

Althusius 56 n140
Aquinas xv, xvi, xx, xxi, xxiii, xxiv, xxxvi, xli, xlv, 8 n19, 50 n120, 72 n186, 76 n199
Argonaut's ship (ship of Theseus) liii n109, 142, 173
Aristotle xv, xx, xxvi n43, xliii, xliv, 23, 29, 53 n131, 55 n137, 69, 72, 73, 75, 76 n199, 77, 85, 163, 176 n22, 190, 193, 199 n49, 213; *de Anima* xliii, 69 n170, 72, 76 n199
Atticus, Pomponius xv
Averroes xv, xliv, xlv, 69, 70, 72, 73, 75, 77
Avicenna xv, xliv, 69 n170, 73

Bacon, Francis 176 n22
Bacon, Roger xv, xliii, 72 n186, 73 n191, 76
Bodin, Jean xxxii, lv and n113, 10 n23, 213
Bonaventure xliii
Bracton xxiv, xxvii, 142, 181, 219
Bury St Edmunds xvii, xviii

Cicero, Marcus Tullius (Tully) xx, 23, 29, 50 n120, 181 n37, 188
Coke, Sir Edward xxvi, xxxix, xlviii, lii n104, lv n111, 153 n78, 185, 220 n41, 224, 230 n81, 233 n100
Cromwell, Oliver xvi, xvii, lix
Cromwell, Richard xvi, xvii, lx
Culverwell, Nathanial xx, xxii–xxiii

Davies, Sir John xxv n41, xxviii n47
Descartes, René xv
Duns Scotus xv, 50 n120

Edward (King—"The Confessor"; "Saint Edward") 130 n3, 140–1, 202, 216
Edward I (King—"The English Justinian") 130 n3, 132, 146, 162, 202
Epictetus xlii n76, 29, 35, 161 n10, 163 n24
Epicurus 5 n8, 28, 53 n130, 122

Finch, Sir Henry xxv n41
Fortescue, John xxiv

Gassendi, Pierre xv, 5 n8
Glanville 142, 181
Gratian 136
Grosseteste, Robert 76 n199
Grotius, Hugo xx, xxxii n54, xxxiv, 4 n6, 50 n120, 53 n132, 54 n133, 56 n140

Hargrave, Francis xix
Harold Godwin xxvii–xxviii, lix, 130 n3, 196, 211, 216, 217 n24
Heliogabalus 119
Hobbes, Thomas ix, xvi, xx, xxix–xxxi, xxxii, xxxiv, xli n72, xlviii, xlix, li, lvi n116, lvii, 4 n6, 5, 8 n19, 10 n23, 24 n58, 48 n115, 52 n126, 53 n129, 185, 186
Hooker, Richard xxiv–xxv, xxvii, lv n111

John I (King) 131, 142, 144, 202
Juvenal 98

Locke, John xx, xxxiv n60, 64 n158
Lucian 28

Maimonides, Moses xv, 70 n175, 75–6 and n198
Marsh, Adam (de Marsico) 76 n199
Matthew of Pari 131–2

Nero 119
New-Platonists xv, 69, 73, 75, 86

Ockham, William of xxi–xxii, 50 n120
Ovid 8 n20

Plato xv, 23, 56, 57 n141, 80–1 and n220, 119 n333, 190, 193
Plotinus 69 n169
Pufendorf, Samuel xx

Richard I (King) 129–30 131, 133
Richard II (King) 219, 225
Rolle, Sir Henry 157, 159
Rump Parliament xvi

Selden, John xvi, xx, xxvii n44, xxxii n56, xxxv n65, xxxvi n66, xxxvii n67, 11 n27, 31 n78, 73, 75, 76, 102, 120, 137, 142 n47, 159, 207 n1, 218 n27
Seneca 23, 29

Socrates 119 n333
St German xxiv
Stoics xlii, xliii, xliv, 19, 23, 85, 86, 119
Suarez, Francisco xv, xvi, xx, xxii, xxxiii, xli n72, lvi n115, 4 n6, 50 n120, 63 n155, 64 n158

Themistius xliv n87, 69 n170, 72, 75

William of Auvergne xliii, 72 n186, 76 and n199
William I (King—"The Conqueror") xxvii–xxviii, liii n107, lix, 128, 130 and n3, 141, 144, 147, 150, 154, 155, 170, 186, 196–7, 202, 211, 216, 217, 218

Zeno of Citium 116, 119

Subject Index

absolutism xxix
accountable xxiii, xxix, xxxii, 63
no man can hold himself accountable xxxii, 5, 9–10, 63
actions—natural vs moral 5–7
active intellect, see *intellectus agens*
allegiance l, liv, 54, 59, 223–5
amendment, *see* common law
ancient constitution xxvi, xxvii
Argonaut's ship 142, 173
Aristotelian philosophy of mind xliii–xlv
Augustinian philosophy of mind xliii, xlv
authority xxi, xxviii–xxix, xxx, xxxii, 11–14
civil/political xlix, li–liv, 13–14, 55–7, 58, 196, 205, 207–12
divine right xxviii
natural, of God l–li, 12, 17–18, 39–40
natural, of parents xxxiv n60, 12–13, 54, 207
nomothetical 11–14, 228

civil society, arguments for 53–7
Civil War, English xvi
cognition, Hale's account of xlv–xlvii
common law
amendment of 160–1, 167–83
as constitution of English people xxvi
before time of memory 130
certainty of 161
changing circumstances and 163, 172
civil (Roman) law and 135–8, 149
common custom and xxv–xxvi, xxxviii, xxxix, 134
common judicial practice 159–60
common reason xxvi, 148, 157, 160
common to the kingdom xxxviii, 139–41
custom and 130, 135, 147
custom of courts xxxviii, 135
ecclesiastical law and 135–8, 149
fits constitution of the people xxvi, xxxviii, 139–41, 167–8 and n2
formal constituents of 146–8
formal force of xxxix, 134, 145–6
Hale's understanding of xxxviii–xl
immemorial usage 134
judicial decisions xxxix, 147–8
lacking method 161–2, 164
lex non scripta xxxi, xxxix, 129, 133, 148
lex prerogativa 135
lex scripta xxxix, 129, 131–5, 146
origin of 141–6
particularity of 161
practical reasoning and xxv–xxvi, xl–xlii, xlvii–xlix, 163–4, 175, 185, 187–95
product of wisdom, time, and experience xxv–xxvi, 160–3, 165, 168–9, 192
seventeenth-century politics and xix, xxvii–xxix
systematic character of 176, 177
tradition xxiv–xxvii
wisdom of 160
common notions (anticipations, preconceptions) xlii, xliii, xliv, xlvi, xlviii, 23–4, 28–9, 35 and n85, 68, 76, 83, 85–6, 92–3, 94, 96, 161, 163, 190
Common Pleas, Court of xvi
conquest xxix, lii–liii, 13, 196, 210–11
victoria in regem vs *victoria in populum* liii, 152–5, 196, 211, 214, 216–17
consent as foundation of authority and obligation xxiv, xxvi, xxvii, xxix, li–liv, 10, 14, 19, 58–9, 151–2, 196, 205, 208–14, 219, 228
as agreement or consensus 26–7, 29, 68–9, 76, 190
conscience xxiv, xxxii n55, xli, xlvii, lvi, 7, 18, 19, 23, 25, 29, 30, 33, 34, 37, 38, 51, 58, 65, 67, 97–9, 105, 110, 111, 114, 206, 221, 230
constitution of England xxvii–xxix, 198–201, 215–22, 226–34, 244–5
custom and usage xxiii, 14, 214–15, 228
and common law xxiv, xxv, xxxviii, 130, 134, 140, 146
institutive power of 215
the political constitution and 214–15

Decretum 136 and n25
Discourses (Epectitus) 35, 161, 163
divine law xxi n24, xxiv, xxv, xxvi, xxviii, xxxi, xxxii, xxxiii, xxxv n65, lvi n116, 11, 19, 20–1, 58, 99, 105, 109, 111, 114
divine lawgiver xxii, xxiii, xxix
divine positive law xxxiii, xl, 2, 20–1

equality
moral xxxiv–xxxv, 42, 46–7, 52
political 48, 208–9 and n3
right to all things in common xxxiv–xxxv, 49–51
Exchequer, Court of xvii

fidelity, principle of(*fides est servanda*) xxxiv, xxxv, xxxvii, lii–liv, lvi, 10, 11 and n27, 19, 36, 48, 58–9, 209; *see also* consent
fides publica 205, 209
Forests, Charter of the 131–2, 202

Hale Commission xvi, 165
human law, need for 108–12

illumination, divine xlvi–xlvii, 68, 73–4; *see also* intellect, active
imagination (phantasy/*phantasia*) xliii, xlvi, 6 and n15, 8, 44, 70, 71, 72 and n182, 74, 75, 80, 88, 89, 90
intellect (understanding/intellective faculty) xli, xlv–xlvii
  acquired 70, 175
  active (agent) xlii, xliv–xlv, 69 n167, 70 n173, 71 n177, 72 n182, 75 and n194
  material (passive/potential) xliii, xliv, xlv, 70 n173, 72 n184
intellectus agens xlii–xlvi, 29, 69, 70–3, 75–7, 79, 80, 81, 114; *see also* intellect, active
intervenient law (*lex interveniens*) xxxvii, 11, 51
invalidating power (*potestas irritans*) lvi–lvii, 10, 197 and n41, 206, 221–2, 230

King's Bench xvii

law
  amendment of 160–1
  author of 9
  authority and xxiii, 3–5, 9–10
  certainty of 161
  civil (human/secular) xxxvi–xxxvii
  and command xxx, 4–5, 14
  customary 14, 130
  definition of xxxi–xxxii, 3–16, 122–5
  executing power of (*dynamis*) 14
  force of xxi, xxxix, 14, 134
  formal character of xxiii, 5
  given to persons with understanding and will 7–8
  instituted xxiii, xxxiii, xxxvi–xxxviii, 11, 109–12; see also *lex permissiva*
  and moral (free) action 5–7
  nullifying power of, *see* invalidating power
  potestas coerciva, directiva, and *irritans* lvi and n115, lvii, 10, 197 and n41, 221–2, 230
  promulgation of 7
  rule of action 3–5
  sanction of (punishment) xxxii, 15–16
  as *summa ratio* xxvi, xxx
  thetic conception of xxxii–xxxiii
  vis indicativa and *vis preceptiva* xxxi, lvi, 4–5, 63–4; *see also* common law, natural law

law-giving (*nomothetical*) power 10, 11–13
  absolute 12
  limited 12–13

Magna Carta 131, 202, 240
marital rape xviii n12
moral law 37; *see also* natural law
moral necessity xxii
morality, complexity of xxxvi, xlviii, 24, 26, 37, 163, 172, 189–92

natural law
  determination xxxvi
  discovering its content vs discovering the ground of its obligation 25
  duties to God 38–41, 47
  duties to others xxxiv, 48–59
  duties to others—existing prior to the institution of government xxx, xxxiv–xxxv, 48–54
  duties to others—regarding established government and law 57–9
  duties to others—regarding the establishment of government 54–7
  duties to self xxxiv, 42–7
  end of 112–14
  fides est servanda, see fidelity, principle of
  God's will and xxxiii
  human law and xxiii, xxx, xxxvii, 59, 108–12
  human nature and 22–4, 42–7, 54–7
  hybrid conception of xxi, xxii, xxxi, xxxiii, 63, 95–6
  in English jurisprudence xxiv–xxv
  in English politics xxviii
  inclinations (rational instincts) to obey xli, 82–3, 87–92
  indeterminacy of xxxv–xxxvi, xxxvii, 14, 37, 108–11
  intrinsic good and evil and xxi–xxiii, xxxiii
  lex permissiva xxxv, xxxvii, lv, 14, 108–10
  nomothetes xxxii, 9
  order of nature 21
  primary truths of (self-evident and immediately evident entailments thereof) xxxv, 24, 35–6, 82, 96
  priority of to civil law 59, 109
  promulgation (publication) of xxi, xl–xli, 25–6, 68–107
  promulgation by common irradiation 68–81
  promulgation through conscience 97–9
  promulgation through implanting 81–93
  promulgation through reason 93–7
  promulgation: supplementary means 99–107
  property rights and xxxiv, 48–51, 56–7
  rationalists vs voluntarists xx–xxi, xxxiii

secondary truths of (derived by discursive reasoning) xxxv, 37–8, 96–7
and self-defence 42–3, 52
self-preservation xxxiv, 24, 42–3

Noachide laws xxxiii, xl, 30–2, 57, 101–2
nomothetes xxxii, 9, 10
Norman Yoke xxviii

obligation xxi, xxii, xxiii, xli, l–li, liv, lvi, 9, 13, 17–18, 59, 64–5
consent as foundation of 10
and fear of punishment xxxii, xli, li, 4–5, 14, 64
to God 12–13, 17–18, 39–42, 59
no man can oblige himself 9–11, 63
of natural law 62–9
obligation *ad officium* vs *ad poenam* 64–7
relational conception of xxiii, xxxii, l–li, 9, 39, 64–5; *see also* allegiance

parliament 226–7, 238
House of Lords' jurisdiction 238–45
permissive law (*lex permissiva*) 109–11
phantasy (*phantasia*) xlvi, 6 and n15, 8, 44, 70, 71, 72 and n182, 74, 75, 80, 88, 89, 90; *see also* imagination
prerogative, royal powers xxvii, 135
property 49–51, 56–7

reason (reasoning)
artificial xxvi, xl, xlviii–xlix
common xxv, xxvi, xlviii
common law xlvii–xlix
disciplined practice of xl, xlviii, 188–9
discursive xxvi, xxxv, xl, xlvi, xlvii, xlviii, xlix, 35, 36, 55, 85, 88, 91, 92, 188
Hale's three conceptions of xl, 187–90
natural xxvi, xxx, xl–xlii, xlvii–xlviii, 111–12, 185, 187, 189, 191, 194
right reason xxi, xxii, xxx
Restoration xvi, xix
rule of law xxiv–xxv, xxx, liv–lvii, 220
no man is above the law xxv, 9, 10

self-defence xxxiv, 42–3, 49, 52
act at one's peril 49, 52
self-preservation xxxiv, 24, 42–3
sociability, human 53, 55, 57
sovereign powers xxix, liv–lv, 186, 196, 198, 207–8, 220, 227–34
limits of 197–204, 220–2
sovereignty xxix, liv–lv, lvii, 199–203

understanding, *see* intellect

will xxiii, xli–xlii, xlv–xlvi, 8
freedom of 8–9
witch trial (Bury St. Edmunds) xviii